Montréal & Québec City

"All you've got to do is decide to go
and the hardest part is over.

So go!"

TONY WHEELER, COFOUNDER – LONELY PLANET

PHILLIP TANG, STEVE FALLON

Contents

COVID-19

We have re-checked every business in this book before publication to ensure that it is still open after the COVID-19 outbreak. However, the economic and social impacts of COVID-19 will continue to be felt long after the outbreak has been contained, and many businesses, services and events referenced in this guide may experience ongoing restrictions. Some businesses may be temporarily closed, have changed their opening hours and services, or require bookings; some unfortunately could have closed permanently. We suggest you check with venues before visiting for the latest information.

(left) **Montréal Pride p22** Held in August, it attracts hundreds of thousands of visitors.

(right) **Bagels p118** A Montréal obsession.

Little Italy, Mile End & Outremont
p114

Plateau Mont-Royal & the Northeast
p99

Rue St-Denis & the Village
p87

Lachine Canal, Little Burgundy & the Southwest
p127

Downtown
p71

Old Montréal
p46

Parc Jean-Drapeau
p66

4

Right:
Old Montréal
(p46)

HENRYK SADURA/GETTY IMAGES ©

WELCOME TO

Montréal

It's the Frenchness of Montréal that works its slow magic on me. The francophone rhythms are there in its music, film festivals and sense of humor. I love the thoughtful appreciation of everything from theater to pastries. I could linger for hours in cafes and terraces, or stroll the city seeking street murals. Locals have enlightened me as to Montréal's winter pleasures – its coziness, outdoor thrills and apple ice cider. And this city that's mastered winter also knows how to go nuts in summer.

By Phillip Tang, Writer
🐦 @philliptang 📷 mrtangtangtang
For more about our writers, see p288

Montréal's Top Experiences

1 YESTERDAY TODAY

The splendid buildings of Vieux-Montréal (Old Montréal, pictured above) tell an illustrious tale of Anglo-French history on its streets. Peer inside the grand buildings around the Place d'Armes and you will see a fresh take on Montréal's past, helping you understand what makes the city tick today. Victorian stone houses are turned into galleries and craft-beer pubs, while lightshows and street art use today's lingo to tell Montréal's fascinating story of architecture and intrigue near the waterfront.

Basilique Notre-Dame laser show

Montréal's celebrity icon, Basilique Notre-Dame, has wowed visitors with its showy display of carved wood and stained-glass windows since 1892. For modern-day awe, the high-tech orchestral laser show Aura Basilica projects a shower of sparkles and fairytale scenes onto the ceiling (pictured right). p63

Glimpse the heart of giants

Architectural giants flank the streets of the Old Town with their handsome-but-impenetrable, facades. Crew Café (pictured above) gives us mere mortals a rare peek into the heart of the old Royal Bank, now a cafe, under its golden honeycomb ceilings. p58

Archaeology or art?

Don't think of Pointe-à-Callière as an archaeology museum so much as a contemporary art installation in cool underground locations. Laser projections, a pirate ship, circus costumes and dolled-up artefacts tell the story of Montréal's development. History is fun here. p50

Above: Exhibit, Pointe-à-Callière Cité d'archéologie et d'histoire de Montréal

2 GREEN CITY

Nature is never far away in Montréal. It's what happens when you make a green mountain the heart of your city. Across Montréal are a network of cycling paths, waterways and islands. No wonder Montréalers grow up jogging, paddling canals and skating in the fresh air. Sometimes it's hard to tell if the city was built to worship nature, or if the forested paths were cleared to admire the city.

Top right: Canal de Lachine

Bottom right: Parc du Mont-Royal

Parc Jean-Drapeau

This pair of island parks in the St Lawrence River is a great place for a view of the city in the fresh air. After walking the green paths of Parc Jean-Drapeau (pictured above left), get active kayaking off the beach of Plage des Îles or kick back to the electro summer beats of Piknic Électronik. p66

Parc du Mont-Royal

It doesn't get more Montréal than picnicking, sunbathing and jogging on the 'mountain' Parc du Mont-Royal. Admire the city with panoramic views from the Belvédère Kondiaronk lookout or from the Observatoire de l'Est, a favorite rendezvous for lovebirds. p102

Canal de Lachine

A 14km-long cycling and pedestrian pathway, with picnic areas (load up on Marché Atwater) and outdoor spaces. Hire a bike to cruise along the Canal de Lachine path, parallel with the flotillas of kayaks and pleasure boats gliding along the canal's calm waters. p130

3 WINTER LOVE

Celebrate the cold in friendly pubs, at steaming sugar shacks, and on the slopes of local mountains on skis, snowboards and toboggans. To see Montréal in winter is to witness another city awaken, with the waters of the Vieux-Port transformed into an outdoor *patinoire* (rink), snow sculptures decorating the white streets and the Québécois spirit warm and alive.

Lac aux Castors

Outdoor ice-skating bliss starts at the slopes above the Lac aux Castors (pictured bottom left). Rent the skates, cross-country skis, snow-shoes and sleds you need to get involved right away. p102

Sugar fix

Head to *cabanes à sucre* (sugar shacks) and do the taffy pull, where steaming maple syrup is cooled in the snow and onto popsicle sticks (pictured top left). p147

Snow festivities

Fête des Neiges turns Parc Jean-Drapeau into a winter paradise with curling, ice-sculpting contests, dogsled races (MAPAQ humane regulated) and snow games (pictured above right). p68

4 EASYGOING STYLE

INSPIRED BY MAPS/SHUTTERSTOCK ©

CAGKAN SAYIN/SHUTTERSTOCK ©

There is a touch of the slower European pace of life that Montréal has over its big-city siblings. This city appreciates slow, cosy times in cafes, museums and local stores in its neighbourhoods. Take your time, and you'll find that this is the capital of French charm in the Americas.

Village life

The village charm of Montréal's neighborhoods is the city's secret magic. Visit bohemian Plateau Mont-Royal (pictured top left) for artsy cafes, street art, and unusual boutiques; Mile End for bagel bakeries and hip bars; and Westmount for Victorian homes and leafy parks. p99

Magnificent museums

Strolling away hours in museums is a proud Montréaler hobby. Start at the Musée des Beaux-Arts de Montréal (pictured bottom left; p73) taking in a showcase of old masters and contemporary artists. Then for those 'only in Montréal' artists, see Québécois legends of Musée d'Art Contemporain (p75) and the history of the fur trade at Lachine National Historic Site (p131).

Cool cats

If hosting the world's largest jazz festival isn't enough, Montréal oozes cool every other night of the year in jazz bars and dens, such as Casa del Popolo, to folk guitarists and spoken-word poets. p111

5 SUMMER FESTIVALS

From June to August, Montréalers get high on sunshine in parks, beaches, mountaintop forests and endless festivals. The steamy outdoors is more alive than ever with arts-loving visitors filling the streets. Rooftop bars turn into parties, punctuated with the fireworks shows of L'International des Feux Loto-Québec on Parc Jean-Drapeau.

Montréal Pride

Paris who? The largest LGBTIQ+ Pride Week in Canada and the Francophone world is in Montréal. Bar rooftops fill up in the Village and fabulous events culminate with a parade drawing 300,000 spectators. p22

Top right: Montréal Pride

JOSEPH S L TAN MATT/SHUTTERSTOCK ©

Festival International de Jazz de Montréal

Big band, bebop, swing or gypsy jazz, you are sure to find your groove at over 1000 concerts in the world's largest jazz festival (pictured above left). p22

Just for Laughs Festival

Montréal hosts the largest standup comedy festival in the world, drawing big names like Laverne Cox and Trevor Noah and launching the careers of newcomers (pictured bottom right). p22

6 POUTINE AND BAGELS

LIAM HILL-ALLAN/SHUTTERSTOCK ©

Baguettes in a bicycle basket and other French patisserie fantasies are a reality everywhere your hungry eyes look in Montréal. Regional specialties like *kouign amann* (Breton butter cake) let you taste your away across France. This is modern Montréal though. Lovers of gluten-free or plant-based treats can find eating bliss in the blossoming number of forward-looking restaurants and bakeries.

Poutine

A comforting hug of French fries, cheese curds and gravy, but oh so much more than that. Poutine (pictured above) is a delicious symbol of Québéc and Canada, and Montréal is a poutine paradise. Try it at La Banquise. p30

Bagels

Chewy, thin and with a hint of sweetness, the bagels in Montréal are the best in the world. Or are they? St-Viateur serves some of the city's best. p117

So tasty, so chic

There are plenty of on-trend food movements happening in Montréal. Innovative vegetarian and allergen-free dishes are served up in style at LOV with flavors that reflect the European, Asian, Latino and other communities of the city. p76

What's New

A rush of activity back to public events after the first rough patches of the pandemic has shown the unstoppable spirit of this social city. There are new neighborhoods to discover and food events that reflect a restored global appreciation for different cultures. There is even a new urban beach, just in time for the city's renewed love of nature.

Verdun beach

It's not everyday that a new beach is created in the city, but water-facing Verdun got just that in 2021 (technically 2019). It might not be the largest of swims but it has a halo effect of creating newness all around it – new cafes, restaurants and bars such as Bar Social Verdun (p135). Even if you don't swim, it's a relaxing spot to appreciate the shore of the much-loved Saint-Lawrence River.

Skaters' trail

More than a home to Grand Prix du Canada, Parc Jean-Drapeau (p66) in the St Lawrence River is now even better for fresh air in any season. A skaters' ice trail has been created so that ice skating fans can do laps on the 3m-wide and 500m-long path. It is especially pretty after a small snowfall. Here you can also watch the sun setting behind the city's skyscrapers.

La Guinguette

In summer, Parc Jean-Drapeau (p66) offers a new open-air space to relax in with friends. Outdoor dining tables and a performance stage create a vacation vibe amid warm evening lights along the river. There is a new vegan restaurant for burgers, tapas and snacks.

For holiday entertainment there are ping-pong tables, pétanque grounds, swings alongside the river and picnic areas.

Espace Paddock

Fans of the Grand Prix du Canada (p70) now have a new space for fine dining and events among the roar ngin . The spacious and contemporary Espace Paddock opened in late 2020 as a private hall. Look out for events at the two immense terraces on the islands of Parc Jean-Drapeau.

LOCAL KNOWLEDGE

WHAT'S HAPPENING IN MONTRÉAL & QUÉBEC CITY

Phillip Tang, Lonely Planet writer

In a city that is often used as a faux New York City backdrop, it's no surprise that the anti-racism rallies of its US neighbors resonated with Montréalers.

Diversity is key to the pop-up food events that have sprung up all over the city. After some tough years of being stuck inside, people are embracing new flavors, especially ones that they can't cook themselves.

There is a new appreciation for outdoor spaces to enjoy these new cuisines, around the new beach of up-and-coming neighborhood Verdun, and year-round on the islands of Parc Jean-Drapeau.

When they do sit down to eat, Montréalers seem to think about health more than ever and the effect they have on the planet. Yet they also want to get away from home cooking. Nothing better encapsulates this than the delicious rise of vegan fine dining in the city.

Cultural food pop-ups

The years 2020 and 2021 saw the Black Lives Matter movement gain attention around the world. In already progressive Montréal, inaugural events were held in 2021 that gave a nod to this renewed appreciation of diversity. It is part of a larger continuing trend to highlight real diversity in the city.

➡ La Maison Onyx was a pop-up restaurant event that gave a space to black and indigenous chefs at Marché Jean-Talon (p116). It also became simply a great place for summer street food.

➡ Outdoor eating continued with the food trucks of Sudbest pulling up along the Canal de Lachine (p130) in late 2021. Over three weeks, more than 30 kiosks popped up to help stimulate artists and food merchants in the southwest. Diverse and delicious food was accompanied by cultural and musical events.

REM light rail

After many delays, the 67-km (41.6-mile) REM Light rail network will begin partial service in 2022 with full operation in 2024. The South Shore (Brossard) to Central Sation segment is set to start rolling by summer 2022.

There will be 26 stations connecting downtown Montreal to the South Shore, North Shore, West Island and Montreal-Trudeau International Airport. Each car will have free WiFi and expansive windows for panoramic views of Montreal's skyline, the Saint-Lawrence River, and Mont-Royal.

Plant-based fine dining

The global anti-racism rallies had the effect of focusing on new diverse tastes. Overlooked cuisines such as Syrian and Ethiopian have started to receive some well-deserved attention. Meanwhile the plant-based food movement has only strengthened but, after years of home cooking, Montréalers want to eat out.

FAST FACTS

Food trend Vegan fine-dining

St-Viateur bagel-maker training 3 months

English and French bilinguals 44.5%

Pop 4.1 million

MONTRÉAL   QUÉBEC

≈ 105 people per sq km

Dishes that can be made at home are too mundane, while elaborate vegan fine dining, at places such as LOV (p76), is hot on the menu.

Paris–Québec City flights

Air France created a new Paris–Québec City route for May 2022. Flights run three times a week between Aéroport International Jean-Lesage de Québec (p241) and Paris-Charles de Gaulle. It also opened a passage in central and eastern Québec to France and beyond.

Need to Know

For more information, see Survival Guide (p239)

Currency
Canadian dollar ($)

Language
French, English

Visas
Not required for citizens of Australia, New Zealand, United Kingdom and the United States, among others. See www.cic.gc.ca.

Money
ATMs are widely available. Major credit cards are widely accepted.

Cell Phones
Buy local prepaid SIM cards for use with unlocked international phones.

Time
Eastern Time (GMT/UTC minus five hours)

Tourist Information
Centre Infotouriste Montréal (p249) Provides maps, info about attractions and booking services (hotels, car hire, tours).

Tourisme Montréal (p249) Has reams of information and a last-minute hotel search engine with guaranteed best price.

Daily Costs

Budget:
Less than $100

➡ Dorm bed: $22–32

➡ Supermarkets, markets, fast-food restaurants: $30

➡ Bixi bike rental, 24 hours: $5

➡ Movie tickets: $12

Midrange:
$100–$200

➡ Double room in a B&B: $130–180

➡ Two-course dinner with glass of wine: $60

➡ Theater ticket: $40

Top End:
More than $200

➡ Boutique hotel room: $200–350

➡ *Table d'hôte* (fixed-price, multicourse meal) in deluxe restaurant with wine: $80

➡ Canadiens de Montréal hockey ticket: $200

Advance Planning

Two months before Book tickets for hockey games and major festivals such as the Festivale International de Jazz de Montréal, and make reservations for top restaurants.

Three weeks before Scan web listings for festivals and events; book hotels and rental bikes. Be sure to have adequate clothing for winter.

A few days before Check the weather at www.weather office.gc.ca.

Useful Websites

MTL Blog (www.mtlblog.com) Opinionated local voices on the latest in dining, drinking, festivals and daily life in the city.

Lonely Planet (www.lonely planet.com/montreal) Destination information, hotel reviews and more.

Tourisme Montréal (www.mtl. org) Useful multilingual info, travel ideas and events calendar from the city's modern, official website.

Montreal Gazette (www.mon trealgazette.com) Montréal's English-language newspaper has interesting arts, opinion and video sections online.

WHEN TO GO

Despite the high humidity, summer is the best season, followed by spring then fall. Winter can be spectacular if you're up to the cold temperatures.

Montréal, QC

°C/°F Temp — Rainfall inches/mm

J F M A M J J A S O N D

Arriving in Montréal

Montréal-Pierre Elliott Trudeau International Airport
Buses and taxis run to downtown Montréal around the clock; buses $10, taxis $40. It takes 45 minutes to an hour to get downtown by bus, and around 30 minutes by taxi. All 747 airport buses stop first at Lionel-Groulx metro and terminate at Berri-UQAM metro station.

Gare Centrale Trains pulling into Montréal arrive at this downtown terminus, within easy reach of many parts of the city by taxi.

Gare d'Autocars de Montréal
Most long-distance buses arrive at this station in the Quartier Latin, with handy connections to the Berri-UQAM metro station.

For much more on **arrival** see p240

Getting Around

Bus Buses cover central parts of the island with well-marked routes. They run from 5am to 1am, with separate night services.

Metro There are four lines, blue trains and unique rubber wheels. Trains run approximately from 5am to midnight and until 1:30am on Friday and Saturday nights.

Bicycle The city's popular Bixi bike-rental system has more than 500 stations, covering central and outlying areas. There is an extensive network of bike paths too.

Boat Good for day trips to Parc Jean-Drapeau and cruises on the St Lawrence River.

Walking Subway stations are fairly close in the city center; save a little cash by walking if you only need to go one stop.

For much more on **getting around** see p242

Sleeping

Montréal's accommodation scene is blessed with a tremendous variety of rooms and styles. Though rates aren't particularly cheap, they are reasonable by international standards – or even compared with other Canadian cities such as Toronto or Vancouver. Reserve at least a month in advance, especially from June to September, for budget accommodations, or to snap up any discounts. French- and Victorian-style inns and independent hotels cater to a variety of budgets.

Useful Websites

Book your hotel well in advance. Good places to browse listings:

Lonely Planet (www.lonely planet.com/canada/montreal/hotels) Recommendations and reviews.

BBCanada (www.bbcanada.com) B&Bs in Montréal and beyond.

Tourisme Montréal (www.mtl.org) Extensive listings from the city's tourism authority.

For much more on **sleeping** see p153

Perfect Days

Day One

Old Montréal (p46)

 Take the subway to Place-d'Armes and make a beeline for the stunning **Basilique Notre-Dame**. Explore the cobblestoned streets of the old town, winding your way to the sailors' church, **Chapelle Notre-Dame-de-Bon-Secours**. Stroll up **Place Jacques-Cartier** with its many buskers and artists, into the **Château Ramezay** museum.

> ✕ **Lunch** Grab a tasty baguette sandwich at Titanic (p56).

Old Montréal (p46)

 Deepen your understanding of the city's history at the excellent **Pointe-à-Callière Cité d'archéologie et d'histoire de Montréal** before crossing Pl d'Youville to **Fonderie Darling** for its innovative contemporary-art installations.

> ✕ **Dinner** Garde-Manger (p59) for a fun crowd, and tasty cocktails and dishes.

Old Montréal (p46)

Walk off dinner with a stroll into **Chinatown** (by the way, if you want cheap eats, slurp down some pho or grab some dumplings here) before catching a show at **Cirque du Soleil** in the Old Port. You might also consider watching the sky turn various colors at sunset while downing an old-fashioned on the rooftop patio at **Terrasse Nelligan**. Party the night away at scenester magnet **Velvet** or **Philémon**, which will rock you until 3am.

Day Two

Downtown (p71)

 Start your tour of at **Musée des Beaux-Arts de Montréal** for its excellent collection of Old Masters and contemporary art. Architecture aficionados will dig the contemporary Desmarais pavilion as well as the **Claire & Marc Bourgie Pavilion** in an 1890s church. Next stroll down **Rue Sherbrooke Ouest**, home to tiny shops and heritage mansions, toward **McGill University**.

> ✕ **Lunch** Vegetarian-friendly Lola Rosa (p78) has great food and ambience.

Canal de Lachine (p127)

Hop on the metro to Lionel-Groulx and walk down to **Marché Atwater** for a look at the farmers' produce, croissants and cheese. If you have the energy, rent a Bixi bike from a nearby station and pedal the **Canal de Lachine**. If not, consider a cruise on the canal.

> ✕ **Dinner** For incredible Québécois fare, try Joe Beef (p135) if you can get in.

Downtown (p71)

Upstairs has nightly jazz performances, or better yet the jazz festival will be rocking the blocks around **Place des Arts** if your timing is right. Otherwise grab a postdinner glass at the **Dominion Square Tavern** or catch some live jazz at Upstairs.

Chinatown

La Ronde (p69)

Day Three

Little Italy, Mile End & Outremont (p114)

 Make for Little Italy to explore the mouthwatering **Marché Jean-Talon**. Stroll down to the local church, the **Église Madonna della Difesa**, and be sure to spot Mussolini on the ceiling. Browse the old-world shops along Blvd St-Laurent before hopping a bus (or Bixi) to Mile End.

> **Lunch** Enjoy market-fresh fare at the charming little Arts Cafe (p117).

Little Italy, Mile End & Outremont (p114)

Ramble along St-Viateur and Bernard, visiting **Drawn & Quarterly** for its whimsical book selections, hipster curiosities at **Monastiraki** and eye-catching curios from the past at **Style Labo**. Before dinner, grab a taxi to **Parc du Mont-Royal** for a panoramic view of the city from **Belvédère Kondiaronk lookout**.

> **Dinner** Inventive Vietnamese fusion and drinks at Hà (p107).

Plateau Mont-Royal (p99)

 Head down to **Casa del Popolo** and see what the hipster kids are cheering for on stage. Afterward, take a late-night bar crawl down Blvd St-Laurent. Stop in **Big in Japan** for elegance and high-end libations, **Majestique** for oysters and cocktails, or **Whisky Cafe** for, well, you can guess.

Day Four

Parc Jean-Drapeau (p66)

 A river runs through it, dividing Parc Jean-Drapeau into two isles. Begin at **Île Ste-Hélène** with a tour of remarkable buildings from yesteryear. Learn about the environment and our impact on it at the **Biosphère**, housed in Buckminster Fuller's geodesic dome built for Expo '67. Not far away, the **Musée Stewart** is the site of an authentic British garrison.

> **Lunch** Snacks along the forested paths.

Parc Jean-Drapeau (p66)

Wander the island's walking paths, taking in the outdoor sculptures before kicking up your heels at **Piknic Électronik**, a summertime electronica dance fest. If it's not on, try for some thrills on the world's tallest wooden roller coaster at **La Ronde**. You can grab panoramic but decidedly slower views of the city from 45m up on the Ferris wheel.

> **Dinner** High-end fare at a restaurant in the Casino de Montréal (p69).

Parc Jean-Drapeau (p66)

 The island is a perfect spot to watch the sky explode with fireworks during **L'International des Feux Loto Québec**. Even if there's no pyrotechnics going off, take a long walk or quick taxi ride to **Habitat 67**, the block-city left over from Expo '67. The winking lights of the Old Port will be beckoning you back across the water.

Month By Month

January

Montréal kicks off the year with a bang, with New Year's Eve parties at restaurants and clubs, and fireworks at Old Montréal's Quai de l'Horloge. Temperatures start to really plummet and ski season begins.

✨ Fête des Neiges

Montréal's family-friendly Snow Festival (p68) features ice-sculpting contests, dog-sled races and snow games. It's held over four consecutive weekends in Parc Jean-Drapeau. A great place for sledding, ice-skating, zip-lining, curling and skiing. Access and most activities are free.

February

Amid the deep freeze, snow piles up and Montréalers beat the blahs by cheering on the Canadiens hockey club. Temperatures can fall below -20˚C.

✨ Montréal en Lumière

Created to help shake off the late-winter doldrums, Montréal en Lumière (www.montrealenlumiere.com) is a kind of wintry Mardi Gras with concerts, exhibitions and fireworks. Place des Arts becomes an illuminated fairground with a Ferris wheel and zip line. Most events happen downtown.

March

Spring break brings families outdoors for a still-frosty, but sunny staycation; but unpredictable March can also bring blankets of snow back to cover the city.

☆ Nuit Blanche

On the first Saturday night in March, Montréal becomes one giant performance space, with film screenings, art installations and concerts. Hundreds of venues participate in the week lead-up. The challenge is choosing where to go (www.montrealenlumiere.com/nuit-blanche).

April

One sign that winter is over is when the Bixi rental bicycles are deployed and bike lanes are reinstated. Spring is here...though bring layers, a last blast of snow is possible.

☆ Blue Metropolis – Montréal International Literary Festival

This festival brings together 200-plus writers from all over the globe for five days in late April of literary events in English, French, Spanish and other languages. There are even events for kids (www.bluemetropolis.org).

May

With the snow gone, rainy, windy weather sets in but doesn't last. A few weeks of mild weather preface rising temperatures, which can soon reach the high 20°Cs.

◉ Biennale de Montréal

One of Montréal's most creative events showcases the best and the brashest of the Canadian art scene, including conferences and seminars on contemporary art. It happens on even-numbered years (biennale montreal.org).

☆ Piknic Électronik

On Sundays from mid-May to late-September, you can enjoy outdoor revelry (p68) out on Parc Jean-Drapeau. House-spinning DJs work the decks on two stages, while young friends gather and dance on the grass (piknicelectronik.com).

🏃 Tour de l'Île

Also known as the Montréal Bikefest, the Tour de l'Île (www.velo.qc.ca) draws 30,000 cycling enthusiasts for a 50km spin around the island of Montréal and a big party in the city afterward (there's also a 25km route). It's staged in late May or early June, with preregistration required.

☆ Metro Metro Festival

This two-day rap-music festival kicked off in 2019 headlining with top pop-rap artists Cardi B, Snoop Dogg and Future. Beyond the big names, it draws attention to the strong rap scene that has been brewing in Montréal by Québécois artists such as Fouki and Loud. Venues include the Olympic Stadium.

June

Amid this hot, festival-packed month, Québecers celebrate their 'national' day, the Fête Nationale du Québec, on June 24. Everyone is out for a drink, some good food and fireworks.

☆ Grand Prix du Canada

Formula One (p70) is going strong in Montréal. It's usually held in early or mid-June on the Circuit Gilles-Villeneuve. Don't forget your earplugs. It brings huge crowds to race and nonrace areas alike, which includes a Family Zone; book accommodations well in advance (www.gpcanada.ca).

🍷 Montréal Beer Festival

Here's your chance to quaff brews from around the globe over five days in mid June. It's held inside the Palais des Congrès in downtown (festivalmondi albiere.qc.ca).

☆ Festival International de Jazz de Montréal

With more than 1000 concerts and nearly two million visitors every year, North America's hippest music fest (p225) just gets bigger and better, with world music, rock and even pop music sharing the program with jazz legends and upstarts over 10 days from late June to early July (www.montrealjazz fest.com).

July

The heat is on in July, humidity sets in and Montréalers long for surrounding lakes and distant beaches. Tourists throng the city for the jazz fest and other festivals.

☆ Just for Laughs Festival

More than 650 artists perform in over 1000 shows at this comedy festival (p38) which runs for two weeks. Past events have featured The Muppets, Kevin Hart, Margaret Cho, Ali Wong, Bob Saget and Bill Hader.

☆ L'International des Feux Loto-Québec

Thousands camp out on rooftops and on the Pont Jacques-Cartier for the planet's hottest pyrotechnics display (p68). The shows last 30 minutes each and are timed to music.

August

Steamy days, heat and thunderstorms mark August, when many Montréalers leave town for seaside resorts. It's high season for travel.

☆ Osheaga Festival Musique et Arts

In early August, Parc Jean-Drapeau is transformed into a giant stage for one of the city's grand rock festivals (p68). More than 100,000 music fans turn up to witness the powerhouse lineup of performers, whichhas included heavy hitters such as the Yeah Yeah Yeahs, St Vincent, Lorde and Muse (www.osheaga.com).

🏳️‍🌈 Montréal Pride

This is *the* event on the Village calendar (p246), drawing more than a million people, even in slow years. The streets around Pl Émilie-Gamelin pulse with dancing, art exhibits, concerts and parades. It's held over one week in August.

☆ Montréal World Film Festival

Over 10 days in late August and early September Montreal brings the movie-star power with big-name actors, directors, producers and writers coming to town. This event (www.ffm-montreal. org) draws 400,000 visitors to screenings (www. ffm-montreal.org).

October

Temperatures begin to fall quickly in October as trees put on a spectacular display of color. It's a perfect time to see the Laurentians and the Eastern Townships.

☆ Festival du Nouveau Cinéma de Montréal

This festival (https://nou veaucinema.ca) highlights who is up-and-coming in feature films, documentaries, experimental shorts, videos, narrative features and electronic art forms during 11 days in October.

🏳️‍🌈 Black & Blue Festival

One of the biggest events (p246) for the LGBTIQ+ community, with major dance parties, along with cultural and art shows, all in the second week of October.

Travel with Kids

Montréal has many sights for young visitors. Depending on the season, you can go boating, cycling and ice-skating, or get some amusement park or skydiving thrills. On warm days, Parc Mont-Royal and neighborhood parks are great places for picnics and exploring.

Live Performances
Cirque du Soleil
World-renowned Cirque du Soleil (p63) combines dance, theater and circus in powerpacked summertime shows. It will thrill the kids, but is truly for all ages.

TOHU
For entertaining shows year-round, head to TOHU (p125), a circular theater in the St-Michel district.

Hands-On Activities
Old Port
At the Old Port (p49) you can hop into a paddleboat, go jet boating on the St Lawrence, or tootle along in a minitrain for a grand tour.

Centre des Sciences de Montréal
Enjoy technological wonders, unusual games and an IMAX cinema at Centre des Sciences de Montréal (p52).

Biosphère
Make a dam and walk on water at hands-on multimedia museum Biosphère (p68) in Parc Jean-Drapeau.

Pointe-à-Callière Cité d'archéologie et d'histoire de Montréal
Go on a simulated archaeological dig at the Mariners' House (p50).

Kid-Friendly Museums
Biodôme
Kids will love Biodôme (p104), a giant indoor zoo with forest, river and marine habitats.

Insectarium
The Insectarium (p104) has 250,000 specimens creeping, crawling or otherwise on display. At the time of writing, the museum was closed for renovations and no reopening date had been announced.

Planétarium
Enjoy the Planétarium (p104), with domed theaters and interactive exhibits on outer space.

Outdoor Fun
La Ronde
At Québec's largest amusement park, La Ronde (p69), kids will experience chills and thrills galore – plus fireworks on some summer nights.

Parks & Gardens
Enormous Parc du Mont-Royal (p102) in the heart of the city is fun for kids year-round, with boating in summer and sledding in winter.

Under the Radar

Real Québec magic happens in discovery – green urban spaces, cafes where locals linger, and snacks that friends tell you about. Many of these places are just one step beyond where most tourists will tread. Once there, immerse yourself in local life and get a taste of what excites the Québécois.

Villeray

Verdun, Montréal

Verdun is a fascinating look at the Montréal of yesteryear. Verdun's grittiness is vanishing but is still visible on the back streets with row houses that were once homes to factory workers. A new beach opened in 2021 that brought a strip of sand to lounge on after strolling and shopping on Wellington street.

Villeray, Montréal

All the ingredients for a charming neighborhood were already in Villeray – abundant green spaces, tree-lined streets, and a village vibe – but wonderful cafes and neighborhood restaurants have turned Villeray into the coolest place to hang out.

In summer, follow the scent of barbecues to Jarry Park, then head down one of the many *ruelles vertes*, green laneways dressed in plants and flowers. In winter, the *ruelles vertes* hide snow sculptures while locals congregate in cocktail lounges, natural-wine establishments and dive bars.

Local Québec Life

If historical tourism fatigue sets in while traipsing around Old Québec, get a glimpse of real life in St-Jean-Baptiste and St-Roch. Other towns where the village vibe has been rediscovered include working-class neighborhood St-Sauveur ('Saint-Sô' to locals) and Limoilu with its tree-lined streets and old brick homes.

Overtourism

Overtourism is a growing concern in Québec City where, before the pandemic, there were government plans to double cruise-ship visitor numbers by 2025.

The tourism board has tried to nip overtourism in the bud by creating neighborhood itineraries to encourage visitors to stray beyond Old Montréal. For some events that are popular with locals, the board does zero promotion to tourists, so it's worth speaking to a local to find out what's on.

Travelers in Montréal and Québec City can help reduce overtourism by visiting in smaller numbers, planning a trip outside the peak summer tourist season, going to popular sights at quieter times and heading to places that fly under the tourism radar.

Visiting Québec City

With captivatingly picturesque old streets and a cliff-top setting overlooking the St Lawrence River, North America's oldest French-speaking city is a gorgeous, seductive place. An easy excursion from Montréal, Québec City has enough magnetism to keep you occupied for days.

AUDETPHOTO ©

onhomme, the ambassador of Carnaval de Québec (p193)

Getting to Québec City

Two superhighways link Québec City with Montréal: Hwy 40 north of the St Lawrence River and Hwy 20 south of the river. Both routes are arrow-straight and easy (if boring) to drive, and each takes just over three hours.

A nicer way to travel between the two cities is by rail; VIA Rail (p241) runs four to five trains daily from Montréal's Gare Centrale to Québec's Gare du Palais (3¼ hours, from $44/87 one way/return). Frequent and economical bus service (3¼ hours, from $55/89 one way/return) is also offered by Orléans Express (p242).

When to Go

Summer (July to August) is the liveliest (and most expensive) time to visit Québec City, with a jam-packed events calendar. Winter (December to February) is its 'other' peak season, coinciding with Winter Carnival and the ski season.

Québec City Festivals & Events

Carnaval de Québec (p193) Spanning 10 days in January/February, the world's biggest winter carnival features an ice palace, snow sports, parades, ice canoe races, music and lots of drinking.

Fête Nationale du Québec (p238) Québec City parties hard on June 23 and June 24. Originally honoring John the Baptist, this holiday has evolved into a celebration of Québec's distinct culture. Major festivities take place on the Plains of Abraham.

Festival d'Été de Québec (p238) With 300 shows on 10 stages, this 11-day festival in July attracts musicians and top new talent from all over the world.

Les Fêtes de la Nouvelle-France This five-day festival (www.nouvellefrance.qc.ca) in August commemorates the province's colonial period with historical reenactments and period costumes.

Les Grands Feux Loto-Québec (p205) A spectacular three-week fireworks and international music show in July/August, with pyrotechnics on Wednesday and Saturday nights along the river at

10pm. Jazz, opera and other musical events are also scheduled.

Fête Arc-en-Ciel (p247) This Gay Pride celebration rocks Québec City in early September with three nights of free shows in Place d'Youville.

Top Sights

In Québec City, just walking down the street is an aesthetic treat. The city's historic core is unlike anyplace else in North America, with hundreds of gorgeous mansard-roofed old stone buildings clustered inside a perfect frame of crenellated town walls. Québec's dramatic cliffside setting enhances its appeal, with picture-postcard views of the St Lawrence River unfolding from the Terrasse Dufferin (p172) boardwalk, and scenic stairways connecting the Upper and Lower Towns.

The most memorable sight for first-time visitors is the castle-like Château Frontenac (p166), dominating the Upper Town from its lofty perch. The city also boasts a fine collection of museums, most notably the Musée National des Beaux-Arts du Québec (p179) and the eclectic Musée de la Civilisation (p167). History buffs will love Québec's 19th-century hilltop Citadelle (p165) and two museums offering graphic representations of the battles between France and Britain for control of the city. Just outside the town walls, the vast Battlefields Park is ideal for cycling, cross-country skiing, snowshoeing and other outdoor activities.

Québec City for Kids

Youngsters go giddy over the ubiquitous street performers and guides in period costume, the uniformed soldiers beating the retreat at the Citadelle (p165) and the antique cannons sprinkled around Battlefields Park (p179). Walking the Fortifications (p173) or rampaging down the pedestrian-friendly Terrasse Dufferin (p172), with its river views and buskers, always delights children. Place d'Armes and Place-Royale are also good for street performers. A slow tour of the Old Town in a *calèche* (horse-drawn carriage) appeals to the whole family.

In winter children will be mesmerized by the Glissade de la Terrasse (p204) toboggan run on Terrasse Dufferin, the ice palace, ice slides and snow tubing at Winter Carnival (p193), the whimsically decorated rooms at the Ice Hotel (p206) and the outdoor ice-skating rinks at Place d'Youville and the Plains of Abraham.

Eating

Dozens of *boulangeries* (bakeries) and patisseries, such as Paillard (p185) and Le Croquembouche (p191), dazzle the eyes and taste buds with perfect croissants and abundant, beautiful displays of éclairs, strawberry tarts and *chocolatines (pain au chocolat)*. For other affordable French-inspired treats, sample the quiches and savory snacks at *traiteurs* (delis) along Ave Cartier or the *crêperies* along Rue St-Jean, or head to the lively Marché du Vieux-Port (p200), where purveyors of artisanal cheeses and sausages mingle with farmers selling fresh produce from nearby Île d'Orléans. If it's fine cuisine you're after, prepare to be spoiled at top-of-the-line restaurants such as Chez Boulay (p188) and Le St-Amour (p188), classy brunch hangouts like Café du Clocher Penché (p192), or trendy bistros like Bistro B (p194) and L'Échaudé (p190).

Drinking & Nightlife

From top-notch microbreweries like Griendel Brasserie Artisanale (p195) to outdoor stalls selling the potent wintertime elixir known as *caribou*, Québec City is a fine place to drink up some local color. Raise a frosty glass (literally, it's made of ice!) beside the roaring fireplace at the incomparable Ice Hotel (p208), quench your midsummer thirst with the eight-beer sampler at La Barberie (p196), get cozy in an ancient stone cellar at L'Oncle Antoine (p194), or sunbathe on the outdoor terraces at Le Sacrilège (p195). When it's time to move on, dance the night away at a cluster of renovated mansions-turned-discos on Colline Parlementaire's Grande-Allée Est like Chez Dagobert (p194); catch the eclectic mix of shows at Impérial Bell (p199) in St-Roch; or check out Le Drague (p196)

Terrasse Dufferin (p172) and Château Frontenac (p166)

in St-Jean Baptiste, the lively center of Québec City's LGBTIQ+ scene.

Entertainment

The city boasts a symphony orchestra, the Orchestre Symphonique de Québec (p199), and an opera company, Opéra de Québec (p198). Homegrown Québécois bands perform regularly, as do touring bands from across Canada, the US and Europe, especially during the Festival d'Été (p238) in July.

The Grand Théâtre de Québec (p198) and Le Théâtre Capitole (p199) offer venerable settings for drama, classical music and revues, while bars around town host everything from Québécois ballads with fiddle and accordion to live rock, alternative music and jazz.

In summer outdoor music venues pop up like mushrooms, including Kiosque Edwin-Bélanger (p199) on the Plains of Abraham and the 10 stages dedicated to world-music performances during Festival d'Été.

Shopping

Local clothing, eyewear and jewelry designers, purveyors of specialty foods and homemade chocolate, and the antiques dealers down on Rue St-Paul in the Lower Town crammed with shops offering one-of-a-kind items with a distinctly French Canadian flavor are representative of the city's small-scale, classy approach to commerce.

Striking an equally retro note, North America's oldest grocery store, JA Moisan Épicier (p203), is another browser's delight. On the cobblestone sidewalks below Château Frontenac, artisans spread out jewelry, leather goods and other handicrafts, while trendy homegrown boutiques abound in the less touristy St-Jean Baptiste, Montcalm and St-Roch neighborhoods. Kids will love the miniature entryway built especially for them at the jam-packed toy emporium Benjo (p204), and fashionistas will swoon over everything from designer shoes to the outrageous glasses frames produced by Québécois designer Anne-Marie Faniel and sold at Les Branchés Lunetterie (p200) in the Old Lower Town.

As a general rule, stores in Québec City keep later hours on Thursday and Friday nights.

Sleeping

Québec City is loaded with atmospheric places to spend the night. Top draws include the river-view rooms in the iconic Château Frontenac (p210) and the plethora of mansions-turned-B&Bs lining the pretty Jardin des Gouverneurs, such as Château Fleur-de-Lys (p209). Other peak sleeping experiences include chilling out on a bed of ice at the famous Ice Hotel (p208); enjoying the vintage charm of the 18th-century Maison Historique James Thompson (p209); treating yourself at the lavish Auberge St-Antoine (p210); or economizing at the Auberge de la Paix (p208), one of several excellent hostels in Québec City.

PINKCANDY/SHUTTERSTOCK ©

Dining Out

Montréal is one of the great foodie destinations of the north. Here you'll find an outstanding assortment of classic French cuisine, hearty Québécois fare and countless ethnic restaurants from 80-odd nationalities. Today's haute cuisine is as likely to be conjured by talented young African, Japanese or Indian chefs as graduates from the Académie Culinaire du Québec.

Neighborhoods

Montréal has more eating choices per capita than anywhere in North America except for New York City. The dining scene is marked by dazzling variety and quality, and brash chefs who attack their creations with innovation. Life in Montréal revolves around food, and it's as much about satisfying your sensual fantasies as it is about nourishment.

Nearly every neighborhood has culinary stars, which makes for rewarding dining no matter where you wander. Downtown and Plateau Mont-Royal are a diner's delight, linked by arteries Blvd St-Laurent and Rue St-Denis. 'The Main,' as locals call Blvd St-Laurent, teems with trendy establishments but shades into the alternative as you move north. Still in the Plateau, Rue Prince-Arthur Est and Ave Duluth Est are popular for their good-time bring-your-own-bottle (BYOB) places. Mile End and Outremont have a wide selection of bistros and ethnic eateries, with new places popping up all the time. The key streets here are Ave Laurier, Ave St-Viateur and Rue Bernard. Head to Little Italy for great Italian trattorias along Blvd St-Laurent and Rue Dante. Or find award-winning restaurants hidden down cobblestone streets in atmospheric Old Montréal.

Specialties

Montréalers enjoy an enormous variety of locally produced ingredients and delicacies: raw cheeses, game and maple syrup, to name a few. Outdoor markets carry exotic food-stuffs that weren't available even a decade ago alongside tasty produce from local farms.

Residents argue heatedly over which places serve the best of anything – chewy bagels, espresso, comfort soup, fluffy omelets or creamy cakes. Montréal smoked meat and bagels, of course, have a formidable reputation that stretches across the country and are a constant source of friendly rivalry with New Yorkers. Montréal loyalists insist the secret to the hometown bagel's success is all in the time-tested preparation.

A popular yet controversial component of Montréal cuisine is foie gras, a food product made from the fattened livers of ducks or geese. The production of foie gras involves force-feeding the animals via a feeding tube, often in amounts far exceeding what they would eat voluntarily. Animal-welfare groups argue that the process is cruel and inhumane, and the production and import of foie gras is banned in several countries around the world.

Classic Cooking

Traditional Québécois cuisine is classic comfort food, heavy and centered on meat. The fact that the ingredients are basic is said to be a historical legacy, as French settlers only had access to limited produce. A classic Québécois meal might center on game meat (caribou, duck, wild boar) or the *tourtière,* a meat pie usually made with pork and another meat such as beef or veal along with celery and onions. Another favorite lowbrow staple is poutine (fries smothered in cheese curds and gravy), with inventive versions served across the city.

The city has a fine choice of French food, with bistros and brasseries of all types and price ranges. Many incorporate the best of Québec's produce and market ingredients.

For local recipes and tips on mastering the great dishes of the province, pick up the cookbook *The Art of Living According to Joe Beef* (2011) by Frederic Morin et al.

How Much?

Dining out in Montréal doesn't have to be costly. On average, a multicourse dinner for two (including a glass of wine, taxes and a tip) at a midrange place will cost about $80 to $120. At the city's more famous establishments, expect to pay about twice that for a multicourse meal. At the other end of the scale, you can eat delicious dishes at casual spots – vegetarian cafes, Jewish delis and simple ethnic eateries – for less than $40 for two people.

Keep an eye out for the *table d'hôte*, a fixed-price meal – usually three or four courses – that can be a good way to sample the chef's top dishes of the day. Prices start at around $20. Some restaurants offer a discount menu for late dining (usually starting at 10pm), while others have a policy of *apportez votre vin* (or bring your own wine). There's rarely a corkage fee, so take advantage of this.

Taxes amounting to 15% apply at all restaurants. Most don't include the taxes in their menu prices, but check the fine print.

Food Markets & Groceries

For a slice of old-world Europe, don't miss Montréal's sprawling food markets. You'll find a broad selection of fruits, vegetables, fresh bakery items, cheeses and more. It's also a chance to interact with the proud farmers, butchers and cheese makers behind these tasty provisions. The big markets have plenty of stands selling prepared foods (crepes, smoothies, coffees, pastries, sandwiches, pizza slices and more).

The biggest market is Marché Jean-Talon in Little Italy. Runner-up Marché Atwater, just west of downtown near the Canal de Lachine, is a fine spot for a picnic.

Blvd St-Laurent in Plateau Mont-Royal, between Ave des Pins and Ave Mont-Royal, is renowned for ethnic food shops. Little Italy has small groceries and deli shops on Blvd St-Laurent, a few blocks south of Rue

NEED TO KNOW

Opening Hours & Meal Times

➡ Restaurants open 11:30am to 2:30pm and 5:30pm to 10pm. Many places close on Monday.

➡ Breakfast cafes open around 8am.

➡ On weekends two dinner sittings are common, at 5:30pm to 6pm and 8pm to 8:30pm. Places fill up from 8pm.

Price Ranges

The following price ranges represent the average cost of a main meal.

$ under $15

$$ $15–$25

$$$ over $25

Paying

Credit and debit cards widely accepted. Some restaurants accept cash only.

Tipping

A tip of 15% of the pretax bill is customary in restaurants. Your bill will show the total with tax in bold. Some waiters may add a service charge for large parties; in these cases, don't pay a tip unless service was extraordinary.

Websites

Montréal Eater (www.montreal.eater.com)

Shut Up & Eat (www.shutupandeat.ca)

MTL Blog (www.mtlblog.com)

Tourisme Montréal (www.mtl.org)

PLAN YOUR TRIP DINING OUT

Jean-Talon. For a journey through Asia, wander through Chinatown; you'll find tea shops, groceries from across Asia and loads of Chinese and Vietnamese eateries.

Food in French

Menus in Montréal are often – but not always – bilingual. Regardless, if you need help with *la langue française,* don't be shy to ask (the waiters are used to it). Important note: in French, an *entrée* is an appetizer, not a main course – that's *le plat principal.* Another thing to watch out for is recognizing the difference between *pâte,* which means pasta, and *pâté,* which means

POUTINE!

Broach the topic of poutine with a native Montréaler, and either a look of utter rapture or vomitous disgust will likely cross the face of your interlocutor. One of the world's most humble dishes, poutine was invented in rural Québec sometime in the 1950s. According to legend, a restaurateur experienced an epiphany while waiting on a customer who ordered fries while waiting for his cheese curds. The word poutine itself derives from an Acadian slang term for 'mushy mess' or 'pudding.'

For the uninitiated, poutine at first glance looks like the leftovers from a large dinner party all slopped into one giant pile, scraped onto a plate and plunked down on the table. While recipes and imaginations run wild when it comes to poutine, the basic building block of the Québécois dish is fries smothered in cheese curds and gravy. Varieties include 'all dress' (sautéed mushrooms and bell peppers), 'richie boy' (ground beef), Italian (beef and spaghetti sauce), barbecue or even smoked meat. In the past, going out for poutine had about as much sex appeal as chowing down on boiled hot dogs and tap water; these days, however, even exalted restaurants such as Au Pied de Cochon serve the well-known dish.

La Banquise (p106) Serving 25 different types of poutine round the clock, this is the gold standard for classic poutine.

Au Pied de Cochon (p108) Changes the simple dish with the addition of foie gras (p28).

L'Gros Luxe (p107) Serves a good vegetarian option, as well as filling options topped with bacon, pulled pork or fish and chips.

Patati Patata (p107) The house special is Patat-ine, with cheese curds served in an edible crispy potato basket.

that spreadable stuff often made of goose liver – though there are also vegetarian pâtés, such as *pâté aux champignons et tofu* (mushrooms and tofu).

Eating by Neighborhood

Old Montréal (p56) Irresistible old-world setting, rooftop patios and some of Montréal's best restaurants. Chinatown is next door.

Parc Jean-Drapeau (p69) Very limited eating options. Plan to eat meals elsewhere or bring a picnic with you.

Downtown (p76) Ample options, from inexpensive ethnic fare to stylish dining rooms, hidden down the backstreets.

Rue St-Denis & the Village (p91) Best for brasseries and bohemian cafes, as well as great budget eats.

Plateau Mont-Royal & the Northeast (p106) Cosmopolitan and hip, with excellent dining options in all price ranges.

Little Italy, Mile End & Outremont (p116) A top Montréal food destination; has everything from bagels to market-based fine dining.

Lachine Canal, Little Burgundy & the Southwest (p132) The outer districts are off the beaten path, but foodie gems continue emerging.

Lonely Planet's Top Choices

Garde-Manger (p59) Celebrated Old Montréal haunt with a festive vibe.

Joe Beef (p135) Creative meats and seafood, excellent wines and knowledgeable staff.

Au Pied de Cochon (p108) Offers foie gras poutine.

L'Express (p107) Captivating Parisian-style bistro.

Olive + Gourmando (p56) Delicious baked goods and outstanding lunch fare.

Best by Budget

$

Satay Brothers (p132) Asian street food and fusion in a colorful setting.

L'Gros Luxe (p107) Dine in style (and on a budget) in the Plateau.

Kazu (p132) Ramen noodles and Japanese comfort food.

$$

Foodlab (p78) Creative, ever-changing small plates atop a media and arts center.

Le Serpent (p58) Well turned out plates in a minimalist setting.

Café Parvis (p78) Delicious salads and pizzas.

$$$

Toqué! (p59) Innovative cuisine and a great tasting menu.

Le Filet (p108) Delectable seafood plates by a celebrated chef.

Impasto (p119) Beloved outpost for Italian cooking.

Best Vegetarian

LOV (p76) Boutique looks on a budget downtown.

Kupfert & Kim (p56) Old Montréal gets healthyz and cool.

Foodchain (p76) Run like a fast-food joint for raw-veg bowls.

Sushi Momo (p107) Vegan sushi as pretty as tasty.

La Panthère Verte (p118) Casual spot with great salads and sandwiches.

Invitation V (p56) Creative vegan fare in a posh setting.

Best for Breakfast

Arts Cafe (p117) Market-fresh ingredients and delicious recipes in an artful setting.

Sparrow (p119) A buzzing spot in Mile End for weekend brunch.

La Croissanterie Figaro (p118) The best place to linger over coffee and croissants.

Best Bagels

St-Viateur Bagel (p117) Contender for best bagels in the city.

Fairmount Bagel (p117) Mile End institution with outdoor public seating.

St-Viateur Bagel & Café (p106) Cosy, bohemian cafe.

Best Teahouses

Camellia Sinensis (p98) A tea-lover's paradise.

Cardinal Tea Room (p120) Sip from fine porcelain in an elegant upstairs hideaway.

Best Old-School Classics

Schwartz's (p106) Long-running Jewish deli serving the best smoked meat on earth.

La Banquise (p106) A must for poutine lovers.

Beauty's (p107) Old-school 1950s-style diner.

Best Bakeries

Patrice (p133) Superb pastries and cakes.

Kouign Amann (p106) Famous for its Breton butter cake.

Guillaume (p117) British scones and pastries with a French twist.

Hof Kelsten (p107) The St-Laurent spot for pastries, sandwiches and soups.

Best Small Plates

Le Vin Papillon (p134) Inventive tapas plates and great wines.

Orange Rouge (p57) Creative Asian cooking tucked down a quiet Chinatown lane.

Tapas, 24 (p59) The city's best tapas, from Catalan star Carles Abellán.

Hà (p107) Brilliant Vietnamese dishes take center stage.

Best for Atmosphere

Barroco (p59) Flickering candles, great cocktails and market-fresh fare.

Le Fantôme (p134) Industrial chic with tasting plates.

Best for Fine Dining

Toqué! (p59) Locally sourced ingredients create one of Montréal's best tasting menus.

Le Club Chasse et Pêche (p61) Elegant new-wave French in Old Montréal.

Joe Beef (p135) Hearty Québécois dishes in up-and-coming foodie hot spot, Little Burgundy.

Brewpub, Rue St-Paul

 # Bar Open

Montréalers love a good drink. Maybe it's the European influence: this is a town where it's perfectly acceptable, even expected, to begin cocktail hour after work and continue well into the night. Montréal nightlife is the stuff of legend: from underground dance clubs to French hip-hop, dub reggae to breakbeat, comedy shows to supper clubs and Anglo indie-rock.

Bars

Montréalers treat their bars like a second home, unwinding after work for the legendary *cinq-à-sept* (5pm to 7pm) happy hour on Thursdays and Fridays, quaffing wine, beer and cocktails; the 7pm cutoff oftens extends until the wee hours. In late spring and summer this is often done on a rooftop patio as temperatures rise. Come winter, Montréalers are undaunted by snowstorms and long, frigid nights. In fact, that's the best time to find a warm, cozy bar (preferably with a roaring fire) and while the night away among friends and a few creative libations. One caveat: many bars have a table service rule, which means that if you're not sitting at the bar, you have to be seated and waited on by waitstaff. This is an annoying policy – well intentioned it may be, but it seems to limit customers' ability to move and mingle.

The cocktail craze has swept through Montréal and many bars have elevated the humble mixed drink to a work of art, blending housemade syrups, high-quality ingredients and top-shelf liquors.

Clubbing & After Hours

Nightlife in Montréal is a vibrant, exciting and ever-evolving scene on the cutting edge of international trends. While established events and club nights have a following, the appeal of one-off concerts and parties (including raves) depends on who's putting it on (and the talent on the bill), rather than the location. Beloved party brands throw events regularly, while indie concert promoters book shows of all musical genres virtually every night. You can catch big names and local up-and-comers before they top the charts.

Blvd St-Laurent and Rue St-Denis are the two main club strips, with Rue Ste-Catherine in the Village housing a strip of gay clubs. Fancier clubs have selective door policies and cover charges, but anything goes at most underground spots. Things tend to start late (after midnight) and close at 3am, but Montréal's after-hours scene is very happening, with clubs, plus private warehouse and loft parties; they don't serve alcohol but are made for dancing and all-night club experiences.

Dining & Drinking

Wherever you go to drink, food is likely to be a part of the experience. You might come across oysters, fish tacos, gourmet poutine (p30), fois gras (p28) or even *tartare de cheval* (raw horsemeat), along with the usual assortment of *frites* (fries), *moules* (mussels) and bistro bites.

Likewise, some of Montréal's best restaurants also serve great cocktails, and a party crowd tends to arrive late in the evening at some places, such as Garde-Manger (p59), as the focus shifts from food to drink.

Brewpubs

Locals have always been fond of good beer. But the microbrewery scene has picked up momentum in recent years, with the opening of excellent, creative brewpubs across town. The most famous is Dieu du Ciel (p120) in Mile End, a must-visit for anyone who remotely likes beer. You'll find daring beers among the growing roster of microbreweries – some successful, some not. The settings have evolved, too, from sudsy beer halls to brew spots with vintage style, industrial fixtures, reclaimed lumber bars, exposed Edison bulbs and flickering candles.

PLAN YOUR TRIP BAR OPEN

NEED TO KNOW

Practicalities

➡ The legal drinking age in the province of Québec is 18.

➡ Buy alcohol from the government-run liquor stores all over town: Societé des Alcools du Québec (SAQ). Opening hours vary, but *dépanneurs* (corner stores) sell wine and beer until 11pm. Some supermarkets sell alcohol.

Opening Hours

➡ Bars open around 5pm and close by 3am.

➡ Clubs typically open between 10pm and midnight (some open only Thursday to Saturday).

➡ Pubs, bistros, cafes and other establishments have varied opening hours; check websites.

Tipping

It's common to tip 15% of your bill, or between $1 and $2 for each drink you order.

Costs

You can often find midweek specials; some will waive cover before 11pm. Admission can be as low as $5 or free, but expect to pay $10 to $15 in larger clubs.

Tickets & Guest Lists

Lining up in freezing temperatures can be a real drag, so check club websites for a chance to get on the guest list to reserve tables, or get advance tickets to events.

Dress Code

Nearly all clubs and bars in the city have a relaxed dress code. Coat-check services cost about $2 and take heavy winter wear, so you don't need to ruin your look.

Websites

Nightlife.ca (www.nightlife.ca)

MTL Blog (www.mtlblog.com)

Cafes

Coffee is big here, and most locals start the day with strong, espresso-based drinks at their neighborhood cafes. It's not uncommon for artists, students and self-employed types to hang out all day at their favorite cafes, electronic devices in tow. Many places

QUÉBEC'S TOP ARTISANAL BEERS

Dieu du Ciel From its Mile End location in Montréal, this microbrewery cranks out a superb selection of beers. A perennial favorite is the Moralité, an American-style IPA.

Unibroue Fin du Monde (End of the World) is a triple-fermented monster with 9% alcohol that more than lives up to its name; La Maudite (the Damned) is a rich, spicy beer that clocks in a close second at 8%; Blanche de Chambly is a light wheat ale.

McAuslan Brewing Keep an eye out for its apricot wheat ale and especially its St-Ambroise oatmeal stout and St-Ambroise Pale Ale.

L'Alchimiste This Joliette-based brewer (about 60km northeast of Montréal) turns out a stable of different brews but its Bock de Joliette, an amber beer, is the star of the bunch.

Les Trois Mousquetaires Based in Brossard (across the St Lawrence River to the southeast of Montréal), this small brewery's Baltic Porter has won awards overseas for its bold taste.

Charlevoix This microbrewery in Baie St Paul (95km north of Québec City) makes excellent Belgian-style beers as well as a creamy imperial milk stout and an unusual Domus Vobiscum Brut, a so-called 'champagne de bière' made in the traditional champagne fermenting method.

roast their own beans, and you can buy fair-trade and specialty blends in shops around town.

Drinking & Nightlife by Neighborhood

Old Montréal (p61) Amid posh lounges and DJ bars is a mix of local scenesters, the fashion crowd and 30s to 40s mob, who have more money to spend.

Downtown (p79) Rue Crescent is *très* touristy but vibrant bars hide among mainstream options. Along Notre-Dame Ouest at Rue Charlevoix is a satellite downtown eating and drinking scene.

Rue St-Denis & the Village (p94) Frenetic Rue St-Denis packs in students with pubs and patio beer pitchers. Along Rue Ste-Catherine Est, the Village has buzzing bars and gay clubs.

Plateau Mont-Royal & the Northeast (p108) Along Blvd St-Laurent is a major anglophone bar scene, with drunk 20-somethings (and police to keep order). Bars get more sophisticated along Aves Roy and Mont-Royal.

Little Italy, Mile End & Outremont (p120) From hipster cafes to whiskey lounges, here you'll find some of the most interesting drinking options. Several cluster around Ave Laurier and Rue Beaubien.

Lachine Canal, Little Burgundy & the Southwest (p135) Sophisticated boho cocktail bars with dinner.

Lonely Planet's Top Choices

Barfly (p108) Legendary dive bar and a great spot to catch live bluegrass.

Big in Japan (p108) Enchanting candlelit hideaway known for its perfectly made cocktails..

Dieu du Ciel (p120) Fantastic microbrews, all made in-house.

Philémon (p62) Rip it up with great club beats and a huge bar in a heritage space.

Confessionnal (p61) Sinfully tempting cocktails and a fun crowd in Old Montréal.

Majestique (p110) Great cocktails, excellent bites and a dash of style.

Best Pubs

Dominion Square Tavern (p79) Gorgeous old-world tavern; a fine setting for a drink (or a bite).

Burgundy Lion (p137) Trendy British-style pub near the Marché Atwater.

Sir Winston Churchill (p81) A downtown anchor on bar-lined Rue Crescent.

Best Terraces

Terrasse Nelligan (p62) Great spot for a sundowner with views over Old Montréal.

Terrasse Place d'Armes (p62) An open-air rooftop bar that draws a stylish crowd.

Le Saint Sulpice (p96) The outdoor garden is a great spot on warm days in the Quartier Latin.

Pub Ste-Élisabeth (p81) A downtown favorite for its lush courtyard.

Best Clubs

Stereo (p96) A mecca for lovers of house music.

La Porte Rouge (p111) Upscale partying in the Plateau.

Bar Datcha (p124) Fun and fog-filled dance club in Mile End.

Velvet (p62) Uberhip club beneath an 18th-century stone cottage.

Best Bars

Philémon (p62) Cocktails, hip-hop and views over Rue St-Paul in Old Montréal.

La Buvette Chez Simone (p120) Artsy-chic wine bar oozing Mile End vibes.

Whisky Café (p120) Step into the 1930s for Scotch and cigars in Mile End.

L'Île Noire (p94) A stylish Rue St-Denis spot for wine, beer and whiskies.

Plan B (p111) Francophone schmoozers and lovers sip cocktails in Plateau Mont-Royal.

Best Gay Bars & Clubs

Le Date Karaoke (p96) Sing your heart out in this Village saloon.

Sky Pub & Club (p94) A full night of amusement with dance floors and roof terrace.

Circus (p97) A massive after-hours club with a celebratory crowd.

Unity (p97) A three-story Village favorite.

Renard (p96) Stylish mixed bar for cocktails and craft beer.

Best Brewpubs

Isle de Garde (p120) A Little Italy gem with great beer and a friendly crowd.

Vice & Versa (p124) Easygoing beer bar with a good selection of Québécois quaffs.

Les Soeurs Grises (p62) A classy brasserie in Old Montréal.

Benelux (p82) Excellent rotating selection of brews near Place des Arts.

Le Cheval Blanc (p94) Easygoing spot near the Quartier Latin, with an outdoor patio.

Best Cocktails

Le Mal Necessaire (p61) Tasty libations stirred up in a hidden Chinatown drinking den.

La Distillerie (p111) East Plateau charmer; its huge range of drinks is served in jars.

Big in Japan (p108) Magical setting for a fancy drink.

SuWu (p111) Easygoing spot with a friendly vibe and good bar food.

Best Wine Bars

Pullman (p81) Extensive wine list and buzzing early-evening gathering spot in downtown.

La Buvette Chez Simone (p120) The best place in town for wine and small plates.

Le Vin Papillon (p134) Much lauded wine-focused eatery.

Best Sports Bars

Fabuleux Chez Serge (p124) Festive Mile End bar that's wild for hockey.

ALINA REYNBAKH/SHUTTERSTOCK ©

Free summer jazz concert

 # Showtime

Montréal is Canada's unofficial arts capital, with both French and English theater, stand-up comedy, dance, classical and jazz music, and all sorts of interesting blends of the above on stage virtually every night of the week. The city's bilingualism makes it creatively unique and encourages creative collaborations and cross-pollinations that light up the performing-arts scene.

Live Rock, Pop, Jazz & Blues

Montréal is a music powerhouse, fostering an incredible variety of talent from cabaret pop stars such as Patrick Watson to Leonard Cohen; jazz legends such as Oscar Peterson; and ex–Mile End resident, electro-pop artist Grimes. Catch rising stars of the underground and indie music community in artsy Plateau venues such as Casa del Popolo; while major acts from elsewhere in Canada and overseas perform at the Bell Centre or occasionally at special venues like the Stade Olympique.

There are dozens of concerts on every week at bars, clubs and concert halls. During summer, major music festivals such as Osheaga showcase big-name bands that bring fans from around the globe. Check local listings for details and try to buy tickets in advance.

Performance Power

While the city is small compared to other artistic capitals (such as New York and London), Montréal boasts some world-class companies renowned on the international circuit: a symphony orchestra (Orchestre Symphonique de Montréal), an opera (Opéra de Montréal) and a ballet company (Les Grands Ballets Canadiens de Montréal). And don't forget Cirque du Soleil, the magical, Québec-born circus of dance, music and acrobatics that forever changed the art form. Speaking of circuses, Montréal has its own year-round dedicated circus-arts venue, TOHU, in the St-Michel district, that hosts an eclectic lineup of shows and circus events, with both homegrown groups and international acts.

Film Hub

The presence of Québec's large French-language film and TV industry, and US productions that shoot here, have made the picturesque city a hotbed of film and TV production. Montréal has been the unnamed backdrop in blockbusters such as *Avatar* and *X-Men: Days of Future Past;* dressed to resemble NYC for other flicks; and featured in films of homegrown auteur Xavier Dolan. Especially during spring and summer, you're likely to see movie shoots on downtown streets and Hollywood stars nonchalantly roaming around – they may show up in unexpected places.

Cinemas

Montréal has its share of multiplex cinemas, but many also include foreign or independent films in their repertoire. More interesting are the several independent movie houses and repertory theaters. The Cinema Montréal website (www.cinemamontreal.com) is excellent, with reviews and details of discount admissions. The repertory houses offer double bills and midnight movies on weekends. These cinemas are sometimes cheaper than the chains showing first-run films.

Film Festivals

Montréal has so many film festivals that it's hard to keep track. The mainstays are Montréal World Film Festival (p22) and Festival du Nouveau Cinéma de Montréal (p22).

Les Rendez-Vous du Cinéma Québécois (www.rvcq.com; ☺mid-Feb) This event showcases the best of Québécois film.

Festival International du Film sur l'Art (www.artfifa.com; ☺Mar) A festival devoted to films and documentaries about art from all over the world.

NEED TO KNOW

Tickets

➡ Book tickets well in advance for live performances.

➡ Book online through Admission (www.admission.com), Ticketmaster (www.ticketmaster.ca) or Evenko (www.evenko.ca).

➡ Beware of touts selling forgeries at venues.

➡ Cinema tickets are around $12. Some art-house theaters have discounted times and days.

➡ *Montreal Gazette,* and French-language *La Presse* and *Voir* are great listings resources.

Websites

Nightlife.ca (www.nightlife.ca)

Festival International de Jazz de Montréal (www.montrealjazzfest.com)

Cirque du Soleil (www.cirquedu soleil.com)

La Scena (www.scena.org)

Tourisme Montréal (www.mtl.org/en/what-to-do/festivals-and-events)

33mag (www.33mag.com)

Vues d'Afrique (www.vuesdafrique.org; ☺Apr/May) Held in April or May, this growing festival celebrates films about Africa.

Fantasia International Film Festival (http://fantasiafestival.com; ☺mid-Jul–early Aug) This leading festival features works from Asia and beyond, appealing to lovers of anime, cult, horror and other genre films. Tickets available for individual films.

Montréal Stop-Motion Film Festival (www.stopmotionmontreal.com; ☺Sep/Oct) For three days in mid September or early October, fans of stop-motion animation gather to see painstakingly crafted works from around the world.

Cinemania (www.festivalcinemania.com; ☺Nov) This two-week festival features films from French-speaking countries, all subtitled in English for non-native speakers. Screenings take place at venues downtown, in the Latin Quarter and in Outremont.

MLUNGU/SHUTTERSTOCK ©

Just for Laughs Festival

Dance

Considered Canada's dance capital, Montréal boasts an avant-garde and extremely vibrant dance scene. These days styles such as ballet, modern, jazz, hip-hop, Latin social dancing and tango exist side by side with cutting-edge contemporary dance that fuses various styles and incorporates theater, music and digital art. Montréal is home to many internationally renowned companies, such as Les Grands Ballets Canadiens de Montréal (www.grandsballets.com), O Vertigo Danse (www.overtigo.com), Tangente (www.tangente.qc.ca), Les Ballets Jazz De Montréal (www.bjmdanse.ca) and the popular theatrical touring dance company Cirque Eloize (www.cirque-eloize.com). The fact that Canada's National Circus School (www.ecolenationaledecirque.ca) is based here certainly helps feed fresh, unconventional talent into the dance and performing-arts scene.

Comedy

With so many potholes in its roads, long winters and a multiethnic brew, humor comes naturally to Montréal. In July the city plays host to the world's largest comedy festival – homegrown **Just For Laughs Festival** (www.hahaha.com; ◷mid-Jul). The laugh-fest has been going strong since 1983, attracting top comics such as Sarah Silverman, Jerry Seinfeld, Hannah Gadsby, John Cleese and Jon Stewart, and even exporting itself to Toronto, Chicago and Sydney.

When Just For Laughs is not on, you can still get knee-slapping laughs at dedicated venues. Comedy Nest (comedynest.com) specializes in stand-up and open-mic nights. Improv specialty venue Montréal Improv (www.montrealimprov.com) has free classes for those who want to be funnier.

Spoken Word

The spoken-word scene is quite popular in Montréal, often linked to the hip-hop community. Some of the most exciting and interesting stuff is being done on university campuses. Since these events tend to move around from bar to bar, it's best to check out the bulletin boards or flyers at McGill or Concordia Universities where new and underground performances are regularly announced. Venues such as Divan Orange also hold spoken-word events, and hip-hop crews and improvisational music collectives such as Kalmunity (www.kalmunity.com) organize special spoken-word and improv events. Throw Collective (www.throwcollective.com) is a poetry-based collective that holds a monthly poetry slam and other events.

Lonely Planet's Top Choices

Place des Arts (p82) Performing-arts complex, home to everything from jazz to ballet and opera.

Casa del Popolo (p111) One of the best indie-music venues in the city.

Usine C (p97) Former industrial space hosting innovative avant-garde theater and dance.

Théâtre St-Denis (p97) Century-old venue hosting everything from comedy to rock and theater.

Cinémathèque Québécoise (p98) Focused on avant-garde and Québécois features.

Gesú (p82) Intimate church-basement venue downtown with everything from stand-up comedy to kids shows and the Montréal Gay Men's Chorus.

Best Circus Arts

TOHU (p125) Great place to see creative groups from around the globe.

Old Port (p63) The summertime venue for Cirque de Soleil.

Best Classical-Music Ensembles

Orchestre Symphonique de Montréal (p83) Outstanding repertoire with performances inside the high-tech Maison Symphonique de Montréal on Place des Arts.

Orchestre Métropolitain (p83) A first-rate orchestra that plays in Place des Arts and around the city.

Opéra de Montréal (p84) Good, sometimes spectacular productions; a must for opera fans.

I Musici de Montréal (p84) A 12-member chamber ensemble that plays all over town.

Best Jazz

Dièse Onze (p112) Atmospheric basement jazz den in the Plateau.

Place des Arts (p82) Free outdoor concerts during Jazzfest.

L'Astral (p82) A larger jazz-focused music space near Place des Arts.

Upstairs (p81) A downtown gem with an outdoor terrace.

Best Cinemas

Cinéma du Parc (p83) Cult classics and indie films as well as new releases.

Cinéma Banque Scotia Montréal (p84) High-tech movie screens and IMAX theater.

Cinéma IMAX du Centre des Sciences de Montréal (p63) 3-D IMAX films down in the Old Port.

Best Live Rock & Pop Venues

Mtelus (p84) A 2300-seat downtown venue that hosts big-name bands.

Club Soda (p83) An icon of the music scene, featuring bands from around the globe.

Foufounes Électriques (p83) An edgy St-Catherine venue for punk, metal and rock.

Best Theater

Centaur Theatre (p63) Top English-language performances in a memorable Old Montréal locale.

Monument National (p82) Showcases theater, dance and comedy in a grand 19th-century building.

Théâtre St-Denis (p97) Touring Broadway shows, musicals and other big-production fare.

Cabaret Mado (p97) Uproarious drag shows in the heart of the gay Village.

Théâtre Ste-Catherine (p97) Drama, comedy and a wide variety of cultural fare.

Théâtre Outremont (p124) Restored 1920s concert hall with an excellent lineup of music, dance and film.

Best Dance

Les Grands Ballets Canadiens de Montréal (p82) Dazzling performances from one of Canada's best dance companies.

Agora de la Danse (p83) Features eclectic and experimental artists and dance troupes.

Treasure Hunt

Style is synonymous with Montréal living. The city itself is beautiful and locals live up to the standard it sets. Maybe it's that much-touted European influence, but most Montréalers seem to instinctively lead stylish lives regardless of income level, enjoying aesthetic pleasures such as food, art and, of course, fashion.

Fashion City

Montréal is Canada's unofficial fashion capital and many of the country's most talented and internationally successful designers have roots here. Locally based lines include Frank & Oak, Denis Gagnon, Nadya Toto, Christian Chenail and Travis Taddeo. For more information, check out Québec fashion magazines such as *Clin d'Oeil, Lou Lou* and *Elle Québec*. Better still, visit during Montréal's August Fashion & Design Festival (http://festival modedesign.com), which showcases new collections.

Something for Everyone

Beyond fashion, Montréal is an ideal shopping city, full of goods you'll want to take home. You'll find the cream of the crop in this shopping paradise – from big international department stores to high-fashion designers, vintage clothing boutiques to weird one-of-a-kind antique shops, used-music stores and booksellers, chic home decor and more. As well, many international megastore chains have shops here, but with a local or European flair.

Sales

Montréal's prices can be high. To save cash, plan your shopping around big sales events. Keep an eye out for sample sales, when designers offload new productions and showroom pieces at rock-bottom prices. Warehouse sales, featuring big reductions on old stock (with savings of 50% to 90%), are another draw.

When it comes to fashion, bargain hunters shouldn't miss **La Braderie de Mode Québécoise**. Held in April and October, the four-day sale brings big savings on more than 100 brands. It's held in the Marché Bonsecours.

For upcoming sales, check out these sites: MTL Warehouse (www.mtlwarehouse.ca), All Sales (www.allsales.ca) and I Love Sample Sales (www.ilovesamplesales.com).

Shopping by Neighborhood

➡ **Old Montréal** (p63) Upscale Rue St-Paul is home to galleries, designer furnishings and clothing shops.

➡ **Downtown** (p84) Busy Rue Ste-Catherine has the big names, department stores, and some specialty shops and local fashion boutiques. For antiques head to Rue Notre-Dame Ouest.

➡ **Plateau Mont-Royal & the Northeast** (p112) Hip clothing and home-decor boutiques are located on Blvd St-Laurent. Ave du Mont-Royal has used books and records.

➡ **Rue St-Denis & the Village** (p98) Eclectic clothes and books on Rue St-Denis and adult toys in the Village.

➡ **Little Italy, Mile End & Outremont** (p125) Great for groceries and cooking items. Prices soar on Rue Laurier, Ave Bernard and elegant Westmount Sq.

➡ **Lachine Canal, Little Burgundy & the Southwest** (p138) Fine antiques and budget vintage on Ste-Catherine Ouest.

Lonely Planet's Top Choices

Le Marché des Saveurs du Québec (p126) A splendor of Québécois goodies: beer, maple syrup, sweets, jams and more.

Frank & Oak (p125) Handsomely crafted (and affordable) men's clothing by a Montréal fashion label.

Monastiraki (p125) Avant-garde art zines to eclectic antiques: this hipster retro shrine fascinates.

Drawn & Quarterly (p125) A fine collection of literary works and graphic novels, including its own imprint.

Best Markets

Marché Jean-Talon (p116) The city's biggest and best food market is in Little Italy.

Marché Atwater (p130) The city's second-largest produce market stands near the Canal de Lachine west of downtown.

Marché de Maisonneuve (p123) A good option when out visiting the sights near the Olympic Park.

Best Art

Galerie Simon Blais (p125) A prestigious gallery with top-name artists in Mile End.

Galeries d'Art Contemporain du Belgo (p75) An intriguing building in downtown with galleries and artist studios.

Fondation Phi (p53) An Old Montréal spot featuring cutting-edge works by contemporary artists.

Parisian Laundry (p131) A massive space near the Marché Atwater often featuring large-scale installations.

Galerie Le Chariot (p64) Huge collection of Inuit arts and crafts.

Best Food & Drink

Camellia Sinensis (p98) Tea lovers shouldn't miss this welcoming shop (and adjoining teahouse).

Candylabs (p138) Flavorful housemade candies almost too pretty to eat.

Best Fashion

Rooney (p63) Stylish garments and accessories in Old Montréal.

Roots (p85) A great variety of clothing and gear from one of Canada's best-known brands.

Holt Renfrew Ogilvy (p85) A high-end department store with a top selection of well-known brands.

Best Gifts

Artpop (p113) Eye-catching T-shirts, bags and frame-worthy prints of Montréal landmarks.

Au Papier Japonais (p126) Gorgeous collection of handmade paper from Japan.

Best Design

Style Labo (p126) Vintage chic and curios from the past.

Espace Pepin (p63) Artful housewares and fashion pieces.

Best Vintage

Eva B (p85) Step into an alternate universe in this wild vintage emporium

Marché Underground (p138) Affordable hip vintage clothing, accessories and furniture.

NEED TO KNOW

Opening Hours

➡ Most stores open from around 10am to 6pm Monday to Wednesday, and close at 9pm Thursday and Friday.

➡ Weekend hours are 10am to 5pm on Saturday and noon to 5pm on Sunday.

Taxes

In Québec, there is a sales tax of nearly 15% on most items (including a 9.975% province tax, plus a 5% goods and services tax).

Websites

Tourisme Montréal (www.mtl.org/en/what-to-do/shopping)

Montreal Fashion Blog (www.themontreal fashionblog.com)

MTL Blog (www.mtl blog.com)

HONESTTRAVELLER/GETTY IMAGES ©

Explore Montréal & Québec City

MONTRÉAL & QUÉBEC CITY'S TOP EXPERIENCES

Neighborhoods at a Glance

❶ Old Montréal p48

On the edge of the St Lawrence River, Old Montréal is the city's birthplace, composed of picturesque squares, grand old-world architecture and a dense concentration of camera-toting tourists. The narrow Rue St-Paul, the old main street, teems with art galleries, shops and eateries, while the broad concourse of the Old Port is lined with green parkland and cafes along Rue de la Commune. Nearby Chinatown is a small, wonderful dose of Pacific Rim cosmopolitanism in eastern Canada.

❷ Parc Jean-Drapeau p66

Worlds away from the city bustle, this park stretches across two leafy islands in the midst of the mighty St Lawrence, about half a mile east of the Old Port. The prime draws are out-

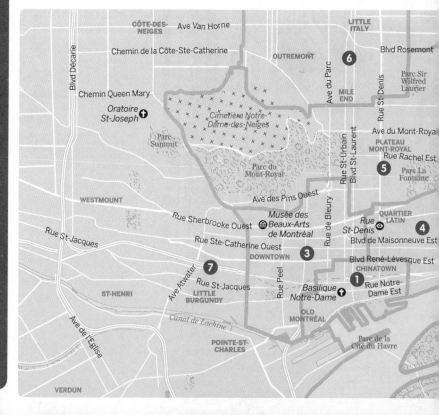

door activities such as cycling and jogging, though you'll also find some noteworthy museums, and lake swimming and weekly dance parties in the summer.

❸ Downtown p71

At the feet of its modern skyscrapers and condo developments lie heritage buildings and old-time mansions, top-notch museums and numerous green spaces. The two most common species here are businesspeople, and students from McGill and Concordia Universities. The city's major shopping district is downtown, as is the performing-arts complex, Place des Arts.

❹ Rue St-Denis & the Village p87

Rue St-Denis in the Quartier Latin is a gateway to theaters, lively cafes and low-key bars packed with students from the French-speaking Université du Québec à Montréal. Closed shopfronts in recent years have created a treasure hunt for gems amongst the grunge. Continue west to reach the Village, a major icon for LGBTIQ+ travelers. Shops, restaurants and bars proudly fly the rainbow colors here, and the nightlife and cafe scene rarely slows down.

❺ Plateau Mont-Royal & the Northeast p99

The cool Plateau Mont-Royal neighborhood houses a wealth of sidewalk cafes, excellent restaurants, bars and boutiques. For many Montréalers and visitors alike, exploring the Plateau is the essence of experiencing Montréal. The former immigrant neighborhood is handily located next to the city's beloved 'mountain,' Mont-Royal, home to walking and cycling trails, a pretty lake and great views over the city. The northeastern part of the city also has some popular attractions, including Olympic Park, home to a planetarium, botanical gardens, a kid-friendly ecosystems museum and an eye-popping stadium.

❻ Little Italy, Mile End & Outremont p114

Mile End and Outremont are two leafy neighborhoods where both upscale and old-world boutiques and restaurants come together ever so fashionably, just up from the Plateau; nearby, Little Italy is a slice of the old world, with classic Italian trattorias and espresso bars, neighborhood churches and the sprawling Marché Jean-Talon, the city's best market.

❼ Lachine Canal, Little Burgundy & the Southwest p127

This area has at its heart the Marché Atwater and the adjacent Canal de Lachine, one of the best cycling paths in the city and a top summer picnic spot. The surrounding working-class districts Little Burgundy (Petite-Bourgogne), St-Henri and Monkland Village have top eating and good coffee, creating a bohemian vibe that is tipping into gentrified. Sometimes sleepy, this is where Montréal's homely atmosphere is at its relaxed best.

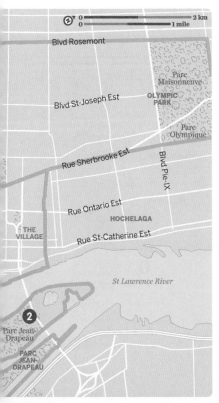

Old Montréal

Neighborhood Top Five

❶ Basilique Notre-Dame (p50) Soaking up the beautiful craftwork and soaring architecture of the city's spiritual jewel.

❷ Old Port (p51) Taking in a circus performance, river cruise, or waterfront stroll at the Vieux-Port de Montréal.

❸ Place d'Armes (p51) Getting your bearings amid heritage architecture and a monument to Montréal's founder.

❹ Pointe-à-Callière Cité d'archéologie et d'histoire de Montréal (p50) Journeying back to Montréal's early foundation on a fascinating subterranean walk.

❺ Chapelle Notre-Dame-de-Bonsecours (p54) Visiting a charming sailors' chapel, as immortalized in lyrics by Leonard Cohen in the song 'Suzanne'.

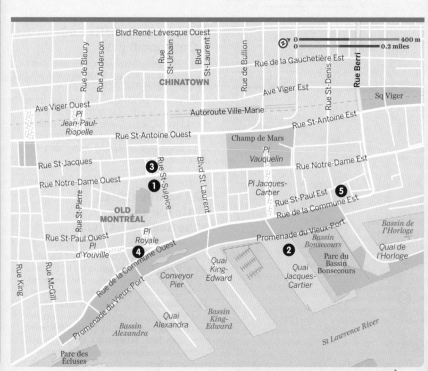

For more detail of this area see Map p268 ➡

Explore Old Montréal

Begin your tour of Vieux-Montréal (Old Montréal) in its heart – the historic Place d'Armes. Admire the renovated square, with its statue of city founder Paul de Chomedey, *sieur* de Maisonneuve, and then head inside the iconic Basilique Notre-Dame. Take your time viewing its finely crafted interior before crossing the square and visiting the Bank of Montreal's 1847 headquarters, with its neo-classical facade and vaulted marble interior.

Next head down Rue St-Sulpice past the basilica to Rue St-Paul Ouest and turn left. It's lined with art galleries, plush boutiques and eateries, but these give way to tacky souvenir shops before you reach Place Jacques-Cartier, a grand square dedicated to the French explorer that's full of artists and buskers. At one end is the photogenic Hôtel de Ville (City Hall) while one block to the north, along Rue St-Paul Est, is the equally pretty Marché Bonsecours with its silver dome. Just past it is the beautiful Chapelle Notre-Dame-de-Bonsecours, a humble sailors' church that is the perfect counterpoint to the basilica.

One block east is Rue de la Commune Est, a breezy waterfront street that gives you access to the Old Port and its museums, the Cirque du Soleil big top and river cruises. Proceed northwest up Blvd St-Laurent for 15 minutes to reach Montréal's small Chinatown. It's an excellent place to grab a cheap but satisfying plate of dumplings.

Local Life

→ **Happy hour** In summer Montréalers love to enjoy *cinq à sept* (5pm to 7pm) happy hour on rooftop patios in Old Montréal.
→ **Fine dining** Locals flock to the atmospheric stone-walled dining rooms in Old Montréal as well as the cheapie noodle eateries in Chinatown.
→ **Biking** Rent a Bixi (p243) bike and ride from the Old Port to the Canal de Lachine bike path.

Getting There & Away

→ **Metro** For Old Montréal or Chinatown, take the metro to Square-Victoria, Place-d'Armes or Champ-de-Mars.
→ **Bus** Bus 14 runs along Rue Notre-Dame in Old Montréal between Rue Berri and Blvd St-Laurent; bus 55 stops on Blvd St-Laurent.
→ **On foot** While it is expansive, the area can be easily explored on foot, and accessed from downtown via streets such as Rue de Bleury.
→ **Biking** The Old Port is an entry point to a bike path that leads to the Canal de Lachine, which connects to the fringes of downtown at Rue Charlevoix.

Lonely Planet's Top Tip

As with many streets in the city, east and west (*est* and *ouest* in French) labels on street signs don't reflect true compass orientations. Remember that 'east–west' streets such as Rue Notre-Dame actually run closer to north–south, and this can be confusing if you like ori-enteering with maps.

Best Places to Eat

→ Olive + Gourmando (p56)
→ Orange Rouge (p57)
→ Barroco (p59)
→ Garde-Manger (p59)
→ Toqué! (p59)
→ Tapas 24 (p59)

For reviews, see p56.

Best Places to Drink

→ Le Mal Necessaire (p61)
→ Confessionnal (p61)
→ Les Sœurs Grises (p62)
→ Philémon (p62)
→ Terrasse Place d'Armes (p62)
→ Terrasse Nelligan (p62)

For reviews, see p61.

Best Activities

→ Ça Roule Montréal (p64)
→ Bota Bota (p64)
→ Saute-Moutons (p64)

For reviews, see p64.

MARC BRUXELLE/SHUTTERSTOCK ©

MARVEL AT THE BASILIQUE NOTRE-DAME

This grand dame of Montréal's ecclesiastical treasures is a must-see when exploring the city. The looming Gothic Revival church can hold up to 3200 worshippers and houses a collection of finely crafted artworks, including an elaborately carved altarpiece, vibrant stained-glass windows and an intricate pulpit. All creating a canvas for the city's best multimedia lightshow.

The Sulpicians commissioned James O'Donnell, a New York architect and Irish Protestant, to design what would be the largest church north of Mexico. It opened in 1829. He converted to Catholicism so he could have his funeral in the basilica, and is buried in the crypt.

The basilica has a spectacular interior with a forest of ornate wood pillars and carvings made entirely by hand (and constructed without the aid of a single nail). Gilt stars shine from the ceiling vaults and the altar is backlit in evening-sky blues. The stained glass windows are conspicuous for their depiction of events in Montréal's history rather than the usual biblical scenes.

The massive 7000-pipe **Casavant Frères organ** provides the powerful anthem at the famous Christmas concerts.

The **Chapelle du Sacré Cœur**, located behind the main hall, is nicknamed the Wedding Chapel for the constant flow of couples tying the knot here. The curious mix of styles emerged after a 1978 fire, when the chapel was rebuilt with a brass altar with abstract-modern motifs.

While decoration is fairly minimal on the stone facade, you'll note three prominent statues: the Virgin Mary in the center (patron saint of Montréal), St John the Baptist (representing Québec) to the right, and St Joseph (for Canada) to the left.

The spectacular orchestral light show Aura Basilica (p63) happens here weekly, and there are periodic choral and orchestral concerts throughout the year.

DON'T MISS

➡ Casavant Frères organ
➡ Chapelle du Sacré Cœur

PRACTICALITIES

➡ Map p268, C4
➡ ☎846-842-2925
➡ www.basiliqueno tredame.ca
➡ 110 Rue Notre-Dame Ouest
➡ adult/child $8/5
➡ ⊘8am-4:30pm Mon-Fri, to 4pm Sat, 12:30-4pm Sun
➡ Ⓜ Place-d'Armes

⊙ SIGHTS

The oldest section of the city is a warren of crooked cobblestone lanes flanked by colonial and Victorian stone houses filled with intimate restaurants, galleries and boutiques. A stroll around here will delight romantics and architecture fans, especially at night when the most beautiful facades are illuminated. And the waterfront is never far away. Old Montréal is anchored by lively Place Jacques Cartier and dignified Place d'Armes, which are linked by busy Rue Notre-Dame. The southern end of Place Jacques-Cartier gives way to Rue St-Paul, the district's prettiest and oldest street.

BASILIQUE NOTRE-DAME   CHURCH
See p48.

★ OLD PORT   PARK
Map p268 (Vieux-Port de Montréal; 🚇) Montréal's Old Port has morphed into a park and fun zone paralleling the mighty St Lawrence River for 2.5km and punctuated by four grand *quais* (quays). Locals and visitors alike come here for strolling, cycling and in-line skating. Cruise boats, ferries, jet boats and speedboats all depart for tours from various docks. In winter you can cut a fine figure on an outdoor ice-skating rink (p64).

Historical relics include the striking white Tour de l'Horloge at the northern end of Quai de l'Horloge. Built in 1922 to honor sailors who died in WWI, it affords commanding views of the river and city.

A perennial family favorite is the Centre des Sciences de Montréal (p54). There are plenty of buttons to push, knobs to pull and games to play as you make your way through the high-tech exhibition halls. The permanent exhibit – Mission Gaia – seeks solutions to environmental or social disasters, while idTV allows you to write your own news story with a virtual editor and report it live.

The center also includes an IMAX cinema (p63) showing vivid nature and science films in 2D or 3D.

PARC DU BASSIN BONSECOURS   PARK
Map p268 (Ⓜ Champ-de-Mars) Perched over the river, the Parc du Bassin Bonsecours is a grassy expanse enclosed by a waterway and crisscrossed with footbridges. In summer you can rent paddleboats or remote-control model sailboats; in winter the ice-skaters take over at the Patinoire (p64). There's a well-placed bistro with outdoor seating in the summer.

TOUR DE L'HORLOGE   MONUMENT
Map p268 (Sailors' Memorial Clock Tower; Quai de l'Horloge; ⊙10am-7pm mid-Mar–Dec; Ⓜ Champ-de-Mars) **FREE** At the eastern edge of the historic port stands the 45m-high white Clock Tower. This precise clock, a replica of Big Ben in London, commemorates all of the sailors and shipmen who died in the world wars. Visitors can climb the 192 steps for a view over Old Montréal and the river.

★ PLACE D'ARMES   HISTORIC SITE
Map p268 (Ⓜ Place-d'Armes) This open square is framed by some of the finest buildings in Old Montréal, including its oldest bank, first skyscraper and Basilique Notre-Dame. The square's name references the bloody battles that took place here as religious settlers and indigenous groups clashed over control of what would become Montréal. At its center stands the **Monument Maisonneuve**, dedicated to city founder Paul de Chomedey, *sieur* de Maisonneuve.

The red sandstone building on the north side of the square is the **New York Life Building** (511 Pl d'Armes), Montréal's first skyscraper (1888). It's said to be built with the blocks used for ballast on ships bringing goods to Montréal. Next door, the **Aldred Building** is made of limestone and was designed to emulate the Empire State Building. Completed in 1931, it has an opulent, L-shaped, art-deco lobby. On the west side of the square, the Bank of Montréal was Canada's first permanent bank. On the south side, two statues by Montréal artist Marc-André J Fortier flank the Banque Nationale and give some comedic relief: one of a French woman in a Chanel suit carrying a poodle and turning her nose up at the English commerce of the Bank of Montréal; the other of a pug-carrying Englishman, offended by the religious grandeur of Basilique Notre-Dame.

BANK OF MONTREAL   HISTORIC BUILDING
Map p268 (119 Rue St-Jacques Ouest; ⊙9am-5pm Mon-Fri; Ⓜ Place-d'Armes) **FREE** Modeled after the Pantheon in Rome, the grand colonnaded edifice of Canada's oldest chartered bank, built in 1847, dominates the north side of Place d'Armes and is still a working bank. The imposing interior has 32

marble columns and a coffered 20m ceiling in Italian Renaissance style over a long row of tellers behind glass partitions. The helmeted marble lady is Patria, representing a minor Roman goddess of patriotism to honor the war dead.

A snoozy **money museum** (admission free) inside the bank has a replica of a cashier's window, old banknotes and an account of early banking in Canada.

★POINTE-À-CALLIÈRE CITÉ D'ARCHÉOLOGIE ET D'HISTOIRE DE MONTRÉAL
MUSEUM

Map p268 (Museum of Archaeology & History; ☑514-872-9150; www.pacmuseum.qc.ca; 350 Pl Royale; adult/child $22/8; ☉10am-5pm Tue-Fri, from 11am Sat & Sun; ♿; ⓂPlace-d'Armes) One of Montréal's most fascinating sites, this museum takes visitors on a historical journey through the centuries, beginning with the early days of Montréal. Visitors should start with *Yours Truly, Montréal*, an 18-minute multimedia show that covers the arrival of the Amerindians, the founding of Montréal and other key moments. Afterward, head to the **archaeological crypt** where you can explore the remains of the city's ancient sewage and river system, and the foundations of its first buildings and public square.

Interactive exhibits allow visitors to hear what life was like in the 17th and 18th centuries from characters on video screens.

Kids will get a kick out of the 'Pirates or Privateers?' exhibit, which explores the world of early-18th-century sailors.

Hands-on displays cover the food, navigational gear, tools and weaponry used by the recruits of Captain Iberville. Other attractions include a restored 1915 pumping station. Across the street is the **Mariners' House** (Maison-des-Marins; Map p268; ☑514-872-9150; https://pacmusee.qc.ca; 165 Pl d'Youville; admission with ticket to Pointe-à-Callière Cité d'archéologie et d'histoire de Montréal; ☉10am-5pm Tue-Fri, from 11am Sat & Sun; ♿; ⓂPlace-d'Armes), which hosts a simulated archaeological dig (great for kids) and temporary exhibitions, including some of Montréal's top gallery shows.

The **lookout** at the top of the tower (free to visit) provides an excellent view of the Old Port.

CENTRE PHI
ARTS CENTER

Map p268 (☑514-225-0525; www.phi-centre.com; 407 Rue St-Pierre; ☉box office 9am-5pm Mon, to 7pm Tue-Fri, noon-7pm Sat, 1-7pm Sun; ⓂSquare-Victoria) One of Old Montréal's most innovative art incubators, Centre Phi stages thought-provoking exhibitions, embracing a wide range of styles and genres. Four or five nights a week, Phi (pronounced 'fie') screens art films, obscure documentaries, experimental shorts and other works you won't see elsewhere. The center also hosts poetry readings, album launches, foodie events and much more.

PLACE JACQUES-CARTIER
SQUARE

Map p268 (ⓂChamp-de-Mars) FREE The liveliest spot in Old Montréal, this gently inclined square hums with performance artists,

---

A CAPITAL EXPERIMENT

Montréal would have a very different place in history but for a boozy rabble and a few newspaper articles. When the city became the capital of the United Provinces of Canada in 1844, the government moved into a two-story limestone building on the elongated Place d'Youville, which at the time was a public market. It was here that Canada's first prime minister, John A Macdonald, made his inaugural speech to a joint French–English parliament.

Montréal's tenure as capital came to an abrupt end in 1849. Egged on by inflammatory editorials in the *Gazette*, an anglophone mob set fire to the assembly and the building burned to a crisp. The crowd was protesting a law that would require the Crown to compensate French Canadians for damages inflicted by the British army in the rebellion of 1837. As a consequence Montréal lost its status as capital, and the seat of government shifted back and forth between Québec City and Toronto until 1858, when Queen Victoria declared Ottawa the new capital.

Nothing was saved from the flames except a legislative mace and a portrait of Queen Victoria; the latter now hangs in the federal parliament building in Ottawa. The location of the first Canadian parliament (the east end of the square) is today a parking lot.

street musicians and the animated chatter from terrace restaurants lining its borders. A public market was set up here after a château burned down in 1803. At its top end stands the **Colonne Nelson**, a monument erected to Admiral Lord Nelson after his defeat of Napoleon's fleet at Trafalgar.

Nelson's presence is a thorn in the side of many French Québécois, and there have been many attempts to have it removed. Francophones later installed a statue of an obscure French admiral, Jean Vauquelin, in the nearby **Place Vauquelin**, just west of Hôtel de Ville (p54) on Rue Notre-Dame.

ROYAL BANK TOWER   NOTABLE BUILDING

Map p268 (Royal Bank Building; 360 Rue St-Jacques; ◎8am-8pm; MSquare Victoria) FREE
The most glamorous building along Rue St-Jacques is probably the Royal Bank Building, the city's tallest building (22 stories) when it was built in 1928. Pass under the royal coat of arms into a banking hall that resembles a Florentine palace; the coffered ceilings are of Wedgwood porcelain tiles and the walls display insignias of eight provinces, Montréal (St George's Cross) and Halifax (a yellow bird).

The Crew Cafe (p58) is one of the businesses here, and is a head-turning place (literally: upwards) to take in all the architectural features inside.

RUE ST-PAUL OUEST   STREET

Map p268 (MPlace-d'Armes) This narrow cobblestone street, the oldest in Montréal, was once a dirt road packed tight by horses laden with goods bound for the Old Port. Today it's a shopping street with galleries, boutiques and restaurants, touristy in spots but undeniably picturesque and enjoyable to wander.

CHINATOWN   AREA

Map p268 Although this neighborhood, perfectly packed into a few easily navigable streets, has no sites per se, it's a nice area for lunch or for shopping for quirky knickknacks. The main thoroughfare, Rue de la Gauchetière, between Blvd St-Laurent and Rue Jeanne-Mance, is enlivened with Taiwanese bubble-tea parlors, Hong Kong–style bakeries and Vietnamese soup restaurants. The public square, **Place Sun-Yat-Sen** (cnr Rue de la Gauchetière & Rue Clark; MPlace-d'Armes), attracts teens, crowds of elderly Chinese and the occasional gaggle of Falun Gong practitioners.

Newspapers first recognised this as a *quartier chinois* in 1902. It started as a mostly Cantonese community of people who had worked on building the Canadian Pacific Railway, but who had faced racism and fled British Columbia. Expo '67 helped the area become a tourist attraction, which continues to the present day with a revamping of the temple at Place Sun-Yat-Sen and the painting of a mural on Blvd René-Lévesque Ouest at the corner with Blvd Saint-Laurent.

FONDERIE DARLING   ARTS CENTER

Map p268 (☑514-392-1554; www.fonderiedarling.org; 745 Rue Ottawa; $5, Thu free; ◎noon-7pm Wed & Fri-Sun, to 10pm Thu; MSquare-Victoria) Tucked away in a little-visited corner of Old Montréal, the Darling Foundry hosts avant-garde, often large-scale exhibitions and installations in its two sizable showrooms. The brick industrial building, which dates back to the early 1900s, once housed a prosperous iron foundry and is today home to the gallery and live-work studios for artists.

In the summertime the foundry hosts occasional Thursday-night street events (with free admission). Check the website for upcoming exhibitions. Also in the foundry is the first-rate restaurant Le Serpent (p58), with its entrance on Prince St.

CHÂTEAU RAMEZAY   HISTORIC BUILDING

Map p268 (☑514-861-3708; www.chateauramezay.qc.ca; 280 Rue Notre-Dame Est; adult/child $11/5.75; ◎9:30am-6pm daily Jun-Oct, 10am-4:30pm Tue-Sun Nov-May; MChamp-de-Mars) A home of French governors in the early 18th century, this mansion is one of the finest examples from the ancien régime. It was built for the 11th governor, Claude de Ramezay, and includes 15 interconnecting rooms with a ballroom of mirrors, as well as mahogany galore. Ramezay went broke trying to maintain it.

American generals used it as a headquarters during the revolution, and Benjamin Franklin held conferences here when attempting (and failing) to convince the Canadians to join the cause.

In 1903 turrets were added to give the 'château' its fanciful French look. The building is a repository of Québec history with a collection of 20,000 objects, including valuable Canadian art and furniture. The **Governor's Garden** (open June to September) in the rear re-creates a horticultural garden

PROMENADE DU VIEUX-PORT

In warm weather the Old Port Promenade is a favorite recreation spot for both joggers and in-line skaters, while cyclists can take in the view from the city bike path that runs parallel to it. There is also plenty of green space for those seeking a little relaxation or for phenomenal views of the L'International des Feux Loto-Québec. In winter skating at the outdoor *patinoire* (rink; p64), with the St Lawrence River shimmering nearby, may well warm your soul, but it will leave the rest of you quite chilly.

from the 18th century, including many heritage varieties of fruit trees and vegetables.

★CHAPELLE NOTRE-DAME-
DE-BON-SECOURS   CHURCH
Map p268 (☎514-282-8670; https://marguerite
bourgeoys.org; 400 Rue St-Paul Est; chapel free, museum adult/student/child $12/9/7; ⊙10am-6pm Tue-Sun May-Oct, 11am-4pm Tue-Sun Nov–mid-Jan & Mar-Apr; ⬤; ⓂChamp-de-Mars) Known as the Sailors' Church, this enchanting chapel derives its name from the sailors who left behind votive lamps in the shapes of ships in thanksgiving for safe passage. The restored interior has stained-glass windows and paintings depicting key moments in the life of the Virgin Mary (for whom Montréal – aka Ville-Marie – was originally named). The attached **Musée Marguerite-Bourgeoys** relates the story of Montréal's first teacher and the founder of the Congregation of Notre-Dame order of nuns.

The **crypt** has artifacts believed to date back 2000 years and foundations of the original chapel from 1773. The **observation tower** of the museum offers grand views of the Old Port.

HÔTEL DE VILLE   HISTORIC BUILDING
Map p268 (City Hall; 275 Rue Notre-Dame Est; ⊙8:30am-5pm Mon-Fri; ⓂChamp-de-Mars) **FREE** Montréal's handsome City Hall was built between 1872 and 1878, then rebuilt after a fire in 1926. Its rigid square-based dome and nod to the baroque makes it a fine example of Second Empire–style architecture. It's steeped in local lore: in 1967 French leader Charles de Gaulle famously yelled from its balcony to the crowds outside '*Vive le Québec libre!*' ('Long live free Québec!'). Those four words fueled the fires of Québécois separatism and strained relations with Ottawa for years.

Peer into the Great Hall of Honor for some scenes of rural Québec and busts of Jacques Viger, the first French-speaking mayor (1833–36), and Peter McGill, the first English-speaking mayor (1840–42).

PLACE JEAN-PAUL-RIOPELLE   SQUARE
Map p268 (cnr Ave Viger Ouest & Rue de Bleury; ⊙ring of fire hourly 6:30-10:30pm mid-May–mid-Oct; ⓂPlace-d'Armes) The big draw of this square by the Palais Des Congrès is the **fountain** that releases a ring of fire (and an ethereal mist) at certain times of year. The fountain and sculpture by Jean-Paul Riopelle (1923–2002), called *La Joute* (The Joust), was inaugurated here in 2003. During the day this area is filled with nearby office workers having lunch, but summer nights are a big draw – that's when the pyrotechnics take place.

CENTRE DES SCIENCES
DE MONTRÉAL   MUSEUM
Map p268 (Montréal Science Centre; ☎514-496-4724; www.montrealsciencecentre.com; King Edward Pier; adult/teen/child $20/15/10, with IMAX 3D movie $30/22.50/15; ⊙9am-4pm Mon-Fri, 10am-5pm Sat & Sun; ⬤; ⓂPlace-d'Armes) This sleek, glass-covered science center houses virtual and interactive games, technology exhibits and an 'immersion theater' that puts a video game on giant screens – all made for kids. Note that there is a huge range of different admission prices depending on which combinations of films and/or exhibits you want to take in. The center also has an IMAX cinema that shows vivid nature and science films.

VIEUX SÉMINAIRE
DE ST-SULPICE   CHRISTIAN SITE
Map p268 (116 Rue Notre-Dame Ouest; ⓂPlace-d'Armes) The seminary by the Basilique Notre-Dame and its grounds are closed to the public, but you can look at them through the gate. The Catholic order of Sulpicians was given title to the entire Island of Montréal in 1663. The order built the seminary in 1684 and the 3rd-floor apartments of the old seminary have been occupied ever since.

The clock on the facade was a gift from French king Louis XIV in 1701; it is believed to be the oldest working clock in North America. Ancient oaks shade the rear garden laid out in 1715.

LIEU HISTORIQUE DE
SIR GEORGE-ÉTIENNE CARTIER   MUSEUM
Map p268 (☑514-283-2282; www.parkscanada.
gc.ca/cartier; 458 Rue Notre-Dame Est; adult/
child $4/free; ☺10am-5pm Wed-Sun late Jun–
early Sep, 10am-5pm Fri-Sun early Sep-late Dec;
ⓂChamp-de-Mars) The Sir George-Étienne
Cartier National Historic Site consists of
two historic houses owned by the Cartier
family. Exhibitions in the first detail the
life of Sir George-Étienne Cartier, one of the
founders of the Canadian Confederation,
and illustrate the changes that society saw
in his lifetime. The other house is a faithful reconstruction of his home during the
Victorian era. Staff in period costume run
guided tours throughout the day and hold
dramatic presentations on etiquette and a
servant's life.

In season, the program includes a Victorian Christmas.

FONDATION PHI   ART
Map p268 (https://fondation-phi.org; 451 Rue
St-Jean; ☺noon-7pm Wed-Fri, 11am-6pm Sat &
Sun; ⓂPlace-d'Armes) FREE Opened in 2007,
this excellent contemporary-art gallery in
a heritage building features mind-bending
works by artists such as Valérie Belin, Ryoji
Ikeda and Marc Quinn.

PALAIS DES CONGRÈS   NOTABLE BUILDING
Map p268 (☑514-871-8122; www.congresmtl.
com; 201 Ave Viger Ouest; ⓂPlace-d'Armes)
Entering the hall of this convention center
with its facade of popsicle-colored panes is
akin to strolling through a kaleidoscope.
Day brings out the colors, night the trans-
parency. The exhibition center integrates
several historic buildings: a 1908 fire station, the art-deco Tramways building from
1928 and a Victorian-era office complex.
Immediately east of the Palais lies a landscaped garden with stone pathways linking 31 heaps of earth, each topped off with
Montréal's official tree, the crab apple.

During warmer weather you might catch
public design installations such as painted
pianos. Otherwise ponder the 52 permanent pink tree sculptures of surreal *Lip-
stick Forest* by Québec landscape architect
Claude Cormier – meant to represent the
harmony of nature and city.

MARCHÉ BONSECOURS   MARKET
Map p268 (Bonsecours Market; www.marche
bonsecours.qc.ca; 350 Rue St-Paul Est; ☺10am-
9pm late Jun–Aug, to 6pm Sep-Mar; ⓂChamp-de-
Mars) This sprawling neoclassical building
houses shops selling tourist-targeted arts
and crafts, leather goods and garments,
and several cafes. The upstairs hall hosts
periodic fashion shows and art auctions,
and a number of restaurants front the facade on Rue St-Paul. Opened in 1847, the
building has played a wide-ranging role in
the city's history. It's been everything from
a farmers market to a concert theater, and
even served briefly as Montréal's city hall
(1852–78).

It's also where the government of United
Canada retreated, in order to continue the
legislative session, after the parliament
buildings nearby were burned down by an
angry anglophone mob in 1849. See p52 for
more information.

THE GREY NUNS

Born in Varennes, Québec, in 1701, Marguerite d'Youville was initially known as the
wife of a bootlegger, François d'Youville, who had a bad reputation for selling liquor to
indigenous people on the black market. When he died of illness at age 30, Marguerite
decided to dedicate her life to help the poor in an age where there was no social wel-
fare. Fired by a religious devotion, her work drew other women to her cause. In those
days, drunks were described as being *grisé par l'alcool* (grey from alcohol) and memories of François's profiteering earned the sisters the derisive nickname Les Sœurs
Grises (the Grey Nuns). Undaunted, they founded a religious order in 1737 and 10
years later were granted a charter to run the General Hospital of Montréal, caring for
orphans, prostitutes, the elderly and the poor. Marguerite, who died at the hospital in
1771, retained the name Grey Nuns to remind the sisters of their humble beginnings.
She was canonized in 1990, becoming Canada's first homegrown saint.

You can learn more about Marguerite d'Youville and the grey nuns by visiting the
Musée des Sœurs-Grises (Map p268; ☑514-842-9411; http://sgm.qc.ca; 138 Rue St-
Pierre; ☺appt only 9:30-11:30am & 1:30-4pm Wed-Sun; ⓂSquare-Victoria) FREE.

1. Rue St-Paul Ouest (p51)
Usually packed with tourists, this narrow cobblestone street is the oldest in Montréal.

2. Marché Bonsecours (p53
This sprawling neoclassical building sits on the banks of the St Lawrence River.

3. Place D'Armes (p49)
At the center of Place D'Armes stands the Monument Maisonneuve, dedicated to city founder Paul de Chomedey, *sieur* de Maisonneuve.

MOLSON BANK BUILDING   NOTABLE BUILDING

Map p268 (278-288 Rue St-Jacques) The Molson beer-brewing dynasty had its own bank, but the Molson Bank Building looks more like a royal residence; heads of founder William and his two sons grace the doorway, though you can't enter.

QUAI JACQUES-CARTIER & AROUND   PIER

Map p268 (M Champ-de-Mars) This pier is the anchor of the Old Port area, home to restaurants, an open-air stage and a handicraft center. Every year the port stages a number of temporary exhibits, shows and events. Montréal's world-renowned Cirque du Soleil (p63) performs under its eye-catching big top here in warmer months. Tours of the port area depart from the pier, and a ferry can take you to Parc Jean-Drapeau (p66).

The ferry can also stop at Parc de la Cité-du-Havre, where there's a restaurant and picnic tables, as well as the nearby Habitat 67 building.

QUAI ALEXANDRA & AROUND   PIER

Map p268 (M Place-d'Armes) This easternmost pier in the port is home to the Iberville Passenger Terminal, the dock for cruise ships that ply the St Lawrence River as far as the Magdalen Islands out in the Gulf of St Lawrence. Nearby, the **Parc des Écluses** (Park of Locks) holds exhibitions of landscape architecture, shows and concerts. A bicycle path starts here and runs southeast along the pretty Canal de Lachine (p130).

The abandoned 17-story-tall concrete silo on the south side of the locks is the last big relic of Montréal's heyday as a grain port.

 EATING

Vieux-Montréal has experienced a culinary renaissance, with acclaimed restaurants winning over discerning diners and food critics alike. Here you'll find top-notch Québécois and fusion fare, among some of the city's most atmospheric dining rooms (it's hard to beat the 18th-century backdrop). That said, Old Montréal still has plenty of touristy restaurants, mostly along Place Jacques-Cartier, favoring quantity not quality. The touristy–local divide is roughly Blvd St-Laurent, with the better restaurants in the west.

KUPFERT & KIM   VEGETARIAN $

Map p268 (www.kupfertandkim.com; 417 Rue Notre-Dame Oest; mains $10-15; ⊘10am-8pm; ⚐; M Square-Victoria) Toronto's stylish yet well-priced vegetarian bowls bring the same health-conscious focus to Montréal without losing any of the flavor, while creating an exemplar for quick food in Old Montréal. Nearly everything is made from scratch, even sauces. Standouts are the sweet-potato curry with brown rice, the 'rainbow bowl' of shredded vegetables, and smoothie bowls.

TITANIC   SANDWICHES $

Map p268 (☎514-849-0894; www.titanicmon treal.com; 445 Rue St-Pierre; sandwiches around $12; ⊘8am-4pm Mon-Fri; ⚐⚐; M Square-Victoria) The sandwiches here have office workers scurrying to these cramped basement quarters from all over Old Montréal on their lunch breaks. The varieties are endless and can include grilled veggies with feta, smoked salmon with sweet roasted peppers or roast beef with horseradish. Excellent salads, soup, quiche and *antipasto misto* are popular takeouts that round out the mix.

★**OLIVE + GOURMANDO**   CAFE $$

Map p268 (☎514-350-1083; www.oliveetgour mando.com; 351 Rue St-Paul Ouest; mains $11-18; ⊘8am-5pm Sun-Fri, to 6pm-Sat; ⚐; M Square-Victoria) Named after the owners' two cats, this bakery-cafe is legendary in town for its hot panini, generous salads and flaky baked goods. Excellent choices include the melted goat's-cheese panini with caramelized onions, decadent mac 'n' cheese, and 'the Cubain' (a ham, roast pork and Gruyère sandwich). Try to avoid the busy lunch rush (11:30am to 1:30pm).

You'll also find decent morning choices (poached eggs, granola, housemade ricotta and toast) and fresh loaves for takeout (including olive and rosemary bread).

INVITATION V   VEGAN $$

Map p268 (☎514-271-8111; 201 Rue St-Jacques; mains $15-24; ⊘10:30am-3pm Tue-Sun, 5:30-10pm Tue, Wed & Sat, to midnight Thu & Fri; ⚐; M Place-d'Armes) ⚐ A game-changer in the world of vegan cuisine, Invitation V serves up creative, beautifully presented dishes in an elegant dining room of white brick and light woods. Start with butternut squash

DINING IN CHINATOWN

A few blocks from the cobblestones of Old Montréal, you'll find the the tiny-but-lively Chinatown. It's home to a delectable assortment of Cantonese, Vietnamese and even Mongolian eateries sprinkled along Blvd St-Laurent and the pedestrian Rue de la Gauchetière.

Qing Hua Dumplings (Map p268; ☑514-903-9887; www.qinghuadumpling.com; 1019 Blvd St-Laurent; mains $9-11; ⊙noon-9:30pm Mon-Wed, to 10pm Thu-Sun; ⓂPlace d'Armes) Dumplings are handmade just a few feet from the casual dining room, so you know they're made fresh. Order generous portions of steamed or fried dumplings from a tasty list of fillings including pork, chicken, lamb, shrimp and vegetarian options.

Pho Bang New York (Map p268; ☑514-954-2032; https://phobangnewyork.com; 1001 Blvd St-Laurent; mains $9-16; ⊙10am-9:30pm; ⓂPlace-d'Armes) Near the gateway to Chinatown, the ph[] (noodle soups) here may pander to Westerners with more broccoli, and there are vegetarian options for broken rice, but the great results mean it regularly turns up on people's 'top' lists. The squeezy sauce bottles and herbs are all still here, and it's less manic than nearby Vietnamese joints.

Orange Rouge (Map p268; ☑514-861-1116; www.orangerouge.ca; 106 de la Gauchetière Ouest; mains $15-20; ⊙11:30am-2:30pm Tue-Fri & 5:30-10:30pm Tue-Sat; ⓂPlace-d'Armes) Hidden down a narrow lane of Chinatown, Orange Rouge has a quaint, low-lit interior that's rather nondescript save for the bright open kitchen at one end and a neon-lit crab sculpture on the wall. Grab a seat at the dark lacquered bar or on one of the banquettes for a feast of Asian fusion. Popular dishes include chrysanthemum salad, shrimp-and-cabbage *okonomiyaki* (Japanese pancake) and fried rice with softshell crab. With great cocktails, a speakeasy-like interior and eclectic dishes, there's nowhere else like it.

Little Sheep Hot Pot (Map p268; 50 Rue de la Gauchetière Est; all-you-can-eat lunch/dinner $16/22; ⊙11am-10pm Mon-Thu, to 10:30pm Fri & Sat; ⓂPlace-d'Armes) For something completely different, head upstairs to this clean, well-lit dining room, where you can feast on juicy morsels of lamb, shiitake mushrooms, noodles, watercress and tofu. At dinner there is also seafood. You pick your ingredients, which are brought raw to your tableside for you to cook up in the simmering hot pot.

Restaurant ChinaTown Kim Fung (Map p268; ☑514-878-2888; www.restaurant chinatownkimfung.com; 1111 Rue St-Urbain; mains $10-16; ⊙7am-3pm & 4:30-10pm; ⓂPlace-d'Armes) This is generally considered the best place in town for dim sum, and is especially popular for Saturday and Sunday brunch. Waiters circle the tables with carts of dim sum ($3 to $7 each) – you pick and choose from tender dumplings, spare ribs, mushrooms, spicy shrimp and much more. The entrance is hidden in the rear of a shopping passage up an escalator. Reservations recommended.

Noodle Factory (Map p268; www.restonoodlefactory.com; 1018 Rue St-Urbain; mains $8-12; ⊙11am-10pm Tue-Sun; ⓂPlace-d'Armes) Noodle fanatics roll up to this bustling hole-in-the-wall place for chef Lin Kwong Cheung's famed homemade noodles. You can watch him in the open kitchen whacking and kneading the dough into fine strips before devouring it yourself. Cash only.

Hoang Oanh (Map p268; ☑514-954-0053; 1071 Blvd St-Laurent; sandwiches around $5; ⊙9:30am-6:30pm; ⓂPlace-d'Armes) The Vietnamese *banh mi* (baguette sandwiches) here are the very best in Chinatown. There's an endless choice of fillings but the grilled chicken or the tofu varieties topped with mayonnaise, veggies and coriander are pretty much unbeatable.

and roasted-red-pepper soup and a round of mushroom satay with peanut sauce, before moving onto curry stew with jasmine rice or a tempeh burger with sweet-potato fries.

The founders profess a strong commitment to sustainability and use organic, locally sourced products where possible. Good brunches, too.

CAFE CULTURE

The atmospheric streets of Old Montréal hide some enchanting spots for a pick-me-up. You'll find excellent espressos and inviting ambiance with a side of some fine people-watching at the following locales:

Crew Café (Map p268; http://crewcollectivecafe.com; 360 Rue St-Jacques; ⊗8am-8pm; 🖥; M Square-Victoria) Easily the most spectacular cafe in Montréal, Crew converted the old Royal Bank into a caffeine and laptop powerhouse. Order from a teller, then sip green tea and good lattes at a gilded deposit-slip (remember those?) and gaze way up at the ornate ceiling laden with chandeliers. It's worth popping in just to have a gander, especially for architecture and interior-design fans. There are sofas and nooks galore to crunch numbers or chat and eat a smoked-salmon bagel.

Tommy (Map p268; www.tommymontreal.com; 200 Rue Notre-Dame Oest; ⊗8am-8pm; 🖥; M Place-d'Armes) Tommy feels like a slightly fantastical cafe. It might be the tables at different minimezzanines occupied by laptop clickers, or the dangling plants against velvet couches. Yet it works and people constantly flow in from nearby Place d'Armes for good coffee, pastries and bagels.

Le Cartet (Map p268; www.lecartet.ca; 106 Rue McGill; mains $11-20; ⊗7am-7:30pm Mon-Fri, 9am-4pm Sat & Sun; 🖥; M Square-Victoria) A great anytime place, Le Cartet has a spacious interior where you can stop in for crepes or eggs with smoked salmon or duck's breast in the morning, sandwiches or salads for lunch, and coffee and desserts at other times. There's also a small shop that sells artisanal chocolates, Québec jams and cheeses, and delicious brioche.

Café Différance (Map p268; http://cafedifferance.ca; 449 Ave Viger Ouest; pastries $2-4; ⊗7:45am-5pm Mon-Fri, 9am-4pm Sat; 🖥; M Square-Victoria) Hipster baristas whip up delightfully smooth lattes at this bright little espresso bar on the edge of Old Montréal to a mostly hurried professional crowd. Big windows, tall ceilings and great pastries make Café Différance a fine pit stop before venturing in or out of the old city.

LE SERPENT   ITALIAN $$
Map p268 (☎514-316-4666; www.leserpent.ca; 257 Rue Prince; mains $13-35; ⊗5:45-10:30pm Mon-Wed, to 11pm Thu & Fri, 5-11pm Sat; M Square-Victoria) Industrial style dominates at this renovated factory next to the Fonderie Darling (p53) art space, which draws a creative tech-industry crowd. The menu features an interesting mix of risottos and pastas (such as *bucatini* with pork confit) and a handful of well-executed seafood and meat dishes (veal fillet with ricotta tortellini), plus a changing daily special.

There's a long marble bar, white brick walls, and exposed beams and pipes snaking overhead.

BORIS BISTRO   BISTRO $$
Map p268 (☎514-848-9575; www.borisbistro.com; 465 Rue McGill; mains $20-29; ⊗noon-11pm Jun-Aug, 11:30am-2pm Mon-Fri & 6-10pm Tue-Sat Sep-May; M Square-Victoria) You'll be elbowing your way through everyone from Armani-clad executives to disheveled artists to get a table at this popular bistro. Once settled, however, you can feast on a mouthwatering assortment of dishes, including artfully presented salads, a much-touted duck risotto with oyster mushrooms or favorites such as roasted sea bass on asparagus risotto.

Whether you want to eat inside or in the inviting outdoor courtyard, it's wise to reserve ahead.

STASH CAFÉ   POLISH $$
Map p268 (☎514-845-6611; http://restaurant stashcafe.ca; 200 Rue St-Paul Ouest; mains $15-25; ⊗11:30am-10pm Sun-Thu, to 11pm Fri & Sat; M Place-d'Armes) Hearty Polish cuisine is served up with good humor in a dining room with seats made of church pews and daringly low red lights illuminating the tables. It dishes out consistently quality traditional fare such as pierogi (dumplings stuffed with meat or cheese, with sour cream) and potato pancakes with apple sauce. A live piano player often adds atmosphere.

DA EMMA   ITALIAN $$
Map p268 (☎514-392-1568; 777 Rue de la Commune Ouest; mains $18-45; ⊗noon-2:30pm

Mon-Fri, 6-10:30pm Mon-Sat; MSquare-Victoria) The old stone walls and beamed ceiling of this atmospheric place – a former women's prison – today provide the backdrop to delicious Italian cooking. Osso buco, fresh grilled fish, *agnolotti* stuffed with veal and satisfying homemade pasta with mushrooms are the top picks from the changing menu. Reservations are recommended.

HOLDER
BISTRO $$

Map p268 (☑514-849-0333; www.restaurant holder.com; 407 Rue McGill; mains $20-28; ◎11:30am-11pm Mon-Fri, 10am-3pm & 5:30-10pm Sat & Sun; MSquare-Victoria) High ceilings, a warm color scheme and beautifully turned-out dishes are just part of the appeal of this classic bistro on busy Rue McGill. It's a buzzing place (sometimes quite noisy), where the crowd – good-looking media and corporate types – dines on lobster ravioli, grilled hangar steak, pan-seared tilapia and other bistro classics.

BEVO
ITALIAN $$

Map p268 (☑514-861-5039; http://bevopizza. com; 410 Rue St-Vincent; pizzas $15-22; ◎4-midnight Sun-Thu, to 2am Fri & Sat; MPlace-d'Armes) In a smartly renovated 1850s stone building, this pizzeria delivers reliably tasty pies from its wood-fired oven, including pizzas topped with all manner of prosciutto and pepperoni. Porcini risotto, veal poutine and roasted pork loin round out the menu, while the interior old-world stone and brick contrast with globe lights and a stylish bar.

The scene spills out onto Rue St-Vincent in the summer for alfresco dining.

GANDHI
INDIAN $$

Map p268 (www.restaurantgandhi.com; 230 Rue St-Paul Ouest; mains $14-26; ◎noon-2pm Mon-Fri & 5:30-10:30pm daily; MSquare-Victoria) Gandhi has a core of loyal fans who come here for classics like tandoori chicken as well as the extensive curry menu with adventurous fare such as *malaya*, a curry of pineapple, lychees and cream. The vegetable samosas are finely spiced, and faves such as lamb tikka and butter chicken also go down nicely. Reservations are recommended.

★BARROCO
INTERNATIONAL $$$

Map p268 (☑514-544-5800; www.barroco. ca; 312 Rue St-Paul Ouest; mains $27-41; ◎5-10:30pm Sun-Wed, to 11pm Thu, to midnight Fri & Sat; MSquare-Victoria) Small, cozy Barroco has stone walls, flickering candles and beautifully presented plates of roast guinea fowl, paella, braised short ribs and grilled fish. The selection is small (just six or so mains and an equal number of appetizers), but you can't go wrong here – particularly if you opt for the outstanding seafood and chorizo paella.

Don't miss the exceptional cocktail menu, cleverly pasted into a hardback book. Fun staff and a jazzy soundtrack add to the buzzing atmosphere.

GARDE-MANGER
INTERNATIONAL $$$

Map p268 (☑514-678-5044; www.crownsalts. com/gardemanger; 408 Rue St-François-Xavier; mains $34-40; ◎5:30-11pm Tue-Sun; MPlace-d'Armes) The buzz surrounding Garde-Manger has barely let up since its opening back in 2006. This small, candlelit restaurant attracts a mix of local scenesters and *haute cuisine*-loving out-of-towners who come for lobster risotto, short ribs, Cornish hen stuffed with foie gras (p28) and other changing chalkboard specials. The stage is set with stone walls, great cocktails and a decidedly not-stuffy vibe.

It's loud and festive, so not the place for an intimate dinner. Reservations essential.

TOQUÉ!
FRENCH $$$

Map p268 (☑514-499-2084; www.restaurant -toque.com; 900 Pl Jean-Paul-Riopelle; mains $48-58; ◎11:30am-1:45pm Tue-Fri, 5:30-10pm Tue-Thu, to 10:30pm Fri & Sat; MSquare-Victoria) Chef Normand Laprise has earned rave reviews for his innovative recipes based on products sourced from local farms. The bright, wide-open dining room has high ceilings accented by playful splashes of color, and a glass-enclosed wine cave with suspended bottles looming. The seven-course *menu dégustation* ($142) is the pinnacle of dining in Montréal – allow three hours for the feast.

TAPAS 24
SPANISH $$$

Map p268 (420 Notre-Dame Ouest; tapas $6-20, mains $25-48; ◎5-11pm Tue-Sat, also 11:30am-2:30pm Thu & Fri; MSquare-Victoria) Celebrated Catalan chef Carles Abellan brings a bit of Barcelona magic to the new world with this outstanding addition to Old Montréal – his first foray outside of Spain. Mouthwatering dishes include razor clams, garlic shrimp, Galician-style octopus and Iberian ham, as well as heartier plates of *fideua* (Catalan-style paella).

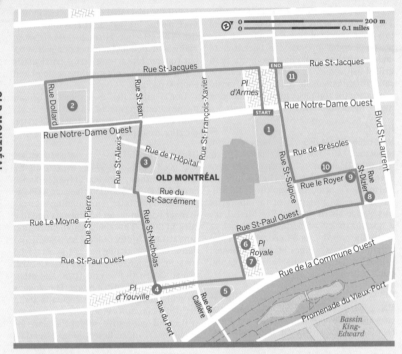

Neighborhood Walk
Reliving History in Old Montréal

START BASILIQUE NOTRE-DAME
END PLACE D'ARMES
LENGTH 2KM; TWO HOURS

On the southeast side of Place d'Armes is the city's most celebrated cathedral, magnificent **①Basilique Notre-Dame** (p50). Inside are a spectacularly carved pulpit and richly hued stained-glass windows.

Cross the Place and head left along Rue St-Jacques, once known as Canada's Wall St. Stop at the grand **②Royal Bank Tower** (p53), Montréal's tallest edifice in 1928, to see its palatial interior.

Loop back onto Rue Notre-Dame then right down Rue St-Jean. On the corner of Rue de l'Hôpital, the **③Lewis Building** has dragons and mischievous gargoyles on the facade.

A few blocks further is **④Place d'Youville**, one of Old Montréal's prettiest squares. Some of the first Europeans settled here in 1642 and an obelisk commemorates the city's founding.

Nearby is fascinating **⑤Pointe-à-Callière Cité d'archéologie et d'histoire de Montréal** (p52). Inside see the city's ancient foundations, or go to the top floor for fine views over the Old Port.

Across the road is the Palladian-style **⑥Old Customs House**. It's in front of **⑦Place Royale**, the settlement's marketplace in the 17th and 18th centuries. Gaze up at the pediment to see the restored bas-relief figure of Albion, representing Britain.

Walk right down Rue St-Paul to see the 2006 bronze sculpture **⑧Les Chuchoteuses** (the Whisperers), tucked in a corner near Rue St-Dizier. This was one of many projects to revitalize the old quarter.

Head up St-Dizier and turn left onto lovely **⑨Cours Le Royer**, a tranquil pedestrian mall. On the north-side passageway is a stained-glass window of **⑩Jérôme Le Royer**, one of Montréal's founders.

Turn right on St-Sulpice and return to Place d'Armes. Note the **⑪New York Life Building** (p51), Montréal's first skyscraper (1888), eight stories tall.

The prix-fixe three-course lunch ($22) menu is a great way to sample the goods.

The two-level dining room boasts an artful, modernist aesthetic, with blond woods, delicate wrought-iron details and tube-like chandeliers.

BOCATA
INTERNATIONAL $$$

Map p268 (☑514-507-8727; www.bocata.ca; 310 Rue St-Paul Ouest; mains $27-36; ☺5pm-10:30pm Mon-Thu, to midnight Fri, 10:30am-2:30pm & 5pm-midnight Sat, to 10:30pm Sun; Ⓜ Square-Victoria) Bocata has abundant old-world charm with stone walls, flickering candles and low ceilings – and a dash of new-world verve with its groovy music selection. The menu is wide-ranging, but the seafood is the highlight, with whole lobster, roasted black cod and squid-ink risotto among the favorites. It has a great wine selection.

L'ORIGNAL
QUÉBÉCOIS $$$

Map p268 (☑514-303-0479; www.restaurant lorignal.com; 479 Rue St-Alexis; mains $22-37; ☺6-11pm; Ⓜ Place-d'Armes) This cozy chalet-style restaurant specializes in exquisitely prepared game meat and fresh seafood. Start with oysters or venison-heart tartare before moving on to braised wild boar or crusted cod with caviar. The service is excellent and the cedar-filled dining room is a great spot to linger over a memorable meal.

Its modest bar makes a great spot for a drink, but the official policy is that customers have to be dining as well.

LE CLUB CHASSE ET PÊCHE
FRENCH $$$

Map p268 (☑514-861-1112; www.leclubchasseet peche.com; 423 Rue St-Claude; mains $34-46; ☺6-10:30pm Tue-Sat year-round, noon-2:30pm Tue-Sat early Jun-Sep; Ⓜ Champ-de-Mars) One of the pillars of Old Montréal's grand dining scene, this elegant restaurant serves fantastic new-wave French fare, including roast suckling pork and sautéed scallops with fennel and citron confit. Given the prices, it's a favorite among execs and Montréalers celebrating a special occasion.

In the summer at lunchtime, dine alfresco in the historic Château Ramezay (p53) garden over the road.

LELOCAL
FRENCH $$$

Map p268 (☑514-397-7737; www.resto-lelocal. com; 740 Rue William; mains $25-32; ☺11:30am-10pm Mon-Wed, to 11pm Thu & Fri, 5:30-11pm Sat & Sun; Ⓜ Square-Victoria) On the western edge of Old Montréal, Lelocal serves delec-

table fare in an architecturally stunning, industrial-chic dining room. Well-dressed 20- and 30-somethings feast on inventive dishes with rich, market-fresh ingredients to the backdrop of unobtrusive electronica. There's an outdoor terrace and an extensive wine list (and an award-winning sommelier). Reservations recommended.

GIBBY'S
STEAK $$$

Map p268 (☑514-282-1837; www.gibbys.com; 298 Pl d'Youville; mains $39-56; ☺5-10pm; Ⓜ Square-Victoria) A purveyor of the good old-fashioned steak, Gibby's serves excellent grilled meats and seafood, including a respected rack of lamb. A mix of corporate types clink glasses inside the elegant stone building (former stables, actually) dating back to the 1700s. There's an open courtyard in the back.

DRINKING & NIGHTLIFE

Old Montréal has the lion's share of the city's best craft-beer pubs, sun-drenched patios and oh-so-dim (and chic) cocktail bars. This area isn't so much about clubs, but there are some old theaters worthy of night entertainment.

LE MAL NECESSAIRE
COCKTAIL BAR

Map p268 (www.lemalnecessaire.com; 1106 Blvd St-Laurent; ☺4:30pm-2am Sun-Wed, to 3am Thu-Sat; Ⓜ St-Laurent) For some of the tastiest cocktails in Montréal, look for the neon-lit green pineapple and descend the stairs to this vaguely Tiki-inspired bar hidden along pedestrian-filled St Laurent. Fruity elixirs are tops here – especially the Abacaxi mai tai, served in a pineapple – whipped up by friendly, chatty bartenders.

You can also order pork dumplings, General Tao chicken and other simple dishes off the menu – it comes from the no-nonsense Chinese restaurant upstairs.

CONFESSIONNAL
BAR

Map p268 (http://barconfessionnal.com; 431 Rue McGill; ☺8pm-3am Wed-Fri, from 9pm Sat & Sun; Ⓜ Square-Victoria) Playing heavily on churchy themes, Le Confessionnal is a tempting spot to wrack up a few sins. It has low red lighting, a glowing alabaster-like bar and low-hanging chandeliers, with old-school R&B playing overhead. Signature cocktails loosely reference the seven deadly sins, and there are DJs spinning on weekends.

LES SŒURS GRISES   PUB

Map p268 (☑514-788-7635; www.bblsg.com; 32 Rue McGill; ⊘noon-midnight Mon-Thu, 11:30am-3am Fri & Sat, 3pm-midnight Sun; Ⓜ Square-Victoria) Named after the famous Montréal religious order of nuns (p55) founded by St Marguerite d'Youville, this swanky concrete-chic bistro-brasserie is equal parts microbrewery and smokehouse, serving a winning combination of brews and bites. Grab some smoked baby-back ribs, candied pheasant thighs or smoked trout, and wash it down with excellent house beers and silky stouts.

Try the Camélia – a white beer with a hint of floral and green-tea finish. Its location near the Old Port bike path makes it a good spot after cycling the Canal de Lachine.

PHILÉMON   CLUB

Map p268 (☑514-289-3777; www.philemonbar. com; 111 Rue St-Paul Ouest; ⊘5pm-3am Mon-Wed, from 4pm Thu & Fri, from 6pm Sat & Sun; Ⓜ Place-d'Armes) A major stop for local scenesters rotating between watering holes in the old city, Philémon was carved out of stone, brick and wood with large windows looking out over Rue St-Paul. Twenty-something fill the space around a huge central bar sipping basic cocktails and nibbling on light fare (oysters, charcuterie plates, smoked-meat sandwiches), while a DJ spins house and hip-hop.

TERRASSE PLACE D'ARMES   BAR

Map p268 (☑514-904-1201; www.terrasseplace darmes.com; 8th fl, 710 Côte de la Pl d'Armes; ⊘11am-3am summer; Ⓜ Place-d'Armes) The rooftop terrace above the boutique Hôtel Place-d'Armes is a requisite stop on the nightlife circuit if you're around during the summer. Nicely mixed cocktails, eclectic cuisine and a fantastic view over Place d'Armes and the Basilique Notre-Dame (p48) never fail to bring in the beautiful crowd.

TERRASSE NELLIGAN   BAR

Map p268 (☑514-788-4021; www.terrasse nelligan.com; 106 Rue St-Paul Ouest; ⊘11:30am-11:30pm Jun-Sep; Ⓜ Place-d'Armes) Above heritage Hôtel Nelligan (p156), this delightful patio is the perfect spot to down a mojito while the sun sinks in summer. There's a full menu for lunch and dinner, and splen-did views over the St Lawrence River and the Old Port.

FLYJIN   COCKTAIL BAR

Map p268 (☑514-564-8881; www.flyjinmtl. com; 417 Rue St-Pierre; ⊘7pm-3am Wed-Sat; Ⓜ Square-Victoria) Flyjin walks a fine line between speakeasy and high-end Asian brasserie, serving up tender sashimi, tuna tataki and green papaya salad to a party-minded crowd who are equally interested in the finely crafted cocktails (like sake mojitos and cachaça–dragon fruit combos). It has a barely marked entrance, leading down to the subterranean – but beautifully designed – space.

TAVERNE GASPAR   PUB

Map p268 (www.tavernegaspar.com; 89 Rue de la Commune Est; ⊘7-11am & 5-10pm Sun-Wed, to 11pm Thu-Sat; Ⓜ Champ-de-Mars) Facing the Old Port, this cozy watering hole in the Auberge du Vieux Port has delicious faux-retro decor, a long zinc bar, and a menu with lobster sliders, oysters, fish and chips, and a delish mac 'n' cheese. The house brew is the Gaspar lager, and other local beers include St-Ambroise suds. There's live music on Wednesday evenings.

L'ASSOMMOIR   PUB

Map p268 (www.assommoir.ca; 211 Rue Notre-Dame Ouest; ⊘3pm-1am Sun-Wed, to 3am Thu-Sat; Ⓜ Place-d'Armes) Like its sister pub in Mile End, L'Assommoir is home to a beautiful long bar that makes a great place to start the night with a house cocktail such as the GHB (gin, chartreuse, kiwi, maple syrup and a bit of apple and pear juice) and a few snacks (fried calamari or mixed ceviche).

VELVET   CLUB

Map p268 (☑514-995-8754; www.velvetspeak easy.ca; 426 Rue St-Gabriel; ⊘11pm-3am Thu-Sat; Ⓜ Champ-de-Mars) Who knew that an inn dating from 1754 could be so hip? Beneath restaurant Auberge St-Gabriel, walk through a long, candlelit stone passageway to this grooving grotto of electronic beats done up like a speakeasy of yore. Attracts beautiful people and the people who act like groupies around beautiful people.

PUB ST-PAUL   PUB

Map p268 (☑514-874-0485; www.pubstpaul. com; 124 Rue St-Paul Est; ⊘11am-3am Mon-Fri, from noon Sat & Sun; Ⓜ Champ-de-Mars) In the heart of Old Montréal's most touristy drag is this rock pub, a hit among students, jocks and passersby. A lunch and dinner menu of upscale pub fare is served, live bands rock out weekend nights, and drink specials complete the Top 40 formula.

CLUB PEOPL CLUB
Map p268 (http://clubpeopl.com; 390 Notre-Dame Ouest; ⊗11pm-3am Wed & Fri-Sun; Ⓜ Square-Victoria) With its edgy, art-covered walls and chic lighting, this basement venue reels in 20- and 30-somethings with its electro-house, live jazz and many sofas in the relaxing lounge. Enter on Rue Ste-Hélène.

 ENTERTAINMENT

★**CIRQUE DU SOLEIL** THEATER
Map p268 (www.cirquedusoleil.com; Quai Jacques-Cartier; tickets from $67; Ⓜ Champ-de-Mars) Globally famous Cirque du Soleil, one of the city's most famous exports, puts on a new production of acrobats and music in this marvelous tent complex roughly once every two years in summer. These shows rarely disappoint, so don't pass up a chance to see one on its home turf.

★**AURA BASILICA** ARTS CENTRE
Map p268 (☏866-842-2925; www.aurabasilique montreal.com; 110 Rue Notre-Dame Ouest; adult/child $26.50/15.50; ⊗shows 6pm Mon-Thu, 6pm & 8pm Fri, 7pm & 9pm Sat; Ⓜ Place-d'Armes) A unique immersive multimedia show where the interior of the Basilique Notre-Dame becomes the canvas for a light show set to surging orchestral music. The columns, ceiling and statues seem to pulse with life as video and lasers are projected all around you in a dazzling 20-minute show. You also receive another 20 minutes to take in the basilica in a calmer light show.

If you intend to watch this show, you don't need to bother visiting the Basilica by day also. Reserve online.

CENTAUR THEATRE THEATER
Map p268 (☏514-288-3161; www.centaurthea tre.com; 453 Rue St-François-Xavier; Ⓜ Place-d'Armes) Montréal's chief English-language theater presents everything from Shake-spearean classics to works by experimental Canadian playwrights. It occupies Montré-al's former stock exchange (1903), a striking building with classical columns.

CINÉMA IMAX DU CENTRE DES SCIENCES DE MONTRÉAL CINEMA
Map p268 (☏514-496-4724; www.montreal sciencecentre.com; Quai King-Edward; Ⓜ Place-d'Armes) Located in the Centre des Sciences de Montréal (p54), this theater brings specially produced adventure, nature and historical films to oversized screens. Watch faraway galaxies, dinosaurs or marine life come tumbling into your lap with the aid of 3D glasses. Great for kids.

 SHOPPING

If buying (or browsing) artwork is on your list, there are some worthy galleries here. Otherwise tourist-heavy Old Montréal is mostly about fashion aimed at tourists. Souvenirs and trinkets abound in Chinatown.

GALERIE LEROYER ART
Map p268 (GLR24; ☏514-845-8411; www.galerie leroyer.com; 24 Rue St-Paul Ouest; ⊗10am-6pm Mon-Sun; Ⓜ Champ-de-Mars) This spacious old gallery has always been at the forefront of the avant-garde scene in Montréal, previously under the moniker of Galerie St-Dizier. Works are split between local and heavyweight artists known abroad, including Besner, St-Pierre and Tetro. Its forte is naive and modernist art and sculpture.

ESPACE PEPIN HOMEWARES
Map p268 (☏514-844-0114; www.thepepinshop. com; 378 Rue St-Paul Ouest; ⊗10am-6pm Mon-Sat, 11am-5pm Sun; Ⓜ Square-Victoria) Boasting a vintage-chic aesthetic, Espace Pepin is a fun place to browse for gift ideas. You'll find items such as wood-branch pepper and spice mills, elegant glassware, lambswool blankets and colorful baskets of hand-woven hemp. A few doors down (at 370 Rue St-Paul Ouest) is Pepin's fashion store, with high-end clothing and accessories.

ROONEY FASHION & ACCESSORIES
Map p268 (☏514-543-6234; www.rooneyshop. com; 395 Rue Notre-Dame Ouest; ⊗11:30am-6pm Mon-Wed, to 8pm Thu & Fri, noon-5pm Sat & Sun; Ⓜ Square-Victoria) Rooney is an inviting shop with lots of stylish streetwear and accessories, with plenty of ideas to help gents score a new look. You'll find Rag & Bone button-downs, nicely cut Levis Vintage denim jackets and jeans, classic Chuck Tay-

lors, soft Mismo wallets, classy Filson duffles and a table of art-minded fashion mags.

GALERIE LE CHARIOT   ART

Map p268 (446 Pl Jacques-Cartier; ☺10am-6pm; MChamp-de-Mars) Browse the Inuit collection at this large emporium. Choose from First Nations art carved mainly from soapstone, as well as fur hats, mountain-goat rugs and fleecy moccasins.

U&I   FASHION & ACCESSORIES

Map p268 (☑514-508-7704; www.boutiqueuandi.com; 215 St-Paul Ouest; ☺10am-6:30pm Mon-Sat, to 6pm Sun; MSquare-Victoria) Specializing in outerware, this eye-catching boutique features beautifully made men's and women's garments – as well as footwear, fragrances and handbags. High-quality brands from Canada are well represented, including Canada Goose, Montréal-based Soia & Kyo and Krane Design (out of Toronto).

MY CUP OF TEA   FOOD & DRINKS

Map p268 (☑514-861-8800; www.mcot.ca; 1063 Blvd St-Laurent; ☺11am-7pm Mon-Sat; MPlace-d'Armes) This stylish Chinatown tea shop has more than 50 tea varieties in loose and teabag form, including its popular blooming tea, which opens up from a ball once immersed. It also has a range of attractive glassware and tea containers.

SPORTS & ACTIVITIES

ÇA ROULE MONTRÉAL   CYCLING

Map p268 (☑514-866-0633; www.caroulemontreal.com; 27 Rue de la Commune Est, Old Port; bikes per hour/day from $9/40, in-line skates 1st/additional hour $9/4; ☺9am-7pm, reduced hours winter; MPlace-d'Armes) Near the Old Port, Ça Roule Montréal has a wide selection of bicycles, in-line skates, spare parts and a good repair shop. Each rental includes a lock, helmet, patch kit and cycling map. You can rent children's bikes, tandems and bike trailers for pulling the little ones along while you pedal. Tours are also available.

Prices are for weekday rentals; weekend rentals cost slightly more.

BOTA BOTA   SPA

(☑514-284-0333; www.botabota.ca; 358 Rue de la Commune Ouest, Old Port; ☺10am-10pm, from 9am Fri-Sun; MSquare-Victoria) This unique floating spa is actually a 1950s ferry that's been repurposed as an oasis on the water. It's permanently docked by the Old Port with great city views, offering a range of treatments on its five beautifully redesigned decks. The Water Circuit admission (from $40) gives you access to saunas, hot tubs and the outdoor terraces.

Treatments run the gamut from manicures and pedicures to facials, wraps and full-body massages (one hour $100). There's also a restaurant on-site, serving healthy seasonal cuisine (open 11am to 8pm) and periodic yoga and pilates classes. Admission varies depending on day and time (it's cheapest on weekdays before 10.30am).

SAUTE-MOUTONS   BOATING

Map p268 (☑514-284-9607; www.jetboatingmontreal.com; 47 Rue de la Commune Ouest, Old Port; per adult/child jet boat $62/52, speedboat $20/17; ☺10am-6pm May-Oct; MChamps-de-Mars) Thrill-seekers certainly get their money's worth on these fast, wet and bouncy boat tours to the Lachine Rapids. The aluminum jet boats take you through foaming white water, from Quai de l'Horloge, on hour-long tours. There are also speedboats that take 20-minute spins around the Parc des Îles from the Jacques Cartier pier. Reservations are a must; minimum age six.

LA PATINOIRE NATREL DU VIEUX PORT   SKATING

Map p268 (Parc du Bassin Bonsecours; adult/child $6/4, skate rental $7; ☺10am-9pm Mon-Wed, to 10pm Thu-Sun; ☑14, MChamp-de-Mars) This is one of Montréal's most popular outdoor-skating rinks, located on the shore of the St Lawrence River next to the Pavilion du Bassin Bonsecours. DJs add to the festivities. At Christmas time there's a big nativity scene.

PLAGE DE L'HORLOGE   BEACH

Map p268 (www.oldportofmontreal.com/activity/clock-tower-beach; Old Port; fireworks evenings $5; ☺11am-7pm Mon-Wed, to 9pm Thu-Sun, to 11pm fireworks evenings late Jun-early Sep; MChamp-de-Mars) FREE Montréal opened this 'urban beach' along the Quai de l'Horloge in 2012, trucking in sand, Adirondack chairs, parasols and a bar. Unfortunately, there's no swimming, but it's a fine spot to take in views of the river and to catch some rays.

AML CRUISES   BOATING

Map p268 (☎514-842-9300, 866-856-6668; www.croisieresaml.com; 200 Rue de la Commune Ouest, ticket office; adult/youth/child under 4yr $30/18/free; ⊙departures 11:30am, 2pm & 4pm May–mid-Sep; MPlace-d'Armes) These 1½-hour river tours in a glassed-in sightseeing boat take in the Old Port and Île Ste-Hélène. Other options include brunch cruises and night cruises with a band, dancing and a multicourse dinner. Early and late cruises are in high season only.

ACADÉMIE
CULINAIRE DU QUÉBEC   COOKING

Map p268 (☎877-393-8111, 514-393-8111; www.academieculinaire.com; 360 Rue du Champ de Mars; MChamp-de-Mars) This esteemed cooking academy conducts regular cooking workshops and short courses encompassing classic French themes such as Parisian bistro cooking, sauces and artisanal baking, along with more international fare. Some classes at the main Montréal branch are offered in English. The Québec City branch (p190) has fewer courses, all in French.

LES FANTÔMES DU
VIEUX-MONTRÉAL   WALKING

Map p268 (☎514-844-4021; www.fantommontreal.com; 360 Rue St-François-Xavier, ticket office; adult/youth $25/16; ⊙scheduled tours 8:30pm Sat May-Jun, daily Jul-Aug & late Oct-early Nov, Fri & Sat early Sep–mid-Oct) Gives 90-minute evening tours tracing historic crimes and legends, led by guides in period costume. You'll hear talk of hangings, sorcery, torture and other light bedtime tales on this good-time evening outing.

AMPHI TOURS   BOATING

Map p268 (☎514-849-5181; www.montreal-amphibus-tour.com; boarding location 2 Rue de la Commune Ouest; 1hr tour adult/youth/child $39/25/18; ⊙May-Oct) This brightly painted 'amphibus' tootles around Old Montréal before plunging into the St Lawrence for a cruise along the waterfront. In summer there are fireworks tours.

LE PETIT NAVIRE   BOATING

Map p268 (☎514-602-1000; www.lepetitnavire.ca; Quai Jacques-Cartier; adult/child 45min tour $20/10, 90min tour $27/20; ⊙10am-7pm mid-May–mid-Oct; MChamp-de-Mars) Aside from rowing a boat yourself, this outfit offers the most ecologically friendly boat tours in Montréal. The silent, electric-powered Le Petit Navire takes passengers on 45-minute tours departing hourly around the Old Port area. Equally intriguing are the 1½-hour cruises up the Canal de Lachine (p130), departing Friday, Saturday and Sunday at 11:30am from Quai Jacques-Cartier and 2pm from Marché Atwater.

GUIDATOUR   WALKING

Map p268 (☎514-844-4021; www.guidatour.qc.ca; ticket office 360 Rue St-François-Xavier; adult/child $30/17; ⊙scheduled tours Fri-Sun May & daily Jun-Oct, private tours year-round) In business for more than three decades, the experienced bilingual guides of Guidatour paint a picture of Old Montréal's eventful history with anecdotes and legends. They also offer culinary tours, plus a 'Christmas Secrets of Old Montréal' tour in December.

LE BATEAU MOUCHE   BOATING

Map p268 (☎514-849-9952; www.bateaumouche.ca; ticket office Quai Jacques-Cartier; 1hr tours adult/child $26/13, 90min tours adult/child $30/16; ⊙1hr tour 11am, 2:30pm, 4pm, 5:30pm May-Oct, 90min tour 12:30pm May-Oct; MChamp-de-Mars) This comfortable, climate-controlled sightseeing boat with a glass roof offers narrated cruises of the Old Port and Parc Jean-Drapeau. Dinner cruises are also available. Phone ahead for reservations and make sure you board the vessel 15 minutes before departure.

MTL ZIPLINE   ADVENTURE SPORTS

Map p268 (☎514-947-5463; http://mtlzipline.com; 363 Rue de la Commune Est; adult/child from $20/17; ⊙11am-9pm May-Oct) This urban zip-line complex lets you soar over the Old Port – or see it rush toward your face at death-defying speeds via a 'Quick Jump' (basically, a bungee jump). You must be 12 or older.

Parc Jean-Drapeau

ÎLE STE-HÉLÈNE | ÎLE NOTRE-DAME

Neighborhood Top Five

1 **Île Ste-Hélène** (p68) Taking a long breather from the hustle of the city by soaking up some sunshine and fresh air while lounging at the beach.

2 **La Ronde** (p69) Riding the world's tallest wooden roller coaster or getting eye-popping views of the firework-lit city from the Ferris wheel.

3 **Piknic Électronik** (p68) Grabbing a picnic and joining music lovers on the grass, during a laid-back summer fest of electronic rhythms by local DJs.

4 **Musée Stewart** (p69) Fighting the good fight, 18th-century style, with military parades around a British garrison.

5 **Stand-up paddleboard** (p68) Getting active by taking a stand-up paddleboarding yoga class, kayaking off Plage Jean-Doré or wakeboarding.

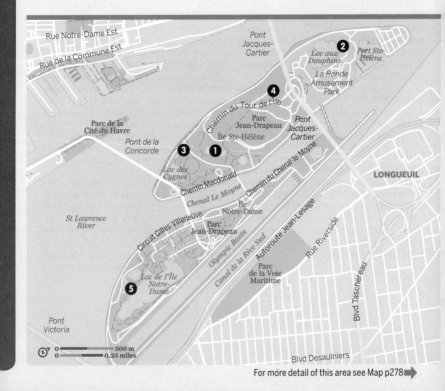

For more detail of this area see Map p278 ➡

Explore Parc Jean-Drapeau

This alluring green space spreads across Île Ste-Hélène and Île Notre-Dame, fringed by the waters of the St Lawrence River. Together, the two islands offer a fine choice of recreational activities, along with some worthwhile museums. The park is also home to a casino, a Formula One racetrack, an old-fashioned amusement park and summer festivals (see www.parcjeandrapeau.com).

You can easily spend the better part of a day exploring Parc Jean-Drapeau. From Jean-Drapeau station, walk north to the Biosphère and take in its unique superstructure and environment-themed exhibits. Continue along Chemin du Tour de l'Île, which winds its way around the center of Île Ste-Hélène, toward Musée Stewart, where you might be able to catch retro military maneuvers in action. Take in the historical pageantry and exhibits before continuing north along the *chemin* (path) to the amusement park La Ronde. While you're walking through the island, note the numerous outdoor sculptures, the most famous of which is Alexander Calder's *L'Homme,* as well as other buildings that are leftovers from Expo '67. The western side of the island offers great views of the city.

If you're looking for thrills of another kind, hop on bus 167 to the Casino de Montréal on Île Notre-Dame.

Local Life

➡ **Festivals** Parc Jean-Drapeau comes into its own during excellent festivals and events such as the Osheaga Festival Musique et Arts (p68).

➡ **Beach bumming** The St Lawrence River doesn't make for good swimming, but there's the decent Plage Jean-Doré (p70) artificial beach on Île Notre-Dame.

➡ **Formula One** The main event in Parc Jean-Drapeau is the Grand Prix du Canada (p70).

Getting There & Away

➡ **Metro** Jean-Drapeau on the yellow line brings you to the heart of the park.

➡ **Bus** Number 767 travels from Jean-Drapeau station to La Ronde when it's open. In the summer, it also stops at the Plage des Îles. Bus 777 travels from Jean-Drapeau station to the Casino de Montréal.

➡ **Ferry** In summer catch a ferry (www.navettes maritimes.com; one-way adult $7.50, child free) to the park from the Jacques-Cartier Pier at the Old Port.

➡ **Bicycle** The best way to get around the park is by bike – access is via the busy Pont Jacques-Cartier or the circuitous but far more peaceful route via Cité du Havre.

Lonely Planet's Top Tip

Parc Jean-Drapeau has a few snack bars and vending machines, but almost no eating options in terms of restaurants (except the food court at the metro station). If you're visiting in early spring, late fall, or winter, you should consider packing a lunch or snacks. In a pinch, try the restaurants at the Casino de Montréal.

PARC JEAN-DRAPEAU

 Best Places for Fun

➡ La Ronde (p69)

➡ Grand Prix du Canada (p70)

➡ Plage Jean-Doré (p70)

 Best Outdoor Activities

➡ Stand-up Paddleboarding (p68)

➡ Swimming (p70)

➡ Kayaking (p70)

➡ Wakeboarding (p70)

☆ **Best Events**

➡ Piknic Électronik (p68)

➡ L'International des Feux Loto-Québec (p68)

➡ Fête des Neiges (p68)

➡ Grand Prix du Canada (p70)

➡ Osheaga Festival Musique et Arts (p68)

◉ SIGHTS

◉ Île Ste-Hélène

There are walkways meandering around this **island** (Map p278; Ⓜ Jean-Drapeau, then bus 777), past gardens and among the old pavilions from Expo '67. The western part of the island was transformed into an open-air stage for shows, concerts and even after-hour parties. A large metal sculpture, **L'Homme** (Humankind), was also created by American artist Alexander Calder for the expo.

It's also here, near the sculpture, that the fantastic **Piknic Électronik** (http://piknic electronik.com; Pl de l'Homme; $14.50; ☺2-9pm Sun mid-May–late Sep) takes place. DJs spin techno and electronic music while you dance or lounge on the grass. Going strong since 2006, **Osheaga Festival Musique et Arts** (www.osheaga.com; Pl de l'Homme; from $325; ☺Aug) is the island's major music festival, showcasing local alternative bands as well as big-name international acts. Other major music festivals include **Heavy Montréal** (www.heavymontreal.com; from $175; ☺Aug), bringing together metal and hard-rock lovers in early August, and **ÎleSoniq** (www.ilesoniq.com; from $210; ☺Aug), an electronic-music fest held in mid-August.

Mainly on weekends from late June to early August, **L'International des Feux Loto-Québec** (Montreal Fireworks Festival; www.internationaldesfeuxloto-quebec.com/en; ☺10pm Wed & Sat Jul–early Aug) fireworks show at La Ronde amusement park lights up the skies with pyrotechnics from around the world.

You can join the wintery action at the **Fête des Neiges** (☎514-872-6120; www.parc jeandrapeau.com; ☺10am-5pm Sat & Sun late Jan–early Feb; ⛄) **FREE**, held over four week-ends from mid- January to early February, this family-friendly event features ice sculpting, horse-drawn sleigh rides, dog-sledding (humane-regulated by MAPAQ), ice skating, tubing and zip lines, plus shows and concerts.

Île Ste-Hélène has had a makeover, with a new riverside promenade and a new amphitheater for shows in summer and winter. The Place des Nations, where cultural events and ceremonies took place during Expo '67, has been given new life with a $73-million restoration, which opened in summer 2019. This included new promenades between the metro, the Calder sculpture and Place des Nations, and the opening of a new large, enclosed food court.

BIOSPHÈRE   MUSEUM

Map p278 (☎514-283-5000; www.ec.gc.ca/biosphere; adult/child $15/free, 25% discount with Musée Stewart ticket; ☺10am-5pm Jun-Nov, Wed-Sun Dec-May; Ⓜ Jean-Drapeau) ⚓ Housed in Buckminster Fuller's striking geodesic dome built for the American pavilion at Expo '67 World Fair, this nature center has its own geothermal energy system and fun interactive displays involving hand-pumps and water spouts. Exhibits focus on urban ecosystems and emerging ecotechnologies; there's a model house outside built using sustainable design principles. Explanations are good (though geared towards older children rather than young kids). The upstairs gallery about Fuller, and the exterior belvederes, offer spectacular river views.

The Biosphere is directly in front of the Jean-Drapeau metro exit with the entrance a short walk to the left. At research time, major renovations were underway on the building, although the museum will remain open throughout the work.

WATER FUN

More-active families and travelers head to the Complexe Aquatique (p70) just near the metro for a summer splash. An outdoor dip with the sounds of birdlife around you is a special Parc Jean-Drapeau moment. For even more strenuous fun, it's possible to try **stand-up paddleboarding** (Map p278; ☎514-595-7873; www.ksf.ca; Pavillon des Activités Nautiques; 1/2hr hire $20/30, 2hr yoga class $49; ☺mid-Jun–Aug; Ⓜ Jean-Drapeau, then bus 767) or sit-down floating **yoga on the lake** on Île Notre-Dame. On the same island in summer, pose and swim at the **Plage des Îles** or watch rowers plough the water in the **Olympic Basin**, the former Olympic rowing basin, at the **Montréal International Dragon Boat Race Festival** (☎514-866-7001; www.22dragons.com; ☺Jul).

★**LA RONDE** AMUSEMENT PARK

Map p278 (☑514-397-2000; www.laronde.com; 22 Chemin Macdonald; season pass $42; ⏰hours vary May-Oct; P ♿; Ⓜ Jean-Drapeau) Québec's largest amusement park, La Ronde has a battery of impressive rides, including **Le Monstre**, the world's highest double wooden roller coaster, and **Le Vampire**, a corkscrew roller coaster with gut-wrenching turns. For a more peaceful experience, there's a Ferris wheel and a gentle minirail that offers views of the river and city.

Concerts and shows are held throughout the summer, and in July and early August fireworks explode overhead on Wednesday and Saturday evenings (when the park stays open later).

★**MUSÉE STEWART** MUSEUM

Map p278 (☑514-861-6701; www.stewart-museum.org; 20 Chemin du Tour de l'Île; adult/child $15/free; ⏰10am-5pm Tue-Sun Jul-Sep, Wed-Sun Oct-Jun) ✎ Inside the old Arsenal British garrison (where troops were stationed in the 19th century), this beautifully renovated museum displays relics from Canada's past in its permanent exhibition, History and Memory. In summer there are military parades outside by actors in 18th-century uniforms; check the website for details. It's a 1km (about 15-minute) walk from Jean-Drapeau metro station.

⊙ Île Notre-Dame

This southern isle emerged from the riverbed in a period of 10 months, atop millions of tons of earth and rock excavated from the new metro created in 1967. The planners were creative with the use of water, carving out canals and pretty garden walkways amid the parklands that stretch across the isle. The **Circuit Gilles-Villeneuve** continues to host the uberpopular Grand Prix du Canada (p70) in summer, while the Casino de Montréal draws punters year-round.

✗ EATING

A sugar shack will hardly satisfy most beachside visitors, so it is best to bring your own food. There are snacks at the sights, otherwise the casino restaurants are the only other options if you're desperate. In summer the Grand Prix and music festivals provide plenty of food-truck/stand options.

LA CABANE CHEZ JEAN QUÉBÉCOIS $$

Map p278 (☑438-382-3335; http://gestion-gsp.com/; Plage des Îles; prix-fixe adult/child $30/20; ⏰7-11pm Fri & Sat, 1-4pm Sat & Sun mid-Apr–mid-Mar, 1-4pm Sat & Sun mid-Mar–mid-Apr) The chalet overlooking Plage des Îles hosts its *cabane à sucre* (sugar shack) during maple season. At long communal tables, diners feast on maple-syrup-tinged dishes such as sausages, beer-braised ham, baked beans, potatoes seared in duck fat and maple-sugar pie. Reserve ahead.

With a flickering fire in the corner and views across the frozen lake, the warmly lit chalet does a fine stand-in for the countryside if you can't get out of town.

LE PAVILLON 67 BUFFET $$$

Map p278 (www.casinosduquebec.com/montreal; 5th fl, 1 Ave du Casino, Île Notre-Dame; buffet $27-36, Sun brunch $25; ⏰4:30-10pm Wed-Sun, 10am-2pm Sun; Ⓜ Jean-Drapeau, then bus 167) Located in the Casino de Montréal, Le Pavillon 67 spreads an excellent buffet. On weekends, you'll find lobster, crab legs, poached salmon, roast lamb, grilled shrimp and many other appealing dishes. The options are more limited on weekdays. On Sundays, there's also a decadent jazz brunch with live music. Note that the casino does not admit children under 18.

There are several other eating and drinking spots in the casino: **Ajia** serves Asian fusion and is open hours similar to Le Pavillon 67; **L'Instant** has sandwiches and other deli fare, and is open 24 hours; there's also sleek modern **Bar Le Poker**, open from 11am to 3am (with food served until 2am).

☆ ENTERTAINMENT

CASINO DE MONTRÉAL CASINO

Map p278 (☑514-392-2746; http://casinos.lotoquebec.com; 1 Ave du Casino; ⏰24hr; 🎷; Ⓜ Jean-Drapeau, then bus 777) Based in the former French pavilion from Expo '67, the Montréal casino opened in 1993 and was so popular (and earned so much money) that expansion occurred almost instantly. It remains Canada's biggest casino, and has quite a sleek design, following a four-year, $300-million makeover completed in 2013.

THE LAST GOOD YEAR

For Montréalers who are old enough, there are few events in the history of the city that evoke such an emotional response as the 1967 International and Universal Exposition, fondly known as 'Expo '67.' For six months that year, what is now Parc Jean-Drapeau hosted 62 nations from around the world and drew 50 million visitors (more than double Canada's population), including VIPs such as Queen Elizabeth II, Lyndon Johnson and Charles de Gaulle. In no small part thanks to the efforts of Mayor Jean Drapeau, Expo '67 became one of the most successful world fairs ever held. It also coincided with the centenary of Canadian confederation, and the country – and Montréal itself – seemed on top of the world. (One of the fair's many legacies was the Expos, Montréal's pro baseball team from 1969 to 2004.)

However, in the decades that followed the Expo, the sovereigntist political movement, an exodus of anglophones and economic stagnation precipitated for many a period of citywide decline. And thus there is a deep longing for Expo '67 and its glories.

It has more than 3000 slot machines and 120 gaming tables.

There are drinks at the Poker Bar in the middle of the casino, and other enticing eating and drinking options. Regular weekend concerts take place here (jazz, folk, blues). Arched footbridges link the casino to the **Jardins des Floralies** (Map p278; 514-872-6120; 1 Circuit Gilles Villeneuve; 6am-10pm; Jean-Drapeau, then bus 777) FREE, a rose garden that is wonderful for a stroll.

SPORTS & ACTIVITIES

GRAND PRIX DU CANADA CAR RACING

Map p278 (www.gpcanada.ca; Circuit Gilles-Villeneuve, Île Notre-Dame; tickets $90-595; Jun; ; Jean-Drapeau) Canada's only Grand Prix race remains one of the most popular motorsport events in the world, selling out and packing Montréal's hotels in early June. It has been held on Île Notre-Dame since 1978, though it went on hiatus in 2009 due to a dispute between the city and Formula One supremo Bernie Ecclestone. Be sure to reserve your tickets early. Ticket-holders have access to a beer-fuelled Beach Zone, complete with DJs, and a Family Zone decked out with games.

PLAGE JEAN-DORÉ BEACH

Map p278 (Plage des Îles; 514-872-0199; www.parcjeandrapeau.com; Île Notre-Dame; adult/child $9/4.50; 10am-7pm daily mid-Jun–late Aug, noon-7pm Sat-Mon late Aug-early Sep; ; Jean-Drapeau, then bus 767) On warm summer days this artificial sandy beach on Île Notre-Dame can accommodate up to 5000 sunning and splashing souls. It's safe, clean and ideal for kids; picnic facilities and snack bars serving beer are on-site. There are also paddleboats, canoes and kayaks for rent.

TTS MONTRÉAL ADVENTURE SPORTS

Map p278 (514-567-2567; www.ttsmontreal.com; Pavillon des Activités Nautiques; per session incl equipment $20; Jun–mid-Sep; Jean-Drapeau, then bus 767) Near the beach on Île Notre-Dame, TTS can set you up with a wakeboard and all the gear you'll need (including a helmet) for an action-packed glide across the water. You hold onto a water-skiing-style grip, which is attached by long cord to a cable that pulls you across the lake. Ramps and other obstacles allow you to get some air on your eight-minute ride.

COMPLEXE AQUATIQUE WATER SPORTS

Map p278 (www.parcjeandrapeau.com; Île Ste-Hélène; adult/child $7.50/3.50; 10am-8pm daily early Jun-late Aug, noon-7pm daily late Aug-early Sep, noon-7pm Sat & Sun late May-early Jun; ; Jean-Drapeau) This pool complex was rebuilt when Montréal scored the 2005 World Aquatic Championships. The magnificent 55m by 44m warm-up pool is open for recreational swimming. There's also a bay-like portion of the pool with a shallow, gently sloping bottom that's great for kids and families.

Turn left upon exiting the metro.

Downtown

Neighborhood Top Five

1 **Musée des Beaux-Arts de Montréal** (p73) Spending a few hours exploring a treasure trove of traditional and contemporary art.

2 **Place des Arts** (p74) Getting your festival freak on with thousands of others when the jazz festival hits town.

3 **Cathédrale Marie-Reine-du-Monde** (p75) Enjoying quiet time inside one of downtown's many beautiful historic churches.

4 **Rue Sherbrooke Ouest** (p75) Browsing this street's eye-catching boutiques and heritage buildings.

5 **Museé McCord** (p74) Examining dance sticks, moccasins and 8500 other archaeological objects from indigenous cultures.

For more detail of this area see Map p272

Lonely Planet's Top Tip

While there's much to see during the day, downtown is also a major nighttime draw for the performing arts. It's worth planning an evening around a concert, play or performance happening in one of the top theaters. If hockey or Canadian football is more your speed, catch a game at the **Bell Centre** (p86) or **Molson Stadium** (p86).

Best Places to Eat

➡ Café Parvis (p78)

➡ LOV (p76)

➡ Foodlab (p78)

➡ Jatoba (p79)

For reviews, see p76.➡

Best Places to Drink

➡ Dominion Square Tavern (p79)

➡ Furco (p79)

➡ Pub Ste-Élisabeth (p81)

➡ Pullman (p81)

➡ Brutopia (p81)

For reviews, see p79.➡

☆ Best Entertainment

➡ Place des Arts (p82)

➡ Monument National (p82)

➡ Les Grands Ballets Canadiens de Montréal (p82)

➡ Foufounes Electriques (p83)

➡ Upstairs (p81)

For reviews, see p82.➡

Explore Downtown

Downtown Montréal's wide boulevards, glass skyscrapers and shopping galleries give the area a decidedly North American flavor, while numerous green spaces, eye-catching heritage buildings and 19th-century churches add a more European character to the bustling city streets. You can explore the area easily in the better part of a day with a pause for lunch.

Begin your tour at the Musée des Beaux-Arts de Montréal, spending the morning taking in its vast collection of Old Masters and modern Canadian art, before grabbing a snack or lunch at nearby spots like Cafe Aunja. Make your way along Rue Sherbrooke Ouest, passing the heritage houses and tiny businesses en route, before reaching McGill University, a bustling haven of green with its own museums.

From the university, you can climb toward Parc du Mont-Royal if you really want to stretch your legs, or turn down Ave McGill College to reach Rue Ste-Catherine Ouest, downtown's main shopping drag. To the west, there's Rue Crescent and Rue Bishop, the traditional anglophone centers of nightlife with an array of bars and restaurants. More shopping centers and the festival-oriented Quartier des Spectacles – including Place des Arts, the performing-arts complex and hub of the jazz festival – are within a short walk to the east along Rue Ste-Catherine Ouest. From Place des Arts, it's easy to walk to Chinatown, and even Old Montréal, for dinner.

Local Life

➡ **Pedaling** Rent a Bixi bike and pedal southwest along Blvd de Maisonneuve to the leafy suburb of Westmount (p77).

➡ **Hiking** Hoof it up hills such as Rue Peel to reach one of the entrances to Parc du Mont-Royal.

➡ **Drinks, theater** Have a drink and a bite at Foodlab (p78), then catch a play or a dance performance across the street at the Monument National (p82).

Getting There & Away

➡ **Metro** Peel and McGill are both central and convenient.

➡ **Bus** Bus 15 runs on Rue Ste-Catherine and Blvd de Maisonneuve, bus 24 on Rue Sherbrooke and bus 150 on Blvd René-Lévesque.

➡ **Bike** Bixi bikes have numerous stations in the area. If you're cycling, head to Blvd de Maisonneuve, which has separate protected bike lanes.

TOP EXPERIENCE
EXPLORE THE MUSÉE DES BEAUX-ARTS DE MONTRÉAL

Montréal's Museum of Fine Arts is an accessible and beautifully updated oasis of art housed in architecturally striking buildings. This is Canada's oldest museum and the city's largest, with works from Old Masters to contemporary artists. Special exhibitions have included the world premiere of works by fashion designer Thierry Mugler.

The collection is housed in five pavilions. The marble-covered **Michal & Renata Hornstein Pavilion** presents everything from ancient African to modern Japanese art.

Behind this building is the **Liliane & David M Stewart Pavilion**, where you'll find an eye-catching decorative-arts collection. Glass, ceramics, textiles, furniture and industrial-design pieces from around the globe have been assembled.

Adjacent to this building on Rue Bishop is the **Michal & Renata Hornstein Pavilion for Peace** (not to be confused with the similarly named pavilion mentioned above), which opened in 2017 and features 750 works from Old Masters to contemporary artists, and the **Michel de la Chenelière International Atelier for Education and Art Therapy**.

Across Ave du Musée, the **Claire & Marc Bourgie Pavilion** is situated in a renovated 1894 church and displays some magnificent works of Canadian and Québécois art. Head to the top floor to delve into Inuit art and its cultural legacy. The church's Bourgie Concert Hall features gorgeous Tiffany stained-glass windows and live shows.

The Moshe Safdie–designed annex across Sherbrooke is the **Jean-Noël Desmarais Pavilion**, home to the Old and Modern Masters, with paintings from the Middle Ages stretching through the Renaissance and classical eras up to contemporary works. It can be reached via an underground passage from the Hornstein Pavilion.

DON'T MISS

➡ Pablo Picasso's *Embrace*
➡ Jean-Paul Riopelle's *Austria*

PRACTICALITIES

➡ Museum of Fine Arts
➡ Map p272, B3
➡ www.mbam.qc.ca
➡ 1380 Rue Sherbrooke Ouest
➡ all exhibitions & pavilions adult over 30yr/21-30yr/under 20yr $24/16/free, after 5pm Wed special exhibition $12
➡ ⊙10am-5pm Tue-Sun, to 9pm Wed special exhibitions only
➡ Ⓜ Guy-Concordia

⊙ SIGHTS

Montréal's modern downtown has a North American look, with wide thoroughfares chopping a forest of skyscrapers into a grid pattern. At street level you'll find some of the city's most beautiful churches, striking buildings, museums, green spaces and major shopping areas. You'll find that an almost Latin spirit pervades the cafes, restaurants and bars, especially along Rue Crescent.

MUSÉE DES BEAUX-ARTS
DE MONTRÉAL   MUSEUM
See p73.

★PLACE DES ARTS   ARTS CENTER
Map p272 (☑box office 514-842-2112; www.place desarts.com; 175 Rue Ste-Catherine Ouest; MPlace-des-Arts) Montréal's performing-arts center is the nexus for artistic and cultural events. Several renowned musical companies call Place des Arts home, including Opéra de Montréal (p84) and the Montréal Symphony Orchestra (p83), based in the acoustically brilliant 2100-seat **Maison Symphonique**. It's also center stage for Festival International de Jazz de Montréal (p225). A key part of the Quartier des Spectacles, the complex embraces an outdoor plaza with fountains and an ornamental pool and is attached to the Complexe Desjardins shopping center via an underground tunnel.

The six halls also include the 3000-seat **Salle Wilfrid-Pelletier**, where Les Grands Ballets Canadiens de Montréal (p82) and the Opéra de Montréal perform. The 1500-seat **Théâtre Maisonneuve** hosts variety shows, dance performances and circus arts, while the smaller **Cinquième Salle** hosts cabaret, experimental theater and small concerts.

★MUSÉE MCCORD   MUSEUM
Map p272 (McCord Museum of Canadian History; ☑514-861-6701; www.mccord-museum.qc.ca; 690 Rue Sherbrooke Ouest; adult/student/child $20/14/free, special exhibitions extra $5, after 5pm Wed free; ◉10am-6pm Tue, Thu & Fri, to 9pm Wed, to 5pm Sat & Sun; MMcGill) With hardly an inch to spare in its cramped but welcoming galleries, the McCord Museum of Canadian History houses thousands of artifacts and documents illustrating Canada's social, cultural and archaeological history from the 18th century to the present day with a small-but-excellent First Nations permanent collection displaying aboriginal dress and artifacts.

MCGILL UNIVERSITY   UNIVERSITY
Map p272 (☑514-398-4455; www.mcgill.ca; 845 Rue Sherbrooke Ouest; MMcGill) Founded in 1828 by James McGill, a rich Scottish fur trader, McGill University is one of Canada's most prestigious learning institutions, with 40,000 students. The university's medical and engineering faculties have a fine

THE UNDERGROUND CITY

Brilliant marketing that conjures up images of subterranean skyscrapers and roads has made the underground city one of the first things visitors seek out when they travel to Montréal.

The underground city doesn't actually have any of these things. What it does have is a network of some 2600 shops, 200 restaurants and 40-odd cinemas, theaters and exhibition halls, all hidden neatly beneath the surface in more than 30km of tunnels and underground spaces. For most travelers, it's a major letdown, because no matter what tourism officials call it, it is basically just a kind of colossal network of interlocking shopping malls. Where it does get interesting, however, is for residents living in downtown Montréal, as it gives them a reprieve from winter – hundreds of thousands use it every day of the year.

The 60-odd distinct complexes that make up this network are linked by brightly lit, well-ventilated corridors; fountains play to maintain humidity and the temperature hovers around 20°C. Add the metro and you have a self-contained world, shielded from the subarctic temperatures. If you move to Montréal and pick the right apartment building, it could literally be the middle of winter and you would be able to go to work, do your grocery shopping, go see a movie and take in a performance at Place des Arts (p82) and never need more than a T-shirt.

reputation and many campus buildings are showcases of Victorian architecture. The campus, at the foot of Mont Royal, is rather nice for a stroll and also incorporates the Musée Redpath.

MUSÉE REDPATH

MUSEUM

Map p272 (⌨514-398-4086; www.mcgill.ca/redpath/; 859 Rue Sherbrooke Ouest; suggested donation adult/child $10/free; ⊗9am-2pm Jun-Aug, 9am-5pm Mon-Fri, 11am-5pm Sat & Sun Sep-May; MMcGill) **FREE** A Victorian spirit of discovery pervades this old natural-history museum, though you won't find anything more gruesome than stuffed animals from the Laurentians hinterland. The Redpath Museum houses a large variety of specimens, including a dinosaur skeleton and seashells donated from around the world. A highlight is the 3rd-floor **World Cultures Exhibits**, which includes Egyptian mummies, shrunken heads and artifacts from ancient Mediterranean, African and East Asian communities.

RUE STE-CATHERINE OUEST

AREA

Map p272 (MPeel, McGill, Place-des-Arts) Lively Rue Ste-Catherine Ouest is one endless orgy of shops, restaurants, bars and cafes on the hyperactive stretch between Rue Crescent and Rue St-Urbain to the northeast. Shopping malls, department stores and multiplex cinemas are sprinkled along the way. Shoppers flood the streets on weekends, slowing pedestrian traffic to a mere shuffle.

MAISON ALCAN

HISTORIC BUILDING

Map p272 (1188 Rue Sherbrooke Ouest; MPeel) This mélange of four carefully restored 19th- and 20th-century buildings integrates the old Berkeley Hotel and three houses, including the Atholstan House, a Québec historic monument. To the rear is an intriguing atrium with a pretty garden. Also on the property stands the **Emmanuel Congregation Church**, which belongs to the Salvation Army.

MUSÉE D'ART CONTEMPORAIN

MUSEUM

Map p272 (⌨514-847-6226; www.macm.org; 185 Rue Ste-Catherine Ouest; adult/child $17/6, 5-9pm Wed half price; ⊗11am-6pm Tue, to 9pm Wed-Fri, 10am-6pm Sat & Sun; MPlace-des-Arts) This showcase of modern Canadian and international art has eight galleries divided between past greats (since 1939) and exciting current developments. A weighty collection of 7600 permanent works includes Québécois legends Jean-Paul Riopelle, Paul-Émile Borduas and Geneviève Cadieux, but also temporary exhibitions of the latest trends in current art from Canadian and international artists. Forms range from traditional to new media, from painting, sculpture and prints to installation art, photography and video.

GALERIES D'ART CONTEMPORAIN DU BELGO

ARTS CENTER

Map p272 (www.thebelgoreport.com; 372 Rue Ste-Catherine Ouest; ⊗vary; MPlace-des-Arts) More than a decade ago the Belgo building was a run-down haven for struggling artists. It has since earned a reputation as one of Montréal's most intriguing exhibition spaces with some 30 galleries and artist studios, along with dance, yoga and photography studios. Check the website for ongoing exhibitions and upcoming openings.

RUE SHERBROOKE OUEST

STREET

Map p272 (MPeel) Until the 1930s the downtown stretch of Rue Sherbrooke Ouest was home to the **Golden Square Mile**, one of the richest residential neighborhoods in Canada. You'll see a few glorious old homes along this drag, including the **Reid Wilson House**, the **Louis-Joseph Forget House** (1195 Rue Sherbrooke Ouest) and the **Mount Royal Club**. There are good interpretation panels outside them explaining their history. The route is also home to visit-worthy churches, some first-rate museums and strings of energetic students en route to McGill University.

CATHÉDRALE MARIE-REINE-DU-MONDE

CHURCH

Map p272 (⌨514-866-1661; 1085 Rue de la Cathédrale; ⊗7:30am-6:15pm; MBonaventure) **FREE** The Cathedral of Mary Queen of the World is a smaller but still magnificent version of St Peter's Basilica in Rome. The architects scaled it down to a quarter of its size, mindful of the structural risks of Montréal's severe winters. This landmark was built from 1870 to 1894 as a symbol of Catholic power in the heart of Protestant Montréal.

ST PATRICK'S BASILICA

CHURCH

Map p272 (⌨514-866-7379; www.stpatricksmtl.ca; 454 Blvd René-Lévesque Ouest; ⊗9am-6pm; MSquare-Victoria) Built for Montréal's booming Irish population in 1847, the interior of St Patrick's Basilica contains huge columns from single pine trunks, an ornate baptismal font and nectar-colored stained-glass windows. The pope raised its status to basilica in 1989, in recognition of its importance to English-speaking Catholics in Montréal. It's a sterling example of French Gothic style and, as you might expect, is classified a national monument.

SQUARE DORCHESTER
SQUARE

Map p272 (2903 Rue Peel; ⓂPeel) This leafy expanse in the heart of downtown was known until 1988 as Dominion Sq, a reminder of Canada's founding in 1867. A Catholic cemetery was here until 1870 and bodies still lie beneath the grass. Events of all kinds have taken place here over the years – fashion shows, political rallies and royal visits.

PLACE DU CANADA
PARK

Map p272 (✆514-879-1010; http://placeducanada.ca; Rue Peel; ⓂBonaventure) This park immediately southeast of Sq Dorchester is best known for its monument of John A Macdonald, Canada's first prime minister, who addressed the maiden session of parliament in Montréal. The two cannons around the base were captured in the Crimean War; if you look closely you'll see the dual-headed eagle of Czar Nicholas I. The statue was decapitated by vandals in 1992 and the head vanished for two years.

The park benches are a quiet spot for a moment's rest from the downtown chaos. Food trucks ring the park in summer.

SQUARE VICTORIA
SQUARE

Map p272 (Rue du Square-Victoria; ⓂSquare-Victoria) In the 19th century this was a Victorian garden in a swanky district of Second Empire homes and offices. Today Square Victoria is a triangle of manicured greenery and water jets in the midst of modern skyscrapers. The only vestige of the period is a statue of Queen Victoria (1872). The art-nouveau entrance railing to the metro station was a gift from the city of Paris for Expo '67.

GARE WINDSOR
HISTORIC BUILDING

Map p272 (✆514-395-5164; 1160 de la Gauchetière Ouest; ⓂBonaventure) FREE The massive Victorian building hugging the slope west of the Marriott Château Champlain is the old Windsor Station, opened in 1889 as the headquarters of the Canadian Pacific Railway. Photo displays show the former station in all its glory. The Romanesque structure inspired a château style for train stations across the country; its architect, Bruce Price, would later build the remarkable Château Frontenac in Québec City.

Take a stroll through the restored Salle des pas perdus, a 25,000-sq-ft concourse, where millions of travelers once set off on train trips. Today, it's hauntingly vacant.

LE WINDSOR HOTEL
ARCHITECTURE

Map p272 (✆514-393-3588; https://lewindsormontreal.com; 1170 Rue Peel; ⓂPeel) The palatial Windsor was Canada's first grand hotel (1878) and played host to all manner of international guests and celebrities, including Mark Twain, Winston Churchill, King George VI, Queen Elizabeth II and John F Kennedy. The original Windsor had six restaurants and 382 sumptuous guest rooms, but a fire that devastated the hotel in 1957 left only the annex – the portion still standing today.

You can stroll down the magnificent main hall, Peacock Alley, and peek at the vast wooden dance floors, chandeliers and high windows that recall turn-of-the-century splendor.

✕ EATING

Plan ahead for eating downtown as it's too easy to wander aimlessly into tourist traps with poor, overpriced poutine. The area has improved dramatically in recent years with ample new, casual vegetarian eating and cafes serving good food beyond the chain offerings. Asian, Indian and Italian food is well represented downtown.

LOV
VEGETARIAN $

Map p272 (✆514-287-1155; www.lov.com; 1232 Rue de la Montagne; mains $14-18; ☎✍; ⓂPeel) The gold floral stylings and large marble tables of LOV might read boutique hotel, but the surprise is that this stylish vegetarian restaurant is well priced and good for both romancing somebody else, or yourself. For a starter, try the mushroom dumplings served with almond butter, or vegan poutine. Then move on to the pasta-free, cashew-cream lasagna or tofu banh-mi burgers.

FOODCHAIN
VEGETARIAN $

Map p272 (www.eatfoodchain.com; 1212 Ave McGill College; mains $9-14; ◷10:30am-8:30pm;

WANDERING IN WESTMOUNT

Though short on traditional sights, the leafy, upper-class neighborhood of Westmount makes for a good afternoon stroll. Here you'll find a mix of sleepy backstreets set with Victorian mansions and manicured parks (parts of the city were named a national historic site in 2012), while the main boulevard, Rue Sherbrooke Ouest, has high-end boutiques, cafes and bistros. Wander about and grab a bite while you're there.

The neighborhood highlight is **Westmount Park & Library** (☏514-989-5300; http://westlib.org; 4574 Rue Sherbrooke Ouest; ⏰10am-9pm Mon-Fri, to 5pm Sat & Sun; Ⓜ Atwater). The lovely Westmount Park encompasses pathways, streams and concealed nooks that recall the whimsical nature of English public gardens. The Westmount Public Library, built in 1899, stands stolid, with its Romanesque brickwork, leaded glass and delightful bas-reliefs dedicated to wisdom. The attached **Westmount Conservatory** is a gorgeous 1927 greenhouse where time stands still among the orchids.

Walking northwest from Westmount Park, you'll pass increasingly large and expensive homes as you climb to **Summit Woods** and **Summit Lookout**, a 57-acre forest and bird sanctuary atop the hill of Westmount with a belvedere commanding views of the St Lawrence River. Following Summit Circle road and Chemin Belvedere, you can soon walk to Parc du Mont-Royal and Cimetière Notre-Dame-des-Neiges.

Back down along Rue Sherbrooke Ouest, the faux-medieval towers of **Westmount City Hall** (Map p286; ☏514-989-5200; 4333 Chemin de la Côte St-Antoine; ⏰8:30am-4:30pm Mon-Fri; Ⓜ Vendôme then bus 104) come as a surprise after the skyscrapers of downtown. This Tudor gatehouse in rough-hewn stone looks like something from an English period drama. A lawn-bowling green lies in the rear.

For a bite to eat, sidewalk cafes and window-shopping, take a stroll along the boutique-lined **Ave Greene** to the northeast of Westmount City Hall. **Westmount Square** (Map p286; cnr Ave Greene & Blvd de Maisonneuve Ouest; Ⓜ Atwater) is a chic 1966 mall by architect Ludwig Mies van der Rohe.

For a bite to eat, stop in Chez Nick (p133), a classic diner on Ave Greene that's been going strong since 1920.

☏⏰; Ⓜ McGill) Foodchain gives a much-needed healthy option downtown with simple, mostly vegan, bowls highlighting raw vegetables. Try a simple curry, or fennel and daikon or cauliflower, mushroom and feta salads. The decoration looks lifted from a stylish kids' picture book, and Foodchain functions like a fast-food joint.

MAJESTHÉ
ASIAN **$**

Map p272 (☏514-840-5128; www.lemajesthe.ca; 2077 Blvd Robert-Bourassa; mains $12-16; ⏰11:30am-10pm Mon-Fri, 12:30-10pm Sat & Sun; ☏; Ⓜ McGill) Fusion numbers are presented on large dishes at this lower-level bistro. The brown-butter-miso-chicken spaghetti and kimchi and braised pork pasta dishes work so effortlessly. This student hangout is also popular for its perfectly crackly Korean fried chicken and boba tea with homemade sweet syrup.

CAFE AUNJA
CAFE **$**

Map p272 (☏514-914-8337; www.aunja.com; 1448 Rue Sherbrooke Ouest; snacks $8-11;

⏰10am-10pm; Ⓜ Guy-Concordia) Despite the location along busy Sherbrooke, Cafe Aunja feels like an oasis from the downtown bustle. Changing artwork adorns the brick walls of this Persian teahouse, and there's a regular lineup of readings and live music. A mix of book- and laptop-absorbed people and quietly chatting friends gather over sandwiches or feta, olive and egg brunches.

PIKOLO ESPRESSO BAR
CAFE **$**

Map p272 (☏514-508-6800; http://pikoloespresso.com; 3418b Ave du Parc; snacks $2-7; ⏰7:30am-7pm Mon-Fri, from 9am Sat & Sun; ☏; Ⓜ Place-des-Arts) Stylish coffee sippers roll up to this friendly split-level joint nestled in a heritage building at the bottom of Ave du Parc for its yummy scones, cookies, nutty bread and the signature drink, the Pikolo. Its *ristretto* shot of espresso goes down very smoothly indeed.

ONG CA CAN
VIETNAMESE **$**

Map p272 (☏514-844-7817; 79 Rue Ste-Catherine Est; mains $10-19; ⏰11:30am-2:30pm

DOWNTOWN EATING

ILLUMINATED CROWD

Constructed of polyester resin, Raymond Mason's sculpture of 65 people is one of Montréal's most photographed pieces of public art. The **Illuminated Crowd** (Map p272; 1981 Ave McGill College; ⊙24hr; MMcGill) shows a rather dark side of humanity. A crowd of onlookers stands pressed tightly together. The first row merely looks off into the distance, while behind them, the mood gradually degenerates as figures show a range of emotions – melancholy, fear, lust, hatred and terror.

A fine vantage point is on the *Secret Bench*, an evocative sculpture by Lea Vivot on the other side of Ave McGill College.

Mon-Fri, 5-9:30pm daily; ☑; MSt-Laurent) Despite its crisp white linens and intricate artwork, this bustling Vietnamese restaurant is only slightly pricier than average but with quality ingredients. The lemongrass rolls and anything involving beef get especially high marks from loyal patrons.

LOLA ROSA   VEGETARIAN $
Map p272 (☑514-287-9337; http://lolarosa.ca; 545 Rue Milton; mains $12-14; ⊙11:30am-9:30pm Sun-Thu, to 10pm Fri & Sat; ☑; MMcGill) On a leafy street near McGill University (p74), students, professors and the odd neighborhood regular not associated with the university flock to this charming vegetarian cafe. Even skeptical carnivores are won over by plates of creamy rich lasagna, vegan sweet-potato and coconut-milk curry, and nachos piled high with black beans, mozzarella, avocado and sour cream.

BOUSTAN   LEBANESE $
Map p272 (☑514-843-3194; http://boustan.ca; 2020 Rue Crescent; mains $5-10; ⊙11am-4am; ☑; MGuy-Concordia) This friendly little Lebanese joint scores high in popularity on the city's *shwarma*-and-falafel circuit because of its delicious toasted-pita sandwiches. Its late hours make it a favorite with pub crawlers in need of sustenance between bars.

★CAFÉ PARVIS   BISTRO $$
Map p272 (☑514-764-3589; www.cafeparvis. com; 433 Rue Mayor; small plates $6-9; ⊙7am-11pm Mon-Wed, to midnight Thu & Fri, 10am-midnight Sat, to 10pm Sun; ☑; MPlace-des-Arts) Hidden on a quiet downtown lane, Café Parvis is set with oversized windows, hanging plants, old wooden floorboards and vintage fixtures. Once part of the fur district, this cleverly repurposed room serves up delicious pizzas ($10 at lunch; about $20 at night) in inventive combinations (such as duck, fennel and squid, ham and eggplant, or roasted vegetables with Gruyère).

These are matched by equally creative salads (such as beet, pear and goat's cheese). Dishes are small; you'll want to order a few.

FOODLAB   INTERNATIONAL $$
Map p272 (☑514-844-2033; http://sat.qc.ca/ fr/restaurant-labo-culinaire; 3rd fl, 1201 Blvd St-Laurent; mains $14-26; ⊙5-10pm Tue-Sat; MSt-Laurent) On the upper floor of the arts center SAT (p83), Foodlab is a creative culinary space where the small menu changes every two weeks, and ranges around the globe. It's a casual but handsomely designed space, where patrons perch on bar stools, sipping creative cocktails and watching fast-moving chefs in the open kitchen.

There's outdoor seating in the summer and a yurt set up in the winter.

LE BALSAM INN   ITALIAN $$
Map p272 (☑514-507-9207; www.lebalsaminn. com; 1237 Rue Metcalfe; small plates $10-16, mains $22-26; ⊙11:30am-11pm Tue-Fri, from 4:30pm Sat; MPeel) A charmer in the downtown dining scene, Le Balsam Inn serves up delectable plates of Italian fare, with standouts such as citrus-drizzled calamari, osso buco with polenta, and pasta with pancetta and parmesan. It's also a great, though noisy, spot for an evening (or afternoon) libation, with a good wine selection and well-executed cocktails.

It has a warm, old-time ambience with wood-paneled walls and a long candle-lined bar.

FURUSATO   JAPANESE $$
Map p272 (☑514-849-3438; 2137 Rue de Bleury; mains $16-34; ⊙noon-1:30pm Tue-Fri, 6-9pm Tue-Sat; MPlace-des-Arts) This humble eatery presents some of the most authentic Japanese in town. Ultrafresh sushi, decent sake, shrimp and vegetable tempura, sukiyaki and grilled *hokke* (horse mackerel) are

some of the stars of the menu, along with black-sesame ice cream for dessert. Reservations recommended.

REUBEN'S
DELI $$

Map p272 (☑514-866-1029; http://reubensdeli. com; 1116 Rue Ste-Catherine Ouest; mains $18-28; ⊗8am-midnight Sun-Thu, to 1:30am Fri & Sat; MPeel) A classic, long-running deli, Reuben's has squishy booths and a long counter, where patrons line up for towering smoked-meat sandwiches served with big-cut fries, or pizza and pasta. Steakhouse favorites such as grilled salmon or fried chicken sit atop salad bowls – that's healthy, right? Try to avoid the busy lunch rush.

LE TAJ
INDIAN $$

Map p272 (☑514-845-9015; www.restaurant letaj.com; 2077 Rue Stanley; mains $14-24; ⊗11:30am-2:30pm Sun-Fri, 5-10:30pm daily; ☑; MPeel) Le Taj throws down the gauntlet for some good, mild Indian dishes. The time to go is at lunch, when downtowners line up for a buffet ($16) featuring a bounty of choice – tandoori chicken, vegetable korma, *palaak paneer* and tender lamb, along with steaming piles of naan bread, custard-like desserts and many other temptations.

MANGO BAY
CARIBBEAN $$

Map p272 (☑514-875-7082; www.mangobay quebec.com; 1236 Rue Mackay; mains $12-21; ⊗noon-10pm Mon-Wed, to 11pm Thu & Fri, 3-11pm Sat, 5-10pm Sun; MGuy-Concordia) A converted Victorian house with simple mango-coloured tablecloths is the setting for serves of authentic chicken jerky or stew, curried goat or island chicken fajitas with a terrific side order of plantain. Watch out for the incendiary hot sauces, and be sure to save room for a slice of the signature mango cheesecake or rum cake.

JATOBA
ASIAN $$$

Map p272 (☑514-871-1184; www.jatobamontreal. com; 1184 Pl Phillips; mains $22-38; ⊗11:30am-2:30pm & 5-10pm Mon-Fri, 5-11pm Sat; ☑; MMcGill) Celebrated chef Antonio Park is behind the menu at this artfully designed space just off Place Phillips. Park, who was born to Korean parents but grew up in South America and went to cooking school in Japan, brilliantly melds flavors from around the globe.

Yellowfin sashimi with Asian pear and jalapeño, king oyster mushrooms in a sweet miso gratin, and beef tataki with truffle peaches and puffed quinoa are among the outstanding dishes.

FERREIRA CAFÉ
PORTUGUESE $$$

Map p272 (☑514-848-0988; www.ferreiracafe. com; 1446 Rue Peel; mains $26-49; ⊗11:45am-3pm Mon-Fri, 5:30-11pm Mon-Wed, 5:30pm-midnight Thu-Sat, 5-10pm Sun; MPeel) This warm and inviting restaurant serves some of Montréal's best Portuguese fare. The *cataplana* (a bouillabaisse-style seafood stew) is magnificent; tender morsels of grilled fish come to the table cooked to perfection, while meat lovers can feast on rack of lamb or spice-rubbed Angus rib-eye steak. Late diners can enjoy two-course, $30 meals from 10pm to close.

DRINKING & NIGHTLIFE

Inviting bistro pubs catering to visitors are found all throughout downtown. Anywhere near the universities is home to bars with budget prices. There are some wine- and cocktail-bars trying to make their way into this space, but that kind of drinking is better saved for Old Montréal or the Plateau Mont-Royal.

DOMINION SQUARE TAVERN
TAVERNA

Map p272 (☑514-564-5056; www.tavernedomin ion.com; 1243 Rue Metcalfe; ⊗11:30am-midnight Mon-Fri, 4:30pm-midnight Sat & Sun; MPeel) Once a down-and-out watering hole dating from the 1920s, this beautifully renovated tavern recalls a classic French bistro but with a long bar, English pub–style. Executive chef Éric Dupuis puts his own spin on pub grub, with mussels cooked with bacon, and smoked trout salad with curry dressing.

FURCO
COCKTAIL BAR

Map p272 (☑514-764-3588; www.barfurco.com; 425 Rue Mayor; ⊗4pm-3am Mon-Sat; MPlace-des-Arts) In a previous life this stylish but industrial hideaway was a fur factory, and its raw concrete pillars, copper bar and modular light fixtures form the backdrop to a buzzing eating and drinking scene just a short stroll from Place-des-Arts. You'll find well-crafted cocktails and upmarket snacks (come for $1 oysters on Sundays and Mondays).

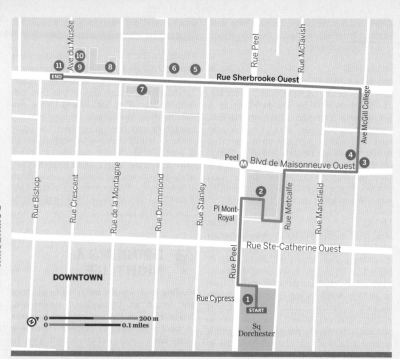

DOWNTOWN

🏃 Walking Tour
Delving into Downtown

START SQ DORCHESTER
END MUSÉE DES BEAUX-ARTS
LENGTH 2.5KM, TWO HOURS

Start at ❶ **Square Dorchester** (p76). Wander south to see the statue of Sir Wilfrid Laurier (1841–1919), one of Canada's most respected prime ministers.

Walk northwest on Rue Peel to the up-scale shopping complex ❷ **Les Cours Mont-Royal** (p85). The central atrium has bird sculptures with human heads by Inuit artist David Ruben Piqtoukun.

Cut through the building and continue up Rue Metcalf. Turn right on Blvd de Maisonneuve Ouest and left on Ave McGill College. About 20m up the block on the right is the ❸ **Illuminated Crowd** (p78) sculpture. Designed by Raymond Mason, it illuminates the darker side of human nature. Head across Ave McGill College to Lea Vivot's ❹ **Secret Bench**, a sensual work with a seated couple that provides a fine counter-point to the unruly mob.

Continue on and turn left at Rue Sherbrooke Ouest, Montréal's most prestigious residential street in the early 20th century. It features glorious old homes, including the ❺ **Mount Royal Club**, once an exclusive men-only club that now opens its doors to all.

Nearby, impressive ❻ **Reid Wilson House** is a mansion with its original carriage house in back and an attached conservatory. Continue along Sherbrooke; you'll soon reach the ❼ **Ritz-Carlton** (p159), which has a lavish afternoon tea in the Palm Court.

Further along Sherbrooke, you'll pass fortresslike apartment complex ❽ **Le Château**, with vestiges of shell fossils in the limestone. Next door is a massive stone church with Tiffany stained-glass windows. It now houses the ❾ **Bourgie Concert Hall**, part of the ❿ **Claire & Marc Bourgie Pavilion** (p73) at the Musée des Beaux-Arts. End your tour with a look at the neoclassical facade of the museum's ⓫ **Michal & Renata Hornstein Pavilion** (p73). Each symmetrical Ionic column took six men three months to cut and shape with pneumatic hammers.

PUB STE-ÉLISABETH   PUB

Map p272 (☑514-286-4302; www.ste-elisabeth.
com; 1412 Rue Ste-Élisabeth; ⏲4pm-3am;
Ⓜ Berri-UQAM) Tucked off a side street, this
handsome little pub is frequented by many
for its heavenly vine-covered courtyard and
drinks menu with a great selection of beers,
whiskeys and ports. It has a respectable
lineup of beers on tap, including imports
and microbrewery fare such as Boréale
Noire and Cidre Mystique.

PULLMAN   BAR

Map p272 (☑514-288-7779; www.pullman-mtl.
com; 3424 Ave du Parc; ⏲4:30pm-midnight Sun-
Tue, to 1am Wed-Sat; Ⓜ Place-des-Arts) This
beautifully designed wine bar is a favorite
haunt of the 30-something set. It's primarily a restaurant, but the downstairs bar of
this two-level space gets jammed (or *jam-
mé,* as they say in Franglais) after work and
becomes quite a pickup spot, so be prepared
to engage in some flirting. Knowledgeable
staff can help you choose from the sprawling wine list.

BRUTOPIA   BREWERY

Map p272 (☑514-393-9277; www.brutopia.net;
1219 Rue Crescent; ⏲2pm-3am Sun-Wed, noon-
3am Thu-Sat; Ⓜ Guy-Concordia) This fantastic
brewpub has eight varieties of suds on tap,
including honey beer, nut brown and the
more challenging raspberry blonde – all
with ingredients from Québécois farms.
The brick walls and wood paneling are con-
ducive to chats among the student crowd.
Live blues bands play nightly (from 10pm).
Things pick up after the night classes from
nearby Concordia get out.

UPSTAIRS   BAR

Map p272 (☑514-931-6808; www.upstairsjazz.
com; 1254 Rue Mackay; ⏲11:30am-1am Mon-Thu,
to 2am Fri, 5:30pm-2am Sat, 6:30pm-1am Sun;
Ⓜ Guy-Concordia) This slick downtown bar
hosts quality jazz and blues acts nightly,
featuring both local and touring talent. The
walled terrace behind the bar is enchanting
at sunset, and the dinner menu features inventive salads and meals such as the Cajun
bacon burger.

BAR PAMPLEMOUSSE   BAR

Map p272 (☑514-543-1579; https://barpample
mousse.com; 1579 Blvd St-Laurent; ⏲4:30pm-
2am; Ⓜ St-Laurent) This hip resto-bar just
east of the popular Quartier des Spectacles

serves an eclectic menu of quality cocktails
and tapas-style bites. With its cool-yet-
casual, friendly vibe and pop-up menus,
it's a good option for both for drinks and
something to eat.

BIIRŪ   BAR

Map p272 (☑514-903-1555; www.biiru.ca; 1433
Rue City Councillors; ⏲11:30am-2:30pm Mon-Fri,
5:30-10pm Tue-Thu & Sun, 5:30-11pm Fri & Sat;
Ⓜ McGill) Despite the name, this colorfully
designed *izakaya* doesn't serve much *biirū*
(beer). What it does have: creative cocktails,
tasty snacks and a festive environment that
draws the after-work crowd. You can nibble
on *gyoza* (dumplings), duck magret salad
or mushroom *okonomiyaki* (Japanese pan-
cake), while admiring the Hokusai-inspired
mural and engaging in the discreet art of
people-watching.

SIR WINSTON
CHURCHILL PUB   PUB

Map p272 (☑514-288-3814; www.winniesbar.
com; 1455 Rue Crescent; ⏲11:30am-3am;
Ⓜ Guy-Concordia) This Rue Crescent staple
is the go-to spot of the block. Winnie's
cavernous, split-level pub draws a steady
crowd of tourists and students and an
older Anglo crowd. Among multiple bars,
pool tables and pulsating music, meals are
served all day and happy-hour drink specials abound.

LE VIEUX DUBLIN PUB
& RESTAURANT   PUB

Map p272 (☑514-861-4448; www.dublinpub.
ca; 636 Rue Cathcart; ⏲11am-3am Mon-Sat,
4pm-midnight Sun; Ⓜ McGill) The city's oldest
Irish pub has the expected great selection
of brews (from $7 to $9 per pint) and live
Celtic or pop music nightly. Curries rub
shoulders with burgers on the menu. It has
50 single malts.

NYKS   PUB

Map p272 (☑514-866-1787; http://nyks.ca; 1250
Rue de Bleury; ⏲11am-3am Mon-Fri, from 3pm
Sat & Sun; Ⓜ Place-des-Arts) Its artsy-chic vibe
makes this warm bistro pub the preferred
lunch and after-work spot of Plateau cool
kids who happen to work in downtown
offices. Daily happy hours and pub finger
foods are a joy to downtowners seeking an
authentic experience. Sometimes it even
has live jazz.

BENELUX MICROBREWERY

Map p272 (http://brasseriebenelux.com; 245 Rue Sherbrooke Ouest; ⊙2pm-3am Sat-Wed, from 11am Thu & Fri; 🕾; Ⓜ Place-des-Arts) Benelux deserves high praise for its beautifully crafted microbrews, with a dozen or so offerings on hand (including one cask ale). Options rotate regularly, though long-time favorites are always on hand, such as Sabotage IPA and the blond Lux. Knowledgeable bartenders are happy to guide you in the right direction.

HURLEY'S IRISH PUB PUB

Map p272 (⌨514-861-4111; www.hurleysirish pub.com; 1125 Rue Crescent; ⊙11am-3am; Ⓜ Guy-Concordia) This cozy place on bar-lined Rue Crescent features live rock and fiddling Celtic folk on the rear stage and beer-soaked football and soccer matches on big-screen TVs. Classic pub grub – Irish lamb stew, fish 'n' chips and burgers – is also served.

MCKIBBIN'S PUB

Map p272 (⌨514-288-1580; www.mckibbins irishpub.com; 1426 Rue Bishop; ⊙11:30am-3am Mon-Fri, from 10am Sat & Sun; Ⓜ Guy-Concordia) With its garage-sale furniture, McKibbin's cultivates a familiar, down-at-heel pub atmosphere. Its live entertainment varies from Celtic and pop to punk music. The office crowd pops in at lunchtime for burgers, chicken wings and salads.

☆ ENTERTAINMENT

The epicenter of entertainment is the outdoor Place des Festivals, outside metro Place-des-Arts. Theater shows and live dance and music in the area as far east as Rue Berri keep any visitor amused for their entire stay, or at least on the weekends. Most options can be heavy on the wallet but smaller venues do offer shows for smaller budgets.

PLACE DES ARTS PERFORMING ARTS

Map p272 (⌨box office 514-842-2112; www.place desarts.com; 175 Rue Ste-Catherine Ouest; Ⓜ Place-des-Arts) Montréal's premier music venue, the storied Place des Arts is at the heart of the growing Quartier des Spectacles.

MONUMENT NATIONAL PERFORMING ARTS

Map p272 (⌨514-871-2224; www.monumentn ational.com; 1182 Blvd St-Laurent; Ⓜ St-Laurent) Québec's oldest theater still in use, the grand Monument National opened in 1893, and has been showing a wide range of cultural fare ever since. Shows here run the gamut from Molière to Sam Shepard, with acting, directing and technical production performed by graduating students of the National Theatre School.

True to the city's bilingual roots, the theater stages works in both French and English. There are two halls, one with 800 seats, the other with 150. The smaller theater stages about three original works a year by student playwrights. Comedy and modern dance are also part of the repertoire.

LES GRANDS BALLETS
CANADIENS DE MONTRÉAL DANCE

Map p272 (⌨514-842-2112; http://grandsbal lets.com; Pl des Arts; Ⓜ Place-des-Arts) You can be assured of a treat if you see Québec's leading ballet troupe. As well as staging six shows per season annually in Montréal at various venues (October through May), the dancers head off on several international tours per year. Its classical and modern programs are both innovative and accessible.

GESÙ JAZZ

Map p272 (⌨514-861-4378; www.legesu.com; 1200 Rue de Bleury; shows $18-57; ⊙box office noon-6:30pm Tue-Sat) This small live-music and events venue at the basement of a church is blessed with character. Its Greek-theater acoustics means you can see and hear well from any seat. The religious setting has no bearing on performances, which include stand-up comedy, jazz, kids' shows, and even the Montréal Gay Men's Chorus.

L'ASTRAL LIVE MUSIC

Map p272 (www.sallelastral.com; 305 Rue Ste-Catherine Ouest; Ⓜ Place-des-Arts) The century-old Blumenthal Building is a polished venue of Montréal's jazz fest as part of the Quartier des Spectacles. With more than 300 seats and standing room for 600, L'Astral nestles in the Maison du Festival Rio Tinto Alcan, which also houses **Le Balmoral**, a jazz club and bistro with a patio on the ground floor.

ORCHESTRE SYMPHONIQUE DE MONTRÉAL
CLASSICAL MUSIC

Map p272 (OSM; ☑514-840-7400; www.osm.ca; 1600 Rue St-Urbain, Maison Symphonique, Pl des Arts; ⏱box office 9am-5pm Mon-Fri & 90mins before shows; ⓂPlace-des-Arts) This internationally renowned orchestra plays to packed audiences in its Place des Arts base, the Maison Symphonique de Montréal, a venue with spectacular acoustics that was inaugurated in 2011. The OSM's Christmas performance of *The Nutcracker* is legendary.

Rock-star conductor Kent Nagano, a Californian with a leonine mane and stellar credentials, took over as music director in 2006 and has proven very popular. Check for free concerts at the Basilique Notre-Dame (p50), the Olympic Stadium (p104) and in municipal parks in the Montréal area.

FOUFOUNES ÉLECTRIQUES
LIVE MUSIC

Map p272 (☑514-844-5539; www.foufounese lectriques.com; 87 Rue Ste-Catherine Est; cover $4-6; ⏱4pm-3am; ⓂSt-Laurent) A one-time bastion of the alternafreak, this cavernous quintessential punk venue still stages some wild music nights (retro Tuesdays, hip-hop Thursdays, rockabilly/metal/punk Saturdays), plus the odd one-off (a night of pro-wrestling or an indoor skateboarding contest). The graffiti-covered walls and industrial charm should tip you off that 'Electric Buttocks' isn't exactly a mainstream kinda place.

AGORA DE LA DANSE
DANCE

Map p272 (☑514-525-1500; http://agoradanse. com; 1435 Rue de Bleury; tickets around $30; ⏱box office noon-5pm; ⓂPlace-des-Arts) One of Montréal's most important names in the contemporary-dance world, Agora de la Danse explores modern and experimental forms, staging both homegrown troupes and performers from around the globe. It's within the Wilder building.

SAT
ARTS CENTER

Map p272 (Société des Arts Technologiques; ☑514-844-2033; www.sat.qc.ca; 1195 Blvd St-Laurent; ⓂSt-Laurent) This slick warehouse and new-media space hosts a range of thought-provoking fare. The 360-degree Satosphere shows cutting-edge audiovisual works, while the Espace Sat stages technology-driven exhibitions and the odd theater troupe and performing artist. Also on-site (on the 3rd floor, next to the Satosphere) is Foodlab (p78), a creative eating and drinking venue.

Throughout the year, SAT holds the occasional party night. DJs and performance artists push the envelope with banks of multimedia installations, while an arty, electro-loving fan base dance and carouse.

ORCHESTRE MÉTROPOLITAIN
CLASSICAL MUSIC

Map p272 (☑514-842-2112; www.orchestre metropolitain.com; 1600 Rue St-Urbain, box office 175 Rue St-Catherine Ouest; ⓂPlace-des-Arts) This hip 60-member orchestra is comprised of young professional musicians from all over Québec, and led by conductor Yannick Nézet-Séguin. The orchestra's mission is to democratize classical music, so aside from playing inside the swish Maison Symphonique at Place des Arts, it may also play Mahler or Haydn in churches or colleges in the city's poorest neighborhoods for reduced admission.

CLUB SODA
LIVE MUSIC

Map p272 (☑514-286-1010; www.clubsoda.ca; 1225 Blvd St-Laurent; tickets $12-40; ⏱box office noon-6pm Mon-Fri, to 5pm Sat; ⓂSt-Laurent) This venerable club hosts some of the city's most eclectic bands. Up-and-coming indie-rock, punk, metal, country and hip-hop groups have all taken the stage, as have well-known stars like Bebel Gilberto and Rufus Wainwright. There are also tribute nights (to Pink Floyd, the Doors, Italian metal bands), evenings of comedy and the odd Muay Thai match.

SALSATHÈQUE
DANCE

Map p272 (☑514-875-0016; www.salsatheque. ca; 1220 Rue Peel; ⏱9:30pm-3am Fri & Sat; ⓂPeel) This bright, busy, dressy place presents large live salsa bands pumping out tropical rhythms. The Latin community (and their admirers) come out in droves to tear up the dance floor. When you need a break, you can refuel with a margarita while watching the 25-to-50s crowd gyrate into exhaustion.

CINÉMA DU PARC
CINEMA

Map p272 (☑514-281-1900; http://cinema duparc.com; 3575 Ave du Parc; adult/child $13/9/9.50, weekdays before 1pm & Tue $9.50; ⓂPlace-des-Arts, then bus 80) Located in the lower level of the Galeries du Parc complex, Montréal's English-language repertory cinema is a tried-and-true favorite of Plateau cinephiles. It shows cult classics as well as cool new releases and lots of foreign films. Despite the shabby decor, its charm and authenticity add to the cinematic experience.

CINÉMA BANQUE SCOTIA MONTRÉAL
CINEMA

Map p272 (www.cineplex.com; 977 Rue Ste-Catherine Ouest; MPeel) This entertainment monstrosity features crowds darting through junk-food kiosks amid flashing lights to get to the IMAX megascreens. Screens and sound system are good. One step up from IMAX is the D-Box cinema, where movie-goers can feel vibrations in their seats, which sync to the action and audio on screen. Hollywood blockbusters are the general fare at this multilevel cinema.

MTELUS
LIVE MUSIC

Map p272 (Metropolis; 514-844-3500; https://mtelus.com; 59 Rue Ste-Catherine Est; MSt-Laurent) Housed in a former art-deco cinema, this beautiful old space (capacity 2300) has featured everyone from indie rockers Interpol to Aussie Courtney Barnett to local favorite Jean Leloup. It's sometimes used as a party venue with DJs and dancing. Buy tickets mainly online, or at the **box office** (1413 Rue St-Dominique) around the corner on show days from 3pm.

OPÉRA DE MONTRÉAL
OPERA

Map p272 (514-985-2258; www.operademontreal.com; Pl des Arts; MPlace-des-Arts) Holds lavish stage productions in the Salle Wilfrid-Pelletier that feature big names from Québec and around the world. The repertoire includes four or five operas each year, with a focus on classics such as *Madame Butterfly, The Barber of Seville* and *Turandot,* as well as contemporary works – such as the Pulitzer Prize–winning *Silent Night,* which premiered in the US in 2011.

I MUSICI DE MONTRÉAL
CLASSICAL MUSIC

Map p272 (514-982-6037; www.imusici.com; 279 Rue Sherbrooke Est; tickets from $55; MSt-Laurent) Under the leadership of Jean-Marie Zeitouni, this 12-member chamber ensemble has won many awards for its baroque and contemporary performances. Over the past 20 years I Musici has recorded more than 30 CDs and toured the world. They play in a variety of venues, including the Chapelle Historique du Bon-Pasteur.

🔒 SHOPPING

The whole of Rue Ste-Catherine Ouest is lined with very commercial stores, many of them franchises, that attract crowds most days, but especially on weekends. Most of the stores can be found elsewhere in the world, but Canadian favorites like Canada Goose, Winners, Hudson's Bay Co. and Roots give visitors an excuse to buy clothes, which is the bulk of the shopping here.

MONTRÉAL BY BIXI

Montréal is one of the most bike-friendly cities in North America, with hundreds of kilometers of bicycle paths across the city. In 2009 the city unveiled **Bixi** (514-789-2494; http://montreal.bixi.com; per 30min $2.95; ⏱24hr mid-Apr–Oct) 🚲, an extensive network of bike-renting stations around town, with bikes available from mid-April through October. For short jaunts, it's great value (24-hour/72-hour subscription fee is $5/12; bikes are free the first 30 minutes), though prices rise quickly ($3 every 15 minutes after 45 minutes). If you're just going to use it once for a quick jaunt, opt for the one-way 30-minute trip – which, at $2.95 costs less than a bus fare. The network includes more than 5000 bikes scattered around 500 stations. Bixi has since inspired bike-rental systems in other cities, including London and New York City.

Checking out a bike from a stand is easy. Just insert a credit card and follow the instructions. The majority of Bixi stands display a network map showing other docking stations across the city. Once you dock the bike, you must wait two minutes before checking out another one. Just reinsert your credit card and go. (Bixi tallies up the charges at the end of a 24-hour period. As long as you always return a bike within 30 minutes, you'll only be charged the one-time fare.) Although the bikes are fine for short hops, the pricing structure discourages longer trips. If you're planning a long day's outing along the Canal de Lachine (p130), it's better to rent from a bike shop.

EVA B
VINTAGE

Map p272 (📞514-849-8246; www.eva-b.ca; 2015 Blvd St-Laurent; ⊙11am-7pm Mon-Sat, noon-6pm Sun; Ⓜ️St-Laurent) Stepping into this graffiti-smeared building on St-Laurent is like entering a theater's backstage, with a riot of vintage coats, bowling shirts, cowboy boots, leather jackets, wigs, suede handbags, summer dresses, wildly patterned sweaters and denim of all shapes and sizes. There's lots of junk, but prices are low, and you can probably unearth a few treasures if you have the time.

The rooms overflow with books and broken typewriters, and bras dangle from the ceiling. There's also a **cafe** with baked goods, samosas and salads.

CHEAP THRILLS
MUSIC

Map p272 (📞514-844-8988; www.cheapthrills.ca; 2044 Rue Metcalfe; ⊙11am-6pm Mon-Wed & Sat, to 9pm Thu & Fri, noon-5pm Sun) It's easy to lose track of time as you browse through this big selection of used books and music (CDs and some vinyl), both with a mainstream and offbeat bent and sold at bargain prices.

HENRI HENRI
FASHION & ACCESSORIES

Map p272 (📞514-288-0109; www.henrihenri.ca; 189 Rue Ste-Catherine Est; ⊙10am-6pm Mon-Fri, to 5pm Sat & Sun; Ⓜ️St-Laurent) Going strong since 1932, this classy millinery sells an impressive assortment of hats, including top global brands such as Stetson, Akubra and Kangol, as well as the Henri Henri house brand. You'll also find gloves, scarves, suspenders and other gentlemanly attire.

ROOTS
FASHION & ACCESSORIES

Map p272 (📞514-845-7995; www.roots.ca; 1025 Rue Ste-Catherine Ouest; ⊙10am-9pm Mon-Fri, 9am-6pm Sat, 10am-6pm Sun; Ⓜ️Peel) One of Canada's best known homegrown brands, Roots started off as a humble shoemaker in the '70s. Now its range includes Roots for kids, Roots athletics, leather and home accessories. Tastes are casual and accessible and geared to teens and 20-somethings; they are sometimes fashionable and innovative, though leaning towards comfy hoodies.

HOLT RENFREW OGILVY
CLOTHING

Map p272 (www.holtrenfrew.com/en/holt-ren frew-ogilvy; 1307 Rue Ste-Catherine Ouest; ⊙10am-6pm Mon-Wed, to 9pm Thu & Fri, 9:30am-6:30pm Sat, 11am-6pm Sun; Ⓜ️Peel) Founded in 1866 as Canada's first department store, Ogilvy has transformed itself into a collection of high-profile boutiques. The store's front window displays mechanical toys that are a Montréal fixture at Christmas.

HUDSON'S BAY CO.
DEPARTMENT STORE

Map p272 (📞514-281-4422; www.thebay.com; 585 Rue Ste-Catherine Ouest; ⊙10am-8pm Mon-Wed, to 9pm Thu & Fri, 9am-7pm Sat, 10am-7pm Sun; Ⓜ️McGill) *La Baie,* as it's called in French, found fame three centuries ago for its striped wool blankets used to measure fur skins. The unique blankets are still available, in wool and fleece, on the ground floor. Take the escalators to reach the clothing boutiques, where you can find all the top labels (Theory, Moschino, Ralph Lauren, Stella McCartney, John Varvatos).

Prices are high, though periodic sales can lead to some great deals.

LES COURS MONT-ROYAL
MALL

Map p272 (www.lcmr.ca; 1455 Rue Peel; ⊙10am-6pm Mon-Wed, to 9pm Thu & Fri, to 5pm Sat, noon-5pm Sun; Ⓜ️Peel) This elegant shopping mall is a reincarnation of the Mount Royal Hotel (1922), at the time the largest hotel in the British Empire. The 1000-room hotel was converted into a snazzy mix of condos and fashion boutiques in 1988. You'll find designer names like Ursula B, DKNY and Desigual among the boutiques here.

Under the skylight you'll see various birdman sculptures by Inuit artist David Ruben Piqtoukun. The spectacular chandelier is from Monte Carlo's old casino. The attractive atrium food court is also a notch above most mall eateries, with sushi, Thai, Tex-Mex and other options on hand.

PLACE MONTRÉAL TRUST
MALL

Map p272 (www.placemontrealtrust.com; 1500 Ave McGill College; ⊙10am-6pm Mon & Tue, to 9pm Wed-Fri, to 5pm Sat, 11am-5pm Sun; Ⓜ️McGill) One of downtown's most successful malls, with enough rays from the skylights to keep shoppers on their day clock. Major retailers here include La Senza lingerie, Indigo books, Winners (outlet for designer labels) and Zara. It has a tremendous water fountain with a spout 30m high, and during the holidays a Christmas tree illuminates the five-story space.

HOCKEY CHAMPS

The **Montréal Canadiens** (Map p272; ☎514-932-2582; www.canadiens.com; 1909 Ave des Canadiens-de-Montréal, Bell Centre; tickets $54-277; ⓂBonaventure) of the National Hockey League have won the Stanley Cup 24 times. Montréalers, especially franco-phones, have a soft spot for the 'Habs' and matches at the **Bell Centre** (Map p272; ☎877-668-8269, 514-790-2525; www.centrebell.ca; 1909 Ave des Canadiens-de-Montréal) sell out routinely. Scalpers hang around the entrance on game days, and you might snag a half-price ticket after the puck drops.

Bring your binoculars for the rafter seats. The center also hosts big-name con-certs, boxing matches, Disney on Ice and visits by the Dalai Lama.

SPORTS & ACTIVITIES

ATRIUM
ICE SKATING

Map p272 (☎514-395-0555; www.le1000.com; 1000 Rue de la Gauchetière Ouest; adult/child $7.50/5, skate rentals $7; ☉11:30am-6pm Mon & Tue, to 9pm Wed-Fri, 12:30-9pm Sat, 12:30-6pm Sun; ⋇; ⓂBonaventure) Enjoy year-round indoor ice skating at this excellent glass-domed rink near Gare Centrale. On Saturdays and Sundays, kids and their families have a special session from 11am to 12:30pm. Special events change regu-larly – such as the summertime 'Bermudas Madness,' a cheesy good time of skating in shorts and T-shirts while DJs spin Hawai-ian and summer-inflected beats.

Check online for operating hours as the schedule changes frequently.

MONTRÉAL ALOUETTES
FOOTBALL

Map p272 (MontréALS; ☎514-871-2255; www.montrealalouettes.com; Ave des Pins Ouest, Molson Stadium; tickets from $20; ⓂMcGill) The Montréal Alouettes, a star franchise of the Canadian Football League, folded several times before going on to win the league's Grey Cup trophy several times over the years. Rules are a bit different from American football: the field is bigger and there are only three downs. Games are held at McGill University's Molson Stadium and sometimes at the Olympic Stadium (p104).

Purchase advance tickets online or at Molson Stadium. On game day, there are free shuttles from Square-Victoria and McGill metro stations.

Rue St-Denis & the Village

Neighborhood Top Five

❶ Rue St-Denis (p89) Sipping *un café*, beer or whiskey and soaking up the ever-changing atmosphere on this colorful street.

❷ Église St-Pierre-Apôtre (p90) Admiring the neo-Gothic interior of this church and its moving chapel dedicated to people who have died of AIDS.

❸ Écomusée du Fier Monde (p91) Stepping back in time to the 1920s for a glimpse of life in working-class Montréal.

❹ Cabaret Mado (p97) Sashaying from the sidelines at a cabaret drag show in the Village.

❺ Usine C (p97) Catching a cutting-edge show followed by drinks and tapas.

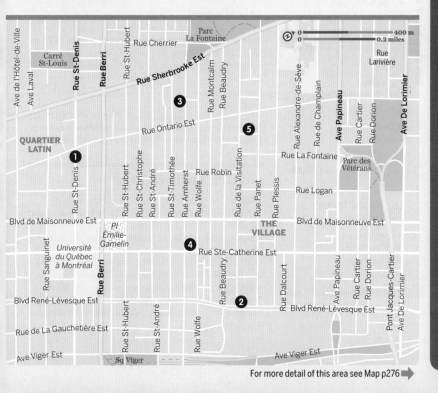

For more detail of this area see Map p276 ➡

Lonely Planet's Top Tip

You can keep a night out in the Village at a manageable budget. Many clubs don't have cover charges if you enter before 10pm or 11pm. Start your night at a pub with cheap drinks and then head to your nightspot of choice while it's still free.

Best Places to Eat

➡ Agrikol (p91)

➡ O'Thym (p94)

➡ Au Petit Extra (p91)

For reviews, see p91. ➡

Best Places to Drink

➡ Le Cheval Blanc (p94)

➡ L'Île Noire (p94)

➡ Le Saint-Bock (p94)

➡ Le Saint Sulpice (p96)

For reviews, see p94. ➡

☆ Best Entertainment

➡ Cabaret Mado (p97)

➡ Usine C (p97)

➡ Théâtre St-Denis (p97)

For reviews, see p97. ➡

Best Places to Shop

➡ Camellia Sinensis (p98)

➡ Priape (p98)

➡ Archambault (p98)

For reviews, see p98. ➡

Explore Rue St-Denis & the Village

The boisterous district of Rue St-Denis and the Village is fairly compact and easy to explore in an afternoon, with the option to kick back and party into the night. Start at Rue Sherbrooke and Rue St-Denis and explore the latter to Rue Ste-Catherine. Be sure to pause for a beverage or snack as you go.

St-Denis picks up at night when local watering holes, restaurants and clubs attract students and other bons vivants who come together over beer and *bouffe* (food). It's best to do a bit of roaming and absorb the free-spirited energy of the quarter. If you want to take a breather during the day, try Carré St-Louis, north of Rue Sherbrooke and off Rue St-Denis, or Place Émilie-Gamelin along Rue Ste-Catherine.

One of the hottest LGBTIQ+ meccas in North America, the Village is quiet during the day, but starts to pick up around 9pm. Packed with eclectic eateries, shops and nightspots, Rue Ste-Catherine is the main thoroughfare here, so it's easy to navigate. August is the most frenetic time as international visitors gather to celebrate the massive annual Montréal Pride Parade.

Local Life

➡ **Eating out** Even starving artists need fuel. Rue St-Denis has some casual-eating brasseries such as Le Saint-Bock (p94), but the best options, such as O'Thym (p94), are further afield.

➡ **Nightlife** Start your evening with a drink on Rue St-Denis, then mosey over to the Village for a drag floorshow at Cabaret Mado (p97) and let the night unfold.

➡ **Festivals** The Montréal World Film Festival (p22) and Montréal Pride (p22) make this neighborhood nearly as festive as downtown on Montréal's celebration circuit.

Getting There & Away

➡ **Metro** The orange and green lines run to Berri-UQAM, with the green line continuing to Beaudry and Papineau.

➡ **Bus** Bus 24 runs along Rue Sherbrooke, the 30 along Rue St-Denis and Rue Berri, and the 15 along Rue Ste-Catherine. The Gare d'Autocars de Montréal (p241) is a hub for intercity and international coach services.

➡ **Walking** It's relatively easy to reach Rue St-Denis from either downtown or Plateau Mont-Royal, and you can also stroll along Rue Ste-Catherine to the Village.

 TOP EXPERIENCE
WANDER RUE ST-DENIS

This street captures the heart of francophone Montréal. A carnivalesque collection of restaurants, brasseries, cafes and arts venues coalesce in four blocks along Rue St-Denis below Rue Sherbrooke. You'll find students from nearby Université du Québec à Montréal (UQAM) grabbing a pint after protesting tuition hikes, or big-name US comics doing stand-up at Théâtre St-Denis.

The quarter is a hotbed of activity, especially during summer festivals, when energy spills from the streets 24 hours a day. The terraced cafes and restaurants of Rue St-Denis are great spots to watch the world go by, over coffee, croissants or even a bowl of borscht. Popular with students at UQAM, who number in the tens of thousands, the street is all about budget dining, inexpensive bistro fare and meals in a hurry.

There are also abundant bars nearby, making for an easy transition from dinner to nighttime amusement. Rue St-Denis is one of the few streets to cross the entire island of Montréal and the bars become a little more upmarket-cool as it heads west toward Mont-Royal.

Rue St-Denis is an entry of sorts to the Village, one of the largest LGBTIQ+ communities in North America. Packed with eclectic eateries, shops and outrageous nightspots, Rue Ste-Catherine is the Village's main thoroughfare, and it closes to traffic periodically in the summer.

In the 19th century, the neighborhood was an exclusive residential area for wealthy francophones. Although many original buildings burned in the great fire of 1852, there are a number of Victorian and art-nouveau gems hidden on the tree-lined streets.

The street and its surrounds (between Rue St-Denis and south to Blvd St-Laurent) are dotted with street art, including spectacular murals that are social-media friendly.

DON'T MISS

➡ People-watching with a drink
➡ Just for Laughs comedy festival
➡ Montréal Pride Parade
➡ Street art

PRACTICALITIES

➡ Map p276, B2
➡ Ⓜ Berri-UQAM

⊙ SIGHTS

The streets themselves are attractions here – student-hotbed Rue St-Denis with its pubs, music clubs and record shops; and Rue Ste-Catherine Est, the heart of the (gay) Village, which has a small open-air art gallery and an LGBT-related museum, library and church. It sees thousands of international visitors gather to celebrate the major annual LGBT Montréal Pride parade. Starting from one street and strolling to the other is a good way to cover it all.

RUE ST-DENIS   AREA

See p89.

**BIBLIOTHÈQUE ET ARCHIVES
NATIONALES DU QUÉBEC**   LIBRARY

Map p276 (BAnQ; www.banq.qc.ca; 475 Blvd de Maisonneuve Est; ☉10am-10pm Tue-Fri, to 6pm Sat & Sun; ⓂBerri-UQAM) FREE Opened in 2005, this stunning building houses both the library and national archives of Québec. Everything published in Québec (books, brochures, sound recordings, posters) since 1968 has been deposited here. Visit for changing exhibitions,

film screenings, performances (poetry, jazz), workshops or some peace (and free wi-fi) among glass and high ceilings. There is also a gift store and a kids reading area.

The library's footprint is 33,000 sq meters, connected to the metro and underground city.

RUE STE-CATHERINE EST   STREET

Map p276 (ⓂBeaudry) Montréal's embrace of the LGBTIQ+ community is tightest along the eastern end of Rue Ste-Catherine, a one-time bed of vice and shabby tenements. This strip of restaurants and clubs has been made so presentable that middle-class families mingle with drag queens on the pavements, all part of the neighborhood scenery.

★ÉGLISE ST-PIERRE-APÔTRE   CHURCH

Map p276 (☏514-524-3791; www.saintpierre apotre.ca; 1201 Rue de la Visitation; ☉noon-4pm Mon-Fri, to 5:15 Sat, 10am-4pm Su; ⓂBeaudry) Located in the Village, this neoclassical church from 1853 has a number of fine decorations – flying buttresses, stained glass, statues in Italian marble – but nowadays

---

THE METRO MUSEUM OF ART

Primarily a mover of the masses, the Montréal metro was also conceived as an enormous art gallery, although not all stations have been decorated. Here are a few highlights from the central zone; many more await your discovery.

Berri-UQAM

A set of murals by artist Robert LaPalme representing science, culture and recreation hangs above the main staircase leading to the yellow line. These works were moved here from the *Man and His World* pavilion of Expo '67 at the request of mayor Jean Drapeau, a buddy of LaPalme.

Champ-de-Mars

The station kiosk boasts a set of antique stained-glass windows by Marcelle Ferron, an artist of the Refus global (Total Refusal) movement. The abstract forms splash light down into the shallow platform, drenching passengers in color as their trains roll through.

Peel

Circles, circles everywhere: in bright single colors on advertising panels, in the marble of one entrance, above the main staircases, as tiles on the floor – even the bulkhead vents are circular. They're the work of Jean-Paul Mousseau of the Québécois art movement Les Automatistes.

Place-des-Arts

The station's east wall has a backlit stained-glass mural entitled *Les Arts lyriques*, by Québécois artist and Oscar-winning filmmaker Frédéric Back. It depicts the evolution of Montréal's music from the first trumpet fanfare played on the island in 1535 to modern composers and conductors.

is more known for its gay-friendly Sunday services. It houses the Chapel of Hope, consecrated in 1997, the first chapel in the world dedicated to the memory of victims of AIDS. The Church of St Peter the Apostle belonged to the monastery of the Oblate fathers who settled in Montréal in the mid-19th century.

★ÉCOMUSÉE DU FIER MONDE   MUSEUM

Map p276 (☑514-528-8444; http://ecomusee. qc.ca; 2050 Rue Amherst; adult/child $8/6, $2 discount with STM tickets; ⊘11am-8pm Wed, 9:30am-4pm Thu & Fri, 10:30am-5pm Sat & Sun; ⓜBerri-UQAM) This striking ex-bathhouse explores the history of Centre-Sud, an industrial district in Montréal until the 1950s and now part of the Village. The museum's permanent exhibition, *Triumphs and Tragedies of a Working-Class Neighborhood*, puts faces on the industrial era through a series of photos and multimedia displays.

The 1927 building is the former Bain Généreux, an art-deco public bathhouse modeled on one in Paris. Frequent modern-art exhibitions are also held here.

CHAPELLE NOTRE-DAME-DE-LOURDES   CHURCH

Map p276 (☑514-845-8278; www.cndlm.org; 430 Rue Ste-Catherine Est; ⊘11am-6pm Mon-Fri, 10:30am-6:30pm Sat, 9am-6:30pm Sun; ⓜBerri-UQAM) Now hidden among the university buildings, this Romanesque gem was built by the Sulpicians in 1876 to cement their influence in Montréal. The chapel was designed by Rue St-Denis resident and artist Napoléon Bourassa. His frescoes, which are dotted about the interior, are regarded as his crowning glory.

GALERIE BLANC   PUBLIC ART

Map p276 (http://galerieblanc.com; 1114 Rue St-Catherine Est; ⊘24hr; ⓜBeaudry) **FREE** Sun, snow and lack of sobriety are no barrier at this free open-air art gallery smack in the middle of the Village's bar street. The often-abstract works can make more sense coming out of a club at 3am.

UNIVERSITÉ DU QUÉBEC À MONTRÉAL   UNIVERSITY

Map p276 (☑514-987-3000; www.uqam.ca; 405 Rue Ste-Catherine Est; ⓜBerri-UQAM) The modern, rather drab buildings of Montréal's French-language university blend into the cityscape and are linked to the underground city and the Berri-UQAM metro station. The most striking aspect here is the old Gothic steeple of the **Église St-Jacques**, which has been integrated into the university's facade.

EATING

A good place to eat out with a wide range of cuisines in restaurants of all budgets, though leaning away from the budget end. A little digging in the back streets is required: Rue St-Denis and Rue Ste-Catherine Est are not the only streets with good eating.

JULIETTE ET CHOCOLAT   CAFE $

Map p276 (☑514-287-3555; www.julietteetcho colat.com; 1615 Rue St-Denis; ⊘11am-11pm Sun-Thu, to midnight Fri & Sat; 🖬; ⓜBerri-UQAM) When the urge to devour something chocolaty arrives, make straight for Juliette et Chocolat, a bustling little cafe where chocolate is served in every shape and form – drizzled over crepes, blended into creamy milkshakes and coffees, or straight up in a blood-sugar-boosting chocolate 'shot.'

The setting is charming but small and busy. For less hustle and bustle, visit the branch at 377 Ave Laurier Ouest.

AGRIKOL   CARIBBEAN $$

Map p276 (☑514-903-6707; www.agrikol.ca; 1844 Rue Amherst; mains $12-25; ⊘5pm-midnight, also 11am-3pm Sun; 🕿; ⓜBeaudry) This Haitian restaurant was originally opened by musicians of Arcade Fire (and Montréal locals), who have now moved on but the food and ambience stand on their own. A casual but elevated diner vibe with hip young staff serving up dishes like small plates of plantains and *chiktay* (smoked herring), fried fish, and of course the namesake rum drink.

AU PETIT EXTRA   FRENCH $$

Map p276 (☑514-527-5552; http://aupetit extra.com; 1690 Rue Ontario Est; mains $22-35; ⊘11:30am-2:30pm Mon-Fri, also 5:30-9:30pm Sun-Wed, to 10:30pm Thu-Sat; ⓜPapineau) This sweet little place serves traditional bistro fare to a garrulous local crowd. The blackboard menu changes frequently but features simple, flavorful dishes – *steak frites,* foie gras (p28), duck confit, fish soup – and staff can expertly pair wines with food. Reservations are advised.

1. Lac aux Castors, Parc du Mont-Royal (p102)
2. Jardin Botanique (p103)
3. Magic of Lanterns festival (p103)
4. Parc Jean-Drapeau (p66)

ESPACE POUR LA VIE (RAYMOND JALBERT) ©

Montréal Across the Seasons

Montréal thrives in summer and excels at good times in winter. Unlike other cities that lie dormant in the cold, the Québécois spirit is alive, warm and well, keeping active, and making the most of warmer months and the colorful autumn days.

Spring

Montréal comes alive in April at the first signs of spring. The ice has mostly melted – and off come the coats. Cafes fill up the first sunny weekend and there is a buzz in the air, especially along **Rue St-Denis** (p89), Rue St-Laurent, **Plateau Mont-Royal** (p108), and in **Mile End** (p120) and **Little Burgundy** (p135).

Summer

When the long summer days arrive, Montréal awakens for a full calendar of festivals and outdoor entertainment. Joggers and cyclists take to the **Old Port** (p52). Locals cool off at the **Plage Jean-Doré** (p70) and **Complexe Aquatique** (p70) on Parc Jean-Drapeau, or in the shaded trails of **Parc du Mont-Royal** (p102).

Fall

At parks around town, the fiery colors of autumn arrive. Photogenic settings for a stroll include Parc du Mont-Royal, **Parc La Fontaine** (p101) and the **Jardin Botanique** (p103) – particularly during the Magic of Lanterns, when hundreds of handmade silk lanterns sparkle at dusk. Cooling weather brings an excuse to gather in cozy drinking dens over wine, microbrews or apple cider.

Winter

Locals celebrate winter in cozy pubs, steaming sugar shacks or on the slopes of local mountains skiing, picnicking and tobogganing. The slopes above the **Lac aux Castors** (p113) are popular for sledding and cross-country skiing. At the **Old Port** (p52), skating at the outdoor rink is iconic, as is family-friendly **Fête des Neiges** (p68), for ice-sculpting contests, dogsled races and snow games.

O'THYM
FRENCH $$

Map p276 (☎514-525-3443; www.othym.com; 1112 Blvd de Maisonneuve Est; mains brunch $16-24, dinner $23-37; ⊙10am-2pm Sat & Sun, 5:30-10pm nightly; MBeaudry) O'Thym buzzes with foodies who flock here from all over town. It features an elegant but understated dining room (exposed-brick walls, floodlit windows, oversized mirrors), and beautifully presented plates such as Eastern Township rabbit with mustard and a fusion kimchi-sumac duck breast. Bring your own wine.

SALOON
BISTRO $$

Map p276 (☎514-522-1333; www.lesaloon. ca; 1333 Rue Ste-Catherine Est; mains $16-28; ⊙11:30am-2pm & 5-10pm Mon-Wed, 11:30am-11pm Thu-Fri, 10am-11pm Sat & Sun; MBeaudry) With nearly 20 years under its belt, this gay bar-bistro has earned a spot in Village hearts for its chilled atmosphere, live DJs, patio seating, cocktails and wide-ranging menu, including salmon bowls, steaks, burgers, pizzas and some good vegetarian options. A stylish preclub pit stop or a good-value spot the next day for set lunches (from $12.75).

LES 3 BRASSEURS
ALSATIAN $$

Map p276 (☎514-845-1660; www.les3brasseurs.ca; 1658 Rue St-Denis; mains $12-17; ⊙11:30am-midnight Sun-Wed, to 1am Thu, to 2am Fri & Sat) If you'd like to cap a day of sightseeing with belly-filling fare and a few pints of handcrafted beer, stop by this convivial brewpub with its stylized warehouse looks and rooftop terrace. The house specialty is the 'flamm,' a French spin on pizza.

USINE C CAFÉ
FRENCH $$

Map p276 (☎514-521-6002; http://usine-c. com/cafe; 1901 Rue de la Visitation; mains $17-19; ⊙4pm-midnight Tue-Thu, to 3am Fri & Sat; MBeaudry) On the lower level of the creative performing center Usine C (p97), you'll find this low-lit bistro serving up a short menu of French classic-inspired dishes such as mushroom fettucine and steak tartare. Some escargots and wine make a nice preshow snack before sliding next door.

🍷 DRINKING & NIGHTLIFE

Rue St-Denis features pubs catering to students, though this area is changing quickly with lots of closures. Nearby, the Village is one of the busiest areas in Canada for LGBTIQ+ nightlife, with plenty of swish cocktail bars and old-school pubs that cater to people of all sexualities (and karaoke singing talent).

★SKY PUB & CLUB
LGBTIQ+

Map p276 (☎514-529-6969; www.complexesky. com; 1474 Rue Ste-Catherine Est; ⊙10pm-3am Thu-Sun, bar & roof 11am-late daily; MBeaudry) FREE A popular three-level Village complex designed to suck you in for an entire Friday or Saturday night of partying. If you're a gorgeous guy or looking for one, start on the chilled 1st-floor pickup bar before heading up to the dance floors (pop hits and energized house/hip-hop). The legendary roof terrace is a perfect place to catch fireworks in summer.

LE CHEVAL BLANC
MICROBREWERY

Map p276 (☎514-522-0211; http://lechevalblanc.ca; 809 Rue Ontario Est; ⊙3pm-3am; MSherbrooke) An icon of Montréal's brewery scene, Le Cheval Blanc has about 10 drafts on hand, all brewed in-house, as well as some Belgian options by the bottle. It's a lively, easygoing place with a friendly all-ages crowd, smiling bartenders and an outdoor patio in the summer.

L'ÎLE NOIRE
PUB

Map p276 (☎514-982-0866; www.ilenoire.com; 1649 Rue St-Denis; ⊙3pm-3am; MBerri-UQAM) Roll into this slice of the Scottish Highlands in the heart of the Quartier Latin and sip from the selection of more than 140 scotches and whiskeys, as well as 15 varieties of beer on tap and several dozen wine choices.

The vibe here is decidedly less bohemian than other watering holes on Rue St-Denis, perfect if you want to take a breather from the surrounding carnival.

LE SAINT-BOCK
PUB

Map p276 (☎514-680-8052; www.saintbock.com; 1749 Rue St-Denis; ⊙11:30am-3am Fri & Sat, to 1am Thu-Sun; MBerri-UQAM) The craft beers on tap at this convivial, low-lit brasserie are its speciality – there are about 50! Menu

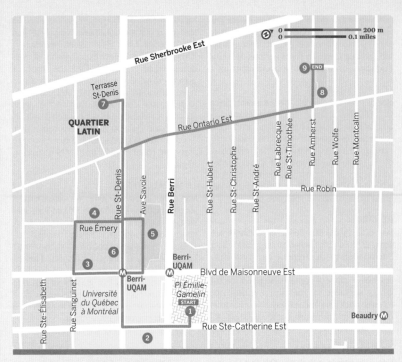

🏃 Neighborhood Walk
Bohemian Life in the Quartier Latin

START PLACE ÉMILIE-GAMELIN
END ÉCOMUSÉE DU FIER MONDE
LENGTH 2.5KM; ONE TO TWO HOURS

Begin your walk in **1 Place Émilie-Gamelin**, site of spontaneous concerts, wacky metal sculptures and outdoor chess.

Head southwest along Rue Ste-Catherine. Peek inside **2 Chapelle Notre-Dame-de-Lourdes** (p91), commissioned in 1876. This Romanesque gem has imaginative frescoes by Napoléon Bourassa.

Head up to Blvd de Maisonneuve Est and turn left to the **3 Cinémathèque Québécoise** (p98). Look at the cinema exhibits on the 1st floor and check out the latest screenings – you can catch rare films here.

Loop around the block and head right along tiny Rue Émery. Stop for a pick-me-up in **4 Camellia Sinensis** (p98), one of Montréal's best-loved teahouses.

Cross Rue St-Denis and continue down the narrow lane. You'll reach the impressive **5 Bibliothèque et Archives Nationales**

du Québec (p90), a massive library housing an astounding collection of all things Québécois. Go into the main hall and downstairs to the gallery, which often hosts fascinating (and free) exhibitions.

Turn right down Blvd de Maisonneuve Est until Rue St-Denis, then turn right again. You'll soon pass two of the neighborhood's cultural mainstays. On the left, **6 Théâtre St-Denis** (p97) is the city's second-largest theater. Continue up the street, noting the terrace cafes, lively pubs and quirky shops. The little side street on the left, **7 Terrasse St-Denis**, was a meeting place of Montréal's bohemian set at the turn of the 20th century.

Walk back down Rue St-Denis and turn left on Rue Ontario Est, then left onto Rue Amherst. On your right is a grand **8 art-deco building**, site of the former Marché St-Jacques.

Up the street is the **9 Écomusée du Fier Monde** (p91), a small museum about working-class life in the neighborhood prior to the 1960s. It's in a former bathhouse built in 1927.

offerings stick mainly to conventional pub fare – burgers, good poutines and pizza. It's a good spot to watch hockey on the screens before getting down to some serious drinking elsewhere, or to linger in a booth chatting.

LE SAINT SULPICE
PUB

Map p276 (📞514-844-9458; www.lesaintsulpice. ca; 1680 Rue St-Denis; ⏰3:30pm-3:30am Tue-Sun; Ⓜ Berri-UQAM) This student evergreen is spread over four levels in an old Victorian stone house – a cafe, several terraces, a disco, karaoke and a sprawling back garden for drinks and chats. The music changes with the DJ's mood, from hip-hop and ambient to mainstream rock and jazz.

RENARD
BAR

Map p276 (📞514-903-0648; http://bar-renard. com; 1272 Rue Ste-Catherine Est; ⏰3pm-3am) Surrounded by the frenetic bars and clubs of Rue St Catherine, stylish cocktail and craft-beer sippers come to Renard for the glossy surfaces in the dim lighting and to mix with the mixed gay-straight-other crowd. Weekends get busy, so dress for standing and posing.

RANDOLPH PUB
BAR

Map p276 (www.randolph.ca; 2041 Rue St-Denis; ⏰4pm-1am Mon-Thu, noon-2am Fri & Sat, to 1am Sun; Ⓜ Berri-UQAM) For something completely different, head to Randolph Pub. You pay a $6 cover, which gives you all-night access to the pub's vast selection of board games (over 1500 in its library). Then you can spend the evening playing games, drinking microbrews and noshing on nachos, sandwiches and salads. Queues are long on weekends.

No reservations, and it's age 18 and up.

LE DATE KARAOKE
PUB

Map p276 (www.ledatekaraoke.com; 1218 Rue Ste-Catherine Est; ⏰8am-3am; Ⓜ Beaudry) This gay tavern knew exactly what it was doing when it karaokefied the spot. A mixed crowd cheers on aspiring vocalists from all walks of life, from the hilariously awful to the downright star-worthy. Reasonably priced drinks and a weird saloon vibe guarantee you a night to remember – or forget. Fridays and Saturdays are standing room only by 9pm, when singing begins.

LE MAGELLAN BAR
BAR

Map p276 (📞514-845-0909; www.pelerinmagel lan.com; 330 Rue Ontario Est; ⏰11am-9pm Sun-Wed, to 10:30pm Thu-Sat; Ⓜ Berri-UQAM) A good spot to enjoy an evening of eclectic offerings, from jazz to chansons with a craft beer, cocktail or digestif in hand. The interior is sprinkled with maritime doodads (there's an interesting gallery of antique maps upstairs), the front terrace is great for people-watching, while the back terrace is perfectly verdant in summer.

It's joined to Le Pèlerin restaurant.

STEREO
CLUB

Map p276 (📞514-658-2646; www.stereonight club.net; 858 Rue Ste-Catherine Est; cover $25-45; ⏰2am-11am Sat-Mon; Ⓜ Berri-UQAM) Montréal's giant of underground house music has opened and closed for various reasons throughout the years. Featuring a sound system so amazing that regulars gush about out-of-body experiences, Stereo is open for business once again, attracting anyone looking to lose sleep in style at an after-hours party.

MIXED MEMORIES

On every car in Montréal, you'll notice the motto 'Je me souviens' (I remember). Officially adopted as part of Québec's coat of arms in 1939, it has been the subject of intense debate as to its meaning. Some say it represents Québec's French heritage before the British victory on the Plains of Abraham in 1760. Others believe it has to do with perceived constitutional injustices that Québec has suffered in the 20th century. Actually, Québec bureaucrat Eugene Taché had it carved in the province's coat of arms on the Parliament building in Ottawa in 1883. Though he did not explain its meaning, it appears to originate in a poem he wrote, part of which runs as follows: *'Je me souviens que né sous le lys, je fleuris sous la rose.'* (I remember that I was born under the fleur de lys, but I blossomed under the rose.) It would suggest that Québec should remember that it was born from France (the lily) but matured under the institutions inherited from Britain (the rose). The motto's cryptic meaning is far from universally agreed upon, however. Montréal's aggressive drivers are usually too busy honking at each other to discuss it.

CIRCUS
CLUB

Map p276 (http://circushd.com; 917 Rue Ste-Catherine Est; ⏰2am-8am Thu-Sun; Ⓜ Berri-UQAM) Sometimes featuring circus performers and dancers, this hot spot is more glamorous than you might expect from an after-hours joint; in fact, it ranks as the biggest of its kind in Canada. More than 200 visiting DJs a year appear behind the decks, to the dancing delight of glow-stick-brandishing ravers and clubbers who are not ready to call it a night.

Get there early to avoid the long line; alcohol served before 3am.

UNITY
LGBTIQ+

Map p276 (http://clubunity.com; 1171 Rue Ste-Catherine Est; after 11pm Fri & Sat cover $8, Thu free; ⏰10pm-3am Thu-Sun; Ⓜ Beaudry) This three-floor Village favorite features not only a club and pub but a VIP lounge, pool tables and rooftop terrace. Saturdays are the best nights, while Fridays are given over to a posey, mostly 20-something crowd. Music alternates between club dance and Latin.

AIGLE NOIR
BAR

Map p276 (☎514-529-0040; 1315 Rue Ste-Catherine Est; ⏰8am-3am; Ⓜ Beaudry) The Black Eagle is a bar for the leather-and-fetish crowd where hairy barmen are topless and porn plays on the screens. It's dependable for having other patrons at the bar, no matter what day or time of the year. Anybody is welcome to visit for the relaxed pub atmosphere and good bears, er beers.

STUD
LGBTIQ+

Map p276 (☎514-598-8243; www.studbar.com; 1812 Rue Ste-Catherine Est; ⏰5pm-3am; Ⓜ Papineau) This Village bar attracts older men, and its dark, down-at-the-heels design might bring to mind New York gay bars of the 1970s. The upside is that it's not pretentious at all, there's cheap beer and no cover charge, and the upstairs Saturday disco can be lots of fun.

 ## ENTERTAINMENT

The Rue St-Denis is a buzz of activity when a film festival is held at its many cinemas. There is plenty of performing arts to draw visitors, and the gay Village is excellent for a drag or cabaret show.

★ CABARET MADO
CABARET

Map p276 (☎514-525-7566; www.mado.qc.ca; 1115 Rue Ste-Catherine Est; tickets $5-15; ⏰4pm-3am Tue-Sun; Ⓜ Beaudry) Mado is a flamboyant celebrity who has been featured in *Fugues*, the gay entertainment mag. Her cabaret is a local institution, with drag shows featuring an assortment of hilariously sarcastic performers in eye-popping costumes. Shows take place Tuesday, Thursday and weekend nights; check the website for details.

★ USINE C
PERFORMING ARTS

Map p276 (☎514-521-4493; www.usine-c.com; 1345 Ave Lalonde; Ⓜ Beaudry) This former jam factory in the Village is home to the award-winning Carbone 14 theatrical dance troupe that performs here regularly. Its two flexible halls (450 and 150 seats) can be rejigged to accommodate circuses or concerts, but you're more likely to find interesting international drama collaborations.

To bump into its talented performers, head for the cozy cafe (p94) downstairs.

THÉÂTRE ST-DENIS
PERFORMING ARTS

Map p276 (☎514-849-4211; www.theatrestdenis.com; 1594 Rue St-Denis; ⏰box office noon-6pm Mon-Sat; Ⓜ Berri-UQAM) This Montréal landmark and historic movie house hosts touring Broadway productions, rock concerts and various theatrical and musical performances. Its two halls (933 and 2218 seats) are equipped with the latest sound and lighting gizmos and figure prominently in the Just for Laughs Festival (p38).

LE 4E MUR
LIVE MUSIC

Map p276 (http://le4emur.com; 2021 Rue St-Denis; ⏰5pm-3am, from 7pm Sun; Ⓜ Sherbrooke) This bar is literally behind an unmarked door – look for a big intimidating bouncer or the beautiful folks walking past him. Follow on, into a basement bar of low lighting and wicker chairs where the cocktails are expertly mixed, live music pops off regularly, and burlesque is a regular fixture.

THÉÂTRE STE-CATHERINE
PERFORMING ARTS

Map p276 (☎514-284-3939; www.theatre saintecatherine.com; 264 Rue Ste-Catherine Est; Ⓜ Berri-UQAM) From film to theater, stand-up comedy to music concerts, this venue presents a variety of shows: Oscar

RUE ST-DENIS & THE VILLAGE ENTERTAINMENT

Wilde one night, burlesque dance the next. Its Sunday Night Improv (sketch and comedy) performances are quite popular with the city's theatrical community; the **Montréal Sketch Comedy Festival** is in late May.

BISTRO À JOJO BLUES

Map p276 (☎514-843-5015; www.bistroajojo. com; 1627 Rue St-Denis; ☺noon-3am; ⓂBerri-UQAM) This brash venue on lively Rue St-Denis has been going strong since 1975. It's the nightly place for down 'n' dirty French- and English-language blues and rock groups.

CINÉMATHÈQUE QUÉBÉCOISE CINEMA

Map p276 (☎514-842-9763; www.cinematheque.qc.ca; 335 Blvd de Maisonneuve Est; adult/student $11/10; ☺10am-9pm Mon-Fri, from 2pm Sat & Sun; ⓂBerri-UQAM) This is a university-flavored venue noted for showing Canadian, Québécois and international avant-garde films. In the lobby there's a permanent exhibition on the history of filmmaking as well as a TV and new-media section.

LE NATIONAL LIVE MUSIC

Map p276 (☎514-845-2014; www.latulipe.ca; 1220 Rue Ste-Catherine Est; ☺box office noon-5pm Oct-May, from 3pm on presentation days Jun-Sep; ⓂBeaudry) This 750-capacity concert venue situated in the Village was one of the first professional French theaters in Montréal. In tandem with sister venue **La Tulipe** on Ave Papineau, it hosts a variety of acts, from hard-core bands to pop shows. Check the website for listings.

CINÉMA QUARTIER LATIN CINEMA

Map p276 (www.cineplex.com; 350 Rue Émery; ☺11:30am-10:15pm; ⓂBerri-UQAM) This large cinema plays French films and French versions of some Hollywood movies, as well as live broadcasts of performances from the Metropolitan Opera in New York several times a month (check www.cineplex.com/Events/MetOpera for the schedule). It's also a host theater for the Montréal World Film Festival (p22).

 # SHOPPING

Bookstores, antique dens and tea shops share space with adult toy emporiums in this area. Most of the shopping is concentrated in the Village, as many of the long-standing smaller stores on Rue St-Denis have closed.

★CAMELLIA SINENSIS FOOD & DRINKS

Map p276 (www.camellia-sinensis.com; 351 Rue Émery; ☺noon-10pm Mon-Thu, to 11pm Sat, to 9pm Sun; ⓂBerri-UQAM) Right in front of the Cinéma Quartier Latin, this welcoming tea shop has more than 200 varieties of tea from China, Japan, India and elsewhere in Asia, plus quality teapots, tea accessories, books, and workshops such as pairing tea with chocolate. You can taste exotic teas and carefully selected desserts in the salon next door, which features brews from recent staff travels.

PRIAPE ADULT

Map p276 (☎514-521-8451; www.priape.com; 1311 Rue Ste-Catherine Est; ☺10am-8pm Mon, to 9pm Tue-Thu, to 10pm Fri & Sat, noon-8pm; ⓂBeaudry) Montréal's biggest gay sex store is well plugged into mainstream erotic wares (DVDs, mags and books), and also has high-quality clothing with a titillating edge – shrink-wrapped jeans, but also a vast choice of black leather gear in the basement.

ARCHAMBAULT BOOKS

Map p276 (☎514-849-6202; www.archambault. ca; 510 Rue Ste-Catherine Est; ☺9am-9pm Mon-Fri, to 7pm Sat, 10am-7pm Sun; ⓂBerri-UQAM) Behind the art-deco portals you'll find Montréal's oldest and largest book and record shop, an emporium that boasts books, CDs and gifts, plus assorted musical supplies such as pianos and sheet music.

AUX QUATRE POINTS CARDINAUX MAPS

Map p276 (☎514-843-8116; www.aqpc.com; 551 Rue Ontario Est; ☺10am-6pm Mon-Wed, to 9pm Thu & Fri, to 5pm Sat; ⓂBerri-UQAM) The globe-trotting folks at AQPC pack a range of goods for the seasoned traveler such as atlases, globes, maps, aerial photographs, and travel guides in English and French, including a good selection of Lonely Planet books.

Plateau Mont-Royal & the Northeast

PARC DU MONT-ROYAL AREA | OLYMPIC PARK

Neighborhood Top Five

❶ Parc du Mont-Royal (p102) Enjoying the fresh air, sweeping vistas, cycling or skiing and feathered friends of the beloved heart of Montréal.

❷ Boulevard St-Laurent (p101) Exploring the old-world groceries that rub shoulders with stylish drinking dens.

❸ Parc La Fontaine (p101) Relaxing by the pond in summer and ice-skating in winter in this leafy refuge.

❹ Jardin Botanique (p103) Bringing out your green side at one of the world's largest gardens, showcasing themed Chinese, Japanese and First Nations landscapes.

❺ Biodôme (p104) Chilling out with the penguins and many other fish and fowl through five ecosystems.

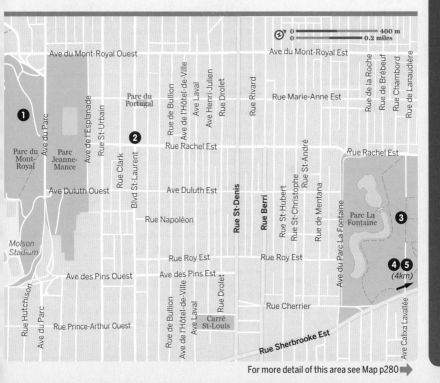

For more detail of this area see Map p280 ➡

Lonely Planet's Top Tip

Enjoying Montréal's famous bagels on the spot doesn't have to be expensive. While sitting down at **St-Viateur Bagel & Café** (p106) to a full bagel meal will cost you over $12, asking for just a bagel and cream cheese will cost you under $4. Even cheaper, some locals will order a $1 bagel from the takeout counter and, if it's not busy, the staff don't mind if you sit and gobble it up (neatly) at a table.

Best Places to Eat

➡ L'Express (p107)

➡ L'Gros Luxe (p107)

➡ Hà (p107)

➡ Le Filet (p108)

➡ Au Pied de Cochon (p108)

➡ Schwartz's (p106)

For reviews, see p106.➡

Best Places to Drink

➡ Big in Japan (p108)

➡ Barfly (p108)

➡ Majestique (p110)

➡ Reservoir (p110)

For reviews, see p108.➡

Best Entertainment

➡ Casa del Popolo (p111)

➡ Dièse Onze (p112)

➡ La Tulipe (p112)

For reviews, see p111.➡

Explore Plateau Mont-Royal & the Northeast

This is a large area, but a good chunk can be explored in a day. Begin at leafy Carré St-Louis, where slate Victorian mansions and duplexes house arty souls and B&Bs.

Make your way along Rue Prince-Arthur Ouest to Blvd St-Laurent, the legendary divide between anglophone and francophone Montréal once known as 'the Main.' Today the Main is a mix of hip cafes and nightspots, European-style delis and grocery stores, and fashionable shops. The stretch to Ave Duluth, known for its Bring Your Own Bottle (BYOB) restaurants, attracts hordes of 20-somethings on weekend nights.

Continuing northwest up Blvd St-Laurent, you'll enter Montréal's Portuguese community, passing Parc du Portugal. Another block to the northwest lies Ave du Mont-Royal. It's worth turning right here and wandering down several blocks, lined with eclectic boutiques, record shops and bookstores.

When you're in the mood for fresh air, hop on bus 11 on the northwest side of Ave du Mont-Royal and ride up to 'the Mountain,' the Parc du Mont-Royal. Hop off at the parking lot near Maison Smith, a visitors center where you can have a drink and learn about the park's history before spending the rest of the day exploring it.

Also easily accessible is Olympic Park – you can take the metro. The big draw here is the massive Olympic Stadium (built for the 1976 Olympic Games), the renovated kid-friendly Biodôme and Insectarium, a planetarium and the verdant Jardin Botanique.

Local Life

➡ **Bar-hopping** Coasting up and down Blvd St-Laurent is the quintessential bar-hopping experience for younger Montréalers.

➡ **Mountainsides** It doesn't get much more Montréal than picnicking, sunbathing and tobogganing (in winter) on the Mountain.

➡ **Foodie faves** You can't go wrong with a bagel, some smoked meat and poutine in your quest to be an authentic Montréaler.

Getting There & Away

➡ **Metro** Metro access is via the orange line, at the stations of Sherbrooke, Mont-Royal and Laurier.

➡ **Bus** The 55 runs along Blvd St-Laurent; bus 30 coasts along Rue St-Denis; bus 80 travels Ave du Parc; bus 11 climbs up to Parc du Mont-Royal from Ave du Mont-Royal.

◉ SIGHTS

East of Parc du Mont-Royal, the Plateau is Montréal's youngest, liveliest and artiest neighborhood. Originally a working-class district, it changed its stripes in the 1960s and '70s when writers, singers and other creative folk moved in. Among them was playwright Michel Tremblay, whose unvarnished look (check out his six-novel series *Chroniques du plateau de Mont-Royal*) at some of the neighborhood's more colorful characters put the Plateau firmly on the path to hipdom.

These days, the Plateau is more gentrified than bohemian, but it's gentrified in a way that still *seems* pretty bohemian. As you stroll through its side streets, admiring the signature streetscapes with their winding staircases, ornate wrought-iron balconies and pointy Victorian roofs, you'll begin to understand why.

The Plateau is bordered roughly by Blvd St-Joseph to the north and Rue Sherbrooke to the south, Mont-Royal to the west and Ave de Lorimier to the east. The main drags are Blvd St-Laurent ('The Main'), Rue St-Denis and Ave du Mont-Royal, all lined with sidewalk cafes, restaurants, clubs and boutiques. Rue Prince-Arthur, Montréal's quintessential hippie hangout in the 1960s, and Rue Duluth are alive with BYOB eateries.

★ PARC LA FONTAINE   PARK

Map p280 (cnr Rue Sherbrooke Est & Ave du Parc La Fontaine; ⊙6am-midnight; ⊞⊛; ⓜSherbrooke) ✎ At 34 hectares, this great verdant municipal park is the city's third largest, after Parc du Mont-Royal (p102) and Parc Maisonneuve. In the warmer months weary urbanites flock to leafy La Fontaine to enjoy the walking and bicycle paths, the attractive ponds and the general air of relaxation that pervades the park. There's also a chalet where you can grab a bite or a drink, **Espace La Fontaine** (📞514-280-2525; https://espacelafontaine.com; 3933 Ave du Parc La Fontaine; mains $10-16; ⊙11am-7pm Wed-Fri, 10am-5pm Sat & Sun; ✎⊞).

The view down the steep banks from Ave du Parc La Fontaine is impressive, especially if the fountains are in play. You can rent paddleboats in summer and go ice-skating in winter. The open-air **Théâtre de Verdure** draws a laid-back crowd on evenings in July.

AVENUE DU MONT-ROYAL   AREA

Map p280 (⊛; ⓜMont-Royal) Old-fashioned five-and-dime stores rub shoulders with a wide array of trendy cafes and fashion boutiques on Ave du Mont-Royal. The nightlife here has surged to the point that it rivals Blvd St-Laurent, with bars and nightclubs ranging from the sedate to uproarious. Intimate shops, secondhand stores and ultramodern boutiques offer eye-catching apparel.

★ BOULEVARD ST-LAURENT   STREET

Map p280 (ⓜSt-Laurent then bus 55) A dividing line between the city's east and west, Blvd St-Laurent (previously 'the Main') has always been a focus of action, a gathering place for people of many languages and backgrounds. In 1996 it was declared a national historic site for its role as ground zero for so many Canadian immigrants and future Montréalers. The label 'the Main' has stuck in the local lingo since the 19th century. Today it's a gateway into the Plateau and a fascinating street to explore.

For a food- and culture-focused tour of the Main, from Chinatown to Little Italy, contact Fitz & Follwell (p113).

CARRÉ ST-LOUIS   SQUARE

Map p280 (cnr Rue St-Denis & Rue Prince-Arthur; ⓜSherbrooke) 🆓 This lovely green square with a three-tiered fountain is flanked by beautiful rows of Second Empire homes. In the 19th century a reservoir here was filled, and a neighborhood emerged for well-to-do French families. Artists and poets gathered in the area back then, and creative types like filmmakers and fashion designers now occupy houses in the streets nearby. The cafe, which opens in summer, is a good spot for a pick-me-up, with occasional musicians creating the soundtrack for the square.

Carré St-Louis feeds west into **Rue Prince-Arthur**, a former slice of 1960s hippie culture that has refashioned itself as a popular restaurant strip.

PARC DU PORTUGAL   PARK

Map p280 (cnr Blvd St-Laurent & Rue Marie-Anne Ouest; ⓜSt-Laurent then bus 55) This quaint little park is dedicated to Portuguese immigrants and their community, founded in Montréal in 1953. At the rear of the park, next to the little summer pavilion, a plaque commemorates the arrival of Portuguese immigrants in search of a new life. The gates and fountain are covered with

ℹ️ MOUNTAIN GUIDE

➡ There's much to experience on Mont-Royal, but it's wise to have a plan before you go.

➡ There are park info centers at Chalet du Mont-Royal and Maison Smith. You'll also find loads of info online (including a handy map). Visit www.lemontroyal.qc.ca.

➡ Head to Lac aux Castors for winter sports and summer boating.

➡ Binoculars are a good idea for the bird feeders set up along some walking trails.

➡ Note that walking in the park after sunset isn't a safe idea.

colorful glazed tiles. Surrounding streets are dotted with Portuguese and Brazilian restaurants.

◉ Parc du Mont-Royal Area

Montréalers are proud of their 'mountain,' so don't call it a hill as Oscar Wilde did when he visited the city in the 1880s. The The charming, leafy expanse of **Parc du Mont-Royal** (Map p280; ☑514-843-8240; www.lemontroyal.qc.ca; 1260 Chemin Remembrance; 🖼; Ⓜ Mont-Royal, then bus 11) 🖋 FREE is charged for a wide range of outdoor activities. The wooded slopes and grassy meadows have stunning views that make it all the more popular for jogging, picnicking, horseback riding, cycling and throwing Frisbees. Winter brings skating, tobogganing and cross-country skiing. Binoculars are a good idea for the bird feeders that have been set up along some walking trails.

The park was laid out by Frederick Law Olmsted, the architect of New York's Central Park. The idea came from bourgeois residents in the adjacent Golden Square Mile who fretted about vanishing greenery.

Contrary to what people may try to tell you, this place is not an extinct volcano. Rather, Parc du Mont-Royal is a hangover from when magma penetrated the earth's crust millions of years ago. This formed a sort of erosion-proof rock, so while time and the elements were wearing down the

ground around it, the 232m-high hunk of rock stood firm.

Note that walking in the park after sunset isn't such a safe idea.

CHALET DU
MONT-ROYAL   HISTORIC BUILDING
(☑514-843-8240; www.lemontroyal.qc.ca; 1196 Voie Camillien-Houde; ◷10am-5pm Mon-Thu, to 8pm Fri-Sun; Ⓜ Mont-Royal, then bus 11) FREE Constructed in 1932, this grand old white villa, complete with bay windows, contains canvases that depict scenes of Montréal history. You'll also see carved squirrels in the rafters. Big bands strut their stuff on the huge balcony in summer, reminiscent of the 1930s. Most people, however, flock here for the spectacular views of downtown from the **Belvédère Kondiaronk lookout** (☑514-872-3911; 1196 Voie Camillien-Houde, Mont-Royal; ◷6am-midnight) FREE fronting the chalet. It's an easy 10-minute walk (700m) from the car park at bus 11 stop Remembrance/Chemin du Chalet.

BELVÉDÈRE
CAMILLIEN-HOUDE   VIEWPOINT
(Voie Camillien-Houde; Ⓜ Mont-Royal, then bus 11) This is the most popular lookout on Mont-Royal thanks to its accessibility and large parking lot. Naturally enough, it's a magnet for couples once night falls, making it nearly impossible on summer nights to find a parking space – try taking the bus that stops right here. To get to the lookout, take the stairs that lead from the parking lot.

You can walk to Chalet du Mont-Royal, about 2km away.

LAC AUX CASTORS   LAKE
(www.lemontroyal.qc.ca; 🚍11) Created in a former marsh as part of a work-creation project, Beaver Lake is a center of activity year-round. You can rent paddleboats on the lake or, in winter, ice skates, cross-country skis, snowshoes and sleds from **Le Pavillon** (2000 Chemin Remembrance; ◷10am-6pm Mon-Fri, 9am-6pm Sat & Sun). The slopes above the lake are popular for sledding. Refreshments and sandwiches are sold at a snack bar; there's also a restaurant with more elaborate dishes.

MAISON SMITH   HISTORIC BUILDING
(http://ville.montreal.qc.ca; 1260 Chemin Remembrance; ◷9am-5pm; 🚍11) Constructed in 1858 by a merchant who wanted to get away from the pollution and overpopulation of

the rest of Montréal, this house contains a small permanent exhibition on the history of surrounding Parc du Mont-Royal and its flora and fauna. There's also a visitors center, the headquarters of Les Amis de la Montagne, and a cafe, with a pleasant outdoor terrace (open mid-May to mid-October) where you can have grilled sandwiches, soups, desserts, coffees, beer and wine.

CROIX DU MONT-ROYAL   MONUMENT

(Chemin Olmsted; MMont-Royal, then bus 11) About 550m north of Kondiaronk lookout stands the Mont-Royal Cross, one of Montréal's most familiar landmarks. Made of reinforced steel, the 31-meter-tall cross was erected in 1924 on the very spot where Maisonneuve placed a wooden cross.

According to legend, when floods threatened the fledgling colony in 1643, Maissonneuve prayed to the Virgin Mary to save the town. When the waters receded, out of gratitude Maisonneuve carried a cross up the steep slopes and planted it there.

⊙ Olympic Park

★JARDIN BOTANIQUE   GARDENS

(☎514-872-1400; www.espacepourlavie.ca/jardin-botanique; 4101 Rue Sherbrooke Est; adult/child $21/10; ☺9am-6pm mid-May–early Sep, 9am-5pm Tue-Sun early Sep–mid-May; ♿; MPie-IX) ♠ Montréal's Jardin Botanique is the third-largest botanical garden in the world, after London's Kew Gardens and Berlin's Botanischer Garten. Since its 1931 opening, the 75-hectare garden has grown to include tens of thousands of species in more than 20 thematic gardens, and its wealth of flowering plants is carefully managed to bloom

in stages. The rose beds are a sight to behold in summertime. Climate-controlled greenhouses house cacti, banana trees and 1500 species of orchid. Bird-watchers should bring their binoculars.

A popular drawcard is the landscaped **Japanese Garden** with traditional pavilions, tearoom and art gallery; the bonsai 'forest' is the largest outside Asia. The twinning of Montréal with Shanghai gave impetus to plant a **Chinese Garden**. The ornamental penjing trees from Hong Kong are up to 100 years old. A Ming-dynasty garden is the feature around Lac de Rêve (Dream Lake). In the northern part of the Jardin Botanique you'll find the **Frédérick Back Tree Pavilion**, a permanent exhibit on life in the 40-hectare arboretum. Displays include the yellow birch, part of Québec's official emblem. The **First Nations Garden** reveals the bonds between 11 Amerindian and Inuit nations and indigenous plants such as silver birches, maples, Labrador and tea. The **Orchidée Gift Shop** in the main building has a wonderful selection, including handmade jewelry and crafts, stuffed animals and beautifully illustrated books.

In fall (mid-September to early November), the Chinese Garden dons its most exquisite garb for the popular **Magic of Lanterns**, when hundreds of handmade silk lanterns sparkle at dusk. Montréalers are devoted to this event and it can feel like it's standing-room only even though it's held in a huge garden.

The best way to get around this huge place is by the hop-on, hop-off trolley that makes its rounds every 35 minutes or so (summer only). Free guided tours leave at 10:30am and 1:30pm daily (except Monday

---

MOUNTAIN MAUSOLEUMS

On the north side of the park lie two enormous cemeteries: **Cimetière Mont-Royal** (☎514-279-7358; www.mountroyalcem.com; 1297 Chemin de la Forêt; ☺9am-8pm May-Aug, to 5pm Sep-Apr; MÉdouard-Montpetit) is Protestant and nondenominational, while **Cimetière Notre-Dame-des-Neiges** (☎514-735-1361; www.notredamedesneiges cemetery.ca; 4601 Chemin de la Côte-des-Neiges; ☺8am-5pm, office 8:30am-4:30pm; MCôte-des-Neiges) is Catholic. The latter has several interesting mausoleums. The Pietà Mausoleum contains a full-scale marble replica of Michelangelo's famous sculpture in St Peter's Basilica in Rome. Other mausoleums in the cemetery emit solemn music, including that of Marguerite Bourgeoys, a nun and teacher who was beatified in 1982 – for more details on her life, visit the Chapelle Notre-Dame-de-Bonsecours (p54). Built in 2007, the Esther Blondin Mausoleum is a modern facility housing 6000 crypts and niches, reflecting the increasing popularity of communal memorial spaces.

from November to May) from the reception center. All facilities are accessible to people in wheelchairs.

The admission ticket includes the gardens, greenhouses and the Insectarium.

★ BIODÔME   MUSEUM

(☎514-868-3000; www.espacepourlavie.ca; 4777 Ave du Pierre-De Coubertin; adult/child $20/10; ☉9am-6pm late Jun-Sep, 9am-5pm Tue-Sun rest of year; ♿; Ⓜ Viau) At this captivating exhibit you can amble through a rainforest, explore Antarctic islands, view rolling woodlands, take in aquatic life in the Gulf of St Lawrence, or wander along the raw Atlantic oceanfront – all without ever leaving the building. The five ecosystems house many thousands of animal and plant species; follow the self-guided circuit and you will see everything. Be sure to dress in layers for the temperature swings. You can borrow free strollers; and interactive exhibits are at small-child height.

After a 2019 makeover the space is bathed in natural light and features raised walkways. Penguins frolic in the pools a few feet away from groups of goggle-eyed children; the tropical chamber is a cross section of Amazonia with mischievous little monkeys teasing alligators in the murky waters below. The Gulf of St Lawrence has an underwater observatory where you can watch cod feeding alongside lobsters and sea urchins in the tidal pools. The appearance of the Laurentian Forest varies widely with the seasons, with special habitats for lynx, otters and around 350 bats.

The Biodôme is wildly popular, so try to visit during the week, avoiding the middle of the day if possible. Plan two hours to do it justice. You can bring a packed lunch for the picnic tables or dine in the cafeteria. In summer there are educational day camps for kids.

The Biodôme is unrelated to the Biosphère (p68) on Île Ste-Hélène.

INSECTARIUM   GARDENS

(www.espacepourlavie.ca; 4101 Rue Sherbrooke Est; adult/child $29.50/15; ☉9am-6pm; Ⓜ Pie-IX) The Insectarium houses an intriguing collection of creepy crawlies. Closed for remodeling at the time of research, most of its 250,000 specimens are dead and mounted, but there will be an expanded section with living species (including tarantulas, bees and scorpions) alongside plants in the Vivarium.

PLANÉTARIUM   PLANETARIUM

(☎514-868-3000; www.espacepourlavie.ca; 4801 Ave du Pierre-De Coubertin; adult/child $20/10; ☉9am-5pm Sun, Tue & Wed, to 8pm Thu-Sat; ♿; Ⓜ Viau) Opened in 2013, these futuristic metallic buildings bring a bit of the cosmos to Montréal, courtesy of two high-tech domed theaters and interactive exhibits on outer space. The round theaters have slightly different layouts and agendas: the Milky Way Theatre is more traditional, with comfy seats and films that give an eye-opening glimpse of what lies beyond earth, while the Chaos theater has beanbags and Adirondack chairs and takes a more philosophical look at the universe.

OLYMPIC STADIUM   STADIUM

(Stade Olympique; ☎514-252-4141; http://parcolympique.qc.ca; 4141 Ave Pierre-De Coubertin; tower adult/child $24/12; ☉1-6pm Mon, 9am-6pm Tue-Sun mid-Jun–early Sep, 9am-5pm rest of year; Ⓜ Viau) The Olympic Stadium seats 56,000 and remains an architectural marvel. Nowadays it hosts mostly concerts and trade shows, though in preparation for the 2026 World Cup, it will receive a retractable roof. The main attraction is the short (three-minute) ride on the bilevel cable car, which goes up the **Montréal Tower** (Tour de Montréal, also called the Olympic Tower) that lords over the stadium. It's the world's tallest inclined structure (165m at a 45-degree angle). Still, many don't find the overall experience worth the price.

Alternatively, ticketed 90-minute tours of the stadium – the only way to get a peek inside aside from the **Centre Aquatique** (per adult/child $7/5.50; ☉6am-9pm Mon-Fri, 8am-6pm Sat & Sun) – start at the ticket office. The Centre Aquatique is the Olympic swimming complex, with six pools, diving towers and a 20m-deep scuba pool.

The glassed-in observation deck (with bar and rest area) isn't for the faint of heart but it does afford a bird's-eye view of the city. In the distance you'll see the pointy modern towers of the Olympic Village, where athletes stayed in 1976.

The Tourist Hall is a three-story information center with a ticket office, restaurant and souvenir shop, as well as the cable-car boarding station.

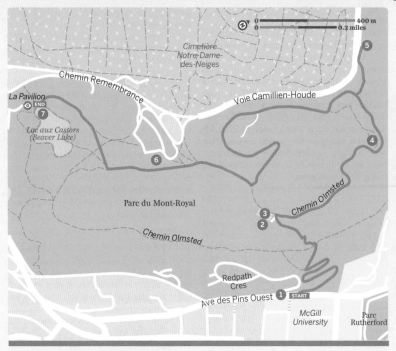

🏃 Neighborhood Walk
Montréal's Favorite Mountain

START AVE DES PINS OUEST
END LAC AUX CASTORS
LENGTH 6KM; TWO HOURS

Many of Montréal's neighborhoods hug the foot of Parc du Mont-Royal, making everyone feel like they have a bit of green space in their backyard. 'The Mountain,' as Mont-Royal is affectionately known by locals, is cherished for its winding trails, fresh air and views.

The starting point for this walk is on ❶ **Ave de Pins Ouest** at the staircase into the park near the corner with Rue Peel. It's a fairly steep 10- to 15-minute climb alternating between steps and inclined, unpaved trail.

When you reach the large path, turn right and you'll soon see yet more stairs heading up to the ❷ **Belvédère Kondiaronk lookout** (p102). The overlook offers stunning panoramic views of the downtown area and even beyond to Parc Jean-Drapeau. A few paces from the lookout is the ❸ **Chalet du Mont-Royal** (p102), which has paintings of

some key scenes from local history. This is a good cafe and bathroom stop.

From the chalet, walk north along the trail named Chemin Olmsted about 600m to the ❹ **Croix du Mont-Royal** (p103). This is where city founder Maisonneuve planted a cross in thanksgiving to the Virgin Mary for saving the city from flood.

Further along you can descend a set of stairs to reach the scenic lookout of ❺ **Belvédère Camillien-Houde** (p102), one of the most romantic views in the city.

Returning to the path, head south toward ❻ **Maison Smith** (p102), an 1858 building that houses a permanent exhibition on the history and ongoing conservation of Mont-Royal. A visitor center doles out information; there is also an on-site cafe.

Another 500m further south, the artificial pond ❼ **Lac aux Castors** (p102) is a haven of toy-boat captains in summer and ice-skaters in winter. Refreshments are available at the pavilion, and in warm weather the meadows around the pond are full of sunbathers.

✕ EATING

Plateau Mont-Royal has a fantastic variety of bistros, upscale restaurants and bohemian-style cafes. Rue Prince-Arthur Est is a narrow residential street that has been converted into a dining-and-entertainment enclave. The restaurant segment runs west from leafy Carré St-Louis (just north of Rue Sherbrooke) to a block west of Blvd St-Laurent. Many of the small, inexpensive and mostly international restaurants here aren't licensed to serve alcohol, so bring your own wine.

SCHWARTZ'S
SANDWICHES $

Map p280 (☎514-842-4813; www.schwartzs deli.com; 3895 Blvd St-Laurent; sandwiches $10.50, mains $13-26; ⏰8am-12:30am Sun-Thu, to 1:30am Fri & Sat; ⓂSherbrooke) Reuben Schwartz, a Romanian Jew, opened this Montréal icon in 1928, and it's been going strong ever since. Schwartz's meat goes through a 14-day regime of curing and smoking before landing on your plate after a final three-hour steam. It's widely considered the best smoked meat in Montréal, whether it's brisket, duck, chicken or turkey, all piled high on sourdough rye bread.

You can order it fat, medium (recommended) or lean. Expect the usual long lines. If you don't feel like waiting, head across the street to the **Main** (Map p280; ☎514-849-3378; www.mainlinetheatre.ca; 3997 Blvd St-Laurent; tickets $10-24; ⓂMont-Royal), which serves a reputable smoked-meat sandwich.

OMNIVORE
MEDITERRANEAN $

Map p280 (www.omnivoregrill.com; 4351 Blvd St-Laurent; mains $6-14; ⏰noon-9pm; ✓; ⓂMont-Royal) Amid rustic wood tables and potted plants, the friendly staff at little Omnivore whip up delicious Middle-Eastern mezze plates of hummus, tabbouleh, baba ghanoush, meat skewers and other Lebanese classics. There are also grilled pita sandwiches. Everything is fresh, generous and delicious and can be made vegetarian.

LA BANQUISE
QUÉBÉCOIS $

Map p280 (☎514-525-2415; www.labanquise. com; 994 Rue Rachel Est; mains $8-15; ⏰24hr; ♿; ⓂMont-Royal) A Montréal legend since 1968, La Banquise is probably the best place in town to sample poutine. More than 30 varieties are available, including a vegan poutine, the boogalou (with pulled pork) and straight-up classic poutine. There's an outdoor terrace, a full breakfast menu and a selection of microbrews, plus the kitchen never closes. Expect long lines on weekends.

KOUIGN AMANN
BAKERY $

Map p280 (322 Ave du Mont-Royal Est; pastries $2-3; ⏰7am-7pm Tue-Fri, to 6pm Sat & Sun; ⓂMont-Royal) The name of this bakery – challenging even for some French speakers – comes from its famous Breton cake (flaky on the outside, rich and tender on the inside), which justifiably draws fans from near and far. The friendly staff also serve soups, quiches and excellent croissants. The tiny space has just three tables; most people get their treats to go.

ST-VIATEUR BAGEL & CAFÉ
BAGELS $

Map p280 (☎514-528-6361; www.stviateur bagel.com; 1127 Ave du Mont-Royal Est; sandwiches $9-12; ⏰6am-10pm; ⓂMont-Royal) A splendid cafe that serves its signature bagels, grilled or *nature,* with soup or salad. There are about a dozen sandwiches but most popular are the traditional smoked lox with cream cheese, and roast beef with Swiss cheese and tomato. You can also find breakfast bagels with eggs and ham.

ROYAL PHO
VIETNAMESE $

Map p280 (☎514-522-7888; http://phomont royal.ca; 1235 Ave Mont-Royal Est; mains $10-16; ⏰11am-10pm Sun, Mon & Wed, 4-10pm Tue, 11am-11pm Thu-Sat; 🤶✓; ⓂMont-Royal) The pho (rice-noodle soup) is the standout at this Vietnamese restaurant, with all the right herbs and touch of anise. This is Mont-Royal not Chinatown, so it's also comfortable, warmly lit, and popular with small groups and local solo diners. The grilled pork and lemongrass chicken dishes are also tempting.

MA POULE MOUILLÉE
CHICKEN $

Map p280 (☎514-522-5175; http://mapoule mouillee.ca; 969 Rue Rachel Est; mains from $7-16; ⏰9am-10pm; ⓂMont-Royal) The moist, roasted and spiced Portuguese-style chicken brings lineups on weekends at this local favorite. Though it might also be the sweet egg tarts or poutine. There is limited, basic seating but then large Parc La Fontaine (p101) is nearby.

SUSHI MOMO
VEGETARIAN **$**

Map p280 (📞514-825-6363; 3609 Rue St-Denis; 5-piece rolls $6-8; ⏱5-10pm Tue-Thu, 3-10pm Fri-Sun; 🖋; Ⓜ St-Laurent, then bus 55) There are just five tables in this art-filled vegan sushi joint, but you can always grab a spot along the counter, and join the mostly student crowd for delicious inexpensive rolls. The excellent meat-free rolls are created with inventive combos, such as the Mangue Patate with sweet potato, mango, cucumber, avocado and more.

Orders come with steaming spiced bowls of edamame, and you should definitely opt for the miso soup.

BEAUTY'S
DINER **$**

Map p280 (📞514-849-8883; http://beautys.ca; 93 Ave du Mont-Royal Ouest; breakfasts $8.50-14; ⏱7am-3pm Mon-Fri, 8am to 4pm Sat & Sun; Ⓜ Mont-Royal) This sleek, retro '50s diner serves what some consider Montréal's best breakfast – all day long. Ask for 'the Special' – a toasted bagel with lox, cream cheese, tomato and onion. Lineups on Saturday and Sunday mornings can run up to 40 minutes long, even in winter (arrive before 10am).

PATATI PATATA
QUÉBÉCOIS **$**

Map p280 (📞514-844-0216; 4177 Blvd St-Laurent; mains $7-11; ⏱9am-11pm; Ⓜ St-Laurent, then bus 55) This matchbox-sized, bohemian-style eatery is known for its good-value poutine, borscht and miniburgers. It's a Montréal classic with rocking music and young efficient staff, and there's almost always a line snaking out the front. Grab a seat at the window and watch the city stroll past.

HOF KELSTEN
BAKERY **$**

Map p280 (📞514-649-7991; http://hofkelsten. com; 4524 Blvd St-Laurent; pastries $2-3, sandwiches $8-10; ⏱8am-7pm Wed-Sun; 🖋; Ⓜ Mont-Royal) This sweet bakery has delectable pastries, tasty sandwiches (including an egg-and-cheese breakfast option) and a tempting selection of loaves. At lunchtime, join Montréalers at the long communal table for lox, roast beef or veggie sandwiches – or get it to go and head to nearby Parc Jeanne-Mance.

There's also soup (borscht, matzo ball, latke) and first-rate espresso drinks. Plus, you can come for weekend brunch – challah French toast, schnitzel and eggs – served from 10am to 3pm.

★L'EXPRESS
FRENCH **$$**

Map p280 (📞514-845-5333; www.restaurant lexpress.com; 3927 Rue St-Denis; mains $19-29; ⏱8am-2am Mon-Fri, from 10am Sat & Sun; Ⓜ Sherbrooke) L'Express has all the hallmarks of a Parisian bistro – black-and-white checkered floor, art-deco globe lights, papered tables and mirrored walls. High-end bistro fare completes the picture, with excellent dishes such as grilled salmon, bone marrow with sea salt, roast duck with salad and beef tartare. The waiters can advise on the extensive wine list. Reservations are essential.

L'GROS LUXE
BISTRO **$$**

Map p280 (📞514-447-2227; www.lgrosluxe. com; 451 Ave Duluth Est; small plates $5-10; ⏱5-11:30pm Mon-Fri, from 11am Sat & Sun; 🖋; Ⓜ Sherbrooke) With classy vintage decor, booths or tables and inexpensive comfort fare, L'Gros Luxe has obvious appeal. The small dining room is always packed with young Plateau residents who come for pork tacos, veggie burgers, and fish and chips. Plates are small, but nothing costs more than $10, and there's an extensive drinks menu (with much higher prices than the food).

HÀ
VIETNAMESE **$$**

Map p280 (📞514-848-0336; http://restaurant ha.com; 243 Ave du Mont-Royal Ouest; mains $14-28; ⏱noon-3pm & 5:30-10pm Tue-Fri, 5:30-10pm Sat & Sun; 🖋; Ⓜ Mont-Royal) Inspired by the street food (and beer) of Vietnam, this neighborhood charmer showcases simple but delectable recipes, near the foot of Mont-Royal. The menu is small, with highlights such as grilled beef with watercress salad, lemongrass pork ribs and spicy papaya salad.

It's set in a minimal, warmly lit dining room (illuminated by sculptural light fixtures), with a lovely terrace in front. The restaurant was opened by the late chef and local personality Hong Hà Nguyen.

ROBIN DES BOIS
FUSION **$$**

Map p280 (📞514-288-1010; www.robindes bois.ca; 4653 Blvd St-Laurent; mains $15-25; ⏱11:30am-10pm Mon-Sat; 📶♿; Ⓜ St-Laurent, then bus 55) 🌿 Montréal's own 'Robin Hood,' restaurateur Judy Servay donates all profits and tips from this reliable favorite to local charities. The relaxed, spacious diner vibe and varied menu is inviting to all, solo or in groups. Customisable dishes include brown rice, mashed potato, noodles or soup topped with grilled salmon or vegan tempeh. Sandwiches and salads keep everybody happy.

Sharing and kids' menus draw families. Cut the servers some slack – most are young volunteers.

CHUCHAI · THAI $$

Map p280 (☏514-843-4194; www.chuchai.com; 4088 Rue St-Denis; mains $16-23; ⏲11am-2pm & 5-10pm Tue-Thu, to 11pm Fri & Sat; ☑) In Montréal's first vegetarian upscale eatery, zippy Thai-inspired stir-fries and coconut soups explore the potential of fragrant kaffir lime, lemongrass and sweet basil. The fake duck could fool even the most discerning carnivore.

LA SALA ROSA · SPANISH $$

Map p280 (☏514-844-4227; www.facebook.com/lasalarosa; 4848 Blvd St-Laurent; mains $13-17; ⏲5-11pm Tue & Wed, to 2am Thu-Sat, to 10pm Sun; ☑; Ⓜ Laurier) A festive, local and often Spanish-speaking crowd comes to this little Iberian gem. La Sala Rosa is best known for its five tasty varieties of paella (including vegetarian) as well as numerous tapas dishes and a changing lineup of Spanish specials. On Thursday nights (from 8:45pm) there's a live flamenco show and the place gets packed.

LE FILET · SEAFOOD $$$

Map p280 (☏514-360-6060; www.lefilet.ca; 219 Ave du Mont-Royal Ouest; mains $25-42; ⏲5:45-11pm Tue-Sat; Ⓜ Mont-Royal) Le Filet presents masterfully crafted fish and seafood with Japanese touches in a low-lit setting facing Parc Jeanne-Mance. Small plates are meant for sharing (two people typically order four to five dishes) and mains showcase risotto, spaghetti and duck with maple syrup. The grilled octopus with Israeli couscous will make you wish there were more than just eight legs.

The menu is market-based and changes often, but other favorites include the misogratin oysters, crab risotto and cavatelli with veal cheeks. Reserve well in advance.

AU PIED DE COCHON · QUÉBÉCOIS $$$

Map p280 (☏514-281-1114; www.aupieddecochon.ca; 536 Ave Duluth Est; mains $28-48; ⏲5pm-midnight Wed-Sun; Ⓜ Mont-Royal) One of Montréal's most respected restaurants features extravagant pork, duck and steak dishes, along with its signature foie gras (p28) plates.

Irreverent, award-winning chef Martin Picard takes simple ingredients and transforms them into works of art. Dishes are rich and portions are large, so bring an appetite. Reservations are essential.

The famous *canard en conserve* (duck in a can) is half a roasted duck magret served with foie gras, cabbage, bacon, venison and spices, sealed and cooked in a can – then opened tableside and dumped over celery-root puree on toast.

MOISHES · STEAK $$$

Map p280 (☏514-845-3509; www.moishes.ca; 3961 Blvd St-Laurent; mains $26-67; ⏲5:30-10pm Mon & Tue, to 11pm Wed, to midnight Thu & Fri, 5pm-midnight Sat, 5-10pm Sun; Ⓜ St-Laurent, then bus 55) Moishes feels a bit like a social club, although guests from all backgrounds come to consume its legendary grilled meats and seafood. Closely set tables and old-fashioned hardwood paneling set the backdrop to the feasting. Skip the appetizers and launch straight into a gargantuan rib eye served with tasty fries or a Monte Carlo potato. Reservations are essential.

🍷 DRINKING & NIGHTLIFE

This area is a Montréal hot spot for nightlife, drawing people from across the city to its grungy cool pubs sitting alongside up-and-coming cocktail bars on the Plateau or St-Laurent. Weekend evenings can get rowdy as revelers wander (or stagger) between drinking establishments. The artisanal-beer craze has hit the area hard.

★ BIG IN JAPAN · COCKTAIL BAR

Map p280 (☏438-380-5658; 4175 Blvd St-Laurent; ⏲5pm-3am; Ⓜ St-Laurent, then bus 55) Completely concealed from the street, Big in Japan always amazes first-timers. There you are walking along bustling St-Laurent, you find the unmarked door (looking for its small window) by the address, walk down a rather unpromising corridor and emerge into a room lit with a thousand candles (or so it seems). Everything is Japanese-inspired – cocktails, whiskey, beer and bar food.

★ BARFLY · BAR

Map p280 (☏514-284-6665; www.facebook.com/BarflyMtl; 4062 Blvd St-Laurent; ⏲4pm-3am;

🏃 Neighborhood Walk
Strolling the Plateau

START CARRÉ ST-LOUIS
END RUE CHERRIER
LENGTH 3KM; ONE TO TWO HOURS

Start at the ❶ **Carré St-Louis** (p101), a shady oasis with a splashing fountain that's a popular spot for lazing and people-watching. It's surrounded by beautiful houses built for wealthy French residents in the 19th century.

Walk around the park, then turn left up Rue St-Denis. On your right you'll pass the majestic buildings of the former ❷ **Institut des Sourdes-Muettes** – note the little silver cupola. The institute was dedicated to the education of deaf, and later also blind, students, and is now known as the Institut Raymond-Dewar.

Continue up Rue St-Denis and turn left onto Rue Rachel Est. You'll see the baroque ❸ **Église St-Jean-Baptiste**, its enormous interior decorated with gilded wood and pink marble.

Exiting the church, look right to see the winged angel on the imposing Sir George-Éti-

enne Cartier monument, way down the end of the street at the leafy base of Mont-Royal. Directly opposite the church stands ❹ **Les Cours Rachel**, once a boarding school but now converted into condos.

Walk northeast along Rue Rachel Est and turn right onto ❺ **Ave Châteaubriand**. A run-down street in the 1970s, today this narrow lane has been spruced up with blue, green and turquoise paint and potted plants hanging outside the windows. Here you'll spot another of this town's signature objects: the external staircase.

Zigzag down to the corner of Rues Roy and St-André. You'll find ❻ **Place Roy**, a tiny leafy square with an art installation by sculptor Michel Goulet.

Walk one block to the right along Rue Roy and turn left down Rue St-Christophe. Continue to Rue Cherrier to see a lovely ❼ **1918 Italian Renaissance building**. It once housed the Palestre Nationale but now belongs to Université du Québec à Montréal (UQAM) and Agora de la Danse, a key name in Montréal's contemporary-dance scene.

CAFE CULTURE

The Plateau has some of the best cafes in the city. Whether you're after the perfect macchiato or simply a buzzing space to take in the neighborhood, you'll be spoiled for choice.

Flocon Espresso (Café Névé; Map p280; www.cafeneve.com; 781 Ave du Mont-Royal Est; ⊙7:30am-6:30pm Mon-Fri, 7am-6pm Sat & Sun; 🖥; MMont-Royal) Coffee nerds flock to this tiny cafe for outstanding espressos, *cortados* (espresso with a dash of milk) and lattes. There are just two communal tables, but a feel-good vibe prevails, with a mix of anglophones and francophones chatting or typing away in the cozy space. Go early to get a seat.

Moineau Masqué (Map p280; www.facebook.com/lemoineaumasque; 912 Rue Marie-Anne Est; ⊙7:30am-7pm Mon-Fri, from 8:30am Sat, from 9:30am Sun; 🖥; MMont-Royal) Hidden on a peaceful street, the 'Masked Sparrow' whips up tasty, if slightly bitter coffees, which you can enjoy on the outdoor terrace. On cooler days, take a seat at a big communal table or on the comfy sofa in the sun-drenched interior. It's a picture-perfect neighborhood cafe.

Replika (Map p280; ✆514-903-4384; www.cafereplika.com; 252 Rue Rachel Est; sandwiches $7-9; ⊙8am-6pm Mon-Fri, from 9am Sat & Sun; 🖥; MMont-Royal) This spacious coffeehouse has lots of tables for quiet conversation and laptop chatter, plus good coffees, sandwiches, desserts and other snacks. For a jolt, try a Turkish coffee.

Chez José (Map p280; www.chezjosecafe.com; 173 Ave Duluth Est; mains $6.50-8; ⊙8:30am-5pm Mon-Fri, to 6pm Sat, 9am-6pm Sun; MSherbrooke) Jolly owner José often mans the small kitchen of this tiny, colorful cafe set in a mural-covered building. Besides serving some of the hood's best and strongest espresso, it's lauded for its breakfasts, seafood soup and Portuguese sausage. A young, bohemian clientele tends to spill onto the sidewalk to chat while eyeing the cast of characters that meanders by.

Café Névé (Map p280; ✆514-903-9294; www.cafeneve.com; 151 Rue Rachel Est; sandwiches $8-10; ⊙8am-9pm Mon-Fri, from 9am Sat & Sun; 🖥; MMont-Royal) This much-loved neighborhood haunt serves excellent coffees, and the food selection goes far beyond the typical baked goods found in most cafes. Stop in for eggs Benedict or yogurt, granola and fresh fruit in the morning. For lunch, there are tasty sandwiches (including several vegetarian options) and French onion soup.

MSt-Laurent, then bus 55) Cheap, gritty, loud, fun and a little bit out of control – just the way we like our dive bars. Live bluegrass and rockabilly bands and bedraggled hipsters hold court alongside aging rockers at this St-Laurent hole-in-the-wall.

MAJESTIQUE BAR

Map p280 (✆514-439-1850; www.restobarmajestique.com; 4105 Blvd St-Laurent; ⊙4pm-3am daily, also 11am-3pm Sun; MSt-Laurent, then bus 55) The Majestique manages to be both kitschy and classy at the same time, with wood-paneled walls, warm lighting and a buck's head presiding over the tables. The bartenders whip up some beautiful concoctions here, and the food menu is equally creative: try the *bourgots* (snails), the *tartare de cheval* (raw horse meat) or, for something simple, the *huîtres* (oysters) or *frites* (fries).

RESERVOIR PUB

Map p280 (✆514-849-7779; http://reservoir brasseur.com; 9 Ave Duluth Est; ⊙3pm-3am; MSt-Laurent, then bus 55) There's lots to adore at this low-key, friendly brasserie. It's nice but not too pricey and the mixed crowd is artsy but unpretentious. If you appreciate good beer, the owners brew their own on the premises. A small kitchen prepares gourmet lunch, after-work snacks and weekend brunch. In summer the 2nd-floor terrace overlooks this pedestrian-friendly lane.

LE DARLING COCKTAIL BAR

Map p280 (www.facebook.com/restobardarling; 4328 Blvd St-Laurent; ⊙8am-3am; MLaurier) A mix of cafe, cocktail bar and bistro, Le Darling is a one-stop spot for top-notch drinks and bistro-quality eats. Straddling a corner on Blvd St-Laurent, just a few blocks from

Mont-Royal, this vibrant hybrid has lush tropical plants hanging from the ceiling and a seemingly endless collage of vintage decor. Come day or night.

BAR SUZANNE
COCKTAIL BAR

Map p280 (☎438-387-3007; http://barsuzanne. ca; 20 Ave Duluth Est; ☺4pm-3am; Ⓜ Mont Royal) Boasting an original interior design with hanging plants and a large skylight, this tasteful bar, named after a Leonard Cohen song, offers an inspiring selection of drinks and a buzzing ambience. Bar Suzanne is just a few blocks from Mont-Royal and other main attractions.

PUB PIT CARIBOU
MICROBREWERY

Map p280 (☎514-522-9773; www.pitcaribou.com; 951 Rue Rachel Est; ☺2pm-1am Sun-Wed, to 3am Thu-Sat; Ⓜ Mont-Royal) There are some awesome microbreweries in this province, and Pit Caribou is one of the greats. It has an outpost here in Montréal that serves its full line of hearty, sudsy goodness, often accompanied by live music.

PLAN B
BAR

Map p280 (☎514-845-6060; www.barplanb.ca; 327 Ave du Mont-Royal Est; ☺3pm-3am; Ⓜ Mont-Royal) Warm decor, elegant snacks and a fine cocktail menu make this high-end bar a perfect date and pickup spot. It's also perfect for drinking with friends, and usually not too loud to talk. A sophisticated French-speaking crowd flocks here after work and on weekends.

BILY KUN
BAR

Map p280 (☎514-845-5392; www.bilykun.com; 354 Ave du Mont-Royal Est; ☺3pm-3am; Ⓜ Mont-Royal) One of the pioneers of 'tavern chic,' Bily Kun is a favorite local hangout for a chilled evening among friends. First-time visitors usually gawp at the ostrich heads that overlook the bar but soon settle into the music groove of live jazz (from 6pm to 8pm) and DJs (10pm onward). Absinthe cocktails, herbaceous liqueurs and organic beers rule.

Upstairs, **O Patro Vys** (☎514-845-3855; http://opatrovys.com; 314 Ave du Mont-Royal Est; ☺11am-9pm) is a performing-arts hall that features a wide range of bands (folk, French pop, indie rock) as well as electronic installations, poetry slams and other esoteric fare.

SUWU
BAR

Map p280 (www.suwumontreal.com; 3581 Blvd St-Laurent; ☺5pm-3am daily, also 11am-3pm Sat & Sun; Ⓜ St-Laurent, then bus 55) Don't let the unpronounceable name deter you. SuWu carves up a winning formula of inventive cocktails and delicious eclectic comfort food that makes it a fine go-to spot no matter the time of night. Snack on fish tacos, fried chicken bao or pork shoulder ramen while sipping an East Side (gin, cucumbers, mint) – or rather a West Side (tequila, basil, lime).

LA DISTILLERIE
BAR

(www.pubdistillerie.com; 2047 Ave du Mont-Royal Est; ☺4pm-3am Mon-Fri, from noon Sat & Sun; Ⓜ Mont-Royal, then bus 97) Although it's a bit of a hike down Ave du Mont-Royal, La Distillerie is worth the trip for its excellent cocktails (served in Mason jars), friendly bartenders and easygoing crowd. The aesthetic is industrial chic, with exposed bulbs, industrial fixtures and a long wooden bar. There's no food, but you can grab pizza from across the street and eat it here.

LA PORTE ROUGE
CLUB

(☎514-891-5455; http://barlaporterouge.com; 1834 Ave du Mont-Royal Est; ☺11pm-3am Wed & Sun, 10pm-3am Thu-Sat; Ⓜ Mont-Royal) One of the few dance clubs in the Plateau, La Porte Rouge is a magnet for the fashion-minded, who don't mind paying high prices for cocktails (or opting for bottle service) to be among the beautiful people. The floral wallpaper, house-spinning DJs and nice lighting add to the appeal.

☆ ENTERTAINMENT

This area is a favorite of lovers of live music, especially the kind that is grungy in dark bars in Plateau Mont-Royal and along St-Laurent. There is also good jazz and performing arts elsewhere in this part of town attracting creative types.

★CASA DEL POPOLO
LIVE MUSIC

Map p280 (☎514-284-0122; www.casadelpopolo. com; 4873 Blvd St-Laurent; $5-20; ☺noon-3am; Ⓜ Laurier) One of Montréal's most charming live venues, the 'House of the People' has talented DJs and is a venue for art-house films and spoken-word performances. It's

PLATEAU MONT-ROYAL & THE NORTHEAST ENTERTAINMENT

TAM-TAM JAM

Huge crowds of alternative free spirits gather every Sunday afternoon in summer for the legendary 'tam-tam' concerts at the edge of Parc du Mont-Royal, when the pounding rhythms and whirling dancers seem to put everyone in a trance. The action takes place at the **Georges-Étienne Cartier monument** (Map p280; http://ville. montreal.qc.ca; Ave du Parc; MMont-Royal, then bus 97) opposite Parc Jeanne-Mance, at the corner of Ave du Parc and Ave Duluth. The percussionists are tireless in their dedication, with some riffs going on for an hour or more, and other instruments joining in on the odd occasion. Vendors along the grass sell alternative handicrafts (eg dream catchers, crystals and bead jewelry) and sarongs, plus percussion instruments in case you left your tambourine and conga drum at home.

is also known for its vegetarian sandwiches and salads and is associated with the tapas bar La Sala Rosa (p108) and its concert venue La Sala Rossa.

DIÈSE ONZE
LIVE MUSIC

Map p280 (514-223-3543; www.dieseonze. com; 4115 Rue St-Denis; $10; 6pm-late; MMont-Royal) This downstairs jazz club has just the right vibe – with an intimate small stage so you can get close to the musicians. There are shows most nights, with an eclectic lineup of artists. You can have a bite while the band plays, with good tapas options as well as a few heartier mains (goat's-cheese burger, mushroom risotto). Call for reservations.

LA TULIPE
LIVE MUSIC

(514-526-4000; www.latulipe.ca; 4530 Rue Papineau; dance parties cover $6-8; MMont-Royal, then bus 97) Best known for its riotously fun '80s dance parties (Saturday nights), La Tulipe also hosts underground indie bands, musical retrospectives and the odd burlesque show. It all takes place in a beautifully restored and intimate theater in the French-speaking eastern area of the Plateau.

LA ROCKETTE
LIVE MUSIC

Map p280 (Rockette Bar; 514-845-9010; 4479 Rue St-Denis; 10pm-3am Mon, Tue & Sat, from 4pm Wed-Fri) Part bar, part concert venue, all grotty as hell, La Rockette is a grand, intimate (read: sometimes loud and cramped) spot to catch a show, and if a show isn't on, it's a good spot for a cheap beer.

MONTRÉAL IMPACT
SPECTATOR SPORT

(514-328-3668; www.impactmontreal.com; Saputo Stadium, 4750 Rue Sherbrooke Est; tickets $25-115; Mar-Oct; MViau) Although Canadians aren't known for doling out the soccer love, the Montréal Impact has played its heart out to earn a local following. Saputo Stadium is a 14,000-seat venue built in 2008 for the club and the second-largest soccer stadium in Canada.

SHOPPING

Easily the best neighbourhood for quirky giftware with a focus on design, especially along the Plateau and St-Laurent. Here you'll also find everything vintage – clothing, books and vinyl.

LE PORT DE TÊTE
BOOKS

Map p280 (514-678-9566; www.leportdetete. com; 262 Ave du Mont-Royal Est; 10am-10pm Mon-Sat, to 8pm Sun; MMont-Royal) This is a wonderfully curated bookstore that often showcases up-and-coming work from dynamic small publishers. The French and English selection is eclectic as hell: thousands of philosophy titles share space with plays, poetry, graphic novels and kids' books. Nonfiction is across the street.

LIBRAIRIE PLANÈTE BD
COMICS

Map p280 (514-759-9800; www.planetebd.ca; 3883 Rue St-Denis; 10am-6pm Mon-Wed, Sat & Sun, to 9pm Thu & Fri; MSherbrooke) If you have a thing for comics and graphic novels – particularly French-language ones – this is a must-stop store. The owners have a passion for their beloved medium, and carry titles you'd be hard-pressed to find anywhere else.

AUX 33 TOURS
MUSIC

Map p280 (514-524-7397; 1373 Ave du Mont-Royal Est; 10am-7pm Mon-Wed, to 9pm Thu & Fri, to 6pm Sat & Sun; MMont-Royal, then bus 97) Hands down, Aux 33 Tours is the best record shop in the city. You'll find a staggering selection of new and used vinyl covering every genre, and there's also a decent selection of CDs. The staff is knowledgeable, the bins are well organized and the rare finds are easy to unearth. You'll find loads of albums not sold elsewhere.

ARTPOP
ARTS & CRAFTS

Map p280 (☑514-843-3443; 129 Ave du Mont-Royal Est; ⊘10am-7pm Mon-Wed & Sat, to 9pm Thu & Fri, 11am-7pm Sun; ⓂMont-Royal) Though tiny in size, Artpop is full of unique Montréal-themed gift ideas. You'll find graphic T-shirts, bags, pillowcases, iPhone covers, postcards and prints with iconic city signage (Farine Five Roses, the big Orange Julep). Other standouts include pendants, earrings and dolls by local designers.

LIBRAIRIE MICHEL FORTIN
BOOKS

Map p280 (☑514-849-5719; www.librairiemichel fortin.com; 3714 Rue St-Denis; ⊘9am-6pm Mon-Wed, to 9pm Thu & Fri, to 5pm Sat, 11am-5pm Sun; ⓂSherbrooke) A mecca for every foreign-language student and linguist freak in town. You can find children's books, CDs and DVDs, dual-language readers and novels, covering more than 200 languages.

COFFRE AUX TRÉSORS DU CHAINON
VINTAGE

Map p280 (☑514-843-4354; www.lechainon.org; 4375 Blvd St-Laurent; ⊘10am-6pm Mon-Wed & 8pm Thu & Fri, 10am-5pm Sat, 11am-5pm Sun; ⓂSt-Laurent, then bus 55) This small secondhand store has two floors packed with clothing, shoes, housewares, books and records. You might come across some great finds, though you'll have to dig. There is a lot of vintage brand-name clothing, with suitably higher prices. Revenue from the store goes directly to the Montréal women's shelter, Le Chaînon.

LE 63
CLOTHING

Map p280 (www.facebook.com/boutiquele63; 63 Ave du Mont-Royal Est; ⊘11am-6pm Mon-Wed & Sat, to 7pm Thu & Fri, noon-6pm Sun; ⓂMont-Royal) The vibe is motorcycle chic, with stylish helmets, goggles, sew-on patches, leather gloves and other eye-catching gear for sale. The real reason to come though is for the vintage selection, with graphic T-shirts, bomber jackets, fur-lined boots and Hawaiian shirts. Check the back room for vintage Playboys and bad priapic pottery.

🏃 SPORTS & ACTIVITIES

FITZ & FOLLWELL
CYCLING

Map p280 (☑514-418-0651; http://montreal.fitz. tours; 1251 Rue Rachel Est; bike/walking tours $79/55, bike rental per day $35; ⊘10am-4pm Thu-Mon; ⓂMont-Royal) This recommended outfit offers a range of cycling tours around Montréal. Tours have very much a local flavor, as young, knowledgeable guides take you on day and evening rides, stopping for a park picnic, visiting a farmers market or spa, or exploring the leafy paths of Mont-Royal. It's inside La Maison des Cyclistes, Montréal's cycling hub.

There are also walking tours that explore the street art of the Plateau; fascinating rambles through Old Montréal; and curious walks through the underground city.

If you prefer to explore on your own, Fitz & Follwell rents bikes – stylish three-or eight-speed Linus models. If you have small children, you can rent Yuba Mundo bikes that carry up to three kids in back, or Babboe City cargo bikes.

LAC AUX CASTORS
ICE SKATING

(☑514-843-8240; www.lemontroyal.qc.ca; Parc du Mont-Royal; free, ice-skate rentals per 2hr $9; ⊘9am-9pm Sun-Thu, to 10pm Fri & Sat, weather permitting; 🚍11) An excellent place for outdoor ice-skating – it's nestled in the woods near a large parking lot and pavilion. Photo ID is required for skate rental. Check ahead to make sure things are up and running.

LA MAISON DES CYCLISTES
CYCLING

Map p280 (☑514-521-8356; www.velo.qc.ca; 1251 Rue Rachel Est; ⊘11am-5pm Mon-Fri; ⓂMont-Royal) The nerve center of Québec's biking culture, this three-story house in the Plateau is an essential stop for avid cyclists. There's a shop with cycling books, maps and guides; the Vélo Québec association (involved in developing one of the largest bicycling networks in North America); a travel agency for planning biking trips; info on events; and a cozy cafe.

It's right along the bike path above Parc La Fontaine (p101).

Little Italy, Mile End & Outremont

Neighborhood Top Five

❶ **Marché Jean-Talon** (p116) Exploring the fresh produce, hawker stalls, and delightful seafood, sandwiches and desserts at Montréal's premiere market.

❷ **Lawrence** (p118) Spoiling yourself in Mile End with some of Montréal's best dining options.

❸ **Monastiraki** (p125) Trolling quirky neighborhood shops for retro junk – or treasures, depending on your taste.

❹ **Caffè Italia** (p118) Enjoying old-world pleasures by nursing an espresso in Little Italy.

❺ **La Buvette Chez Simone** (p120) Schmoozing with Mile End's well-dressed crowd over wine and tapas.

For more detail of this area see Map p282 ➡

Explore Little Italy, Mile End & Outremont

These three neighborhoods are a foodie's dreamland, distilled from a potent mish-mash of Italian, Portuguese, Jewish and Québécois roots. The good thing is there's plenty of walking to be done to burn off those extra calories. Most of the area can be explored in a day, though you might want to return for dinner.

Start your day at the flavor cornucopia that is Marché Jean-Talon, grabbing fresh fruit or a crepe for breakfast before diving deeper into Little Italy, taking in the 1930s ceiling fresco of Mussolini at the Église Madonna Della Difesa. Stroll down Blvd St-Laurent, where the green-white-red flag is proudly displayed, pausing for an espresso at Caffè Italia and some fine contemporary art at galleries near Rue Beaubien.

A bus along the boulevard can bring you back downtown if you're tired out, or drop you near Ave Fairmount. This area is a good spot to explore Mile End, a multiethnic neighborhood with great dining along Ave Laurier, fantastic bagels and increasingly trendy hangouts at its epicenter: Rue St-Viateur and Blvd St-Laurent.

Further west, Outremont is largely a residence for wealthy francophones. Fabulous old mansions lie on leafy streets northwest of Rue Bernard.

Local Life

➡ **Cafe culture** This area has some of Montréal's most charming cafes and teahouses, including Cardinal Tea Room (p120).

➡ **Catch the game** Purchase provisions at Marché Jean-Talon (p116), then head to a park – such as Parc Outremont (p116) – for a picnic.

➡ **For the kitchen** Cruise the high-end cooking boutiques such as Les Touilleurs (p126) or try a cooking course at Mezza Luna Cooking School (p126).

➡ **International diners** Eat at cheap and cheerful Middle Eastern or Asian restaurants between metro Jean-Talon and the namesake market.

Getting There & Away

➡ **Metro** Though not ideally located, Laurier on the orange line gives you access to Ave Laurier, while Jean-Talon (on the orange and blue lines) puts you within easy reach of Marché Jean-Talon. Outremont has its own station on the blue line.

➡ **Bus** Bus 55 runs along Blvd St-Laurent; bus 46 runs on part of Rue Bernard and Ave Laurier; bus 80 runs along Ave du Parc.

Lonely Planet's Top Tip

While your average visitor whizzes through Marché Jean-Talon and the obvious Little Italy or Mile End strips, locals have started to head to Rue Beaubien, a street sandwiched between both areas. A growing number of bars, restaurants and cafes are popping up along the street, making it a fine place to explore.

LITTLE ITALY, MILE END & OUTREMONT

Best Places to Eat

➡ Impasto (p119)

➡ Provisions (p119)

➡ Arts Cafe (p117)

➡ Sparrow (p119)

➡ Kitchen Galerie (p119)

For reviews, see p116.

Best Places to Drink

➡ La Buvette Chez Simone (p120)

➡ Notre Dame des Quilles (p120)

➡ Isle de Garde (p120)

➡ Dieu du Ciel (p120)

For reviews, see p120.

Best Places to Shop

➡ Drawn & Quarterly (p125)

➡ Monastiraki (p125)

➡ Frank & Oak (p125)

For reviews, see p125.

⊙ SIGHTS

The zest and flavor of the old country find their way into the lively Little Italy district, north of the Plateau, where the espresso seems stiffer, the pasta sauce thicker and the chefs plumper. Italian football games are practically broadcast straight onto Blvd St-Laurent, where the green-white-red flag is proudly displayed. Soak up the atmosphere on a stroll, and don't miss Marché Jean-Talon, which always hums with activity.

Dubbed the 'new Plateau' by the exodus of students and artists seeking a more affordable, less polished hangout, the Mile End district has all the coolness of its predecessor as well as two phenomenal bagel shops, upscale dining along Ave Laurier and tonnes of increasingly trendy hangouts at its epicenter: Rue St-Viateur and Blvd St-Laurent. The flavor here is multicultural: Hasidic Jews live side by side with immigrants from all over Europe – visible in the Greek restaurants along Ave du Parc, and Rue St-Urbain's neo-Byzantine Polish church, Église St-Michel.

Many of celebrated Canadian novelist Mordecai Richler's novels are set in the Mile End, including *The Apprenticeship of Duddy Kravitz.*

★MARCHÉ JEAN-TALON　　　　MARKET

Map p282 (⌨514-937-7754; www.marchespublics-mtl.com; 7075 Ave Casgrain; ☉7am-6pm Mon-Wed & Sat, to 8pm Thu & Fri, to 5pm Sun; P♿; MJean-Talon) 🥐 The pride of Little Italy, this huge covered market is Montréal's most diverse. Many chefs buy ingredients for their menus here or in the specialty food shops nearby. Three long covered aisles are packed with merchants selling fruit, vegetables, flowers and baked goods, all flanked by delis and cafe-restaurants with tiny patios. Even in winter, the market is open under big tents.

Snackers can nibble on sandwiches, crepes, tacos, pastries, ice cream, fresh juices and excellent coffee. Be sure to stop by Le Marché des Saveurs du Québec (p126), one of the few large stores here and devoted entirely to Québec specialties such as wine and cider, fresh cheeses, smoked meats, preserves and a huge number of tasteful gifts.

PARC OUTREMONT　　　　PARK

Map p282 (cnr Ave Outremont & Rue St-Viateur; ♿; MRosemont) One of Montréal's best-kept secrets, this small leafy space is a great place for a bit of quiet time after exploring the neighborhood. Lovely Victorian homes ring the park, and benches provide a nice vantage point for viewing the small pond with fountain. This is a good spot to go with an ice cream from **Le Bilboquet** (Map p282; ☎514-276-0414; www.bilboquet.ca; 1311 Rue Bernard Ouest; cones $2.50-6; ☉9am-midnight Jun-Aug, to 8pm mid-Mar–May & Sep-Dec, closed Jan–mid-Mar; MLaurier), two blocks northwest.

PARC ST-VIATEUR　　　　PARK

Map p282 (cnr Ave l'Épée & Rue Bernard; MOutremont) Just off Rue Bernard a small pedestrian lane leads to this small but handsomely landscaped neighborhood park. It has a bridge over a narrow circular waterway, which draws ice-skaters in winter (bring your own skates).

ÉGLISE MADONNA
DELLA DIFESA　　　　CHURCH

Map p282 (☎514-277-6522; www.facebook.com/MadonnadellaDifesaMTL; 6800 Ave Henri-Julien; ☉Mass 8-11am Sun, 8am Mon, 7:30pm Tue-Fri; MJean-Talon) Our Lady of Protection Church was built in 1919 according to the drawings of Florence-born Guido Nincheri (1885–1973), who spent the next two decades working on the Roman Byzantine structure. The artist painted the church's remarkable **frescoes**, including one of Mussolini on horseback with a bevy of generals in the background. The work honored the formal recognition by Rome of the pope's sovereignty over Vatican City in 1929 and was unveiled a few years later as Hitler came to power.

During WWII, Nincheri and others who had worked on the building were interned by the Canadian authorities. The fresco can be viewed above the high marble altar.

✖ EATING

Little Italy is a neighborhood full of old-fashioned trattorias and lively little cafes, where the heavenly aroma of freshly brewed espresso hangs in the air. Stylish eateries, including some of the best in Montréal, have also established a strong presence here.

Mile End and Outremont are duly blessed in the dining department. Strewn with an impressive variety of Parisian-style bistros, high-end international eateries and low-key cafes, these neighborhoods also boast two oven-baked stars of the city's culinary history: the famous Montréal bagel shops.

★ ST-VIATEUR BAGEL   BAKERY $

Map p282 (🖉514-276-8044; www.stviateur bagel.com; 263 Rue St-Viateur Ouest; bagels 90¢; ⊘24hr; M Place-des-Arts, then bus 80) Currently the bagel favorite of Montréal, St-Viateur Bagel was set up in 1957 and has a reputation stretching across Canada and beyond for its perfectly crusty, chewy and slightly sweet creations. The secret to their perfection seems to be boiling in honey water followed by baking in the wood-fired oven.

Biting into a warm one straight out of the oven is an absolute delight.

ARTS CAFE   INTERNATIONAL $

Map p282 (🖉514-274-0919; http://artscafe montreal.com; 201 Ave Fairmount Ouest; mains $13-16; ⊘9am-6pm Mon-Fri, 10am-4pm Sat & Sun; 🖉; M Laurier) The Arts Cafe has instant appeal with its plank floors, white clapboard walls and sculptural knickknacks (a frenzy of light bulbs above the windows, vintage farmhouse relics). But it's the all-day brunches/breakfasts that warrant the most attention – excellent *fattoush*, falafel, *shakshuka* and cod cakes. Most dishes have a vegetarian option.

FAIRMOUNT BAGEL   BAKERY $

Map p282 (🖉514-272-0667; http://fairmount bagel.com; 74 Ave Fairmount Ouest; bagels $1; ⊘24hr; M Laurier) One of Montréal's famed bagel bakeries – people flood in here around the clock to scoop them up the minute they come out of the oven. Classic sesame- or poppy-seed varieties are hits, though everything from cinnamon to all-dressed is here, too. If you want an immediate fix of these honey-water boiled bagels, there is public seating outside.

GUILLAUME   BAKERY $

Map p282 (🖉514-507-3199; www.guillau.me; 5134 Blvd St-Laurent; snacks $1.50-6; ⊘7am-7pm; M Laurier) It's easy to go overboard with 'just one more pastry' at British-inspired Guillaume when their delicious chocolate scones and orange-blossom balls are casually laid out along the wall racks. The fair prices and minitables or public outdoor

benches are more bakery bait. One extra cruffin won't hurt. There are pics of all its products online, for food voyeurism.

LE BUTTERBLUME   GERMAN $

Map p282 (🖉514-903-9115; www.lebutterblume. com; 5836 Blvd St-Laurent; mains $10-14; ⊘8am-4pm Tue-Fri, 10am-4pm Sat & Sun; 🛜🖉; M) A light-filled bistro with enough space for a small group, or to sit up at the bar, while working through a short but quaint list of brunch items with a German twist, such as four pork-stuffed German ravioli or Nordic-shrimp steamed buns.

CHESKIE'S   BAKERY $

Map p282 (🖉514-271-2253; 359 Rue Bernard Ouest; breads $2-5; ⊘7am-11pm; 🚌160) Cheskie's is a landmark kosher bakery serving Montréal's Jewish community and beyond. Stop by and grab freshly baked challah bread or some traditional pastries. Located in the popular Mile End district, it's a great stop to glimpse one of the city's most eclectic neighborhoods in full swing.

PORCHETTA   SANDWICHES $

Map p282 (🖉514-278-7672; www.facebook.com/ PorchettaMontreal; 6887 Blvd St-Laurent; mains $7-9; ⊘11am-5pm Sun-Wed, to 8pm Thu & Fri, to 6pm Sat) We love Porchetta for its single-minded focus on, basically, one thing: beautiful Italian street food. The signature dishes are porchetta-and-mortadella sandwiches that are slow roasted to melting perfection; you'll want some napkins for all that delicious grease that soaks into the fresh bread.

DÉPANNEUR LE PICK UP   DINER $

Map p282 (🖉514-271-8011; http://depanneur lepickup.com; 7032 Rue Waverly; mains $5-9; ⊘7am-7pm Mon-Fri, 9am-7pm Sat, 10am-6pm Sun; 🖉; M De Castelnau) A hip favorite, unpretentious Le Pick Up began as an authentic 1950s *dépanneur* (convenience store) and snack bar before the current owners took it over and added zines (homemade magazines) to the daily necessities on the shelves and '80s synth-pop to the stereo. Nosh on yummy veggie burgers, or grilled haloumi and pulled-pork sandwiches at the grill counter.

You can also soak up some rays at the picnic tables outside. Outside of spring and summer, hours are restricted to breakfast and lunch.

THE GREAT BAGEL DEBATE

The Montréal bagel has a long and venerable history. It all started in 1915 when Isadore and Fanny Shlafman, Jews from Ukraine, opened a tiny bakery on Rue Roy in the Plateau. They made the yeast bread rings according to a recipe they'd brought from the bakery where Shlafman's father worked. In 1919 they started the Montréal Bagel Bakery in a wooden shack just off Blvd St-Laurent, a few doors down from the Plateau's iconic Schwartz's (p106) deli.

After WWII many Holocaust survivors emigrated to Montréal and the bagel market boomed. Isadore Shlafman decided to build a bakery in the living room of his house at 74 Ave Fairmount, where he opened Fairmount Bagel (p117) in 1950. Meanwhile Myer Lewkowicz, a Polish Jew who had survived Auschwitz, went on to establish St-Viateur Bagel (p117) in 1957. A legendary rivalry was born and scores of other bagel bakeries sprang up in their wake.

Ask any Montréaler whose bagel is best and passions will flare. Year in and year out tireless critics tour the main bagel bakeries to chat, chew and cogitate. In recent years St-Viateur has edged out Fairmount for the number-one slot. But locals do agree on one thing: they believe that Montréal's bagels are superior to their New York cousins. The Montréal bagel is lighter, sweeter and crustier, and chewy but not dense thanks to an enriched eggy dough that looks almost like batter. The dough hardly rises and the tender rings are formed by hand and boiled in a honey-and-water solution before being baked in a wood-burning oven.

CAFFÈ ITALIA
CAFE $

Map p282 (☑514-495-0059; 6840 Blvd St-Laurent; sandwiches $8, coffees $2-3; ⊗6am-11pm; MDe Castelnau) Calling this place old school is like calling the Sahara dry. 'Old school' isn't just a descriptor, but the essence of this little Italian espresso bar – graybeards and guys unironically wearing flat caps seemingly step out of a time warp for a quick coffee on the Formica counter. Grab a panettone and an espresso, and live that *dolce vita*.

LE FALCO
JAPANESE $

Map p282 (☑514-272-7766; www.cafefalco.ca; 5605 Ave de Gaspé; mains $7-13; ⊗8am-5pm Mon-Thu, to 4pm Fri; MBeaubien) Strong coffee, nice sandwiches and Japanese rice bowls – an incongruous mix, but a delicious one.

LA CROISSANTERIE FIGARO
CAFE $

Map p282 (☑514-278-6567; www.lacroissanteriefigaro.com; 5200 Rue Hutchison; sandwiches $10-14; ⊗7am-1am; MLaurier) With its deco fixtures, wrought-iron marble-topped tables and lovely terrace, this charming neighborhood cafe has a Parisian vibe, and has long been a popular meeting spot for well-heeled locals. Stop in for warm, buttery croissants (among Montréal's best), baguette sandwiches or rich

desserts. It's also a fine place to nurse a coffee or a cocktail.

LA PANTHÈRE VERTE
VEGETARIAN $

Map p282 (☑514-508-5564; www.lapantherverte.com; 160 Rue St-Viateur Est; mains $9-15; ⊗10am-10pm Mon-Sat, 11am-9pm Sun; ☞⏏; MLaurier) Green in every sense of the word, La Panthère Verte is a casual vegetarian spot, where you can stop for delicious falafel sandwiches, energy-charging juices and smoothies, and fresh salad specials that change daily. Plants, a zippy green paint job and an elegant chandelier help set the scene in the industrial-chic space.

★LAWRENCE
EUROPEAN $$

Map p282 (☑514-503-1070; www.lawrencerestaurant.com; 5201 Blvd St-Laurent; mains brunch $13-17, dinner $23-36; ⊗11:30am-2:30pm Tue-Fri, 5:30-10pm Tue-Sat, 10am-2:30pm Sat & Sun; MLaurier) This gorgeously designed, high-style hip eatery helmed by British chef Marc Cohen of Sparrow serves up some of the best brunch in Montréal. With high windows looking out over the Main and an airy vibe, it's a perfect spot to sink your teeth into smoked trout with scrambled eggs or scones with jam and clotted cream.

In the evening, you can feast on clam and pig-skin stew or stewed octopus with chickpeas. Just don't expect anything too conventional.

SPARROW
INTERNATIONAL **$$**

Map p282 (☑514-507-1642; http://lesparrow-bar.com; 5322 Blvd St-Laurent; mains $10-16; ◷6pm-3am daily & 10am-3pm Sat & Sun; ☑; ⓂLaurier) In a vintage chic dining room, Mile Enders feast on mussels with white wine and fries, pan-roasted trout, butter chicken and other unfussy but tasty bistro classics. For the price, it's hard to find a better meal in this city. Food aside, Sparrow serves up excellent cocktails, and the festive vibe continues until late into the night.

★DAMAS RESTAURANT
SYRIAN **$$$**

Map p282 (☑514-439-5435; www.restaurant-damas.com; 1201 Ave Van Horne; mains $34-62; ◷5-10pm Mon-Thu, to 11pm Fri, 4-11pm Sat, 4-10pm Sun; ☑; ⓂOutremont) Unique Syrian-inspired cuisine just a few minutes from Mile End and Little Italy, Damas is consistently rated as one of the top restaurants in the city. A warm and welcoming ambience, along with an eclectic menu of Syrian classics (Damascus marinated chicken, tahini seabass), and inspiring new flavors (herbed dumplings, sumac fries), all come together for a complete fine-dining experience.

IMPASTO
ITALIAN **$$$**

Map p282 (☑514-508-6508; www.impastomtl.ca; 48 Rue Dante; mains $19-36; ◷11:30am-2pm Thu & Fri, 5-11pm Tue-Sat; ⓂDe Castelnau) There's much buzz surrounding this polished Italian eatery – largely owing to the heavy-hitting foodies behind it: best-selling cookbook author Stefano Faita and celebrated chef Michele Forgione. Both have deep connections to Italian cooking, obvious in brilliant dishes such as braised beef cheeks with Savoy-style potatoes, arctic char with cauliflower puree and lentils, and housemade pastas like busiate with lobster.

PROVISIONS
EUROPEAN **$$$**

Map p282 (☑514-508-0828; www.restaurant provisions.ca; 1268 Ave Van Horne; 5-/7-course menu $65/75; ◷6-11pm Tue-Sun; ⓂOutremont) Tasting-menu-roulette-style dining where not only are you not told what you will be eating until it's in front of you, but other tables might be served something completely different. Luckily the food is superb, with nuanced flavours in the light crab toast, multicoloured beet salad combining grapefruit and toasted almonds, and the sous-vide cod with leeks.

KITCHEN GALERIE
FRENCH **$$$**

Map p282 (☑514-315-8994; www.kitchen-galerie.com; 60 Rue Jean-Talon Est; mains $26-40; ◷5-11pm Tue-Sat; ⓂJean-Talon) Jovial chefs Mathieu Cloutier and Mathieu Bourdages are well situated by the Marché Jean-Talon for their succulently fresh market offerings, which change daily. Expect carnivore-oriented choices such as *bavette saignant* (flank steak) with mashed potatoes, or foie gras in various incarnations (the most famous of which is prepared in a dishwasher!). Be sure to call and reserve.

LEMÉAC
FRENCH **$$$**

Map p282 (☑514-270-0999; www.restaurant lemeac.com; 1045 Ave Laurier Ouest; mains brunch $15-22, dinner $29-40; ◷11:45am-midnight Mon-Fri, from 10am Sat & Sun; ⓂLaurier) A well-respected name among the well-heeled Laurier crowd, Lémeac has a light and airy setting with huge windows overlooking the street, a lively ambience and beautifully turned-out plates. It's a popular brunch spot on weekends, and at night – the after-10pm multicourse prix-fixe menu (roast duck, chicken, salmon tartare) is excellent value at $28.

LOCAL MONTRÉAL FOOD TOURS

The most important aspect about any walking tour is its guides, and the friendly leaders at **Local Montréal Food Tours** (Map p282; ☑438-600-0501; https://localfoodtours.com; 5555 Ave de Gaspé, Mile End; 2hr tour $52) are full of insights, give attention to everybody on the tour and receive good feedback. The Mile End food tour picks out the local flavor of the area with food samples at all five stops, including craft beer and a bagel.

Other tours explore Mile End by night, as well Old Montréal or a tour just about microbreweries

LITTLE ITALY, MILE END & OUTREMONT EATING

🍷 DRINKING & ⚑ NIGHTLIFE

Mile End is hip and eclectic, attracting former residents, such as electro artist Grimes, to its establishments (generally pubs and bars). Little Italy is famous for its Italian espresso bars and bars that fill up during large soccer matches. Outremont is a good spot for cocktails and tapas bars.

★CARDINAL TEA ROOM
BRITISH $

Map p282 (www.thecardinaltea.com; 5326 Blvd St-Laurent; small teapot $5, snacks $5-10; ⊙11am-7pm Thu & Fri, to 8pm Sat & Sun; Ⓜ Laurier) Above Sparrow (p119) – Cardinal's food-focused sibling – you'll find a two-story tearoom set with a glittering chandelier, velvet couches, framed artwork and fresh flowers on the tables. It's all very prim and proper, right down to the delicate china and tiny teaspoons, worthy of collecting. Of course, this is Mile End, so that means groovy bossa nova tunes and hip waitstaff.

★LA BUVETTE CHEZ SIMONE
WINE BAR

Map p282 (🖉514-750-6577; www.buvettechez simone.com; 4869 Ave du Parc; ⊙4pm-3am; Ⓜ Laurier) An artsy-chic crowd of (mostly) Francophone bons vivants and professionals loves this cozy wine bar. The staff know their vino and the extensive list is complemented by a gourmet tapas menu. Weekends, the place is jammed from *cinq à sept* (5pm to 7pm 'happy hour') into the wee hours.

WHISKY CAFÉ
LOUNGE

Map p282 (🖉514-278-2646; www.facebook. com/whiskycafe; 5800 Blvd St-Laurent; ⊙5pm-1am Mon-Thu, to 3am Fri, 6pm-3am Sat, 7pm-1am Sun; Ⓜ Place-des-Arts, then bus 80) Cuban cigars and fine whiskies are partners in crime at this classy 1930s-styled joint, hidden near the industrial sector of the Mile End. The well-ventilated cigar lounge is separated from the main bar, which stocks 150 Scotch whiskeys, plus wines, ports and tasting trios. Snacks range from duck *rillettes* to Belgian chocolates. Music is as sexy-smooth as the leather chairs.

NOTRE DAME DES QUILLES
BAR

Map p282 (🖉514-507-1313; www.facebook. com/notredamedesquilles; 32 Rue Beaubien Est; ⊙5pm-3am Mon-Fri, from 4pm Sat & Sun; Ⓜ Beaubien) Does drinking improve your bowling game? That seems to be the eternal question at this hip outpost near Little Italy, where two free lanes have been set up with pint-sized pins. There's a good mix of anglophones and francophones here, and there are fun kitsch-filled nights of karaoke, bingo and spinning DJs.

ISLE DE GARDE
BAR

(www.isledegarde.com; 1039 Rue Beaubien Est; ⊙1pm-1:30am Sun-Wed, 11:30am-3am Thu & Fri, 1pm-3am Sat; 🤶; Ⓜ Beaubien) Beer lovers shouldn't miss this buzzing amber-lit brasserie, which has a dazzling (and ever-changing) selection of unique microbrews on tap. Friendly bar staff dole out Belgian-style farmhouse ales, American-style IPAs and creamy stouts, with one-of-a-kind brews (such as Brasseurs Illimités smoked porter that tastes like drinking a campfire) among the options.

DIEU DU CIEL
BREWERY

Map p282 (🖉514-490-9555; www.dieuduciel. com; 29 Ave Laurier Ouest; ⊙11:30am-3am; Ⓜ Laurier) Packed every night with a young, francophone crowd, this unpretentious bar serves a phenomenal rotating menu of its famous microbrews, running from classic ales to rich stouts such as the imperial coffee stout Péché Mortel.

NESTOR
COCKTAIL BAR

Map p282 (🖉514-272-3753; http://nestor-bar.com; 6289 Rue St-Hubert; ⊙3pm-3am; Ⓜ Beaubien) There is plenty of craftsmanship on show at this low-lit bar with exposed brass pipes, polished wood-veneer bar tops and Edison light globes to transport you to another era. Indeed the classic 1920s cocktails have the right balance of whiskey, bourbon and scotch and the craft beers on tap are also good.

LA REMISE
PUB

Map p282 (🖉514-272-0206; 540 Rue Boucher; ⊙11am-3am; Ⓜ Laurier) If you want to catch a cool crowd belt out a francophone classic, head straight to this dive bar (it is heartland Mile End after all). There are English hits on the playlist, too. Cheap drinks and a pool table help make it friendly to visitors; so does the very very dark lighting.

🏃 Neighborhood Walk
Exploring Mile End & Outremont

START BOULEVARD ST-LAURENT
END PARC ST-VIATEUR
LENGTH 2.5KM; ONE TO TWO HOURS

Multicultural Mile End and Outremont are home to Hasidic Jews, Portuguese, Greeks and Italians, among others. You'll find eclectic cafes, eye-catching boutiques, lively bars, leafy parks and great bagels.

Start along **1 Boulevard St-Laurent** (p101) and take in some of the galleries and curio shops, such as Galerie Simon Blais.

Continue along Blvd St-Laurent to one of Mile End's great little bakeries, **2 Guillaume** (p117). Grab a coffee and a chocolate scone for fuel.

Double back along Blvd St-Laurent and turn left onto Ave Fairmount Ouest. Near the corner is **3 Au Papier Japonais** (p126), a sweet little store specializing in handmade paper, art books and more.

On your left, **4 Wilensky's Light Lunch** (sandwiches $4-5; ⏱9am-4pm Mon-Fri, 10am-4pm Sat) hasn't changed much since opening in 1937.

Continue along Ave Fairmount. Stop for a bagel at famous **5 Fairmount Bagel** (p117). The honey-water dipped delights are ever-so slightly sweeter than those of its archrival St-Viateur Bagel.

Continue on Fairmount, turn left on Ave de l'Épee and right on Ave Laurier. The magnificent church on the corner is **6 Église St-Viateur d'Outremont**.

Exiting the church, turn right up Ave Bloomfield and in two blocks you'll reach **7 Parc Outremont** (p116), a beautiful park with a tiny lake and a playground.

Cross the park diagonally, and exit onto Ave Outremont, continuing until Rue Bernard Ouest. Go left to **8 Le Bilboquet** (p116), one of the best ice-cream shops in Montréal. The maple-syrup flavor is a must; dairy haters can try from over a dozen sorbets.

Heading back along Rue Bernard, zigzag over to **9 Parc St-Viateur** (p116), another peaceful green space in the neighborhood, and enjoy your ice cream.

CAGKAN SAYTIN/SHUTTERSTOCK ©

1. Cheese on display at Marché Atwater 2. Marché Atwater (p130)
3. Berry stall, Marché Jean-Talon (p116)

Montréal's Markets

Montréal is famed for its impressive year-round food markets, where you can sample the great bounty of the north. The biggest and best are Marché Jean-Talon in Little Italy and Marché Atwater just west of downtown near the Canal de Lachine. For more visit Marchés Publics de Montréal (www.marchespublics-mtl.com).

Marché Jean-Talon

The city's largest market (p116) has several hundred market stalls selling all manner of produce, plus food counters where you can get juices, crepes, baguette sandwiches and more. Don't miss the Québécois specialty store Le Marché des Saveurs.

Marché Atwater

This market (p130) is located right on the banks of the Canal de Lachine, with scores of vendors outside and high-class delicatessens and specialty food shops inside, in the tiled, vaulted hall under the art-deco clock tower.

Marché de Maisonneuve

About 20 farm stalls (www.fb.me/marchemaisonneuve; 4445 Rue Ontario Est, Maisonneuve; 7am-6pm, to 8pm Thu & Fri, to 5pm Sun; M Pie-IX, then bus 139), and inside, a dozen vendors of meat, cheese, fresh vegetables, tasty pastries and pastas in a beautiful beaux-arts building (1912–14) in Maisonneuve, girded by pretty gardens.

BAR WAVERLY
BAR

Map p282 (http://barwaverly.com; 5550 Blvd St-Laurent; ⊙4pm-3am; MLaurier) With its engaging decor and a great location, Bar Waverly has established itself in the Mile End bar scene. A full selection of cocktails is complemented by a tasty and well-priced food menu. Sit outside on the large patio or enjoy a drink in the warm-yet-happening indoor ambience. Good for a relaxed happy hour or some late-night fun.

CAFÉ CLUB SOCIAL
CAFE

Map p282 (☑514-495-0114; www.facebook.com/cafeclubsocial; 180 Rue St-Viateur Ouest; ⊙6am-11pm; MLaurier) In the heart of Mile End you'll find this throwback cafe and 'social club,' a quaint favorite of Montréal's Italian community. Tucked in between hipster hot spots, it retains most of its old charm, with retro pictures on the wall and a big tree-covered terrace out back. Stop in for a great espresso.

CAFÉ RÉSONANCE
CAFE

Map p282 (www.resonancecafe.com; 5175A Ave du Parc; ⊙8:30am-midnight Mon-Fri, from 10am Sat & Sun; ⬜80) A favorite with local writers, artists and students, this cafe-restaurant does fair-trade coffee, a homemade vegan menu, and daily live shows ranging from jazz to poetry. It's an ideal spot to get some work done or to just hang out. You will be charmed.

BAR DATCHA
CLUB

Map p282 (www.bardatcha.ca; 98 Ave Laurier Ouest; ⊙10pm-3am Thu-Sun; MLaurier) Datcha is a small night spot with a tiny dance floor that draws a laid-back, groove-loving crowd enveloped in the fog machine. Eclectic DJs from around the globe spin; and on Thursdays you can groove to jazz while having your tarot read. Party like it's 1987, while sipping Moscow Mules (vodka, ginger syrup, lime juice) from the adjoining bar **Kabinet** (☑514-274-3555; www.barkabinet.com; ⊙5pm-1am Mon, 4pm-2am Tue & Wed, 4pm-3am Thu & Fri, 3pm-3am Sat, 3pm-1am Sun).

CAFÉ OLIMPICO
CAFE

Map p282 (☑514-495-0746; 124 Rue St-Viateur; coffees $2-4; ⊙7am-midnight; 🗢; MLaurier) Its espresso is excellent, yet this rocking, no-frills Italian cafe is all about atmosphere, as young good-looking baristas whip up smooth caffeinated drinks for the jumble of hipsters, tourists and elderly gentlemen who pass through. It's big on sports (especially the Italian football league), so there are TVs inside.

FABULEUX CHEZ SERGE
SPORTS BAR

Map p282 (☑514-663-4227; www.facebook.com/ChezSergeMontreal; 5301 Blvd St-Laurent; ⊙5pm-3am; MSt-Laurent, then bus 55) How can you go wrong with a bra-adorned moose head on the wall? Hockey games, unbridled kitsch and a mechanical bull reel in neighborhood kids. With cold beer, flashing lights and staff who love dancing (sometimes on the bar), this homey spot gets out of control during hockey and soccer seasons. Reserve ahead (for a table) on game nights.

VICE ET VERSA
BAR

Map p282 (http://vicesetversa.com; 6631 Blvd St-Laurent; ⊙11:30am-3am; MDe Castelnau) Vices et Versa is a laid-back spot that draws a loyal neighborhood following who come for the first-rate craft-beer selection. There are 40 varieties on tap, with a strong emphasis on local and regional brews. You can match those quaffs with bison burgers, cheese platters, smoked-meat sandwiches and pulled-pork poutine.

☆ ENTERTAINMENT

THÉÂTRE RIALTO
CONCERT VENUE

Map p282 (☑514-770-7773; www.theatrerialto.ca; 5723 Ave du Parc; ⊙box office noon-6pm Tue-Sat; MRosemont) This grand 1920s theater was inspired by the Paris Opera house and, since 2010, has undergone restoration to its former glory following years of neglect. The repertoire is a bit hit-or-miss, with nights devoted to Prince and Beatles impersonators, along with swing dancing, burlesque balls and tango shows.

THÉÂTRE OUTREMONT
THEATER

Map p282 (☑514-495-9944; www.theatreoutremont.ca; 1248 Rue Bernard Ouest; ⊙box office 2-7pm Mon-Sat, 10am-4pm Sun; MOutremont) Built in 1929, this theater was both a repertory cinema and a major concert hall until it was shuttered in the late 1980s. The municipality of Outremont later brought it back to life and the theater was reopened in

---

WORTH A DETOUR

CIRCUS CENTER

Montréal's circus mecca of **TOHU** (☎514-376-8648, 888-376-8648; www.tohu.ca; 2345 Rue Jarry Est, St-Michel; parking $8; ⊙9am-5pm; Md'Iberville, then bus 94) resides in the working-class St-Michel district, and is a great place to see a show. This innovative complex (from the French expression *tohu-bohu*, for 'hustle and bustle'), includes an arena designed only with circus arts in mind, Cirque du Soleil's international head-quarters and artists' residence and the National Circus School. It was built on the site of North America's second-largest waste dump and the complex is now powered completely by methane gas from the landfill garbage beneath it.

You can visit the complex on your own via a map and English audioguide available from reception, or downloadable (http://tohu.ca/en/activities). TOHU also hosts special exhibitions and outdoor activities (such as *pétanque* tournaments and bike rallies), and you can catch live performances here throughout the year. Visit the web-site or contact TOHU. Take the blue metro line to d'Iberville station and then hop onto bus 94 north (or walk 1km northwest up Rue d'Iberville).

Attached to the TOHU theater, a small **cafe** (snacks $5-10; ⊙8am-2pm Mon-Fri, from 10am Sat) sells sandwiches, salads, bagels and other light fare.

2001. Today, the repertoire is wide-ranging, with concerts (jazz, folk, flamenco, blues), dance performances (ballet, modern) and family events (marionettes, animated films).

There are also regular Monday film screenings (usually at 4pm and 7:30pm), which features indie cinema from around the globe.

 SHOPPING

Gallery-filled Mile End has interesting speciality art and origami stores as well as places to buy locally made clothing. There are also vintage-clothing stores galore here but few bargains. Head to the Jean-Talon area in Little Italy for gifts for foodies at the namesake market and surrounding gourmet stores. Outremont has upmarket clothing and gifts for its well-to-do clientele.

★**DRAWN & QUARTERLY**   BOOKS

Map p282 (☎514-279-2224; http://mtl.drawn andquarterly.com; 211 Rue Bernard Ouest; ⊙10am-8pm; MOutremont) The flagship store of this cult independent comic-book and graphic-novel publisher has become some-thing of a local literary haven. Cool book launches take place here, and the quaint little shop sells all sorts of reading matter, including children's books, vintage Tintin comics, recent fiction and art books.

★**MONASTIRAKI**   VINTAGE

Map p282 (☎514-278-4879; www.monastiraki. blogspot.ca; 5478 Blvd St-Laurent; ⊙noon-6pm Wed, to 8pm Thu & Fri, to 5pm Sat & Sun; MLau-rier) This unclassifiable store named after a flea-market neighborhood in Athens calls itself a 'hybrid curiosity shop/art space,' but that doesn't do justice to what illustra-tor Billy Mavreas sells: 1960s comic books, contemporary zines, silk-screen posters, and myriad antique and collectible knick-knacks, as well as recent works mainly by local graphic artists.

FRANK & OAK   CLOTHING

Map p282 (☎438-384-0824; www.frankan-doak.com; 160 Rue St-Viateur Est; ⊙10am-7pm Mon-Fri, to 6pm Sat, 11am-5pm Sun; MLaurier) Although the selection isn't huge, this dap-per menswear shop is worth a visit for classic, well-made trousers, button-downs, sweaters, leather belts and footwear. Though high end, the prices are fair con-sidering it's designed and manufactured in Montréal. There's also a coffee bar and a barber on-site – meaning you can get a pick-me-up, a trim and a new wardrobe all in one place.

GALERIE SIMON BLAIS   ART

Map p282 (☎514-849-1165; www.galeriesimon blais.com; 5420 Blvd St-Laurent; ⊙10am-6pm Tue-Fri, to 5pm Sat; MLaurier) One of the most prestigious galleries in Canada, Simon Blais carries works by well-known inter-national and domestic artists such as Lu-cien Freud, Antoni Tàpies and Jean-Paul

Riopelle as well as emerging contemporary artists from Montréal and Québec like Carol Bernier.

AU PAPIER JAPONAIS ARTS & CRAFTS

Map p282 (☑514-276-6863; www.aupapier japonais.com; 24 Ave Fairmount Ouest; ☉10am-6pm Mon-Sat, noon-4pm Sun; Ⓜ Laurier) You might never guess how many guises Japanese paper can come in until you visit this gorgeous little shop, which stocks more than 800 varieties. Origami kits and art books make great gifts, as do the elegant teapots, pottery and Buddha boards (where you can 'paint' ephemeral works with water).

LE MARCHÉ DES
SAVEURS DU QUÉBEC FOOD & DRINKS

Map p282 (☑514-271-3811; www.lemarche dessaveurs.com; 280 Pl du Marché-du-Nord; ☉9am-6pm Sat-Wed, to 8pm Thu & Fri; Ⓜ Jean-Talon) Everything here is Québécois, from the food to the handmade soaps to one of the best collections of artisanal local beer, maple products, jams and cheeses in the city. The store was established so local producers could gain wider exposure for their regional products, and it's a joy to browse.

STYLE LABO VINTAGE

Map p282 (http://stylelabo-deco.com; 5765 Blvd St-Laurent; ☉10:30am-6pm Tue-Fri, to 5pm Sat, 11:30am-5pm Sun; ☒55, Ⓜ Rosemont) Owners Anne Defay and Romain Castelli mix industrial remnants with quirky antique signage, farmers' furniture and even vintage dentistry equipment in this emporium of tools and gear from yesteryear. They also have accessories ranging from designer clock radios to old flags. An essential stop for feathering your loft.

PHONOPOLIS MUSIC

Map p282 (☑514-270-4442; http://phonopolis. ca; 207 Rue Bernard Ouest; ☉11am-6pm Sun & Mon, to 7pm Wed, Thu & Sat, to 8pm Fri; Ⓜ Outremont) Indie rock, jazz, blues, folk and world music – and hybrids thereof – are the raison

d'être of this little record shop, which sells (and buys) LPs and CDs. Its complete catalog of stock is listed online.

JET-SETTER SPORTS & OUTDOORS

Map p282 (☑514-271-5058; www.jet-setter.ca; 66 Ave Laurier Ouest; ☉10am-6pm Mon-Wed, to 9pm Thu & Fri, to 5pm Sat, noon-5pm Sun; Ⓜ Laurier) A plethora of state-of-the-art luggage and clever travel gadgetry, Jet-Setter has inflatable sacks for wine bottles, pocket-sized T-shirts, 'dry-in-an-instant' underwear, silk sleep sacks, mini-irons and hairdryers, waterproof hats and loads of other items you might find handy when you hit the road.

LES TOUILLEURS HOMEWARES

Map p282 (☑514-278-0008; www.lestouilleurs. com; 152 Ave Laurier Ouest; ☉10am-6pm Mon-Wed, to 7pm Thu & Fri, 11am-5pm Sat & Sun; Ⓜ Laurier) Beautifully designed Les Touilleurs celebrates Mile End's love affair with good food, presenting gorgeous high-end cookware and cookbooks by local and international chefs. There's a very popular teaching kitchen at the back of the shop, but **workshops** sell out well in advance. Most courses are held in French but attendees can usually ask questions in English.

SPORTS & ACTIVITIES

MEZZA LUNA
COOKING SCHOOL COOKING

Map p282 (☑514-272-5299; www.ecolemezza luna.ca; 57 Rue Dante, Little Italy; classes from $80; ⛹; Ⓜ De Castelnau) Offered in French, English and Italian, Mezza Luna's renowned Italian-cooking classes are held in a small apartment facing a high-end kitchen. They're educational, but not very hands on. The best part is eating the pasta, pizza or cake at the end. Classes are held several nights a week and on Saturday mornings. Kids' courses available. Reserve ahead.

Lachine Canal, Little Burgundy & the Southwest

Neighborhood Top Five

1 Oratoire St-Joseph (p129) Witnessing the soaring architecture of one of North America's grandest churches.

2 Canal de Lachine (p130) Walking or cycling off those poutine calories along 14km of bike paths and green spaces.

3 Marché Atwater (p130) Savoring fresh produce and tasty international food stalls surrounded by the buzz of one of Montréal's best markets.

4 Centre Canadien d'Architecture (p131) Pondering the city's architectural past and future

direction or lingering in its sculpture garden with a view.

5 Maison St-Gabriel (p131) Admiring the artifacts and traditional stately architecture of a Québécois farmhouse and its museum.

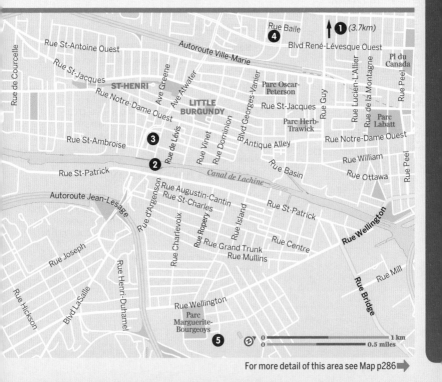

For more detail of this area see Map p286

Lonely Planet's Top Tip

If you are traveling light on luggage and time, consider just popping by Little Burgundy on your way to or from the airport. The 747 Airport Bus makes its first stop here at Lionel-Groulx metro station, from where it's an easy stroll to Marché Atwater, the Canal de Lachine and the center of Little Burgundy.

Best Places to Eat

➡ Liverpool House (p135)
➡ Tuck Shop (p135)
➡ Joe Beef (p135)

For reviews, see p132. ➡

Best Places to Drink

➡ Canal Lounge (p135)
➡ Bar Social Verdun (p135)
➡ La Drinkerie Ste-Cunégonde (p137)

For reviews, see p135. ➡

Best Activities

➡ Ma Bicyclette (p139)
➡ H2O Adventures (p139)
➡ Rafting Montréal (p138)

Explore Lachine Canal, Little Burgundy & the Southwest

Exploring the outlying residential neighborhoods of Montréal allows you to get a deeper experience of life on the island. A good chunk of them lie to the south and west of downtown (remember that Montréal's 'east–west' streets actually run northeast–southwest). Since they're far-flung, it's best to explore them over several days, though it's possible to combine contiguous areas such as Côte-des-Neiges and Notre-Dame-de-Grâce.

A must-do experience is the Canal de Lachine, Montréal's best biking course. In downtown or Old Montréal, find your way to a Bixi stand or bike-rental outfit and roll down to the Old Port. From there, get on the bike path that winds along the canal and out to Lachine, where several museums and a breezy riverside park await.

It will take at least an hour, but if you don't want to go that far, stop at the Marché Atwater, walk to Lionel-Groulx metro station and go to Côte-des-Neiges, which lies off the western slope of Parc du Mont-Royal. The magnificent Oratoire St-Joseph and the buzzing campus of the prestigious Université de Montréal are the main draws here. Notre-Dame-de-Grâce (or simply NDG) is a sleepy residential district, livened up by the cafes and restaurants along Ave Monkland.

Local Life

➡ **Sunning** Rent a bike, scoot along the Canal de Lachine (p130) and pause along its banks to soak up some rays.
➡ **Ahoy there!** Montréal is surrounded by rivers, so why not rent a canoe or kayak and go with the flow?
➡ **Over the hill** For a good workout, hike from downtown over Mont-Royal to Côte-des-Neiges, following the street of the same name.

Getting There & Away

➡ **Metro** Metro access to the area is via Villa-Maria station for NDG, while the Côte-des-Neiges station is for the neighborhood of the same name. To get to the east side of town, take the green metro line to either Pie-IX or Viau.
➡ **Bike** You can rent a Bixi bike to reach NDG, Petite-Bourgogne, St-Henri and Pointe-St-Charles, and to roll along the Canal de Lachine. Bikes are best avoided in hilly Côte-des-Neiges.

ANDRIY BLOKHIN/SHUTTERSTOCK ©

TOP EXPERIENCE
CLIMB THE STEPS TO ORATOIRE ST-JOSEPH

This stunning church built on the flanks of Mont-Royal commands grand views of the the Côte-des-Neiges area and northwest Montréal. The majestic basilica is a tribute to mid-20th-century design as well as an intimate shrine to Brother André, a local saint said to have healed countless people.

The largest shrine ever built in honor of Jesus' earthly father, this Renaissance-style building was completed in 1960 and commands fine views of the northern slope of Mont-Royal. The oratory dome is visible from anywhere in this part of town.

The oratory is also a tribute to the work of Brother André (1845–1937), the determined monk who first built a little **chapel** here in 1904. Brother André was said to have healing powers – as word spread, a larger shrine was needed, so the church began gathering funds to build one. Rows of discarded crutches and walking sticks in the basement **Votive Chapel** testify to this belief and the shrine is warmed by hundreds of candles. When Brother André died at age 91, a million devotees filed past his coffin over the course of six days. His black granite tomb in the Votive Chapel was donated by Québec premier Maurice Duplessis. Brother André was beatified in 1982 and finally canonized in 2010. His **heart** is on display too, in an upstairs museum dedicated to him.

DON'T MISS

➡ Brother André's room and 1904 chapel
➡ Brother André's tomb and heart
➡ The Votive Chapel
➡ The Grand Organ

PRACTICALITIES

➡ St-Joseph's Oratory
➡ ☏514-733-8211
➡ www.saint-joseph.org
➡ 3800 Chemin Queen-Mary
➡ $3, 2-for-1 entry with Opus card, parking $5
➡ ⊘24hr
➡ Ⓟ
➡ Ⓜ Laurier, then bus 51

Religious pilgrims might climb the 300 wooden steps to the oratory on their knees, praying at every step; other visitors take the stone stairs or one of the free shuttle buses from the base parking lot.

⊙ SIGHTS

The outdoor infrastructure linked by the Canal de Lachine constitutes some of the finest urban green space in Canada and is backed up by a fine produce market, which is worth a wander. The architectural draw is the Oratoire St-Joseph, or Habitat 67 for those with a taste for the quirky. Some specialist museums provide spaces dedicated to the history of the fur trade, Holocaust and architecture in Montréal.

ORATOIRE ST-JOSEPH   CHURCH
See p129.

★MARCHÉ ATWATER   MARKET
Map p286 (☑514-937-7754; www.marchespublics-mtl.com; 138 Ave Atwater; ⊙7am-6pm Mon-Wed, to 7pm Thu, to 8pm Fri, to 5pm Sat & Sun; Ⓜ Atwater) ✐ Just off the Canal de Lachine, this fantastic market has a mouthwatering assortment of fresh produce from local farms (some promoting sustainability), excellent wines, crusty breads, fine cheeses and other delectable fare. The market's specialty shops operate year-round, while outdoor eatery stalls open from March to October. It's all housed in a 1933 brick hall, topped with a clock tower, and little bouts of live music pop off with pleasing regularity. The grassy banks overlooking the canal are great for a picnic.

★CANAL DE LACHINE   CANAL
Map p286 (Rue Charles-Biddle; 🚻🚲) ✐ FREE A perfect marriage of urban infrastructure and green civic planning: a 14km-long cycling and pedestrian pathway, with picnic areas and outdoor spaces. Since the canal was reopened for navigation in 2002, flotillas of pleasure and sightseeing boats glide along its calm waters. Old warehouses converted into luxury condos line the canal near Atwater market. The Lachine Canal was originally built in 1825 as a means of bypassing the treacherous Lachine Rapids on the St Lawrence River.

It's well worth hiring a bike or in-line skates (kid sizes and baby trailers available) and heading out along the canal path but try to avoid summer weekends, when it's particularly crowded. For a canalside spin, you can hire bikes from Ça Roule Montréal (p64) in Old Montréal or My Bicyclette (p139) near the Atwater market. Kayaks and boats are also available at nearby H2O Adventures (p139). For a leisurely boat ride where someone else does the work, take a ride with Le Petit Navire (p65).

HABITAT 67   NOTABLE BUILDING
(☑514-866-5971; www.habitat67.com; 2600 Ave Pierre Dupuy; tours adult/child under 12yr $25/free; ⊙tours Tue-Sat May-Oct) The artificial peninsula Cité-du-Havre was created to protect the port from vicious currents and ice. Here, in 1967, architect Moshe Safdie designed a set of futuristic cube-like condominiums for Expo '67 when he was just 23 years old – from a distance, they resemble a microscopic zoom-in on table salt. This narrow spit of land connects Île Ste-Hélène with Old Montréal via the Pont de la Concorde.

THE GREAT HEART HEIST

How much is a holy man's heart worth? Fifty-thousand dollars, according to thieves who broke into a locked room in the Oratoire St-Joseph (p129) in March 1973. They made off with Brother André's heart sealed in a vial and demanded the sum in a ransom note that scandalized Montréal. The purloined organ was the subject of tabloid articles, musical compositions and even an art exhibition. Church officials reportedly refused the ransom demand, and nothing more was seen of the heart until December 1974 when Montréal lawyer to the underworld, Frank Shoofey, received a mysterious phone call asking him if he wanted to know its whereabouts. Shoofey was directed to an apartment building storage locker that contained a box, and inside was the vial housing Brother André's heart. The thieves were never found, and today the heart is secure in the Oratoire behind a metal grille and a sturdy transparent display case. But some believe the Church actually did pay the ransom to get it back. Was Shoofey, who was shot dead in 1985 in a still-unsolved murder, a go-between? Whatever the case, Montréal's great heart heist has continued to inspire artists long after the saint himself died.

Guided tours in English can be booked online. Hours are irregular but usually at 10am or 2:30pm. You can get a distant view of Habitat 67 from the south stretch of the Old Port, especially near Rue du Port.

★ **CENTRE CANADIEN D'ARCHITECTURE** MUSEUM

Map p286 (CCA; www.cca.qc.ca; 1920 Rue Baile; adult/child $10/free, 5:30-9pm Thu & 1st Sun of month free; ⊘11am-6pm Wed-Sun, to 9pm Thu; MGeorges-Vanier) A must for architecture fans, this center is equal parts museum and research institute. The building incorporates **Shaughnessy House**, a 19th-century gray limestone treasure. Highlights in this section include the conservatory and an ornate sitting room with intricate woodwork and a massive stone fireplace. The exhibition galleries focus on remarkable architectural works of both local and international scope, with a particular focus on urban design.

The CCA's **sculpture garden** is located on a grassy lot overlooking south Montréal. There's also a busy, well-stocked bookstore.

There is free admission on Thursday evenings and the 1st Sunday of the month, which also has free guided tours of the current exhibition and an introduction to CCA in English at 1pm. At other times, tours are only available for groups ($5 per person including admission) and must be reserved weeks in advance.

★ **MAISON ST-GABRIEL** MUSEUM

(☎514-935-8136; www.maisonsaint-gabriel.qc.ca; 2146 Pl Dublin; adult/student/child $20/5/5, after 5pm mid-Jun–early Sep free; ⊘1-5pm Tue-Sun early Jan–mid-Jun & early Sep–mid-Dec, 11am-6pm mid-Jun–early Sep; ☐57 est, MCharlevoix) This magnificent farmhouse in Pointe St-Charles is one of the finest examples of traditional Québec architecture. The house was bought in 1668 by Marguerite Bourgeoys to house a religious order. Young women called the Filles du Roy also stayed here – they were sent from Paris to Montréal to find husbands. The 17th-century roof of the two-story building is of particular interest for its intricate beam work, one of the few of its kind in North America.

The museum has an excellent collection of artifacts going back to the 17th and 18th centuries, with unusual items including sinks made from black stone and a sophisticated water-disposal system.

PARISIAN LAUNDRY GALLERY

Map p286 (☎514-989-1056; www.parisian laundry.com; 3550 Rue St-Antoine Ouest; ⊘noon-5pm Tue-Sat; MLionel-Groulx) **FREE** A former industrial laundry turned monster (15,000-sq-ft) gallery, this space is worth a trip for the old building itself even if you're not a fan of contemporary art. Previous exhibitions have included works by New York conceptual artist Adam Pendleton and Québec sculptor Valérie Blass. Be sure to check out exhibits upstairs and in the basement.

MONTRÉAL HOLOCAUST MUSEUM MUSEUM

(☎514-345-2605; http://museeholocauste.ca; 5151 Chemin de la Côte-Ste-Catherine; adult/child $8/5, 1st Sun of month free; ⊘10am-5pm Mon, Tue & Thu, to 9pm Wed, to 4pm Fri & Sun; MCôte-Ste-Catherine) This small museum provides a record of Jewish history and culture from pre-WWII Europe, during Nazi Germany, and after the Holocaust. The museum has many powerful exhibits, including some personal items like earmuffs and letters, and holds seminars and other events; groups of 10 or more can arrange to hear testimonies by Holocaust survivors. The museum is closed on Jewish holidays; see the website to confirm Friday hours between November and March.

FUR TRADE AT LACHINE NATIONAL HISTORIC SITE HISTORIC SITE

(www.pc.gc.ca/en/lhn-nhs/qc/lachine; 1255 Blvd St-Joseph; adult/child $4/free; ⊘10am-5pm mid-Jun–early Sep; ☒; ☐195, MAngrignon) This 1803 stone depot in Lachine is now an engaging little museum telling the story of the fur trade in Canada. The Hudson Bay Company made Lachine the hub of its fur-trading operations because the rapids made further navigation impossible. Visitors can view the furs and old trappers' gear, and costumed interpreters show how the bales and canoes were schlepped by Amerindian trappers. Kids can try all the gear on in interactive exhibitions.

The site is located about 1km west of the Musée de Lachine.

MUSÉE DE LACHINE MUSEUM

(☎514-634-3478; www.ville.montreal.qc.ca; 1 Chemin du Musée; ⊘noon-5pm Tue-Sun, closed Tue late Apr-late Nov, closed Dec-Mar; ☐110, MAngrignon) **FREE** It's a great bike ride to this museum, which is practically on the Canal de Lachine. It is also one of the oldest houses (1669) in the Montréal region, with shooting holes for defense. Back then Lachine was the last frontier for trappers heading west and the final stop for fur shipments. You can see and smell the old fur-storage building from the original trading days.

Adjacent to the museum is a huge waterfront **sculpture garden** that you can visit anytime from dawn to dusk.

MOULIN FLEMING
MUSEUM

(☑514-367-6439; www.ville.montreal.qc.ca; 9675 Blvd LaSalle, LaSalle; ⊙1-5pm Sun mid-May–early Jun, Sat & Sun early Jun-Aug; 🚍110, ⓂAngrignon) **FREE** This restored five-story windmill was built for a Scottish merchant in 1816, and a multimedia exhibit inside covers its two centuries of history. It's a nice diversion if you're out there visiting the other Lachine sites, and a great photo op.

There are free tours of the mill's exterior at 3pm every Sunday in July and August.

AVE DE MONKLAND
STREET

(ⓂVilla-Maria) Since the early noughties, Ave de Monkland in Notre-Dame-de-Grâce has been transformed, with coffee bars, restaurants and condominiums springing up like mushrooms after a warm rain. It certainly has a village character as many people walk to the shops from their homes. Access is via the Villa-Maria metro station, from where you can walk southwest down Monkland.

EATING

Little Burgundy is a great area for up-and-coming cool bistros and unpretentious restaurants with gourmet tasting menus. The Canal de Lachine is a popular place for a picnic with goodies assembled from the nearby market, while the southwest end of downtown is good for budget eats.

SATAY BROTHERS
MALAYSIAN $

Map p286 (☑514-933-3507; www.sataybrothers. com; 3721 Rue Notre-Dame Ouest; mains $9-15; ⊙11am-11pm Wed-Sun; ⓂLionel-Groulx) Amid red walls, hanging lamps and mismatched thrift-store furnishings, this lively and Malaysia-chic bar-bistro serves some of the best 'street food' in Montréal. Crowds flock here to gorge on delicious chicken-satay

sandwiches with peanut sauce served on grilled bread, tangy green papaya salad, braised pork (or tofu) buns, and *laksa lemak,* a rich and spicy coconut soup. It has great cocktails, too.

The 30-something Winnicki brothers quickly gained a cult following after opening a food stall in Marché Atwater (p130), which is still open in the summer.

KAZU
JAPANESE $

Map p286 (☑514-937-2333; www.kazumontreal.com; 1862 Rue Ste-Catherine Ouest; mains $10-17; ⊙noon-3pm Sun, Mon, Thu & Fri, also 5:30-9:30pm Thu-Mon; ⓂGuy-Concordia) Kazuo Akutsu's frenetic hole-in-the-wall in the Concordia Chinatown draws long lines of people waiting for *gyoza* (dumplings), ramen-noodle soup and awesome creations such as the 48-hour pork. Its popularity is well earned, but be warned: it gets cramped inside.

MAI XIANG YUAN
DUMPLING HOUSE
DUMPLINGS $

Map p286 (☑514-931-8880; 1929 Rue Ste-Catherine Ouest; mains $10-15; ⊙11am-9:30pm; ⓂGuy-Concordia) Part of the Asian food hub along Rue Ste-Catherine, this dumpling house is a solid option for traditional Chinese dumplings at affordable prices. The wide selection includes steamed or fried dumplings – the pork and shrimp steamed dumplings are a crowd-favorite – including vegetarian options. There's a second location on Rue St-Laurent in Chinatown.

HOT STAR
FRIED CHICKEN
TAIWANESE $

Map p286 (☑514-543-5588; http://hot-star. ca; 1953 Rue Ste-Catherine Ouest; mains $8-15; ⊙11am-11pm; ⓂGuy-Concordia) Originating in Taipei's Shilin Night Market, this fried-chicken joint is located in downtown Montréal's growing Asian-food epicenter. From giant chicken cutlets to seaweed-flavored fried mushrooms, this simple fast-food counter offers a menu of fast-food delicacies with a touch of Taiwan. A great stop for a quick eat.

MON AMI
KOREAN RESTAURANT
KOREAN $

Map p286 (☑514-934-5500; http://restomonami.com; 2081 Rue Ste-Catherine Ouest; mains $10-18; ⊙11:30am-10:30pm; 🖋🍴; ⓂAtwater) One of the latest additions to Montréal's

HARVARD DE MONTRÉAL

For all the francophiles among us, the **Université de Montréal** (☎514-343-6111; www.umontreal.ca; 2900 Blvd Édouard-Montpetit; Ⓜ Université-de-Montréal) is kind of like the French-speaking Harvard in Canada. The second-largest French-speaking university in the world, it has more than 66,000 students. Maybe because it's on the mountain far from downtown and feels removed from the rest of the city, you'll find an array of cultural events and happenings that remain virtually unknown to those outside the area.

Nearby Chemin de la Côte-des-Neiges is a lively street for strolling, with cafes, bookstores and a green market, the Marché Côtes-des-Neiges (p138), open 24 hours daily in summer.

From here you're also within walking distance of the Oratoire St-Joseph (p129), a great spot to visit at sunset. Two handy metro stations – Côte-des-Neiges and Université de Montréal – provide easy access to the area.

'second Chinatown,' this vibrant Korean restaurant offers classic dishes such as pork-bone soup and kimchi seafood noodles, with modern touches including fried chicken served with large pitchers of beer. The food is tasty and the atmosphere is lively.

PATRICE BAKERY $

Map p286 (http://patricepatissier.ca; 2360 Rue Notre-Dame Ouest; pastries $3-6; ⊙10:30am-6:30pm Wed-Fri, 9:30am-6:30pm Sat, 9:30am-5pm Sun; Ⓜ Lionel-Groulx) This elegantly designed patisserie has a modern, Scandinavian-like design, which makes a fine backdrop to the heavenly creations prepared here. Perennial favorites: the Kouign Amman (a Breton-style butter cake), *choux à la crème* (a mix of chocolate, caramel and banana cream enclosed in pastries), and the chocolate-coffee St-Henri cake. At lunch, you can get soup, salads and sandwiches.

IMADAKE JAPANESE $

Map p286 (☎514-931-8833; www.imadake.ca; 4006 Rue Ste-Catherine Ouest; mains $10-16; ⊙noon-2:30pm Mon-Fri, 5-10:30pm Sun-Thu, 5pm-1am Fri & Sat; Ⓜ Atwater) On the fringes of the Concordia Chinatown, Imadake is the closest thing to an authentic *izakaya* (Japanese pub-eatery) in the city. Staff scream *irrashaimase!* (welcome!) when you walk in, and there's an excellent assortment of *izakaya* standbys such as *tsukune* (chicken meatballs), *takoyaki* (octopus croquettes) and *okonomiyaki* (Japanese pancake with seafood or pork). The ramen noodles are excellent.

CHEZ NICK DINER $

Map p286 (☎514-935-0946; www.cheznick.ca; 1377 Ave Greene; mains $12-20; ⊙7am-8pm Mon-Fri, to 5pm Sat, 8am-5pm Sun; Ⓜ Atwater) This perfect little diner has been smack in the middle of swish Westmount since 1920. Despite the trendy stores and galleries that have mushroomed around it, it has stayed delightfully old-fashioned. The Montréal diner staples are all here, from burgers and fries, to smoked meat and desserts so high and rich they threaten to topple over.

RESTAURANT GREENSPOT DINER $

Map p286 (☎514-931-6473; 3041 Rue Notre-Dame Ouest; mains $8-12; ⊙5am-11pm; Ⓜ Lionel Groulx) This classic Québécois diner is a legend of Montréal greasy spoons. In business for more than 70 years, Greenspot remains a local favorite for hot dogs, smoked meat and poutine. Come day or night to enjoy the tasty fast food and lively ambience.

MELK CAFE $

(https://melk.cafe; 5612 Ave Monkland; baked goods $3; ⊙7am-7pm Mon-Fri, from 8am Sat & Sun; Ⓜ Villa-Maria) This tiny neighborhood gem is a requisite pit stop when strolling Ave Monkland. You can enjoy first-rate coffees, matcha lattes, and heavenly baked goods (buttery scones, gourmet donuts) while taking in the tin ceilings and passing people parade.

THALI INDIAN $

Map p286 (www.thalimontreal.com; 1409 Rue St-Marc; mains $5-10; ⊙11:30am-11pm Mon-Fri, 1-11pm Sat, noon-10pm Sun; ☑; Ⓜ Guy-Concordia) A popular budget gem in the Concordia Chinatown, Thali offers quick plates of delish Indian fare, with three-course specials for about $10. The naan bread, butter chicken and lamb kebab are particularly delectable. There are also wraps and good vegetarian options.

LE BON VIVANT
BISTRO $$

Map p286 (☑514-316-4585; https://lebv.ca; 2705 Rue Notre-Dame Ouest; mains $15-30; ☺5-11pm Mon-Fri, from 11am Sat & Sun; MLionel Groulx) Part of the lineup of great restaurants on Rue Notre-Dame in Little Burgundy, this locally owned bistro has a welcoming atmosphere and friendly staff, serving up a select menu from grilled octopus to freshly made beef or salmon tartare, plus weekend bagel brunches.

LE VIN PAPILLON
INTERNATIONAL $$

Map p286 (www.vinpapillon.com; 2519 Rue Notre-Dame Ouest; small plates $7-17; ☺3pm-midnight Tue-Sat; ☑; MLionel-Groulx) The folks behind Joe Beef continue the hit parade with this delightful wine bar and small-plate eatery next door to Liverpool House – another Joe Beef success. Creative, mouthwatering veggie dishes take top billing with favorites such as tomato-and-chickpea salad, sautéed chanterelles and smoked-eggplant caviar, along with roasted cauliflower with chicken skin, guinea-fowl confit, and charcuterie and cheese platters.

No reservations – so go early!

LE FANTÔME
EUROPEAN $$

Map p286 (☑514-846-1832; www.restofantome. com; 1832 Rue William; tasting menus from $55; ☺6-10pm; ☑; MLionel-Groulx) This industrial-chic restaurant does a fantastic tasting menu for $55 and further polishes the rising star of the Little Burgundy area as a relaxed foodie go-to. Young, knowledgeable staff

can help pair organic wines to artful dishes – like beef tartare in fennel, fresh tarragon mushroom risotto, and truffle spaghetti. There is a good vegetarian option.

FOIEGWA
QUÉBÉCOIS $$

Map p286 (☑438-387-4252; http://foiegwa. com; 3001 Rue Notre-Dame Ouest; mains $15-25; ☺5pm-2am; MLionel Groulx) Foiegwa is a trendy Québécois-French fusion restaurant dressed in the aesthetic of a classic diner. Taking over the location of a longtime neighborhood greasy spoon, it serves decadent dishes with a casual touch. Poutine, gourmet burgers and more feature foie gras (typically duck or goose liver produced by force-feeding). Cozy seating, hand-crafted cocktails and a lively ambience.

MAISON BULGOGI
KOREAN $$

Map p286 (☑514-935-9820; 2127 Rue Ste-Catherine Ouest; mains $10-15; ☺11am-10pm; MAtwater) This simple eatery is a reliable option for delicious Korean classics at reasonable prices. Be sure to try the *kimchi jigae* (kimchi stews) and homemade noodle dishes.

SU
TURKISH $$

(☑514-362-1818; www.restaurantsu.com; 5145 Rue Wellington, Verdun; mains $18-26; ☺5-10:30pm Tue-Wed, to 11pm Thu-Sun, also 10am-3pm Sat & Sun; MVerdun) Chef Fisun Ercan takes her home-style but inventive Turkish cuisine beyond your expectations of kabobs and coffee. She prepares feather-light fried calamari, beef *manti* (dumplings) with garlic yogurt and spiced tomatoes, rich seafood rice (with shrimp, mussels and fish) and delicious *lokum* (Turkish delight). It's worth the trip to Verdun; be sure to reserve.

RETURN OF THE MONTRÉAL MELON

In its heyday it was truly the Queen of Melons. A single specimen might easily reach 9kg and its spicy flavor earned it the nickname 'Nutmeg Melon.' The market gardeners of western Montréal did a booming business in the fruit.

After WWII, small agricultural plots in Montréal vanished as the city expanded, and industrial farms had little interest in growing a melon with ultrasensitive rind. By the 1950s the melon was gone – but not forever. In 1996 an enterprising Montréal journalist tracked down Montréal melon seeds held in a US Department of Agriculture collection in Iowa. The first new crop was harvested a year later in a new collective garden in Notre-Dame-de-Grâce, the heart of the old melon-growing district.

To sample this blast from the past, visit local markets such as Marché Atwater (p130) or Marché Jean-Talon (p116) after the harvest every September.

PHAYATHAI
THAI **$$**

Map p286 (☑514-933-9949; www.phayathai.ca; 1235 Rue Guy; mains $17-25; ⊙11:30am-2:30pm Tue-Fri, 5-10pm Mon-Sun; ✔; Ⓜ Guy-Concordia) Just off the beaten track, this elegant little restaurant serves some of the best Thai cuisine in town. Fresh-tasting curries, crispy boneless duck and seafood plates are among the many delicacies from the East. A dozen vegetarian options include eggplant red curry.

LA LOUISIANE
CAJUN **$$**

(☑514-369-3073; www.lalouisiane.ca; 5850 Rue Sherbrooke Ouest; mains $16-32; ⊙5:30-10:30pm Tue-Sat; Ⓜ Vendôme, then bus 105) Montréal meets the Big Easy in this casual Cajun eatery, with amazing results. The menu bears the hearty, delicious flavors of jambalaya, shrimp Creole or chicken étouffée (stew-like rice dish), all armed with mysterious peppers and spices. The rich 'voodoo pasta' has spicy Cajun sausage and tomatoes in white wine and cream. Go early, as La Louisiane accepts no reservations.

While you're here, be sure to check out paintings of street scenes by New Orleans native James Michelopoulos.

★ LIVERPOOL HOUSE
QUÉBÉCOIS **$$$**

Map p286 (☑514-313-6049; www.joebeef.ca; 2501 Rue Notre-Dame Ouest; mains $24-50; ⊙5-11pm Tue-Sat; ✔) Liverpool House sets the standard so many Québec restaurants are racing for: an ambience that feels laid-back, like a friend's dinner party, where the food is sent from angels on high. Expect oysters, smoked trout, braised rabbit, lobster spaghetti and various other iterations of regional excellence. There is usually a vegetarian main, but sometimes just one choice.

★ TUCK SHOP
QUÉBÉCOIS **$$$**

(☑514-439-7432; www.tuckshop.ca; 4662 Rue Notre-Dame Ouest; mains $30-36; ⊙5-11pm Tue-Sat; ✔; Ⓜ Place-St-Henri) ✔ Set in the heart of working-class St-Henri, Tuck Shop could have been plucked from London or New York if it weren't for its distinctly local menu, a delightful blend of market and terroir (locally sourced) offerings such as Kamouraska lamb shank, fish of the day with Jerusalem-artichoke puree and a Québec cheese plate, all prepared by able chef Theo Lerikos.

The lively atmosphere, warm service and excellent dishes are pitch-perfect, so it's no wonder this place fills up fast. Be sure to reserve.

JOE BEEF
QUÉBÉCOIS **$$$**

Map p286 (☑514-935-6504; www.joebeef.ca; 2491 Rue Notre-Dame Ouest; mains $30-55; ⊙6pm-late Tue-Sat; Ⓜ Lionel-Groulx) In the heart of the Little Burgundy neighborhood, Joe Beef remains a darling of food critics for its unfussy, market-fresh fare. The rustic, country-kitsch setting is a great spot to linger over fresh oysters, braised rabbit, roasted scallops with smoked onions and a changing selection of hearty Québécois dishes – all served with good humor and low pretension.

In summer some of the best seats are in the backyard garden. Reserve weeks in advance.

DRINKING & NIGHTLIFE

The Little Burgundy area has great bars along Rue Ste-Catherine Ouest. Head to the southwest of downtown for student-friendly, busy pubs, and in summer, watch the sun go down on a boat-bar or BYO beer to the grassy edges of the Lachine.

★ CANAL LOUNGE
COCKTAIL BAR

Map p286 (☑514-451-2665; www.canallounge.com; 22 Ave Atwater; ⊙3-11pm Tue-Sat, to 10pm Sun late May-early Oct; Ⓜ Lionel Groulx) This permanently docked boat-bar nestles along the canal in front of a lovely pedestrian bridge. The over-45-year-old vessel has been converted into an upscale cocktail lounge. Sit on the rooftop for some fresh air or inside for maritime ambience. The friendly owners moonlight as bartenders and whip up finely crafted cocktails.

BAR SOCIAL VERDUN
BAR

(☑438-387-7828; 3819 Rue Wellington, Verdun; ⊙3pm-3am; Ⓜ De l'Eglise) A fun neighborhood spot with outdoor seating, an impressive central bar and live music, Bar Social Verdun is a welcome addition to this up-and-coming residential district. There's a wide selection of drinks including microbrews, and a food menu highlighted by fresh-roasted chicken.

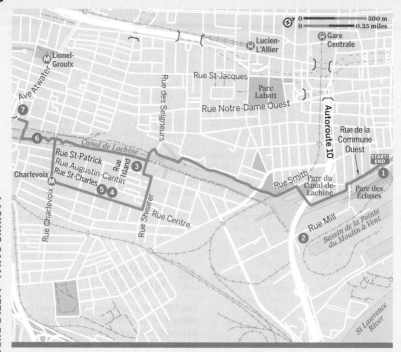

⚲ Cycling Tour
⚙ Cycling the Canal de Lachine

START CANAL LOCKS
END CANAL LOCKS
LENGTH 7KM; TWO HOURS

The prettiest cycle path in Montréal stretches along the Canal de Lachine (p130). On warm days you'll see sunbathers on the grass, families at picnic tables, and cyclists and in-line skaters gliding along.

Start at the ❶ **Canal Locks** at the southwestern end of the Old Port. This area has an industrial feel thanks to the abandoned grain silo southeast of the locks.

Pedaling southwest along Rue de la Commune Ouest, you'll pass under Autoroute 10. Continue along the downtown side of the canal, lined with strips of greenery. The enormous neon sign ❷ **Farine Five Roses** crowns a former flour mill across the canal.

The path switches sides at the bridge at Rue des Seigneurs, where you come to a ❸ **former silk mill** that ran its operations on hydraulic power from the canal. The redbrick factory has been reborn as lofts.

Continue south on Rue Shearer and turn right on Rue Centre. You'll come to Romanesque ❹ **Église St-Charles** on your right. Push your bike over to French-style ❺ **Église St-Gabriel**, taking in the charm of this little-visited neighborhood.

Continue to Rue Charlevoix, turn right and you'll soon be on the bike path again. Turn left, and you'll come to ❻ **H2O Adventures** (p139), a kayak-rental outfit. If you're interested in getting out on the water, this is the place to do it,.

Continue on the bike path and turn right at the pedestrian bridge to head to ❼ **Marché Atwater** (p130), one of the city's best markets. Assemble a picnic here to enjoy by the water where there are green spaces and outdoor picnic tables, followed by an easy pedal back to your starting point.

If you want to explore further, continue heading west. Another 10km along the path will take you to a sculpture garden at the edge of scenic Lac St-Louis – a favorite spot at sunset. To head back, simply follow the canal path back to the Canal Locks.

LA DRINKERIE
STE-CUNÉGONDE   BAR
Map p286 (www.facebook.com/drinkerie; 2661 Rue Notre-Dame Ouest; ⊙3pm-3am; MLionel Groulx) Along the popular Rue Notre-Dame you'll find this locally owned bar that's perfect for a relaxing evening drink or a late-night party. Well-crafted cocktails, original menu options, and a summertime patio have made La Drinkerie a popular spot with Little Burgundy and St-Henri residents. Walking distance from the Lachine Canal, the Marché Atwater and many restaurant options.

KAMPAI GARDEN   BEER GARDEN
Map p286 (☎514-379-6161; https://kampaigarden.com; 1616 Rue Ste-Catherine Ouest; ⊙5pm-1am; MGuy-Concordia) This large Asian-inspired beer garden serves tapas-style plates and trendy cocktails, making it a worthy option for a birthday dinner or other events. Weekend nights can get quite busy with a younger crowd, so plan accordingly.

BAR DE COURCELLE   BAR
(www.bardecourcelle.com; 4685 Rue Notre-Dame Ouest; ⊙3pm-3am; MSt-Henri) A favorite with St-Henri locals, this former working-class watering hole turned cool cocktail bar has managed to upgrade itself without losing its original charm. Dark and mellow with a touch of rock 'n' roll, friendly staff, live music and good snacks, Courcelle is a great neighborhood joint for everything from cheap beer to finely crafted cocktails.

BAR GANADARA   BAR
Map p286 (☎514-379-3009; www.facebook.com/BarGanadara; 1900 Rue Ste-Catherine Ouest; ⊙5:30pm-3am; MGuy) Part cocktail-party bar and part Japanese-Korean fusion eatery, this happening hybrid offers late-night drinks and bites in a lively atmosphere. A fun night out.

CAFÉ LILI & OLI   COFFEE
Map p286 (www.facebook.com/liliandoli; 2713 Rue Notre-Dame Ouest; ⊙7am-10pm Mon-Thu, to 8pm Fri, 8am-8pm Sat & Sun; 🖫; MLionel Groulx) This family-owned cafe is a Little Burgundy mainstay, delivering delicious coffee and a welcoming ambience. Freshly baked muffins and one of the best iced coffees in town are just some of the highlights. Bring your dog or your laptop and hang out with some locals, chances are you'll be charmed.

BURGUNDY LION   PUB
Map p286 (☎514-934-0888; www.burgundylion.com; 2496 Rue Notre-Dame Ouest; ⊙11:30am-3am Mon-Fri, 9am-3am Sat & Sun; MLionel-Groulx) This trendy take on the English pub features British pub fare, beers and whiskeys galore, and an attitude-free vibe where everyone (and their parents) feels welcome to drink, eat and be merry. Things get the good kind of crazy on late-night weekends. Tip your cap to Queen Elizabeth, whose portrait adorns the bathroom door.

TERRASSE ST-AMBROISE   BEER GARDEN
(http://mcauslan.com/en/terrace/about/; 5080 Rue St-Ambroise; ⊙noon-11pm Thu-Sun, from 4pm Mon-Wed May-Oct; 🖫; MPlace St-Henri) This outdoor beer garden at the McAuslan Brewery, one of Quebec's most successful microbreweries, makes the most of summer with family-friendly picnic tables and a barbecue restaurant in a wide green, no-smoking space near the Lachine Canal. A large selection of beers are available fresh from the brewery.

☆ ENTERTAINMENT

WHEEL CLUB   DANCE
(☎514-489-3322; www.thewheelclub.wordpress.com; 3373 Blvd Cavendish; ⊙8pm-1am; 🚌105, MVendôme) Going strong for more than 50 years, this venerable country-and-western bar is famous for its Hillbilly Night on Mondays, featuring bluegrass, cowboy and fiddle music. House-band Vintage Wine, which plays late '60s and '70s covers, can also get your heels hopping. Otherwise, there are dartboards, a pool table and a full bar. Dress verycasual. Call ahead for live-music schedules.

SEGAL CENTRE   PERFORMING ARTS

(☎514-739-7944; www.segalcentre.org; 5170 Chemin de la Côte-Ste-Catherine; plays $15-65; Ⓜ Côte-Ste-Catherine) Montréal's Jewish theater stages dramatic performances in English and Yiddish – although as one of the city's most prominent professional theater venues, plays presented are by no means exclusively Jewish. Past productions have included *The Apprenticeship of Duddy Kravitz* (based on Mordecai Richler's novel), Tom Stoppard's *Travesties,* and Dora Wasserman's Yiddish masterpiece *The Dybbuk.*

 SHOPPING

Little Burgundy has some budget vintage gems in its markets. Elsewhere in this area there are antiques, books and sweet treats.

MARCHÉ UNDERGROUND   VINTAGE

Map p286 (☎514-820-2117; https://marche-underground.business.site; 3731 Rue Notre-Dame Ouest; ◔noon-6pm Mon-Wed, to 9pm Thu, to 5pm Fri, 11am-5pm Sat & Sun; Ⓜ Lionel-Groulx) Vintage doesn't have to be pricey, especially outside of Mile End and the Plateau. Visit this collective of nearly 10 sellers of clothes, furniture, toys, homewares and other collectibles from yesteryear. You'll pay near what you would at thrift stores, but here it's pleasingly curated.

LES ANTIQUITÉS GRAND CENTRAL   ANTIQUES

Map p286 (☎514-935-1467; www.grandcentralinc.ca; 2448 Rue Notre-Dame Ouest; ◔9:30am-5pm Mon & Tue, to 5:30pm Wed-Fri, 11am-5pm Sat; Ⓜ Lionel-Groulx) The most elegant store on Rue Notre-Dame's Antique Alley is a pleasure to visit for its English and continental furniture, lighting and decorative objects from the 18th and 19th centuries. Get buzzed in to see the Louis XIV chairs, full dining-room suites and chandeliers in Dutch-cathedral or French Empire style, with price tags in the thousands.

CANDYLABS   FOOD

Map p286 (www.candylabs.ca; 2305 Rue Guy; ◔10am-6pm Tue & Wed, to 7pm Thu & Fri, 11am-6pm Sat & Sun; Ⓜ Guy-Concordia) Head to this bright little shop for jewel-like hard candy. You can watch the candy makers in action since these artful sweets are made on-site, and then packaged in pretty glass jars that make great gifts. There are some 40 flavors available, and the friendly staff are happy to let you sample a wide assortment.

MARCHÉ CÔTES-DES-NEIGES   MARKET

(Jean-Brillant; cnr Chemin de la Côte-des-Neiges & Rue Jean-Brillant; ◔7am-6pm Nov-Dec & mid-Mar–early Apr, 24hr early Apr-Oct; Ⓜ Côte-des-Neiges) This is a much-loved neighborhood market in Côte-des-Neiges, known for its budget-priced fresh produce, flowers and herbs.

MONTRÉAL'S WHITE WATER

The **Parc des Rapides** (☎514-367-1000; cnr Blvd LaSalle & 7e Ave; 🚌58, Ⓜ De l'Église) on the St Lawrence is the spot to view the Lachine Rapids (and the jet boats that ride them). The park attracts hikers and anglers, and cyclists who pedal the riverside trail. It's also a renowned bird sanctuary – located on a small peninsula, with what's said to be Québec's largest heron colony. The 30-hectare sanctuary is an important site for migratory birds, with some 225 species passing through each year.

Some information displays relate the history of the rapids and of the old hydro-electric plant on the grounds. You can rent kayaks and sign up for classes where you'll learn to surf or kayak the Lachine Rapids – scaredy-cats need not apply. An adrenaline-rushing experience can be had with **Rafting Montréal** (☎514-767-2230; www.raftingmontreal.com; 8912 Blvd LaSalle; jet boat per adult/teen/child $56/46/36, rafting $47/40/29; ◔9am-6pm May-Sep; 🚻; 🚌110, Ⓜ Angrignon), a jet-boating and rafting outfit located 2km west of the Parc des Rapides. Rafting trips last a little over two hours and are also suitable for kids age six and up. Jet-boat trips offer high-speed 75-minute rides. For something a bit different, you can try river boarding (not unlike a boogie-board ride along more than 6.4km of rapids) or tandem rafting (where you and a friend brave the white water in a two-person kayak).

PARC DE LA RIVIÈRE-DES-MILLE-ÎLES

For a scenic paddle far from the bustle of downtown head to the **Parc de la Rivière-des-Mille-Îles** (☏450-622-1020; www.parc-mille-iles.qc.ca; 345 Blvd Ste-Rose; kayak/canoe per hour $12.50/13.50, per day $42/44; ⊗9am-6pm, to 8pm Fri & Sat mid-Jun–mid-Aug; ⓂCartier then bus 73). One of Montréal's loveliest spots for canoeing and kayaking lies along the Rivière des Mille-Îles near Laval. It has 10 islands where you can disembark on self-guided water tours, and about 10km of the river (including calm inner channels) are open for paddling.

You can rent a wide range of watercraft, including 10-seat rabaska ($38/125 per hour/day) – canoes like those used by fur trappers.

SALVATION ARMY CLOTHING
Map p286 (1620 Rue Notre-Dame Ouest; ⊗9am-9pm Mon-Fri, to 5pm Sat; ⓂLucien l'Allier) This sprawling secondhand store has seemingly endless racks of clothes, plus 99¢ books (French and English), records, sports gear (including skis and snowboards) and more.

🏃 SPORTS & ACTIVITIES

The Lachine Canal provides the best water activities in this neighbourhood for kayaking, boating, rafting and canoeing. Out of the water, cycling is very popular for both pros and casual pedalers, who ride the extensive bike path tracing the canal.

MA BICYCLETTE CYCLING
Map p286 (☏514-317-6306; www.mybicyclette.com; 2985 Rue St-Patrick; bicycle per 2hr/day from $22/45; ⊗10am-6pm; ⓂCharlevoix) Located along the Canal de Lachine (p130) – just across the bridge from the Atwater market (p130) – this place rents bikes and other gear during the warmer months. It also sponsors city bike tours, and the repair

shop next door is a good place to go if your bike conks out on the canal path.

H2O ADVENTURES WATER SPORTS
Map p286 (☏514-842-1306; www.h2oadventures.com; 2727b Rue St-Patrick; pedal boat/tandem kayak/electric boat/voyageur canoe per hour $25/35/50/50; ⊗9am-9pm Jun-Aug, noon-7:30pm Mon-Fri, 10am-7:30pm Sat & Sun Sep-May; ⓂCharlevoix) Located across from the Atwater market (p130) on the banks of the Canal de Lachine (p130), H2O rents out kayaks and pedal boats for a gentle glide along the water. There are also a variety of courses on offer.

L'ÉCOLE DE VOILE
DE LACHINE BOATING
(☏514-634-4326; www.voilelachine.com; 3045 Blvd St-Joseph, Lachine; boat rental per 1hr $30-50, per 3hr $60-100; ⊗1-6pm Mon-Fri, 9am-8pm Sat & Sun May-Sep; ☐173, ⓂLionel-Groulx) Located on the edge of Lac St-Louis, the Lachine Sailing School organizes regattas on the St Lawrence River, gives free boat tours in late June and early July, and rents light craft (windsurfing boards, small sailboats and catamarans). Qualified instructors give windsurfing and sailing courses in summer. A 20-hour sailing course (one night and one weekend) costs $405.

1. Lachine Rapids (p138)
A popular spot on the St Lawrence River for rafting and jet-boating.

2. Canal de Lachine (p130)
This picturesque canal was built in 1825 to bypass the Lachine Rapids on the St Lawrence River.

3. Habitat 67 (p130)
Moshe Safdie–designed condominium complex built for Expo '67 when the architect was just 23.

GLASS AND NATURE/SHUTTERSTOCK ©

INSPIRED BY MAPS/SHUTTERSTOCK ©; ARCHITECT: MOSHE SAFDIE

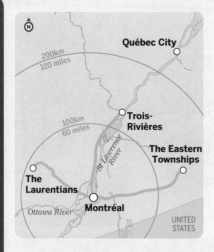

Day Trips from Montréal

Trois-Rivières p143

Midway between Montréal and Québec City, this historic town makes a pleasant stopover, with its attractive riverfront backed by a small cluster of museums and historic buildings. Highlights include a former 17th-century convent packed with artwork and a fascinating folk-art museum.

The Laurentians p144

Montréal's backyard mountain playground, the Laurentians offer countless recreational opportunities, including hiking, downhill and cross-country skiing, and cycling on a 230km converted railway bed. You can stop for a meal or a scenic stroll in Val-David, St-Sauveur-des-Monts, Ste-Agathe-des-Monts and other charming villages in the Laurentians.

The Eastern Townships p148

Québec meets New England in this pretty landscape of rolling hills, sparkling waterways, picturesque villages and farms specializing in cider, wine, cheese and maple syrup. Summer brings fishing and swimming in the region's numerous lakes, and cycling is also extremely popular in the warmer months, with nearly 500km of trails taking in sumptuous landscapes.

Trois-Rivières

Explore

Founded in 1634, Trois-Rivières is North America's second-oldest city north of Mexico, but you'd never know it: a roaring fire that swept through in 1908 left little of the city's historic looks. Still, the city center, right on the north shore of the St Lawrence River, is not without charms and some bona fide tourist attractions. A riverfront promenade leads to the oldest section of town along Rue des Ursulines.

The name, by the way, is a misnomer as there are only two, not three, streams here. There are, however, three branches of the Rivière St Maurice at its mouth, where islands split its flow into three channels.

Cultural highlights include the **Festival International de la Poésie** (International Poetry Festival; www.fiptr.com; ⊘Oct), a 10-day international poetry festival in October.

The Best...

➡ **Sight** Musée Québécois de Culture Populaire

➡ **Place to Eat** Le Poivre Noir

➡ **Place to Drink** Gambrinus (p144)

Top Tip

If you read French, don't miss the interesting interpretive plaques sprinkled around Trois-Rivières' riverfront district, enlivened by vintage photos and engravings tracing four centuries of local history.

Getting There & Away

➡ **Bus** Several buses daily by **Orléans Express** (☑514-395-4000; www.orleans express.com) from Montréal to Trois-Rivières. Buses arrive at Trois-Rivières' **Gare d'Autocars** (Orléans Express station; ☑819-374-2944; 275 Rue St-Georges), within a 10-minute walk of the historic riverfront district.

➡ **Car** Autoroute 40.

Need to Know

➡ **Area Code** ☑819

➡ **Location** 140km northeast of Montréal

➡ **Tourist Office** (☑819-375-1122; www. tourismetroisrivieres.com; 1457 Rue Notre-Dame;

⊙ SIGHTS & ACTIVITIES

MUSÉE QUÉBÉCOIS DE CULTURE POPULAIRE   MUSEUM
(Musée POP; ☑819-372-0406; http://musee pop.ca; 200 Rue Laviolette; adult/child $13/8; ⊘10am-6pm Jul & Aug, to 4pm Wed-Fri, to 5pm Sat & Sun Sep-Jun) One of the most interesting stops in the area, this museum's changing exhibits cover the gamut from folk art to pop culture, delving into the social and cultural life of the Québécois. Previous exhibits include a quirky show on the social significance of garage sales, and woodcarvings of birds commonly sighted in the area.

VIEILLE PRISON   MUSEUM
(☑819-372-0406; http://museeopop.ca; 200 Rue Laviolette; adult/child $21/13; ⊘10am-6pm Jul-Aug, 10am-5pm Sat & Sun Sep-Jun) Tour guides, including some former inmates, bring the harsh realities of the lockup vividly to life during 90-minute tours that include a stop at dank underground cells known as 'the pit.' English tours run between 11:30am and 3:30pm from late June to the end of August, and by reservation the rest of the year. No children under 12!

CROISIÈRES AML   BOATING
(☑866-856-6668; www.croisieresaml.com; 1515 Rue du Fleuve; adult/child $30/18; ⊘mid-Jun–early Sep; ♿) These 90-minute cruises along the St Lawrence River feature historical commentary about the town. Tours depart from Port de Trois-Rivières in Parc Portuaire and run to the Laviolette Bridge, the **Sanctuaire Notre-Dame-du-Cap** (www. sanctuaire-ndc.ca/en; 626 Rue Notre-Dame Est; ⊘8:30am-8pm; ℗) FREE, Île St-Quentin and the confluence of the St Lawrence and St Maurice Rivers. The ticket office is near the departure point, at the foot of Rue des Forges.

✖ EATING & DRINKING

⭐**LE POIVRE NOIR**   FUSION $$$
(☑819-378-5772; www.poivrenoir.com; 1300 Rue du Fleuve; mains $25-34, 3-course menu $46; ⊘11:30am-2pm Wed-Fri, also 5:30-8:30pm

DAY TRIPS FROM MONTRÉAL TROIS-RIVIÈRES

LA DOMAINE JOLY DE LOTBINIÈRE

If you're continuing east from Trois-Rivières toward Québec City, don't miss **La Domaine Joly de Lotbinière** (☑418-926-2462; www.domainejoly.com; Hwy 132, Rte de Pointe-Platon; adult/child $17/free; ◷10am-5pm late May-late Sep; P). This stately museum between Trois-Rivières and Québec City was built for Henri-Gustave Joly de Lotbinière (1849–1908), a premier of Québec. This is one of the most impressive manors built during the seignorial period of Québec and has been preserved in its late-19th-century state. The outbuildings and huge cultivated garden are a treat, and the cafe serves lunch and afternoon teas.

Tue-Sat; ☑) At this upmarket place by the riverfront, chef José Pierre Durand's inspired, often daring, blend of French, Québécois and international influences creates a memorable dining experience. Appetizers such as asparagus and blood-orange salad, or warm goat's-cheese 'snowballs' with tomatoes and pistachios are followed by main dishes such as Québécois deer with pine-nut and squash risotto and cranberry chutney. Reservations suggested.

CAFÉ MORGANE   CAFE $

(☑819-694-1118; http://cafemorgane.com; 100 Rue des Forges; dishes $5-9; ◷6am-11:30pm Mon-Thu, to 12:30am Fri & Sat, 7am-11:30pm Sun; ☎☑) On most afternoons, this branch of a local chain is the busiest spot in Trois-Rivières. Espresso, herbal teas and decadent sweets infuse the airy space with delightful smells. There's a free wi-fi connection here.

GAMBRINUS   BREWERY

(☑819-691-3371; www.gambrinus.qc.ca; 3160 Blvd des Forges; ◷11am-1am Mon-Fri, 3pm-1am Sat) About 3km northwest of the riverfront, this decade-old brewery serves more than a dozen varieties of beer, including seasonal cranberry, raspberry and apple ales, an excellent IPA, and an unconventional hemp-and-honey blend called Miel d'Ange.

🛏 SLEEPING

AUBERGE INTERNATIONALE
DE TROIS-RIVIÈRES   HOSTEL $

(☑819-378-8010; www.hihostels.ca; 497 Rue Radisson; dm/d $32/70; @☎) This wonderfully clean and friendly youth hostel is set in a two-story brick Georgian home,

within easy walking distance of the bus station (p143), the riverfront and all the city's attractions. Dorms have four to eight beds each, and there are also reasonably priced private rooms. Bicycle rentals are available.

LE FLEURVIL   B&B $$

(☑819-372-5195; www.fleurvil.qc.ca; 635 Rue des Ursulines; d $119-159; ☎☑) Operated by a gregarious Harley aficionado with a knack for decorating, this homey inn within a stone's throw of the St Lawrence River and the walking promenade fronts a lush garden with a maple-shaded pool.

The Laurentians

Explore

The Laurentians (Les Laurentides in French) make for an excellent day trip from Montréal, being just an hour's drive from the city. Here you'll find gentle rolling mountains, crystal-blue lakes and meandering rivers bordered by towns and villages too cute for words. A visit to this natural paradise is like putting your feet up after a long day.

Although sometimes criticized for being overcommercialized, Mont-Tremblant offers outstanding skiing, rivaled only by Whistler in the whole of Canada. Speckling the Laurentians are many lower-profile resort villages, whose miniature town centers deliver an air of the Alps, with breezy patios and independent designer-clothing shops.

Expect higher prices and heavy crowds during high season, which includes the summer months and Christmas holidays. Check ahead for opening hours in winter, which are often curtailed severely.

The Best...

➡ **Sight** Parc National du Mont-Tremblant

➡ **Place to Eat** La Tablée des Pionniers (p146)

➡ **Activity** Via Ferrata au Diable (p148)

Top Tip

Even without your own bicycle, you can cycle Canada's longest rails-to-trails route, the 232km Parc Linéaire du P'tit Train du Nord (p147); Autobus Le Petit Train du Nord (p147) will rent you a bike and provide transportation between the start and end points of your choice.

Getting There & Away

➡ **Bus** Galland Laurentides (p242) runs buses from Montréal's Central Bus Station to the Laurentians two to three times a day. Stops along the way include St-Jérôme, St-Sauveur-des-Monts, Ste-Adèle, Val-David, Ste-Agathe-des-Monts and Mont-Tremblant.

➡ **Car** Autoroute 15 (Autoroute des Laurentides) and provincial Hwy 117.

Need to Know

➡ **Area Code** ☑450, ☑819

➡ **Location** 80km to 150km northwest of Montréal

➡ **Tourisme Laurentides** (☑450-224-7007; www.laurentides.com; La Porte-du-Nord, Hwy 15, exit 51; ⊙8:30am-6:30pm Mon-Sat, to 5:30pm Sun late Jun–early Sep, to 5pm rest of year)

◉ SIGHTS

★PARC NATIONAL DU
MONT-TREMBLANT   NATIONAL PARK
(Mont Tremblant National Park; ☑819-688-2281, reservations 800-665-6527; www.sepaq.com/pq/mot; 4456 Chemin du Lac Supérieur, Lac-Supérieur; adult/child $8.60/free; ⛄) ✿ Opened 125 years ago, this wild, wooded national park covers more than 1500 sq

km of gorgeous Laurentian lakes, rivers, hills and woods. You'll find fantastic hiking and mountain-biking trails as well as camping and river routes for canoes. The half-day **Méandres de la Diable** route from Lac Chat to Mont de la Vache Noire is particularly popular. Reserve a canoe and a place on the shuttle bus by calling the park reservations line well in advance.

MONT-TREMBLANT VILLAGE   VILLAGE
(⛄) The village of Mont-Tremblant, some 4km southwest of the Mont-Tremblant Ski Resort (p147), is spread along the shores of pretty Lac Mercier. Here you'll find shops, cafes, B&Bs, restaurants and a pretty lakeside section of the Parc Linéaire du P'tit Train du Nord recreation path, perfect for exploring on foot or cross-country skis. In summer there are cruises out on the water; in winter the lake adjoining the municipal beach is converted into an ice rink, illuminated for skating until 10pm.

VAL-DAVID   VILLAGE
Tiny Val-David was a major hippie mecca in the '60s, a hangover still apparent today. The village has artisanal bakeries, jazz music in its cafes on summer weekends and more than its share of arts and crafts people. Studios and galleries line the main street, Rue de l'Église. The town's tourist office, in a cute old train station, is conveniently located alongside the Parc Linéaire du P'tit Train du Nord recreation trail. Check out the **Val-David farmers market** (Marché d'Été de Val-David; http://marchesdici.org/nos-marches/val-david/#marche-d-ete; Rue de l'Académie; ⊙9:30am-1:30pm Sat late May-early Oct) ✿ if you're in town on a Saturday morning.

STE-AGATHE-DES-MONTS   VILLAGE
This mountain village, located about 9km northwest of Val-David, has a prime location on Lac des Sables. By the beginning of the 1900s, it was a well-known spa town. Later, famous guests included Queen Elizabeth, who came during WWII, and Jackie Kennedy. Ste-Agathe is a stopover point on the Parc Linéaire du P'tit Train du Nord recreation path, making this a great option for cyclists and cross-country skiers.

Croisières Alouette (p148) offers 50-minute cruises on Lac des Sables.

ST-SAUVEUR-DES-MONTS VILLAGE

St-Sauveur-des-Monts (usually just called St-Sauveur) is the busiest village in the Laurentians and is often deluged with day-trippers due to its proximity to central Montréal (70km). A pretty church anchors Rue Principale, the attractive main street, which is lined with restaurants, cafes and stylish boutiques.

ST-FAUSTIN VILLAGE

The gateway to the Mont-Tremblant region, St-Faustin is home to pretty lakes and a gorgeous slice of protected Laurentian wilderness at **Centre Touristique Éducatif des Laurentides** (CTEL; ☏819-326-9072; www.ctel.ca; 5000 Chemin du lac Caribou; adult/child $10/free; ◷8am-5pm Sat-Thu, to 9pm Fri late Jun-early Sep, 8am-5pm Sat-Mon, to 9pm Fri mid-May–late-Jun & early Sep–mid-Oct; 🅿🚼) 🐾 20km to the south. Here you can hike an extensive trail network, and hire a kayak (three hours/day $20/30) or canoe ($25/40).

MUSÉE D'ART CONTEMPORAIN DES LAURENTIDES MUSEUM

(☏450-432-7171; www.museelaurentides.ca; 101 Pl du Curé-Labelle; by donation; ◷noon-5pm Tue- Fri & Sun, from 10am Sat) Less than an hour from Montréal, this contemporary-art museum has small but excellent exhibitions of work by regional artists. You'll also find the re-created study of writer Claude-Henri Grignon (1894–1976), best known for his novel *Un Homme et Son Péché* (The Woman and the Miser), who was born in nearby St-Adèle.

✖️ EATING

LE MOUTON NOIR FUSION $

(☏819-322-1571; www.bistromoutonnoir.com; 2301 Rue de l'Église; mains $7.50-14.50; ◷8am-10.30pm Mon-Thu, to 1am Fri, 10am-10:30pm Sat & Sun, closed Mon & Tue winter) This artsy spot attracts a very Val-Davidian crowd of beards – some hippie-esque, some hipster-esque, some lumberjack-y. Everyone enjoys the funky Canadian fusion on old LP menus; you gotta love a place that serves bibimbap alongside poutine. Open mike on Friday and live music on Saturday keep the 'Black Sheep' baaing till late on weekends.

★LA TABLÉE DES PIONNIERS QUÉBÉCOIS $$

(☏855-688-2101, 819-688-2101; www.latablee despionniers.com; 1357 Rue St-Faustin; 4-/5-/6-course set menu $38/45/55; ◷4:30-9:30pm Thu, 10am-10pm Fri-Sun late Feb-early May) For top-notch traditional Québécois cuisine in rustic country surroundings, don't miss this seasonal roadside eatery between Mont-Tremblant and Ste-Agathe. Multicourse menus, served during maple-sugaring and apple-harvest season, feature such delights as split pea, cabbage and bacon soup; smoked-trout soufflés; pulled-pork and mushroom puff-pastry pies; and maple-walnut tarts – all accompanied by cider from the family's orchard.

★ADÈLE BISTRO FRENCH $$

(☏450-229-4894; www.adelebistro.ca; 1241 Chemin du Chantecler; mains $21-32; ◷5-11pm Thu-Sun, 10am-3pm Sun) This stylish bistro opposite Lac Rond is the place to come if you want serious French dishes: goose liver, bone marrow, blood pudding, *carbonnade* (selection of chargrilled meats). Host Jean-Marc Gandroz from Burgundy will walk you through the extensive wine list. Don't miss the killer bergamot-tea-flavoured crème brûlée. One of our favorite places for a meal in the Laurentians.

★AU PETIT POUCET QUÉBÉCOIS $$

(☏819-322-2246, 888-334-2246; https://aupetit poucet.ca; 1030 Hwy 117; mains $9-21; ◷6:30am-4pm) For the ultimate Québécois dining experience, head for this rustic cabin a couple of kilometers south of the village. In place since 1945, it's every local's go-to place for huge breakfasts and such specialties as *tourtière* (meat pie), ham-hock ragout and cassoulet with smoked ham.

SEB CANADIAN $$$

(☏819-429-6991; www.seblartisanculinaire.com; 444 Rue St-Georges, Mont-Tremblant Centre Ville; mains $32-55, 4-/7-course set menu $49/85; ◷6-11pm Thu-Mon) 🐾 Escape the mediocre and get a little taste of what culinary artisans can create with seasonal, sustainable local ingredients. A flexible, eager-to-please kitchen, an unforgettable menu and a never-ending wine list enhance the jovial atmosphere. sEb is best described as alpine chalet meets globetrotter (think African masks) meets Hollywood chic (Michael Douglas is a regular). Reservations essential.

SUGAR SHACKS

Québec is the undisputed world champion of maple-sugar production, and there's a long-standing tradition of early-spring visits to *cabanes à sucre* (maple-sugar shacks); English-speaking Québecers refer to such trips as 'sugaring off.' With a roaring fire boiling the sap down into syrup, these cozy places can be found all over the province in March and April, including the Laurentians and the Eastern Townships.

For a list of more than 100 sugar shacks open to the public, see www.quebecoriginal. com. Here are a few shacks within easy driving distance of Montréal to get you started:

Cabane à Sucre Au Pied de Cochon (☑450-258-1732; https://aupieddecochon.ca; 11382 Rang de la Fresnière, St-Benoît de Mirabel; adult/child menu $65/20; ⊙5:30-8:30pm Thu & Fri, from 11am Sat & Sun mid-Feb–early May) This high-end version of the sugar-shack experience, 45-minutes west of Montréal, is brought to you by renowned Montréal chef Martin Picard. Tables fill up months in advance for his gourmet menu of maple-based delights; book well ahead.

Cabane du Pic-Bois (☑450-263-6060; www.cabanedupicbois.com; 1468 Chemin Gaspé, Brigham; adult/child $32/18; ⊙by reservation Fri Mar & Apr; ⊕) If you want to really gorge yourself, you can't do better than the all-you-can-eat spread at this traditional sugar shack. You get all the classics – omelettes, pork jowls, ham, maple sausage, beans and potatoes – plus cabbage salad dressed with Pic-Bois' famous maple vinegar. We'll gladly come back, even though they had to roll us out the door. It's about an hour east of Montréal and between Bromont and Cowansville.

Cabane à Sucre Bouvrette (☑450-438-4659; www.bouvrette.ca; 1000 Rue Nobel, St-Jérôme; menus $19-24; ⊙11:30am-8pm Tue-Sun Mar & Apr; ⊕) In business for seven decades, this enormous 'shack' 45-minutes north of Montréal serves a set menu that includes ham, bacon, sausages, *oreilles de crisse* (deep-fried pork jowls), fried potatoes, oven-baked 48-egg omelets, pea soup, baked beans, beet juice and homemade pickles, all slathered in maple syrup. Kids will love the petting zoo, old-fashioned locomotive and horse-drawn sleigh rides. For dessert don't miss the classic *tire d'érable* (maple taffy made by pouring hot, concentrated maple syrup over snow, then rolling the congealed syrup onto wooden sticks).

🏃 SPORTS & ACTIVITIES

★**PARC LINÉAIRE
DU P'TIT TRAIN DU NORD**   CYCLING

(Little Train of the North Linear Park; ☑450-745-0185; www.laurentides.com/parclineaire; cross-country skiing/cycling $14/free; ⊕) This awesome trail system is built on top of old railway tracks and snakes 232km north from Bois-de-Filion to Mont Laurier, passing streams, rivers, rapids, lakes and great mountain scenery. In summer it's open to bicycles and in-line skates, and you'll find rest stops, information booths, restaurants, B&Bs, and bike-rental and repair shops along the way.

Snow season lures cross-country skiers to the 42km-long section between St-Jérôme and Val-David, while snowmobile aficionados rule between Val-David and Mont Laurier (49km).

For bike rentals and shuttle services along the route, contact **Autobus Le Petit Train du Nord** (☑450-569-5596; www.autobus lepetittraindunord.com; rental bike per day/week $25/126; ⊙mid-May–mid-Oct).

MONT-TREMBLANT SKI RESORT   SKIING
(☑514-764-7546; www.tremblant.ca; 1000 Chemin des Voyageurs, Station Tremblant; lift ticket adult/youth/child $99/88/66; ⊙8:30am-4pm late Nov–mid-Apr; ⊕) Founded in 1938, this is among the top-ranked international ski resorts in eastern North America and includes the area's highest peak (875m), more than 100 trails and 14 lifts. Its state-of-the-art summer facilities and activities include golf courses, water sports, cycling, tennis courts, hiking, yoga and zip lines.

Bikes and skates can be rented at the ski center for the 10km skating/cycling path that runs up to the mountain's edge.

VIA FERRATA AU DIABLE CLIMBING

(📞800-665-6527; www.sepaq.com/pq/mot/index.dot; adult/child from $49/37; ⏱mid-Jun–mid-Oct) 🏊 A popular half-day guided climbing tour, the so-called 'Excursion' along the Via Ferrata scales the rock face of La Vache Noire to take in a stunning vista of Rivière du Diable with the Laurentians behind. No rock-climbing experience is needed as guides cover the basics and supply the equipment. Reservations can be made through the park.

Climbs for those with more experience include the 'Intermediary' (adult/youth $64/48) and the 'Great Escape' ($84/63).

À L'ABORDAGE OUTDOORS

(📞819-322-1234; http://alabordage.ca; 2268 Rue de l'Église; 3hr kayak tours adult/child from $35/26; ⏱9am-4:30pm late Jun-early Sep, 10am-3:30pm Sat & Sun May-late Jun & early Sep-Oct) Rents bicycles, kayaks and canoes, and can get you set up with kayaking and canoeing equipment. Also offers excellent guided tours on the Rivière du Nord.

CROISIÈRES ALOUETTE CRUISE

(📞0778-752-5098; www.croisierealouette.com; Quai Municipal; adult/youth/child $22/19/10.50; ⏱Jun-Oct) Croisières Alouette offers 50-minute cruises on Lac des Sables between two and five times a day.

🛏 SLEEPING

★AUBERGE LE LUPIN B&B $$

(📞819-425-5474; www.lelupin.com; 127 Rue Pinoteau, Mont-Tremblant Village; s $27-157, d $143-173; P🐾🍴🛜) Our favorite place to stay in Mont-Tremblant, this log house built in 1945 offers snug digs just 1km from the ski station, with private beach access to sparkling Lac Tremblant. The nine themed rooms are spacious and intelligently organised. The tasty breakfasts whipped up by hosts Pierre and Sylvie in the homey kitchen are a perfect start to the day.

As dog lovers, we wanted to take both resident wheaten terriers Petzl and Fofo home with us.

★AU CLOS ROLLAND B&B $$

(📞450-229-1939; www.auclosrolland.com; 1200 Rue St-Jean; s $115-130, d $120-145; 🍴🛜) Hidden in an otherwise-undistinguished neighborhood, this sprawling 1904 mansion

surrounded by vast grassy lawns is an absolute gem. The public spaces downstairs – a library with piano, living room with fireplace and pretty glass-walled breakfast room – are instantly inviting, while the seven guest rooms, including a couple tucked under the eaves, have cozy beds, wood floors and 'old-house' charm.

The B&B is only 300m from the Parc Linéaire du P'tit Train du Nord recreation path, making this a great option for cyclists and cross-country skiers. Swiss nationals Carolyne and Pierre-André are the consummate hosts; the multicourse breakfasts are the repasts of gourmets.

★LE PETIT CLOCHER B&B $$

(📞450-227-7576; www.lepetitclocher.com; 216 Rue de l'Église; s $165-215, d $185-235; P🍴🛜) A gorgeous inn occupying a converted Dominican monastery on a little hillside above town, Le Petit Clocher has seven rooms decorated in French Country style, many of which have extraordinary views. Our favorite room was once a chapel and has beautiful old wood-paneled walls.

The Eastern Townships

Explore

Lush rolling hills, crystal-clear lakes and checkerboard farms fill the Eastern Townships, or the Cantons-des-l'Est as they're known by French-speaking inhabitants. The region begins 80km southeast of Montréal and is squished between the labyrinth of minor highways that stretch all the way to the Vermont and New Hampshire borders. New Englanders will feel right at home: covered bridges and round barns dot the bumpy landscape, which is sculpted by the tail end of the US Appalachian mountain range.

A visit during spring is rewarding, as it's the season for 'sugaring off' – the tapping, boiling and preparation of maple syrup. In fall the foliage puts on a kaleidoscopic show of colors, to be toasted with freshly brewed apple cider, served in local pubs. The district is also home to a fast-growing wine region that produces some respectable whites and an excellent ice wine – a dessert wine made from frozen grapes.

....

The Best...

→ **Sight** Parc de la Gorge de Coaticook

→ **Place to Eat** Auberge Le Coeur d'Or (p152)

....

Top Tip

During the busy summer and fall foliage seasons, travel midweek to avoid the crowds and the two-night weekend minimum imposed by many B&Bs.

....

Getting There & Away

→ **Bus** Services are operated by **Limocar** (📞514-842-2281; http://limocar.ca) between Montréal's Gare d'Autocars (p241) and Bromont ($26, 1 to 2½ hours, 8:25am and 5:40pm), Lac Brome ($25, 1¾ hours, 8am – call ahead as this service is subject to passenger demand), Sutton ($25, 2¼ hours, 4:15pm weekdays, 8am and 12:30pm weekends), Magog ($32, 1½ to two hours, frequent) and Sherbrooke ($36, two to 2½ hours, frequent).

→ **Car** Autoroutes 10 Est (East) and 55 Sud (South).

....

Need to Know

→ **Area Code** 📞450, 📞819

→ **Location** 80km to 165km east and southeast of Montréal

→ **Tourist Office** (Maison du Tourisme des Cantons-de-l'Est; 📞450-375-8774; www. easterntownships.org; 100 Rue du Tourisme, Hwy 10, exit 68, St-Alphonse-de-Granby; ⏰8:30am-6pm Jun-Aug, reduced hours May, Sep & Oct)

⊙ SIGHTS

★**ABBAYE ST-BENOÎT-DU-LAC** MONASTERY
(📞819-843-4080; www.abbaye.ca; 1 Rue Principale, St-Benoît-du-Lac; ⏰church 5am-8:30pm, shop 9-10:45am & 11:45am-6pm Mon-Sat) Sitting on the western shore of Lac Memphrémagog, about 12km south of Magog, this complex is a striking blend of traditional and modern architecture, including a hallway awash in colorful tiles and a lofty church with exposed structural beams and brick walls. If you can, visit at 7:30am,

11am or 5pm, when the monks practice Gregorian chanting, famous throughout Québec. Equally famous are the monks' apple cider and finely made cheeses, available from the abbey's shop.

There's a hostel for men here and another for women at a nearby nunnery.

**PARC DE LA GORGE
DE COATICOOK** PARK
(📞819-849-2331; www.gorgedecoaticook.qc.ca; 400 Rue St-Marc, Coaticook; adult/child $7.50/4.50; ⏰information desk 9am-5pm; 🚸) Straddling a lovely forested gorge outside the town of Coaticook, this scenic park is famous for having the world's longest pedestrian suspension bridge. Visitors come for hiking, mountain biking and horseback riding in summer, and snow-tubing and snowshoeing in winter. You can also camp or stay in one of the park's cabins. The surrounding area boasts some of the Eastern Townships' prettiest scenery, not to mention some wonderful cheese makers (get the cheese-route brochure from the Coaticook tourist office).

Family-friendly attractions include a minifarm where kids can pet and feed animals and go on pony rides, as well as **Foresta Lumina** (📞819-849-2331; www.forestalumina.com; 135 Rue Michaud, Coaticook; adult/child $19.50/11.50; ⏰8:30-10:30pm Jul & Aug, Fri & Sat Jun, Sep & early Oct; 🚸), a summertime evening event in which forest trails are illuminated with colorful lights, creating magical effects.

NORTH HATLEY VILLAGE
All of the Eastern Townships are cute, but North Hatley is the geographic equivalent of a yawning puppy. It occupies an enchanting spot at the northern tip of the crystal-clear Lac Massawippi, about 17km east of Magog. This was a popular second home for wealthy US citizens who enjoyed the scenery – and the absence of Prohibition – during the 1920s. Many historic residences have been converted into inns and B&Bs. Popular summer activities include swimming, boating, admiring the lakeshore's natural beauty, and browsing the village's galleries, and antique and craft shops.

In summer English-language dramas, concerts and comedy acts play at the **Piggery Theatre** (📞819-842-2431; www.piggery.com; 215 Chemin Simard).

DAY TRIPS FROM MONTRÉAL THE EASTERN TOWNSHIPS

FRELIGHSBURG VILLAGE

(Rte 237, cnr Rte 213) A few kilometers from the Vermont border, this village makes a pleasant stop along the Eastern Townships Route des Vins (Wine Route). A cluster of stone and wood homes straddles the banks of the brook that runs through town, and the surrounding area is filled with apple orchards. Local eateries specialize in smoked fish and maple products; if you have a sweet tooth, don't miss the famous maple tarts at the old general store-cafe in the center of town.

SUTTON VILLAGE

Sutton is a little Loyalist town with a pretty main street where you can shop to your heart's content or let your hair down during après-ski partying – the ski area **Mont Sutton** (☑450-538-2545; www.mont-sutton.com; 671 Rue Maple; day tickets adult/child $68/38; ☺9am-4pm; 🖟) is nearby. One of southern Québec's most attractive villages, Sutton is popular with artsy types, who come to appreciate the scenic beauty of the surrounding landscape, dominated by the northern Green Mountains. The downtown strip is filled with cafes, restaurants, inns and B&Bs, along with a helpful **tourist office** (☑450-538-8455; https://tourismesutton.ca; 24a Rue Principale Sud; ☺11am-4pm, from 10am Fri, to 5pm Sat & Sun).

LAC BROME VILLAGE

A stroll around the cute downtown of Lac Brome, which teems with quality boutiques, art galleries, cafes and restaurants, is a fun way to spend an hour or two. Lac Brome is the name given to what is in fact seven amalgamated villages orbiting the eponymous lake, with Knowlton on the southern shore being the largest, most attractive village and considered its 'downtown.'

A favorite meal in this area is Lac Brome duck, which shows up frequently on the better menus and is celebrated with the town's annual **Canard en Fête** (Brome Lake Duck Festival; www.canardenfete.ca; 270 Victoria, Knowlton; ☺late Sep).

PARC NATIONAL DU MONT-MÉGANTIC NATIONAL PARK

(☑819-888-2941; www.sepaq.com/pq/mme; 189 Rte du Parc; adult/child $8.75/free; 🅿 🖟) 🖉 At the heart of a scenic and delightfully uncrowded area, this park holds megasized appeal for wilderness fans and stargazers. Encounters with moose, white-tailed deer, coyote and other wildlife are pretty much guaranteed as you roam the trails of this park.

PARC NATIONAL DU MONT ORFORD NATIONAL PARK

(☑819-843-9855; www.sepaq.com/pq/mor; 3321 Chemin du Parc, Orford; adult/child $8.75/

TRAVELING THE TOWNSHIPS

There are a number of interesting and well-signposted driving and cycling routes through the Eastern Townships. Visit www.easterntownships.org for more road-trip ideas and cycling itineraries. Full routes by car or bike are available online; click Discover.

Townships Trail (Chemin des Cantons; www.chemindescantons.qc.ca) This 419km driving circuit takes in most of the Townships' prettiest villages and scenery. Coming from Montréal, pick up the route in Granby, Knowlton or Sutton, then simply follow the signs as far as you like.

Route des Vins (www.laroutedesvins.ca) The Route des Vins threads its way past 22 wineries on a 121km ramble through the rolling country between Granby and the Vermont border. The route is well signposted from exits 48, 68 and 90 off Hwy 10. Variants of the route focus on gastronomy, outdoor activities and the arts; see the website for details.

Route des Sommets (Summit Drive; ☑800-363-5515; www.routedessommets.com) The Route des Sommets starts northeast of Sherbrooke at Parc Régional du Mont-Ham and winds 193km along the high mountain slopes north of the New Hampshire border, passing a series of villages and scenic lookouts between La Patrie and St-Adrien. This is a great option for viewing the spectacular fall colors of the Eastern Townships.

free, parking $8.50; ⓟ 🔄) Just outside the town of Magog, Mont Orford (853m) dominates the lush Parc National du Mont Orford. In winter the park is a cross-country and downhill skiing center; summer brings hiking (on 80km of trails), plus swimming, boating and camping on Lac Stukely and Lac Fraser. Canoe, kayak and ski rentals are available.

SHERBROOKE   VILLAGE

Sherbrooke is the commercial center of the area, a bustling city that's perfect for refueling on modern conveniences before returning to the Eastern Townships. The historic center, 'Vieux Sherbrooke,' sits at the confluence of two rivers and is bisected by Rue Wellington and Rue King, the main commercial arteries. Highlights include the city's small but well-conceived **Musée des Beaux-Arts** (☑619-821-2115; http://mbas.qc.ca; 241 Rue Dufferin; adult/student $10/7; ⊙10am-5pm Jul & Aug, noon-5pm Tue-Sun Sep-Jun), with works by Québécois and Canadian artists, and the 18km **Réseau Riverain** walking and cycling path along the Rivière Magog, which starts at Blanchard Park, west of downtown.

✖ EATING & DRINKING

GAÏA RESTO VÉGAN   VEGAN $
(☑450-534-2074; www.legaia.ca; 840 Rue Shefford; mains $9-15; ⊙8am-3pm Thu-Mon, also 5-8pm Fri & Sat; ✐) For vegans, Gaïa is easily the culinary drawcard for the Eastern Townships. Middle Eastern, South Asian and Québécois flavors go into knockout crepes, burgers, bowls and smoothies pretty enough to elicit oohs and ahs when served up. Details like cashew ricotta elevate fresh ingredients into gourmet dishes great enough to convince an omnivore; and staff have a local warmth. Reservations recommended.

LES SUCRERIES
DE L'ÉRABLE   BAKERY $
(☑450-298-5181; www.lessucreriesdelerable. com; 16 Rue Principale, Frelighsburg; mains $9-14; ⊙8:30am-5pm Thu-Sun; 🔄) Best known for its scrumptious maple pies, this bakery in an attractive old brick-walled general

ORFORD MUSIQUE

Each summer this renowned music academy, dating back to 1951, hosts the **Festival Orford Musique** (Centre d'Arts Orford; ☑819-843-3981; www.orford.mu; 3165 Chemin du Parc, Orford), a celebration of music and art that features more than 60 concerts by international musicians, with performances by guest artists as well as the academy's own advanced students. Between September and May, the center also hosts occasional lunch and dinner concerts featuring jazz and classical artists.

Its located just outside the national-park boundaries in the small township of Orford.

store in central Frelighsburg does double duty as a simple restaurant. Breakfast treats include waffles with blueberries, bananas, crème fraîche and maple sugar, while lunch revolves around salads and sandwiches. Try a bagel topped with local maple-smoked salmon, accompanied by a glass of local cider.

Save room for fresh maple ice cream or – of course – maple pie. In summer it's delightful to sit on the outdoor deck near the river out back.

LE RELAIS   FRENCH $$
(☑450-242-2232; www.aubergeknowlton.ca/relais; 286 Chemin Knowlton, Knowlton; lunch $12-21, dinner $14-35; ⊙11am-3pm & 5-10pm Mon-Fri, 8am-10pm Sat; 🕏) At **Auberge Knowlton** (☑450-242-6886; www.auberge-knowlton.ca; 286 Chemin Knowlton, Knowlton; d incl breakfast from $168; 🕏), this restaurant features juicy Lac Brome duck served many ways, such as duck ravioli in mushroom sauce, duck confit in orange sauce and duck livers with blackened butter. The many other options include pork tenderloin with calvados, veal piccata and garlic scampi, along with burgers, salads, soups and pasta. Guests of the hotel get a 10% discount.

In summer the tables on the upstairs terrace are much in demand.

★**AUBERGE LE
COEUR D'OR** QUÉBÉCOIS **$$$**

(✏819-842-4363; www.aubergelecoeurdor.com; 85 Rue School; 4-course meal $47; ⊙6-9pm, closed Mon & Tue Nov-Apr) For a delightful night out, head to this charming farmhouse inn. The restaurant's four- to five-course dinners make abundant use of local ingredients, including cheeses from Sherbrooke, rabbit from Stanstead, duck from Orford and smoked trout from East Hereford. Save room for profiteroles, chocolate mousse cake, or the Coeur d'Or's trademark trio of crème brûlées.

SIBOIRE MICROBREWERY

(✏819-565-3636; www.siboire.ca; 80 Rue du Dépôt; ⊙6am-3am Mon-Fri, from 7:30am Sat & Sun) Sherbrooke's historic train depot houses this atmospheric microbrewery with nearly a dozen beers on tap, including Siboire's own IPA, wheat beer, oatmeal stout, Irish red ale and seasonal maple scotch ale. High ceilings, brick walls and a flower-fringed summer terrace create an inviting atmosphere for drinking everything in and enjoying some of the tastiest fish and chips in the Townships.

 SHOPPING

BROME LAKE DUCK FARM FOOD

(✏450-242-3825; www.canardsdulacbrome. com; 40 Chemin Centre; ⊙8am-5pm Mon-Thu, to 6pm Fri, 9am-6pm Sat, 10am-5pm Sun) Lac Brome is famous for its ducks, which have been bred here since 1912 on a special diet that includes soy and vitamins. Pick up pâté and other products at this shop; there's a second branch in Montréal.

 **SLEEPING**

★**LE PLEASANT
HÔTEL & CAFÉ** HISTORIC HOTEL **$$**

(✏450-538-6188; www.lepleasant.com; 1 Rue Pleasant; r $125-259; ❄@⚡) This luxurious inn is a great place for a weekend escape or romantic interlude. Some of the sleek and modern rooms – well balanced by a classically historical facade – have views of Mont Sutton (p150), and the breakfasts are memorable.

The owners can help you take a shuttle bus to Mont Sutton, which stops conveniently across the road.

À L'ANCESTRALE B&B B&B **$$**

(✏819-847-5555; www.ancestrale.com; 200 Rue Abbott; r incl breakfast $109-139; @⚡) Wake up to a five-course gourmet breakfast at this intimate retreat. The five rooms are dressed in a romantic, countrified way and outfitted with refrigerators and coffeemakers. It's central but on a quiet street.

★**MANOIR HOVEY** RESORT **$$$**

(✏819-842-2421; www.manoirhovey.com; 575 Rue Hovey; d from $300, dinner & breakfast incl from $505; ℗❄@⚡⛱) This lovely resort offers handsomely set rooms in a picturesque lakeside setting. You'll find expansive gardens, a heated pool and an ice rink (in winter), and you can arrange numerous outdoor activities – windsurfing, lake cruises and golfing. The award-winning restaurant **Le Hatley** is among the best in the Eastern Townships, with four-course meals highlighting refined Québécois fare ($80 for nonguests).

Sleeping

Montréal's accommodation scene is blessed with a tremendous variety of rooms and styles. Though rates aren't particularly cheap, they are reasonable by international standards – or even compared with other Canadian cities such as Toronto or Vancouver. Reserve at least a month in advance for budget accommodations, or to snap up any discounts.

Luxury & Boutique Hotels

Montréal has many choices when it comes to high-end lodging. You'll find top names such as Ritz-Carlton, Sofitel, Fairmont and other luxury brands. But you'll also find plenty of homegrown places such as the Hôtel Le St-James and the Hôtel Nelligan. The big full-service luxury hotels are largely downtown.

For more of the boutique experience, Old Montréal has the best selection. Many of the best are set inside 18th-century buildings and blend original details – stone walls, timber ceilings – with updated interiors (big windows and marble-filled baths). While prices tend to be high at these places, you can find some great deals. This is especially true in low season even if you book at the last minute. Keep an eye out for cut-rate weekend deals and online specials.

Small Hotels & B&Bs

Small, European-style hotels are a Montréal specialty. Located downtown and in the Quartier Latin, they occupy Victorian-era homes that are plain and functional or comfy and charming. Prices are graded by facilities (eg with sink, toilet and/or full bath), and all must legally provide heating – but not cooling, with few rooms offering air-con.

B&Bs are a wonderful alternative. Many of them are set in attractive, 19th-century stone houses close to the Plateau's bar-and-restaurant strips of Blvd St-Laurent and Rue St-Denis, or near Rue Ste-Catherine Est in the Village. The many B&Bs offer heaps of character – the precious commodity that can make all the difference – and their owners are often invaluable sources of travel advice. There are many comfortable but bland chain hotels in town, which may be useful in peak season when the B&Bs and guesthouses are booked solid.

Budget Sleeps

Montréal has an abundance of good budget accommodations. Apart from the usual dorm beds, hostels may offer basic single and double rooms – though these are often booked out weeks in advance. In addition, the universities throw open their residence halls to non-students in summer; prices are competitive.

Planning in advance is key to finding accommodations during big events. The summertime festival season, from late June to the end of August, is the peak period, and conventions can crimp availability in late summer.

Sleeping with Locals

Websites such as Airbnb have hundreds of listings in Montréal. If you don't mind sharing, staying with a local is a great way to get an insider's take on the city. If you are visiting in a group, having a whole place to yourselves can be better value than a hotel. And if you're after a flashy apartment for your stay in the city, renting local is one of the best ways to go.

NEED TO KNOW

Price Ranges
The following price ranges refer to the cost of a double room in high season.

$ less than $100

$$ $100–$250

$$$ more than $250

Room Rates
➡ The average room rate is around $150, with some seasonal fluctuations (rates fall by about 30% January through March).

➡ Prices quoted generally do not include taxes – adding another 19% or so.

➡ Hotels charge a premium during the Grand Prix (late May through early June). Check websites for details.

Booking Services
Book your hotel well in advance. Good places to browse listings:

Lonely Planet (www. lonelyplanet.com/canada/montreal/hotels) Find independent reviews, as well as recommendations on the best places to stay.

BBCanada (www. bbcanada.com) B&Bs in Montréal and beyond.

Tourisme Montréal (www.mtl.org) Extensive listings from the city's tourism authority.

Lonely Planet's Top Choices

Hôtel Gault (p156) One of the city's top boutique stays, in a great location in Old Montréal.

L Hotel (p155) A lavish hotel that's packed with artwork by Warhol, Stella and other luminaries.

Hôtel Le Germain (p159) Designer looks for an ultracomfortable stay downtown.

M Montreal (p160) One of the city's best hostels, with a rooftop spa.

Best by Budget

$

Auberge St-Paul (p155) Friendly neat hostel in a great Old Montréal location.

M Montreal (p160) A great place to meet other travelers, with a first-rate roof garden.

Le Gîte du Plateau Mont-Royal (p157) Top pick with its rooftop terrace and location near 'the Mountain'.

$$

Auberge Les Bons Matins (p158) Great value for suites with spas and fireplaces.

Hotel Parc Suites (p159) Spacious, attractively designed suites, all with kitchenettes.

Auberge De La Fontaine (p162) Appealing place, particularly the suites with in-room spas and park views.

$$$

Hôtel Nelligan (p156) With one of the best rooftop patios in the city, the Nelligan wins with its old-world setting and great staff.

Hôtel Le St-James (p156) Refined opulence in a 19th-century building in Old Montréal.

Ritz-Carlton (p159) The Ritz sparkles with elegant decor and world-class service.

Best B&Bs

Accueil Chez François (p162) Delicious breakfasts, friendly hosts and good-value rooms.

Alacoque B&B Revolution (p158) Great value for the attractive rooms and cooked breakfast.

Best Heritage Stays

Auberge Bonaparte (p157) Delve into the past at this inn that would make its namesake proud.

Auberge du Vieux-Port (p156) Original details from the 1880s, plus waterfront views.

Auberge Bishop Downtown (p157) Budget hostel with 1800s manor-house features.

Best Funky Stays

Héritage Victorien (p161) Period-style rooms are named after the 19th-century family members who resided here.

Hôtel de l'Institut (p163) Great prices and hard-working staff at this training ground for aspiring hoteliers.

A la Carte B&B (p162) Get off the beaten path at this lovely inn in Montréal's east.

Le Petit Hôtel (p156) Rooms come in S, M, L and XL at this boutique stay.

La Citadelle (p160) Feels like a new midrange hotel, but it's actually a student dorm outside summer.

Where to Stay

NEIGHBORHOOD	FOR	AGAINST
Old Montréal	Ultraconvenient for many sights, old-world charm, access to Old Port.	Crowded with tourists at peak times, few inexpensive rooms, hard to find parking.
Downtown	Convenient for public transport and sights throughout the city. Plentiful budget eating.	Can be congested, with few inexpensive options compared with other districts.
Rue St-Denis & the Village	Semiresidential area with bohemian charm, restaurants and cafes. The most gay-friendly area. Well-connected transport hub to across the city.	Somewhat remote from central sights; many store closures. Noise on weekend nights from bars and clubs.
Plateau Mont-Royal & the Northeast	Home to the city's most charming B&Bs; atmospheric neighborhood with many parks; top family attractions.	Removed from central downtown and Old Montréal.

🛏 Old Montréal

Old Montréal has the city's most atmospheric – and highest-priced – hotel rooms. Over the last decade or so, many of the area's old buildings have been converted into impeccable boutique hotels with unique ambience and careful, confident service. The proliferation of such distinctive hotels has also inflated the area's B&B and inn rates.

AUBERGE ST-PAUL HOSTEL $
Map p268 (☑438-386-1339; www.aubergesaintpaul.com; 347 Rue St-Paul Est; dm $26-34, d with shared bath $70-77; ⓟ❄️📶; ⓜChamp-de-Mars) In an excellent Old Montréal location, this well-maintained hostel has clean-swept rooms with old stone walls, comfortable mattresses and good natural light, with some windows facing onto the picturesque Marché Bonsecours (p55) across the road. The welcome is warm and friendly, and all the usual hostel features are here: in-room lockers, kitchen and laundry access, free coffee and tea.

This is a good place to meet other travelers; the hostel arranges pub crawls, music jam sessions, weekend trips out of town and other activities.

AUBERGE ALTERNATIVE HOSTEL $
Map p268 (☑514-282-8069; www.aubergealternative.qc.ca; 358 Rue St-Pierre; dm incl tax $21-30, r $80-105; @📶; ⓜSquare-Victoria) This laid-back hostel near the Old Port has a bohemian vibe with an inviting cafe-restaurant where you can mingle with other travelers or enjoy an organic breakfast ($5 extra). Guests bunk in trim, colorfully painted dorms that accommodate anywhere from four to 20 people. There's a laundry and no curfew.

★L HOTEL BOUTIQUE HOTEL $$
Map p268 (☑514-985-0019; www.lhotelmontreal.com; 262 Rue St-Jacques Ouest; d $219-379; ⓟ❄️📶; ⓜSquare-Victoria) Inside a grand 1870 building, L Hotel is a major draw for art lovers. Georges Marciano, founder of Guess jeans, opened the hotel in 2010, showering great artworks throughout the rooms and common areas. You might sleep in a room with an original piece by Andy Warhol, Roy Lichtenstein or Frank Stella, or one of scores of other famed artists.

The rooms themselves are uniquely designed (though most tend toward a more refined classical look than a pop-art aesthetic); all have big windows, high ceilings and luxury finishings.

LOFTS DU VIEUX-PORT APARTMENT $$
Map p268 (☑514-876-9119; www.loftsduvieuxport.com; 97 Rue de la Commune Est; apt $252-499; ❄️) Run by the Auberge du Vieux-Port (p156), these lofts are a good-value option for those who need more space and want to remain in Old Montréal. You'll find small studios and one- and two-bedroom apartments. Book online or at the Auberge.

★ HÔTEL GAULT
BOUTIQUE HOTEL $$$

Map p268 (☑514-904-1616; www.hotelgault.com; 449 Rue Ste-Hélène; r from $245; P ✳ @ 🛜; M Square-Victoria) The Gault delivers beauty and comfort in its 30 spacious rooms. Lovely 19th-century architectural details figure in some rooms, with exposed brick or stone walls, though for the most part it boasts a fashion-forward, contemporary design. Rooms have extremely comfortable beds, ergonomic chairs, high ceilings, huge windows and spotless bathrooms (some with two-person bathtubs) with heated tile floors.

iPads are available upon request.

★ HÔTEL NELLIGAN
BOUTIQUE HOTEL $$$

Map p268 (☑514-788-2040; www.hotelnelligan. com; 106 Rue St-Paul Ouest; d/ste from $225/360; P ✳ @ 🛜; M Place-d'Armes) Housed in two restored buildings and named in honor of Québec's famous and tragic poet, Émile Nelligan (p230), this Old Montréal beauty has original details (such as exposed brick or stone) and luxurious fittings (down comforters, high-quality bath products, and Jacuzzis in some rooms). **Verses**, a plush bar and restaurant, is next door, with a magnificent roof patio, **Terrasse Nelligan**.

HÔTEL LE ST-JAMES
BOUTIQUE HOTEL $$$

Map p268 (☑514-841-3111; www.hotellestjames. com; 355 Rue St-Jacques; r/ste from $342/413; P ✳ @ 🛜; M Square-Victoria) Housed in the former Merchants Bank, the Hôtel Le St-James is a world-class establishment. Lavish guest rooms have beautiful antique furnishings, with oil paintings adorning the walls. There's a candlelit spa, a library and high-tea service. The concierge and staff are particularly kind and helpful, but for dining you're better off looking elsewhere.

PLACE D'ARMES
HOTEL $$$

Map p268 (☑514-842-1887; www.hotelplace darmes.com; 55 Rue St-Jacques; r/ste from $270/378; P ✳ 🛜; M Place-d'Armes) Spread among three regal buildings on the edge of Place d'Armes (p51), this luxury hotel has stylish rooms, excellent service and a historic location. Rooms have first-class fittings – antique moldings, brick or stone walls, black granite and white marble in the bathrooms, and an entertainment system. Even small quarters feel spacious thanks to views of Mont-Royal or the Basilique Notre-Dame.

There's a full-service spa, fitness center, restaurant and bar, but the crowning touch is the splendid rooftop patio, Terrasse Place d'Armes (p62), which on a summertime night is a magnet for the beautiful crowd.

AUBERGE DU VIEUX-PORT
BOUTIQUE HOTEL $$$

Map p268 (☑888-660-7678; www.aubergedu vieuxport.com; 97 Rue de la Commune Est; r $290-430; P ✳ 🛜; M Champ-de-Mars) Set in an 1882 warehouse, this is a stylish boutique hotel with exposed brick or stone walls, wooden beams, wrought-iron beds, high-quality furnishings (including occasional antiques) and big windows overlooking the waterfront. For more space and seclusion (a kitchen, multiple rooms), you can book one of its minimalist lofts (p155) in a separate building around the corner.

LE PETIT HÔTEL
BOUTIQUE HOTEL $$$

Map p268 (☑514-940-0360; www.petithotel montreal.com; 168 Rue St-Paul Ouest; r $242-372; P ✳ @ 🛜; M Place-d'Armes) Set in a 19th-century building, Le Petit Hôtel uses 'small', 'medium', 'large' and 'extra large' to describe its four room classes – identical save for the size. Owned by the same group as the Hôtel Place d'Armes, rooms boast a sleek, contemporary design (polished wood floors, atmospheric lighting and goose-down comforters), while showcasing the old stone walls in some rooms.

You'll also find iPod docking stations, free bike hire and dashes of color – orange – that give a creative zing to the overall look. There's a small spa here and an enticing little cafe, with down-tempo beats, on the ground floor.

ÉPIK
BOUTIQUE HOTEL $$$

Map p268 (☑514-842-2634; www.epikmon treal.com; 171 Rue St-Paul Ouest; d/ste from $300/2250; P ✳ 🛜; M Place-d'Armes) Set in a 1723 structure, the Épik is a boutique hotel with loads of charm. Its 10 beautifully designed rooms have wood-beam ceilings, stone walls and other original details, plus modern flourishes (flat-screen TVs), sleek bathrooms with rain showers, leather armchairs or sofas and elegant bedside lamps.

Enjoy fluffy croissants and fresh-brewed coffee in the morning; in the evening stop in the restaurant for wine and tapas.

HÔTEL ST-PAUL
BOUTIQUE HOTEL **$$$**

Map p268 (☎514-380-2222; www.hotelstpaul. com; 355 Rue McGill; d $284-300, ste $314-490; P✳@🛜; MSquare-Victoria) The lobby greets you with a fireplace flickering inside a wall of glowing alabaster – a fine introduction to this beaux-arts hotel on the edge of Old Montréal. Set along dimly lit hallways, the rooms and suites feature high-end mattresses, ambient lighting and large windows – though the design feels a little sparse in the lower-category accommodations.

AUBERGE BONAPARTE
INN **$$$**

Map p268 (☎514-844-1448; www.bonaparte. com; 447 Rue St-François-Xavier; r $195-289, ste $475; ✳🛜; MPlace-d'Armes) Wrought-iron beds and Louis Philippe furnishings lend a suitably Napoleonic touch to this historic 30-room inn, a former judge's residence built in 1886. The best rooms are warmly decorated and boast high ceilings, dormer windows and bronze lamps. Low-end rooms can seem a little dark and dowdy; some guests are disappointed with the lack of in-room coffeemakers.

Those at the rear overlook a pretty garden with views of the Basilique Notre-Dame (p48). Breakfast is served in the fine **Bonaparte Restaurant**, which has been done up in Napoleonic Imperial style. There's also a pleasant rooftop terrace.

AUBERGE BONSECOURS
INN **$$$**

Map p268 (☎514-396-2662; www.auberge bonsecours.com; 353 Rue St-Paul Est; s/d $180-220; P✳🛜; MChamp-de-Mars) The unusual ambience of these renovated stables lends this secluded hotel particular appeal. All six rooms have exposed-brick walls, a cheerful color scheme, designer lighting and floral linen, but each room is cut differently – the front-facing room with pine floors and sloping ceiling is especially popular. All quarters are set around an inner courtyard, remaining blissfully quiet at night.

INTERCONTINENTAL MONTRÉAL
LUXURY HOTEL **$$$**

Map p268 (☎514-987-9900; www.montreal. intercontinental.com; 360 Rue St-Antoine Ouest; d $286-386; P✳@; MSquare-Victoria) This enormous InterContinental has a unique location between a high-rise and a restored annex of the 19th-century Nordheimer building. The 357 rooms have a modern, contemporary design done in earth tones

and are fairly spacious. The turret suites are particularly attractive, with superb views to Mont-Royal. There are extensive facilities, including a sauna, 15m lap pool, bar and restaurant.

🛏 Downtown

The city center is the bastion of the business hotel and large, upper-end chains, but there are some interesting independent hotels, B&Bs and budget establishments scattered throughout the area.

HÔTEL Y MONTRÉAL
HOTEL **$**

Map p272 (☎514-866-9942; www.hotelymon treal.com; 1355 Blvd René-Lévesque Ouest; r $90-130, r with shared bath $55-90; ✳@🛜; MLucien-L'Allier) The YWCA's hotel welcomes both sexes to rooms that are basic but clean – and good value for the city. If you don't mind sharing a bathroom, opt for the Auberge floor, with clean, quite small private rooms with a sink. Despite the location on busy Blvd René-Lévesque, it's fairly quiet, with rooms on the 6th and 7th floors.

Guests can use the kitchen or laundry facilities, and there's a thrift shop and unaffiliated cafe on the ground floor. Unfortunately, the Y no longer lives up to its name – there's no fitness center or pool. Money raised goes to Y programs.

AUBERGE BISHOP DOWNTOWN
HOSTEL **$**

Map p272 (☎514-508-8870; https://auberge bishop.ca; 1447 Rue Bishop; dm $23-30; 🍴🛜; MGuy-Concordia) You might never guess that this is a hostel, seeing the winding wooden staircase, stained-glass windows and old French fireplaces in this 1800s brick manor house. Metal beds are comfortable and quiet, though it's worth upgrading for fewer people in the room; it can get cramped in the triple-stacked bunks. There's a modern white bathroom and shared kitchen.

LE GÎTE DU PLATEAU MONT-ROYAL
HOSTEL **$**

Map p272 (Auberge du Plateau Mont-Royal; ☎514-284-1276, 877-350-4483; www.hostelmontreal. com; 185 Rue Sherbrooke Est; d & tw from $83, dm/d/tr with shared bath from $28/69/69; @🛜; MSherbrooke) This popular youth hostel at the southern end of the Plateau (and the western edge of downtown) has all the expected hostel features (kitchen access, laundry room and lounge), though rooms and facilities are basic. Staff are friendly, and the rooftop terrace and communal lounge are fine places to meet other travelers.

HI-MONTREAL HOSTEL   HOSTEL $

Map p272 (☎514-843-3317; www.hostelling montreal.com; 1030 Rue Mackay; dm $36-40, r $55-110; ❄@☎; ⓂLucien-L'Allier) This large, well-equipped HI hostel has bright, well-maintained dorm rooms (all with air-con) with four to 10 beds, and a handful of private en suite rooms. Rooms are small and, depending on your bunkmates, can feel cramped. Energetic staff organize daily activities and outings (pub crawls, bike tours, day trips), plus there's a lively cafe-bar on the ground floor.

You'll save cash (around $5 per night) with a HI card. There's no curfew and bike hire is available. Reservations are strongly recommended in summer.

HOTEL ZERO 1   HOTEL $$

Map p272 (☎514-871-9696; www.zero1-mtl.com; 1 Blvd René-Lévesque Est; r from $170; ❄☎; ⓂSt-Laurent) This jazzy updated hotel has modern rooms painted in dark, matte-like tones, each with a small kitchenette (minifridge, microwave and sink) and a tiny table and chairs. Rooms in the lower category (Pop) are quite small. There's a lounge-like vibe throughout, and it's steps away from the eateries of Chinatown, or a short stroll (uphill) to Old Montréal.

Avoid the lower floors due to street noise.

MANOIR AMBROSE   HOTEL $$

Map p272 (☎514-288-6922; https://hotel ambrose.ca; 3422 Rue Stanley; d $97-150; ❄☎; ⓂPeel) This hotel consists of two merged Victorian homes in a quiet residential area. Its 21 rooms are comfortably furnished in neutral tones, and all have flat-screen TVs as well as plenty of natural light. The whitewashed brickwork and vintage doors as decor give Ambrose a converted-loft vibe. The on-site cafe is a nice place to start the day.

The best rooms are upstairs, so you'll have to hoof it up two or three flights (no lift). Staff are friendly and the location is decent.

HOTEL MANOIR SHERBROOKE   HOTEL $$

Map p272 (☎514-845-0915; http://manoir sherbrooke.ca; 157 Rue Sherbrooke Est; d $129-149; ☎; ⓂSherbrooke) This engaging conversion of two fine Victorian houses is replete with atmosphere. Its 30 rooms range from small standards to spacious deluxes. The budget rooms are small but cozy with a warm color scheme and attractive furnishings. The best rooms have oversized gilded mirrors, decorative fireplaces and Jacuzzis. Staff are friendly.

AUBERGE LES BONS MATINS   BOUTIQUE HOTEL $$

Map p272 (☎514-931-9167; www.bonsmatins. com; 1401 Ave Argyle; d/ste from $110/160; ❄☎; ⓂLucien-L'Allier) The Bons Matins has spacious rooms with gorgeous art, hardwood floors, brick walls and delicious breakfasts. The walk-up rooms are spread out over stately traditional town houses, and the entire affair is conveniently located at the edge of downtown.

HOTEL 10   BOUTIQUE HOTEL $$

Map p272 (☎514-843-6000; www.hotel10mon treal.com; 10 Rue Sherbrooke Ouest; d/tw from $195/221; P❄☎; ⓂSt-Laurent) Set in a minimalist art-nouveau building, this designer hotel has contemporary rooms with grays, silvers and creams – giving them an ethereal quality. The bathrooms are sleek and modern (with separate soaking tubs in deluxe rooms), and upper floors have fine views. High marks for the soft, fluffy towels and bathrobes. Avoid the noisy rooms on the lower floors.

L'ABRI DU VOYAGEUR   HOTEL $$

Map p272 (☎514-849-2922; www.abri-voya geur.ca; 9 Rue Ste-Catherine Ouest; r $130-190; P❄☎; ⓂSt-Laurent) It's on a seedy stretch of Rue Ste-Catherine but if you're not turned off by the nearby sex clubs (no pun intended), you can enjoy clean, cozy rooms with exposed-brick walls, wood floors and comfortable furnishings. Some rooms are spacious with tiny kitchenettes, while others could use more natural light. Overall, it's good value for money.

ALACOQUE B&B REVOLUTION   B&B $$

Map p272 (☎514-842-0938; www.bbrevolu tion.com; 2091 Rue St-Urbain; s/d without bath $95/120; P❄☎; ⓂPlace-des-Arts) This little place offers good rates for its simply furnished rooms. Exposed-brick walls and homey touches create a warm ambience, but some beds and furnishings need refreshing. Guests have access to the whole house (kitchen, terrace, garden, dining

THE B&B CONNECTION

For an overview of the many charming B&Bs across the city, visit B&B Canada (www.bbcanada.com). It currently has more than 20 B&Bs listed for Montréal, with photos, room descriptions and reviews.

If you show up in Montréal without a reservation and don't feel like making the rounds, you can always book a place through the city's main tourist office, **Centre Infotouriste** (🖉514-844-5400; www.quebecoriginal.com; 1255 Rue Peel; ⊘9am-5pm; 🛜; Ⓜ Peel). Keep in mind that it can only book you a room in a guesthouse with which it has an affiliation.

---

room and laundry). The included breakfasts are good (croissants, baked goods, homemade jams and eggs cooked to order). There's free parking.

HOTEL PARC SUITES   HOTEL $$

Map p272 (🖉514-985-5656; www.parcsuites.com; 3463 Ave du Parc; r/ste from $159/218; Ⓟ ✳🛜; Ⓜ Place-des-Arts) Although the building doesn't look promising, this eight-room all-suites guesthouse is a great place to base yourself while exploring Montréal. The accommodations range from small studios to only marginally more expensive one-bedroom suites, with a comfy living/dining area and adjoining kitchenette, plus a separate bedroom – all tastefully furnished in a bright, contemporary style.

★HÔTEL LE GERMAIN   BOUTIQUE HOTEL $$$

Map p272 (🖉514-849-2050; www.germainmontreal.com; 2050 Rue Mansfield; r from $255; Ⓟ ✳🛜; Ⓜ Peel) This stylish hotel boasts luxurious rooms with dark wood details (headboard, wood blinds), cream-colored walls, sheer curtains and artful lighting. You'll find all the creature comforts, such as goose-down duvets, gadget docks and rainfall showers; the bathrooms have a touch of the eccentric with one big window into the room. (Superior rooms have only a shower.) Service is friendly and professional.

RITZ-CARLTON   LUXURY HOTEL $$$

Map p272 (🖉514-842-4212; www.ritzmontreal.com; 1228 Rue Sherbrooke Ouest; r from $556; Ⓟ ✳@🛜⊠🛏; Ⓜ Peel) This grande dame of Montréal has been impressing guests ever since Liz Taylor and Richard Burton got married here. For its 2012 centenary, it reopened after a four-year, $200-million renovation, with only half as many rooms as before and a new set of luxury residences. Rooms are ultraopulent, with classic touches and impeccable service.

SOFITEL   LUXURY HOTEL $$$

Map p272 (🖉514-285-9000; www.sofitel.com; 1155 Rue Sherbrooke Ouest; d from $275; Ⓟ ✳@🛜; Ⓜ Peel) A solid link in the French luxury chain (and the only Sofitel in Canada), this hotel has stylish, modern rooms and a European feel. Staff hit the right note of sophistication without too much snobbery and the rooms are modern and bright with oversized windows and a subdued color scheme (save for the rich red duvets) with blond-wood details.

HOTEL LE CRYSTAL   BOUTIQUE HOTEL $$$

Map p272 (🖉514-861-5550; www.hotellecrystal.com; 1100 Rue de la Montagne; ste from $229; Ⓟ ✳🛜🛏; Ⓜ Bonaventure) This all-suite boutique hotel is a great spot for a sleeping splurge. The business-casual rooms have great views over the city and are arranged around a lobby decked out like a modern-art exhibit. To round out the indulgence, hop into the pool and take in the city skyline.

HOTEL BONAVENTURE   LUXURY HOTEL $$$

Map p272 (🖉8514-878-2332; www.hotelbonaventure.com; 900 Rue de La Gauchetière Ouest; d from $249; Ⓟ ✳@🛜🛏; Ⓜ Bonaventure) Once part of the Hilton chain, today the Bonaventure is locally owned and has all the deluxe amenities you'd expect in a luxury hotel. All rooms have on-command movies, mahogany furniture, marbled bathrooms and large working areas – and most have panoramic views of downtown. The highlight is the 1-hectare rooftop garden with heated pool, open year-round.

It's connected to the underground city, so you can move around downtown without braving the cold if you visit in winter.

CASTEL DUROCHER   APARTMENT $$$

Map p272 (🖉514-282-1697; www.casteldurocher.com; 3488 Rue Durocher; 1-/2-bedroom apt

$199/259; P✳@🛜; MMcGill) This family-run establishment occupies a tall, turreted stone house on a peaceful, tree-lined street near McGill University. Those seeking self-sufficiency will find one- or two-bedroom apartments with kitchen units, homey furnishings and artwork covering the walls (the multitalented Belgian owner is an artist, novelist and chocolate-maker extraordinaire). There are discounts for long-term stays.

LOEW'S

HOTEL VOGUE   LUXURY HOTEL $$$

Map p272 (📞514-285-5555; www.loewshotels.com/montreal-hotel; 1425 Rue de la Montagne; d from $269; P✳🛜; MPeel) This upmarket hotel blends French-empire style with modern luxury. You'll find flat-screen TVs attached to the oversized marble Jacuzzis and nicely furnished rooms (though somewhat lacking in individuality). Staff are friendly and efficient, and there's a charming Parisian-style bistro and a small classy bar on-site.

🛏 Rue St-Denis & the Village

You'll find a good mix of options in the nightlife-charged areas of Rue St-Denis and the Village. Delightful, superb-quality B&Bs dominate the choices in this part of town. This is also a good place to base yourself, with excellent metro connections and walking access to both downtown and Old Montréal – plus the Plateau is just up the hill.

★M MONTREAL   HOSTEL $

Map p276 (📞514-845-9803; www.m-montreal.com; 1245 Rue St-André; dm $18-36, d $84-130; ✳🛜❄; MBerri-UQAM) One of Québec's best hostels, M Montreal makes an excellent base while exploring the city. Dorms are nicely outfitted like Japanese sleeping pods, with privacy curtains, beds that don't squeak, underbed lockers and modern en suites. Private rooms resemble snazzy apartments with kitchenettes and microwaves. The rooftop Jacuzzis are

---

LONGER-TERM RENTALS

The universities offer good deals from May to August, though you should not expect much more than dormitory amenities for the longer-term options.

This residence hall at Université de Québec à Montréal (UQAM) offers tidy modern studio **apartments** (Map p276; 📞514-987-6669; www.residences-uqam.qc.ca; 303 Blvd René-Lévesque Est; studio $63-83; ⊘mid-May–mid-Aug; P✳@🛜; MBerri-UQAM) with small, fully equipped kitchens in a convenient location not far from the nightlife along Rue St-Denis. It's set in a rather charmless building, and the quarters are simple, but the price is hard to beat. Rooms are available only during the summer. Private rooms in shared apartments are available from $45. There's a laundry and a cafe on-site. A second location (at 2100 Rue St-Urbain) near Place des Arts has similar features.

In summer McGill also opens its student residence halls to travelers. Lodging is in one of five buildings, each varying in price and features. The pick of the bunch is **La Citadelle** (Map p272; 📞514-398-8650; www.mcgill.ca/accommodations/summer; 410 Rue Sherbrooke Ouest; r/ste $119/149; ⊘mid-May–mid-Aug; P✳🛜; MPlace-des-Arts), a renovated 26-story high-rise with small, handsomely designed rooms with flat-screen TVs, modern bathrooms, plush bedding and superb views (not the dorm rooms we remember). Excellent location.

Other McGill summer options include the nearby hotel-style **Carrefour Sherbrooke** (rooms $109 to $139), the 1960s **New Residence Hall** (rooms $89) at the foot of Mont-Royal, the budget-oriented **Royal Victoria College** (single/double/triple $45/65/85) and the inviting Solin Hall with studios and two-, three- and four-bedroom apartments, near the Atwater market and the Lachine Canal. Check online for details.

The modern high-rise **Trylon Apartments** (Map p272; 📞514-843-3971; www.trylon.ca; 3463 Rue Ste-Famille; apt per day/week from $102/587; P✳🛜❄; MPlace-des-Arts) are a plush alternative to top-end hotels at a fraction of the price. The small studios and one-bedroom apartments have contemporary furnishings with kitchenettes, and access to the indoor swimming pool.

flashy for a hostel. The 747 airport bus passes nearby.

There's usually something on: live music and comedy, movie nights, karaoke or beer pong. You can also join in on regularly scheduled pub crawls and walking tours.

LE GÎTE DU PARC
LA FONTAINE   HOSTEL $

Map p276 (📞514-522-3910; www.hostelmon treal.com; 1250 Rue Sherbrooke Est; dm $22, s/ tw/d with shared bath from $45/68/72; ☉Jun-Aug; @🛜; ⓂSherbrooke) This great summertime option in a converted Victorian house feels more like a guesthouse than a hostel. The rooms are clean, if simply furnished (wood floors and painted wrought-iron beds), and guests can make themselves at home using the kitchen, lounge and laundry. The top-floor terrace, with views over the rooftops, is the best feature.

ALEXANDRIE MONTREAL   HOSTEL $

Map p276 (📞514-525-9420; www.alexandrie-montreal.com; 1750 Rue Amherst; dm $22-30, d with shared bath $50-90; 🛜; ⓂBerri-UQAM) Set in a converted multistory brick building, this friendly, welcoming hostel has a good location near the Village and Rue St-Denis. Rooms are clean and nicely maintained, with four- to eight-bed bunks and sunny private rooms with shared baths. The open kitchen and lounge area is a good place to mingle with other travelers.

SAMESUN
MONTRÉAL CENTRAL   HOSTEL $

Map p276 (📞514-843-5739; www.hostelmon trealcentral.com; 1586 Rue St-Hubert; dm/d from $31/130; ❄@🛜; ⓂBerri-UQAM) This popular hostel is just steps away from the local bus depot and metro station, and a short stroll from the buzz of Rue St-Denis. Four-, six- and eight-bunk dorms are basic but serviceable, with metal bed frames and tile floors, although in-bed reading lights and in-room fridges are thoughtful features.

Private doubles are clean and simple. The usual hostel features are on offer: guest kitchen and laundry. There is also a small terrace and a lobby bar, where you can chat with fellow travelers over a beer.

LA LOGGIA ART
& BREAKFAST   B&B $$

Map p276 (📞514-524-2493; www.laloggia.ca; 1637 Rue Amherst; s/d $155/180, with shared bath $120/140, studio s/d/tr $170/200/220; 🅿❄🛜; ⓂBeaudry) This beautifully maintained B&B has a handful of charming rooms, each with artwork on the walls and attractive furnishings. The best rooms are light and airy with Persian carpets, antique armoires and private baths. Lower-level rooms are a little dark, but still clean. Good firm mattresses and soundproof windows ensure a decent night's rest.

For a bit extra, the 'studio' is the pick of the five rooms, with tall ceilings, skylights and colorful artwork. The hosts offer a warm and friendly welcome. Buffet-style breakfasts are simple but adequate.

HÉRITAGE VICTORIEN   B&B $$

Map p276 (📞514-845-7932; www.montreal bedandbreakfast.ca; 305 Rue Ontario Est; d $179-199, ste $259; ❄🛜; ⓂBerri-UQAM) True to name, this nine-room guesthouse celebrates its Victorian heritage with gorgeous rooms decorated with antiques and boasting period details. You'll find intricately carved wooden headboards, gilt-framed mirrors, clawfoot soaking tubs and portraits from yesteryear, plus modern baths and flat-screen TVs. There's also a garden in back and great buffet breakfasts. Save about $40 per room by staying on weeknights.

Ask the owner about Louise Amelia Monk, who lived with her siblings and parents here in the late 19th century and left behind a diary (on display in the inn).

LE RELAIS LYONNAIS   GUESTHOUSE $$

Map p276 (📞514-448-2999; www.lerelaislyon nais.com; 1595 Rue St-Denis; r/ste $148/163; @🛜; ⓂBerri-UQAM) Set in a beautifully restored 19th-century building, it has seven elegantly furnished rooms. Dark maple floors, exposed-brick walls, touches of artwork and wooden blinds give the rooms a classy, but masculine look, while white goose-down duvets provide a soft complement. The rooms are a bit small, but high ceilings, oversized windows and rain showers add to the appeal.

Light sleepers beware: front-facing rooms get lots of street noise from lively Rue St-Denis. Suites face the rear and are quieter.

LGBTIQ+ STAYS

Any guesthouse in the Village will be gay-friendly. A few perennial favorites include the following:

➡ **Turquoise B&B** (p162) Like stepping into a glossy magazine.

➡ **Alacoque B&B Revolution** (p158) Gorgeous antiques in an 1830s setting.

HÔTEL ST-DENIS
HOTEL $$

Map p276 (📞514-849-4526; www.hotel-st-denis. com; 1254 Rue St-Denis; d from $165; P❄️📶; MBerri-UQAM) In a good location, this hotel receives positive reviews for its clean, well-maintained rooms with wood floors, trim modern furnishings and comfortable beds. Sizes vary from cramped to rather spacious – avoid the budget rooms if you need space.

For a touch of luxury, opt for the newer king suites, which have large TVs, a Jacuzzi tub and bath products from Lord & Mayfair.

AUBERGE LE JARDIN D'ANTOINE
B&B $$

Map p276 (📞514-843-4506; www.aubergele jardindantoine.com; 2024 Rue St-Denis; d/ste from $167/202; ❄️@📶; MBerri-UQAM) You'll find a wide range of rooms at this welcoming four-story hotel, handily located in the thick of the Rue St-Denis action. Some have carpeting, others have nicely polished wood floors. And while some rooms have classic old-world touches such as exposed brick and wrought-iron bedsteads, others tend toward a modern, cheerful design scheme.

TURQUOISE B&B
B&B $$$

Map p276 (📞514-523-9943; www.turquoisebb. com; 1576 Rue Alexandre-de-Sève; s/d with shared bath from $270/330; P📶; MBeaudry) The decor in this plush two-story greystone looks like something out of *Better Homes & Gardens*. Each of the five bedrooms boasts bright colors (yellow, chartreuse or, yes, turquoise) and has a queen-size bed, original moldings and shiny wood floors. Included breakfast is served in the large backyard. Baths are shared – there are three for the five rooms.

🛏 Plateau Mont-Royal & the Northeast

Staying in the most fashionable district of Montréal means being close to some of the best eateries and nightlife in town. Like the Village, the Plateau is packed with B&Bs; hotels are few and far between.

★ACCUEIL CHEZ FRANÇOIS
B&B $$

Map p280 (📞514-239-4638; www.chezfrancois. ca; 4031 Ave Papineau; s/d from $135/160, s/d with shared bath $115/135; P❄️📶; MSherbrooke, then bus 24) Overlooking Parc La Fontaine, François indeed gives a warm *accueil* (welcome) to his pleasant and excellent-value five-room guesthouse in the Plateau east. Many guests are repeat visitors, drawn by the spotless and attractive rooms, the delicious breakfasts and the great location (free parking is a bonus).

A LA CARTE B&B
B&B $$

Map p280 (📞514-593-4005; http://alacartebnb. com; 5477 10th Ave; s/d/apt from $115/135/190; P❄️📶; MLaurier, then bus 47) For something completely different, book one of two rooms or a fully equipped two-bedroom apartment at this charming guesthouse in the leafy neighborhood of Rosemont-La Petite Patrie. Rooms are dated but comfortably furnished, and guests can use the dining or living room, and warm up by the wood-burning fireplace on chilly nights.

It's in the eastern part of the city, not far from the Jardin Botanique (2km away). Hosts Petra and Daniel (and their poodle Monsieur Petit) extend a warm welcome. The pair whip up delicious breakfasts (for a fee) and have loads of insight on exploring the neighborhood.

AUBERGE DE LA FONTAINE
INN $$

Map p280 (📞514-597-0166; www.aubergedela fontaine.com; 1301 Rue Rachel Est; r $122-185, ste from $160; P❄️📶; MMont-Royal) A gem of an inn on the edge of Parc La Fontaine, this guesthouse has cheery rooms with comfy beds and touches of artwork. Standard rooms are small, while the best rooms have park views. The spacious suites also have in-room Jacuzzis. The snack refrigerator with free goodies is a nice touch. There's a wheelchair-accessible room available.

GINGERBREAD MANOR
B&B $$

Map p280 (☎514-597-2804; www.gingerbread manor.com; 3445 Ave Laval; with/without bath from $120/89; P🛜; MSherbrooke) The hosts give a warm welcome at this charming B&B near leafy Carré St-Louis. The house itself is a stately three-story town house built in 1885 with bay windows, ornamental details and an attached carriage house. The elegant rooms – five in all – are uniquely furnished (only one has a private bath, the others share).

The best rooms have king-size beds and a bay window, but all have decent light. Hot cooked breakfasts (which may include banana-walnut pancakes, French toast and fruit salad or croissants) are a bonus.

HÔTEL DE L'INSTITUT
HOTEL $$

Map p280 (☎514-282-5120; www.ithq.qc.ca; 3535 Rue St-Denis; s/d $158/200; P❄🛜; MSherbrooke) Set in a sleek glass cube, this modern hotel is run as a training center for the Québec tourism and hotel board. The 42 neutrally decorated rooms are well appointed, with flat-screen TVs, laptop safes, desks and small couches. They are quite bright, with small balconies – some with decent views. Baths are cramped, but clean and functional.

KUTUMA HOTEL & SUITES
B&B $$

Map p280 (☎514-844-0111; www.kutuma.com; 3708 Rue St-Denis; d/ste from $148/172; P❄🛜; MSherbrooke) In an excellent location on lively Rue St-Denis, the Kutuma has the feel of a boutique hotel. Cozy, well-maintained rooms feature safari-theme decor, including animal-print fabrics, potted palms and colorful artwork. Baths are modern and perhaps overly sleek, but the two-person tub in some is a nice feature. It's worth dining in the Ethiopian restaurant, Le Nil Bleu, on the 1st floor.

Negatives: some rooms have tiny windows, noise can be an issue on lower floors, and there's no elevator – though staff can help you lug your stuff up the stairs.

LE GÎTE
B&B $$

Map p280 (☎514-849-4567; www.legite.ca; 3619 Rue de Bullion; s/d with shared bath from $87/97; ❄🛜; MSherbrooke) In a row house just off restaurant-lined Rue Prince-Arthur Est, Le Gîte is a charming B&B. The four rooms have polished wood floors, an attractive minimalist design and striking works of art covering the walls (created by the owner's son). Other nice touches are the small shaded terrace, kitchen use and free laundry. Small discounts from December to April.

On the downside, the one shared bath for guests causes a bit of a traffic jam in the mornings, making Le Gîte less than ideal for longer stays.

SLEEPING PLATEAU MONT-ROYAL & THE NORTHEAST

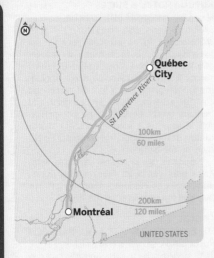

Québec City

Québec City Top Five

❶ Strolling, shopping and admiring the murals, museums and historic buildings in the 17th-century **Quartier Petit-Champlain** (p169).

❷ Soaking up spectacular views of **Le Château Frontenac** (p166) from the panoramic riverside boardwalk in summer or the hair-raising toboggan run in winter.

❸ Visualizing the legendary rivalry between French and English on a tour of **La Citadelle** (p165).

❹ Walking, cycling, cross-country skiing, skating or celebrating Winter Carnival in the city's beautiful and historic **Battlefields Park** (p179).

❺ Embracing Québec City's festive summer spirit and long daylight hours at street performances along **Terrasse Dufferin** (p172) and open-air concerts in the city's parks.

TOP EXPERIENCE
TAKE A LANTERN-LIT TOUR OF LA CITADELLE

Towering above the St Lawrence River, this massive, star-shaped fort is a living museum that offers something for all ages. The exhibits on military life from colonial times to today will appeal to anyone interested in Québécois history, while children will be enthralled in summertime by the daily 10am changing of the guard and the beating of the retreat (6pm Saturday).

French forces started building a defensive structure here in the late 1750s, but what we see today was constructed over 30 years from 1820 by the British, who feared two things: an American invasion of the colony and a possible revolt by the French-speaking population (that's why the cannons point not only at the river, but at Québec City itself).

By the time the Citadelle was completed, things were calming down. In 1871 the Treaty of Washington between the US and the newly minted Dominion of Canada ended the threat of American invasion.

The Citadelle now houses about 200 members of the Royal 22e Régiment. The Vandoos, a nickname taken from the French for 22 *(vingt-deux)*, is the only entirely French-speaking battalion in the Canadian Forces and there's a museum dedicated to them here. The second official residence of the governor-general, who represents the Queen of England in Canada, has also been located here since 1872.

Hour-long guided tours of the Citadelle are excellent and will give you the lowdown on the spectacular architecture; don't miss the King's Bastion with its 9-ton cannon and the reduit used later as a military prison. From late June through October, lantern-lit evening tours are also offered.

DON'T MISS

➡ Changing of the guard in summer
➡ Medals room in the Musée Royal 22e Régiment
➡ Panoramic views from the King's Bastion

PRACTICALITIES

➡ Map p170, D7
➡ ☎418-694-2815
➡ www.lacitadelle.qc.ca
➡ Côte de la Citadelle, Old Upper Town
➡ adult/child $16/6
➡ ◷9am-5pm May-Oct, 10am-4pm Nov-Apr

◉ TOP EXPERIENCE
ENJOY A MEAL AT CHÂTEAU FRONTENAC

This audaciously elegant structure is Québec City's most iconic edifice. Its fabulous turrets, winding hallways and imposing wings graciously complement its dramatic location atop Cap Diamant, a cliff that swoops into the St Lawrence River. Over the years, it's lured a never-ending lineup of luminaries, including Alfred Hitchcock, who shot the opening scene of his 1953 mystery *I Confess* here.

It's probably one of the rare hotels where most people in the lobby aren't even guests but rather tourists visiting to get close to the history and architecture (they say that this is the world's most photographed hotel).

Designed by New Yorker Bruce Price (father of manners maven Emily Post), the château was named after the mercurial Count of Frontenac, Louis de Buade, who governed New France in the late 1600s. Completed in 1893, it was one of the Canadian Pacific Railway's series of luxury hotels built across Canada.

In August 1943 and again in September 1944, the Québec Conferences involving British Prime Minister Winston Churchill, US President Franklin Roosevelt and Canadian Prime Minister William Lyon Mackenzie King were all held here to plot the final stages of WWII. Other illustrious guests have included King George VI, Chiang Kai-shek, Princess Grace of Monaco and Paul McCartney.

Guided tours of the building were discontinued in 2011, but nonguests can still wander through the reception area (there's usually a special exhibition of some sort going on) and stop for a drink or a bite at the hotel's restaurant, bistro or bar. Québec Cicerone Tours (p201) offers tours that focus solely on the Château Frontenac.

DON'T MISS

➡ The panoramas from the hotel's bar 1608

➡ Arriving here by *calèche* (horse-drawn carriage)

➡ Views of the Frontenac illuminated at night

PRACTICALITIES

➡ Map p170, E5

➡ ☎418-692-3861

➡ www.fairmont.com/frontenac-quebec

➡ 1 Rue des Carrières, Old Upper Town

TOP EXPERIENCE
TIME TRAVEL AT MUSÉE DE LA CIVILISATION

This world-class museum wows even before you've clapped your eyes on the exhibits. It is a fascinating mix of modern design that incorporates preexisting industrial buildings along the old port with contemporary architecture. What's inside is quite unique in that this is really the only museum in town that regularly looks at contemporary issues and culture.

The grandiose-sounding 'Museum of Civilization' contains just two permanent exhibits. The first – and arguably more ambitious – is 'People of Québec: Then and Now,' which traces the history of the city and province imaginatively via multimedia from earliest times (12,500 BCE) until today. It's a must-see for understanding Québec today; the postwar drive for an independent Quebec is handled both sensitively and accurately.

The second permanent exhibit, called 'This Is Our Story', focuses on the province's Aboriginals today – 93,000 people from a dozen different indigenous groups. The beautiful objects on display are unique, sensitively curated and highly educational, with some clever interactive elements. Listen to some of the interviews conducted with various members; they are interesting and enlightening.

The museum's focus on contemporary issues and culture sees some stunning special exhibits examining topics as diverse as London and its culture on the eve of Brexit, the transformation of Québec City from a city of trappers to one of entrepreneurs, and the social history of Québec and the Québécois in 400 very ordinary objects.

DON'T MISS

➡ Twentieth-century gallery of 'People of Québec'

➡ Mobile-like low-lit canoe above 'This Is Our Story'

➡ Vaulted 18th-century cellar below museum shop

PRACTICALITIES

➡ Museum of Civilization

➡ Map p170, F3

➡ ☑418-643-2158

➡ www.mcq.org/en

➡ 85 Rue Dalhousie, Old Lower Town & Port

➡ adult/teen/child $17/6/free, with temporary exhibitions $22/7/free

➡ ⏱10am-5pm mid-Jun–early Sep, closed Mon early Sep–mid-Jun

Explore

The crown jewel of French Canada, Québec City is one of North America's oldest and most magnificent settlements. Its picturesque Old Town is a Unesco World Heritage site, a living museum of narrow cobblestone streets, 17th- and 18th-century houses and soaring church spires, with the splendid Château Frontenac towering above it all. There's more than a glimmer of Old Europe in its classic bistros, sidewalk cafes and manicured squares.

You can get a taste of the city in a single day, but linger at least a weekend if you can. The city's compact size makes it ideal for walking, and it shines brightest when you slow down.

The main focus of your visit should be the Old Town, split between the Old Upper Town (Haute Ville), perched above the St Lawrence River on the Cap Diamant cliffs, and the Old Lower Town (Basse Ville), where Samuel de Champlain established the first French foothold in 1608. The Old Town is packed with museums, mansard-roofed houses and cobblestone streets just begging to be explored.

Outside the walls, through the historic town gates of Porte St-Louis and Porte St-Jean, four additional neighborhoods are easily accessible: St-Jean Baptiste, Montcalm, Colline Parlementaire, and St-Roch, each boasting wonderful restaurants, shopping and nightlife. Also noteworthy here are the vast Plains of Abraham, where the British defeated the French in 1759; nowadays enshrined as a national park, this area offers superb recreational opportunities.

Québec City goes to great lengths to entertain visitors. All summer long, musicians, acrobats and actors in period costume take to the streets, while fantastic festivals fill the air with fireworks and song. In the coldest months of January and February, Carnaval de Québec (p193) is arguably the biggest and most colorful winter festival around. Fall and spring bring beautiful foliage, dramatically reduced prices and thinner crowds.

The Best...

➜ **Place to Sleep** Le Monastère des Augustines (p208)

➜ **Place to Eat** Chez Boulay (p188)
➜ **Place to Drink** Griendel Brasserie Artisanale (p195)

Top Tip

Make lunch your main meal. Most restaurants, including some of Québec City's finest, offer midday *tables d'hôte* (fixed-price menus) for about half the price of a comparable dinner.

Getting There & Away

➜ **Train** VIA Rail (p241) runs four trains daily from Montréal's Gare Centrale to Québec's Gare du Palais (3¼ hours, from $44/87 one way/return).
➜ **Bus** Orléans Express (p242) offers frequent bus service from Montréal (3¼ hours, from $55/89 one way/return).
➜ **Car** Driving from Montréal to Québec City takes about three hours, via Autoroute 20 on the south shore of the St Lawrence River, and the slightly longer Autoroute 40 along the north shore.
➜ **Air** Regular Air Canada flights (45 minutes) run from Montréal to Québec City's Jean Lesage Airport. There are some direct flights from the USA and Europe.

Need to Know

➜ **Area code** ✆418
➜ **Location** 260km northeast of Montréal
➜ **Tourist Office** (p249)

⊙ SIGHTS

Most of Québec City's sights are found within the compact cluster of Old Town walls, or just outside them, making this a dream destination for pedestrians.

⊙ Old Town & Port

Québec City's historic kernel is composed of the Old Upper Town and Old Lower Town with its adjoining Vieux-Port (Old Port). The former is where you'll spend most of your time because it's packed with the city's blockbuster sights and museums.

The narrow, winding roads are lined with extraordinary architecture; some buildings date from the 1600s. Sandwiched between the Old Upper Town and the waterfront, the Old Lower Town has some of the city's most intriguing museums, plus numerous statues and plenty of cafes and restaurants along its pedestrian-friendly streets.

LA CITADELLE FORT
See p165.

**LE CHÂTEAU
FRONTENAC** HISTORIC BUILDING
See p166.

**MUSÉE DE LA
CIVILISATION** MUSEUM
See p167.

**GOVERNOR GENERAL'S
RESIDENCE** HISTORIC BUILDING
Map p170 (Résidence du Gouverneur Général; ☑418-648-4322; www.gg.ca/en/visit-us/cita delle; 1 Côte de la Citadelle, Old Upper Town; tours free; ☺11am-4pm late Jun–early Sep, 10am-4pm early Sep–late Jun) Located within Québec's Citadelle (p165), this is one of only two residences in the country (the other is Rideau Hall in Ottawa) where Canada's governor-general, currently French-Canadian and former astronaut Julie Payette, lives and receives foreign dignitaries. Free 60-minute guided tours are available year-round, but you must book ahead, except in the high season (between late June and early September), by phone or email. It's a small bit of Canadiana right in the heart of Québec.

★**LE MONASTÈRE
DES AUGUSTINES** MUSEUM
Map p170 (☑418-694-1639; https://monas tere.ca; 77 Rue des Remparts, Old Upper Town; adult/youth/child $10.50/4.50/free, guided tour $15/9/free; ☺10am-5pm late Jun–Aug, Tue-Sun Sep–late Jun) On no account should you miss this museum, which traces the history of the order of Augustinian nuns who founded Québec's first hospital, the Hôtel-Dieu, in 1644 and ran it for over 300 years. OK, it may not sound like a crowd-pleaser, but the half-dozen rooms around a central cloister are filled with remarkable displays of religious items, crafts (artificial flowers were mandatory where flowers bloom only four months a year), an old apothecary and an 18th-century refectory.

THE INSIDE INFO

Shopping Streets Stroll Rue St-Jean outside the walls in St-Jean Baptiste, Rue St-Joseph in St-Roch, Ave Cartier in Montcalm, or Rue Maguire in Sillery.

Markets For the freshest cheeses, meats and produce, locals head for the Marché du Vieux-Port (p200) down by the waterfront or Les Halles Cartier (p204) in Montcalm.

Hangouts While away a summer evening drinking beer with laid-back locals on the outdoor terrace at La Barberie (p196).

The 18th-century building also has a fantastic boutique hotel (p208) and a restaurant. Don't miss the richly decorated chapel designed by wood-carver and architect Thomas Baillairgé (1791–1859).

ÉDIFICE PRICE ARCHITECTURE
Map p170 (Price Building; www.ivanhoecam bridge.com/en/office-buildings/properties/edi fice-price; 65 Rue Ste-Anne, Old Upper Town) This art-deco 'skyscraper,' modeled after New York City's Empire State Building, opened in 1929 and for decades the 80m, 17-story structure dominated the city skyline. It was named after the Price Brothers Company, a lumber company founded in 1816 that supplied the lucrative paper and pulp industries. Go into the lobby to admire the fine bronze friezes of loggers at work as well as the stunning coffered ceiling and its brass chandeliers.

The building was once owned by the city administration though today it is largely occupied by a large real-estate company. However, it remains the official residence of the premier of Québec, who uses the top two floors.

★**LE QUARTIER
PETIT-CHAMPLAIN** AREA
Map p170 Arguably the city's most picturesque district, this area sandwiched between the Old Upper Town and the waterfront has Québec City's most intriguing museums and galleries, plus numerous plaques and statues and plenty of outdoor cafes and restaurants along its pedestrian-friendly streets.

QUÉBEC CITY SIGHTS

QUÉBEC CITY

Québec City – Old Town

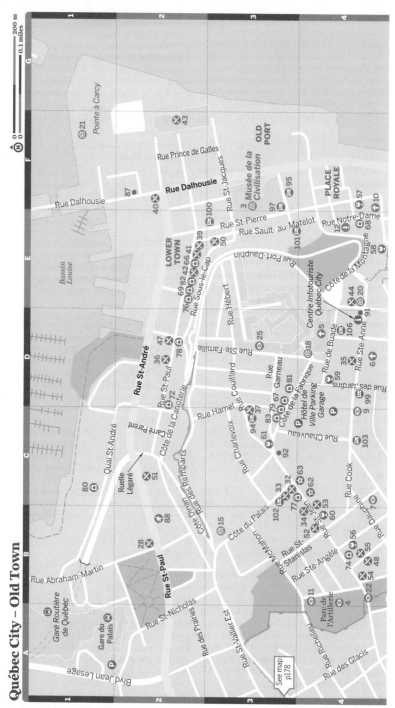

OLD LOWER TOWN

Ferry to Lévis

St Lawrence River
(Fleuve St-Laurent)

93

64
73 89 45
16
70

Rue du Petit-Champlain

13
26
17
46 65
75

Le Château Frontenac
2
27
90

Blvd Champlain

85

Rue des Carrières

14
Rue de la Porte
104 109
96
Rue des Grisons

38
Rue St-Louis
71

Rue Mont Carmel

19
8
30
Rue Donnacona

98
Ave Ste-Geneviève
Ave St-Denis

OLD UPPER TOWN

105
31

Cap Diamant

1
La Citadelle

La Citadelle

107
49
Ruelle des Ursulines
Rue Ste-Ursule

29
Rue d'Auteuil

86
23
24

Côte de la Citadelle

108
Rue Ste-Anne

84
Parc de l'Esplanade

Ave George VI

Battlefields Park
(Parc des Champs
de Bataille)

Ave du Cap Aux Diamant

Place d'Youville

Rue Ste-Julie

COLLINE
PARLEMENTAIRE

Grande Allée Est

Ave Honoré Mercier

Ave George VI

Parc de la
Francophonie

Québec City – Old Town

★**TERRASSE DUFFERIN**   PARK

Map p170 (Rue des Carrières, Old Upper Town) Perched on a clifftop 60m above the St Lawrence River, this 425m-long boardwalk is a marvelous setting for a stroll, with spectacular, sweeping views. In summer it's peppered with street performers; in winter it hosts a dramatic toboggan run (p204). Near the statue of Samuel de Champlain, stairways descend to the excavations of Champlain's second fort, which stood here from 1620 to 1635. Nearby, you can take the funicular (p244) to the Old Lower Town.

ST-LOUIS FORTS & CHÂTEAUX NATIONAL HISTORIC SITE   ARCHAEOLOGICAL SITE

Map p170 (☑418-648-7016; www.pc.gc.ca/eng/lhn-nhs/qc/saintlouisforts/index.aspx; Terrasse Dufferin, Old Upper Town; adult/child $4/free, incl guided tour $15/10; ⊗9am-5:30pm mid-May–early Oct) 🖉 Hidden underneath the Terrasse Dufferin are the ruins of four forts and two châteaus constructed by Samuel de Champlain and other early Québec residents between 1620 and 1694. These structures, excavated between 2005 and 2007, served as residences for the French and English governors of Québec for over 200 years before falling victim to bombardment, fire and neglect. In warm weather, Parks Canada offers twice-daily English-language tours of the archaeological site and the artifacts unearthed there.

Access the forts and châteaus either via the Frontenac Kiosk (p249) or the Lorne Kiosk (Map p170).

CENTRE MORRIN   CULTURAL CENTRE
Map p170 (☑418-694-9147; www.morrin.org; 44 Chausée des Écossais, Old Upper Town; ⊙noon-8pm Tue, to 4pm Wed-Fri & Sun, 10am-4pm Sat) FREE You'd never know from looking at it but this stately early-19th-century stone building held Canada's first modern prison before being converted into Morrin

College in 1868. It later served as the national archives. Guided tours (adult/student $12/10) of two blocks of prison cells (yes, there were executions here), a magnificent Victorian-era library with books going back to the 16th century and College Hall depart at different times and on different days throughout the year; check the website.

FORTIFICATIONS OF QUÉBEC NATIONAL HISTORIC SITE   HISTORIC SITE
Map p170 (☑418-648-7016; www.pc.gc.ca/eng/lhn-nhs/qc/fortifications/index.aspx; 2 Rue d'Auteuil, Old Upper Town; adult/child $4/free;

⊙10am-5pm mid-May–early Oct, to 6pm Jul & Aug) These largely restored old walls are protected as both a Canadian National Historic site and a Unesco World Heritage site. Walking the complete 4.6km circuit around the walls outside on your own is free of charge, and you'll enjoy fine vantage points on the city's historical buildings as you trace the perimeter of the Old Town. There are two other entrances: at **Porte St-Louis** (Map p170; 100 Rue St-Louis) and the Frontenac Kiosk (p249) on the Terrasse Dufferin.

In summer 90-minute guided walks (adult/youth $15/10) are also available, beginning at the Frontenac Kiosk and ending at Artillery Park. Walks depart at 10:30am, 1:30pm and 3:30pm.

ARTILLERY PARK   HISTORIC SITE

Map p170 (🖉418-648-7016; www.pc.gc.ca/eng/lhn-nhs/qc/fortifications/natcul/natcul2.aspx; Rue d'Auteuil, Old Upper Town; adult/child $4/free; ⊙10am-5pm mid-May–early Oct, to 6pm Jul & Aug) Part of the Fortifications of Québec National Historic Site (p173) and open in summer, this park along the Old Upper Town walls was chosen as the site for 18th-century French army barracks due to its strategic position opposite the plateau and the St Charles River, both of which could feed enemy soldiers into Québec City. Visit the **Officers' Quarters** and the **Dauphine Redoubt**, where guides in period dress speak in character about life in the barracks.

Don't miss the huge 19th-century model of Québec City in the **Arsenal Foundry**. After the British conquest of New France, English soldiers moved in and remained here until 1871, when the site was converted into an ammunition factory for the Canadian army. The factory operated until 1964, and thousands of Canadians worked there during the World Wars.

MUSÉE DES URSULINES   MUSEUM

Map p170 (Ursulines Museum; 🖉418-694-0694; www.poleculturaldesursulines.ca; 10 Rue Donnacona, Old Upper Town; adult/youth/child $10/5/free; ⊙10am-5pm Tue-Sun May-Sep, 1-5pm Tue-Sun Oct-Apr) Housed in a historic convent, this thoughtful, well-laid-out and wheelchair-accessible museum tells the fascinating story of the Ursuline nuns' lives and their influence in the 17th and 18th centuries. The sisters established North America's first school for girls in 1641, educating both Aboriginal and French students.

Displays on convent school life are enlivened by a vast array of historic artifacts, including examples of the Ursulines' gold and silver embroidery.

The chapel just opposite dates from 1902 but retains some interiors from 1726. Ursuline sisters, the first order of nuns to come to North America, were cloistered until 1965; there are some 48 nuns today, but only four still live in the convent.

The convent's founder, Marie de l'Incarnation, was one of the most intriguing figures from the order. Leaving a young son in France after she was widowed, she joined the Ursulines and moved to New France, where she lived well into old age. She taught herself Aboriginal languages, and her frequent and eloquent letters to her son back in France are held by historians to be some of the richest and most valuable material available to scholars studying life in the French colony.

CHAPELLE DES URSULINES   CHAPEL

Map p170 (Ursulines Chapel; www.museedesursulines.com; 12 Rue Donnacona, Old Upper Town; ⊙10:30am-noon & 1-4:30pm Tue-Sun May-Oct, 1-4:30pm Sat & Sun Nov-Apr) This glittering chapel just across from the Musée des Ursulines contains some of the finest wood carving in Québec and was gilded by the nuns themselves. French General Louis-Joseph Montcalm was buried here after he died in the decisive 1759 battle on the Plains of Abraham. However, in 2001 his remains were transferred to the cemetery at the Hôpital Général de Québec on Blvd Langelier to rest with those of his comrades-in-arms.

MUSÉE DE L'AMÉRIQUE FRANCOPHONE   MUSEUM

Map p170 (Museum of French-Speaking America; 🖉418-643-2158, 866-710-8031; www.mcq.org/en/informations/maf; 2 Côte de la Fabrique, Old Upper Town; adult/teen/child $10/4/free; ⊙10am-5pm mid-Jun–Aug, Sat & Sun Sep–mid-Jun) Anchor tenant of the 17th-century **Séminaire de Québec** (Map p170; Côte de la Fabrique, Old Upper Town), this breathtakingly thorough museum is purported to be Canada's oldest. Enter via the awesome **Chapelle du Musée** (Museum Chapel), built in 1898 by Joseph-Ferdinand Peachy, who earlier built the Église St-Jean-Baptiste. Access the main building pavilion by underground tunnel and its three floors of exhibits exploring the diaspora of French-speaking

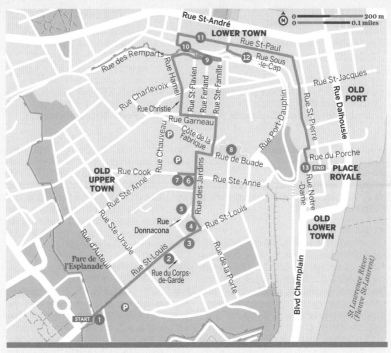

🏃 Neighborhood Walk
Historic Stroll Through the Old Town

START PORTE ST-LOUIS
END FRESQUE DES QUÉBÉCOIS
LENGTH 3KM; ONE TO TWO HOURS

This tour encompasses a mix of well-known and lesser-known Vieux-Québec attractions.

Begin at ❶**Porte St-Louis**, an impressive gate first erected in 1693. Follow Rue St-Louis to the corner of Rue du Corps-de-Garde, where a ❷**cannonball** sits embedded in a tree at its base (allegedly since 1759). Further on at ❸**47 Rue St-Louis** is where French General Montcalm died, a day after being shot by the British during the destiny-changing Battle of the Plains of Abraham.

At 34 Rue St-Louis, a 1676 home houses the Québécois restaurant ❹**Aux Anciens Canadiens** (p190). Its steeply pitched roof was typical of 17th-century French architecture. Follow Rue des Jardins to the ❺**Ursuline Chapel** and museum where generations of nuns educated both French and Aboriginal girls from 1641.

Left down Rue Ste-Anne is the elegant 1870 ❻**Hôtel Clarendon** (p209), Québec City's oldest hotel. Next door is ❼**Édifice Price** (p169), one of Canada's first skyscrapers. Enter to see the art-deco lobby.

A short stroll along Rue des Jardins and Rue de Buade brings you to the heavily restored ❽**Basilique-Cathédrale Notre-Dame-de-Québec** (p176). Detour down pretty Rue Garneau, then descend to ❾**Rue des Remparts** for fine views.

Descend ❿**Côte de la Canoterie**, a historical link between the Lower and Upper Towns. Hope Gate stood atop the *côte* (rise) until 1873 to keep the riffraff from entering the Upper Town. Turn right at Rue St-Thomas and right again onto ⓫**Rue St-Paul**, the heart of Québec City's antiques district. Take a peek at ⓬**Rue Sous-le-Cap**, a former red-light district.

Turn right down Rue Sault-au-Matelot to the 420-sq-meter trompe-l'oeil ⓭**Fresque des Québécois** (p176), where you can pose beside historical figures like Jacques Cartier and Samuel de Champlain.

QUÉBEC BY CALÈCHE

For a scenic journey about town, climb aboard one of Québec City's old-fashioned *calèches* (horse-drawn carriages). While rides are not cheap – $90 for 35 minutes, $180 for 90 minutes, or $270 for two hours (maximum four passengers) – drivers can give you an earful of history as they take you to historic points around the city. Find them primarily at the **Place d'Armes** (Map p170; ☑418-520-1555, 418-683-9222; 35-/80-/120min rides $90/180/270) in front of Le Château Frontenac, though there are also stands in the **Parc de l'Esplanade** (Map p170) and at the **Porte St-Louis** (Map p170).

people in North America, the early years of New France and the work of artists and artisans here since 1930.

There's also a wonderful and telling short film on new-world history from a Québécois perspective.

MUSÉE DU FORT
MUSEUM

Map p170 (Fort Museum; ☑418-692-2175; www. museedufort.com; 10 Rue Ste-Anne, Old Upper Town; adult/child $8.50/6.50; ☺10am-5pm Apr-Jun, Sep & Oct, to 6pm Jul & Aug, 11am-4pm Nov-Mar) Now into its sixth decade, this minimuseum houses a 30-minute multimedia show that chronicles centuries of attacks on Québec City. It's all played out on a model diorama that lights up in the middle of a minitheater. Even with seven projectors, it's not exactly high tech, but it does offer a quick, easy-to-grasp audiovisual survey of the battles that shaped Québec City's history. English-language shows are held on the hour, French-language versions on the half-hour.

CATHEDRAL OF THE HOLY TRINITY
CHURCH

Map p170 (☑418-692-2193; www.cathedral.ca; 31 Rue des Jardins, Old Upper Town; ☺9am-5pm mid-May–mid-Nov, by arrangement out of season) Consecrated in 1804, this handsome church was the first Anglican cathedral built outside the British Isles. Designed by two officers from the British army's military engineering corps, it is modeled on London's St Martin-in-the-Fields, with pews built of oak imported from Windsor Castle's Great Park. The bell tower, an impressive 47m high, competes for attention with the Basilique Notre-Dame to the north. In season, guided tours ($6) depart between 10am and 4:30pm Monday to Saturday and 12:30pm and 4:30pm Sunday.

Upon the church's completion, King George III sent the cathedral a treasure chest of objects, including candlesticks, chalices and silver trays. The elaborateness of the gifts heading toward the New World sent London's chattering classes atwitter. The silver collection is on permanent display. The royal box for the reigning monarch or her representative is located in the upper left balcony if you are facing the altar (look for the royal coat of arms).

BASILIQUE-CATHÉDRALE NOTRE-DAME-DE-QUÉBEC
CHURCH

Map p170 (☑418-694-0665; http://holy doorquebec.ca/en; 16 Rue de Buade, Old Upper Town; ☺8:45am-3:45pm Mon-Fri, to 4:45pm Sat & Sun, to 8:15pm daily summer) Québec's Roman Catholic basilica got its start as a small church in 1647. Despite frequent fires and battle damage over the ensuing years, especially during the Siege of Québec in 1759, the church was repeatedly rebuilt, ultimately becoming the much larger cathedral you see today. The interior is appropriately grandiose, though most of its treasures didn't survive a fire in 1922 that left behind only the walls and foundations. It reopened in 1925.

Between mid-May and early September, guided tours ($5) allow you to visit the basilica's crypt and ossuary; check with the shop to the left of the main entrance for schedules. Everyone from four governors of New France to archbishops and cardinals has been laid to rest down here.

FRESQUE DES QUÉBÉCOIS
PUBLIC ART

Map p170 (Québec City Mural; 29 Rue Notre-Dame, Parc de la Cetière, Old Lower Town & Port) An obligatory photo stop on any tour of the Old Lower Town, this whimsical multistory trompe-l'oeil mural was painted in 1998 by a group of artists from Québec and Lyon in France. Samuel de Champlain stands jauntily in the center of the scene, flanked by kids playing hockey, while Jacques Cartier peeks out through a 3rd-story window. The rest of the characters are famous Québécois writers, artists and religious figures. Step up to the wall and join them!

ÉGLISE NOTRE-DAME-DES-VICTOIRES
CHURCH

Map p170 (Our Lady of Victories Church; ☑418-692-1650; www.notre-dame-de-quebec.org; 32 Rue Sous-le-Fort, Old Lower Town & Port; ⊙9:30am-8:30pm late Jun-Aug, to 4:30pm late May-late Jun, 9:30am-4:30pm Sun Sep-late May) Begun in 1687 and named for French victories over the British in 1690 and 1711, this is North America's oldest stone church. It stands on the spot where Champlain set up his 'Habitation,' a small stockade, more than a century before the small church was completed in 1723. Inside are copies of paintings by Rubens and Van Dyck.

Hanging from the ceiling is a replica of a wooden ship called the *Brézé*, thought to be a good-luck charm for ocean crossings and battles with the Iroquois.

JARDIN DES GOUVERNEURS
PARK

Map p170 (Rue Mont Carmel, Old Upper Town) Overlooking the St Lawrence River is this leafy gem of a city park, with a monument to legendary generals James Wolfe and Louis-Joseph Montcalm on a shared pedestal. Even in peak season, it's a peaceful refuge from the holidaying masses.

MUSÉE NAVAL DE QUÉBEC
MUSEUM

Map p170 (☑418-694-5387; http://mnq-nmq.org; 170 Rue Dalhousie, Old Lower Town & Port; ⊙9am-4pm Jun-Aug, Wed-Sun Sep & Oct) FREE Perhaps not everyone's cup of cha, this small museum in the Old Port area focuses on the shipping industry here, the Canadian navy and the participation of its sailors in WWII, especially D-Day. The semipermanent exhibition *Héritiers des Guerres* (Heirs of Wars) looks at the human cost of wars and the impact they have on our societies.

◉ Outside the Old Town

Most visitors venture through Porte St-Louis to take a peek at Québec City's most significant attraction outside the walls: Battlefields Park. Unfortunately, most then scuttle back to the safety of that fairy-tale land inside the walls. Some of the sights here are certainly more interesting than taking yet another snap of Le Château Frontenac – notably Hôtel du Parlement and Obsérvatoire de la Capitale. The St-Jean Baptiste and St-Roch areas, which offer a taste of everyday Québec, are a depressurization chamber after the onslaught of historical tourism in the Old Town.

FRENCH IN CANADA: THE BACK STORY

Until the 1970s it was the English minority (few of whom spoke French) who ran the businesses, held positions of power and accumulated wealth in Québec; more often than not French Quebecers going into a downtown store couldn't get service in their own language.

But as Québec's separatist movement strengthened, the Canadian government passed laws in 1969 that required all federal services and public signs to appear in both languages. The separatists took things further and demanded the primacy of French in Québec, which was affirmed by the Parti Québécois with the passage of Bill 101 in 1977. Though there was much hand-wringing, the fact is that Bill 101 helped breathe new life into the French language in Canada and boosted Québécois confidence. If you're at a party with five anglophones and one francophone these days, the chances are everyone will be speaking French, something that would have been rare in decades past.

Québec settlers were relatively cut off from France once they arrived in the New World, so the French you hear today in the province, known colloquially as Québécois (and in Montréal as *joual*), developed more or less independently from what was going on in France. The result is a rich local vocabulary, with its own idioms and sayings, and words used in everyday speech that haven't been used in France since the 18th century. Accents vary widely across the province, but all are characterized by a twang and rhythmic bounce unique to Québec.

Québec City – Outside the City Walls

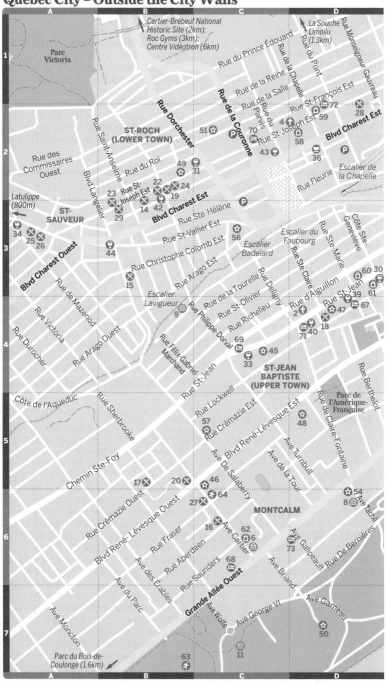

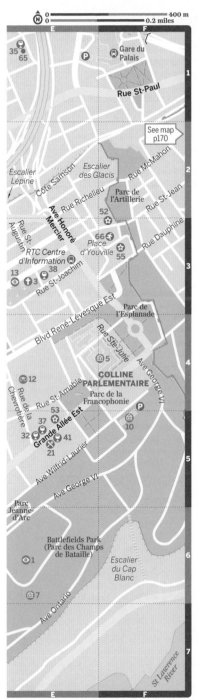

MUSÉE NATIONAL DES BEAUX-ARTS DU QUÉBEC

MUSEUM

Map p178 (Québec National Museum of Fine Arts; ☑418-643-2150; www.mnbaq.org; 179 Grande Allée Ouest, Plains of Abraham; adult/youth/child $20/11/free; ⊘10am-6pm Jun-Aug, to 5pm Tue-Sun Sep-May, to 9pm Wed year-round) Spare at least a half-day to visit this extraordinary art museum, one of the province's best. Permanent exhibitions range from art in the early French colonies to Québec's contemporary artists, with individual halls devoted entirely to 20th-century artistic giants such as Jean-Paul Lemieux, Fernand Leduc and Jean-Paul Riopelle. Arguably the museum's highlight is the **Brousseau Collection of Inuit Art**, a selection of 100 pieces by 60 artists located at the top of the **Pavillon Pierre Lassonde**.

The museum hosts frequent temporary exhibitions from abroad and elsewhere in Canada. Among its four halls is the **Pavillon Charles-Baillairgé**, Québec City's former prison, complete with a block of cells. Audioguides are available for rent for the permanent collections or can be downloaded for free onto your phone. Other events include film screenings (often documentaries on prominent international artists), drawing and painting classes open to the public, and a concert series.

If all this cultural activity is wearing you out, you can grab a snack or the daily lunch special at the cafe in the Pavillon Charles-Baillairgé, or visit the museum's restaurant, Tempéra Québecor (p192), just inside the main entrance, which enjoys superb views of Battlefields Park from its bay windows and outdoor terrace.

★ BATTLEFIELDS PARK

HISTORIC SITE

Map p178 (Parc des Champs-de-Bataille; ☑418-649-6157; www.theplainsofabraham.ca; Ave George VI, Montcalm & Colline Parlementaire; ⊘9am-5:30pm; 🚼) 🖉 One of Québec City's must-sees, this verdant clifftop park contains the **Plains of Abraham**, site of the infamous 1759 battle between British General James Wolfe and French General Louis-Joseph Montcalm that determined the fate of the North American continent. Packed with old cannons, monuments and Martello towers, it's a favorite local spot for picnicking, running, skating, skiing and snowshoeing, along with Winter Carnival festivities and open-air summer concerts. For information

Québec City – Outside the City Walls

and to learn more, visit the Musée des Plaines d'Abraham.

The Plains of Abraham are named for Abraham Martin, a Frenchman who was one of the first farmers to settle in the area. The park was commissioned in 1908 to mark Québec City's tricentennial, and it acquired a reservoir to supply the city with drinking water in 1933. Huts built for soldiers being mobilized during WWII later housed displaced German civilians and POWs. It was here on the Plains of Abraham that 'O Canada,' the Canadian national anthem, written by Sir Adolphe-Basil Routhier with music by Calixa Lavallée, was sung for the first time on June 24, 1880.

MUSÉE DES PLAINES D'ABRAHAM   MUSEUM

Map p178 (Plains of Abraham Museum; ☑418-649-6157; www.theplainsofabraham.ca; 835 Ave Wilfrid-Laurier, Montcalm & Colline Parlementaire; adult/youth/child $12.25/10.25/4, incl Abraham's bus tour & Martello Tower 1 Jul-early Sep $15.25/11.25/5; ☺9am-5:30pm) This museum spread over three levels presents a fine multimedia history show entitled *Battles: 1759–60*. Incorporating maps, scale models, interactive games, period uniforms and an overly long audiovisual presentation, the exhibit immerses visitors in the pivotal 18th-century battles that shaped Québec's destiny during the Seven Years' War between France and England. The experience is enlivened by first-hand accounts from the French, British, Canadian and Amerindian protagonists of the period.

Between July and early September, museum visitors can pay a small extra fee to visit the nearby Martello Tower 1 and take the guided Abraham's Bus Tour (p201).

MARTELLO TOWER 1   HISTORIC BUILDING

Map p178 (Tour Martello 1; ☑855-649-6157, 418-649-6157; www.theplainsofabraham.ca/en/history-heritage/site-history/illustrious-park/#tours; Battlefields Park, Montcalm & Colline Parlementaire; adult/youth/child incl Plains of Abraham Museum & Abraham's bus tour $15.25/11.25/5; ☺9am-5:30pm Jul-early Sep) Despite its small appearance, this defensive tower dating to 1810 on the Plains of Abraham – one of four built by the British – is jam-packed with fascinating exhibits that explore the towers' engineering history and living conditions for the soldiers based here. History buffs can also seek out the nearby Martello Tower 2 (Tour Martello 2;

Map p178) and **Martello Tower 4** (Map p178; Rue Lavigueur, St-Jean Baptiste), which are usually closed to the public but viewable from the outside. (In case you're wondering, Martello Tower 3 was torn down in 1905.)

LA MAISON HENRY-STUART   HISTORIC BUILDING

Map p178 (☑800-494-4347, 418-647-4347; www.maisonhenrystuart.qc.ca; 82 Grande Allée Ouest, Montcalm & Colline Parlementaire; adult/student/child $8/6/3; ☺11am-5pm Tue-Sat late Jun-Aug) This handsomely preserved cottage built in 1850 by an upper-middle-class anglophone family contains period furnishings from the early 1900s. Hour-long guided tours on the hour help elucidate what life was like in those days; tea and lemon cake (included in the tour price) make it that much sweeter.

HÔTEL DU PARLEMENT   HISTORIC BUILDING

Map p178 (Parliament Building; ☑418-643-7239; www.assnat.qc.ca/en/visiteurs; 1045 Rue des Parlementaires, enter from Grande Allée Est, Montcalm & Colline Parlementaire; ☺8:30am-4:30pm Mon-Fri, 9:30am-4:30pm Sat & Sun late Jun-Aug, 8am-5pm Mon-Fri Sep-late Jun) FREE Home to Québec's Provincial Legislature, the gargantuan Parliament building is a Second Empire structure completed in 1886. Free 30-minute tours, offered in English and French, get you into the **National Assembly Chamber**, **Legislative Council Chamber** and **President's Gallery**. The facade is decorated with 26 statues, mostly of significant provincial historical figures, including explorer Samuel de Champlain (1570–1635), New France governor Louis de Buade Frontenac (1622–98) and English and French generals James Wolfe (1727–59) and Louis-Joseph Montcalm (1712–59).

Engraved above the entrance and just below the province's coat of arms is its motto: *Je me souviens* (I remember; 1883).

On the grounds are more recent figures in Québec's tumultuous history, including Maurice Duplessis (1890–1959), who kept a stranglehold on the province during his 20-year-long premiership, and René Lévesque (1922-87), founder of the Parti Québécois (PQ), who first attempted through referendum to negotiate the political independence of Québec. The grounds are also used for staging events during Winter Carnival (p193).

Note the flower-trimmed **Fontaine de Tourny** (Tourny Fountain) facing the grounds, a gift from the Simons department store, installed in 2007 to celebrate Québec City's 400th anniversary the following year. It was built in the mid-19th century and graced the Allées de Tourny in Bordeaux, Québec's sister city, before Simons bought and restored it. It's a fine vantage point for photographing the building.

ÉGLISE ST-MATTHEW (BIBLIOTHÈQUE CLAIRE-MARTIN) CHURCH

Map p178 (Church of St Matthew; ☑418-641-6798; www.bibliothequedequebec.qc.ca/biblio theques/lacitelimoilou/claire_martin.aspx; 755 Rue St-Jean, St-Jean Baptiste; ☺10am-5pm Fri-Tue, 1-8pm Wed & Thu) This Anglican church dating to 1849 closed in 1978 and was subsequently transformed into a public library called Bibliothèque Claire-Martin, retaining its rich ecclesiastical interior. The adjoining cemetery, which functioned as a Protestant burial ground from 1772 until 1860, is now the **Parc St-Matthew**.

ST-JEAN BAPTISTE AREA

Map p178 (St-Jean Baptiste) Strolling along **Rue St-Jean** is a great way to feel the pulse of this bohemian district. The first thing that strikes you, once you've recovered from crossing busy Ave Honoré Mercier, is the area's down-to-earth ambience. Good restaurants, interesting shops and hip cafes and bars, many catering to a LGBTIQ+ clientele, line the thoroughfare as far as Ave Turnbull. Take any side street and walk downhill (north) to the narrow residential streets like Rue d'Aiguillon, Rue Richelieu and Rue St-Olivier.

On these narrow streets, the miniature, scrunched-together wooden houses, some with lovely entrances, are typical of Québec City's residential landscape. The fanciful protruding oriel windows are distinctive too.

To the southwest of Rue St-Jean, the colorful strip of storefronts along **Ave Cartier** in the Montcalm neighborhood has exploded in recent years with mostly chi-chi eateries, cafes and boutiques. It's most buzzing on hot days when the dozen or so terraces open up for business. The epicenter of this little restaurant district is located at the intersection of Ave Cartier and Blvd René-Lévesque Ouest.

OBSÉRVATOIRE DE LA CAPITALE VIEWPOINT

Map p178 (Capital Observatory; ☑418-644-9841, 888-497-4322; www.observatoirecapi tale.org; 1037 Rue de la Chevrotière, Montcalm & Colline Parlementaire; adult/student/child $14.75/11.50/5; ☺10am-5pm Feb–mid-Oct, Tue-Sun mid-Oct–Jan) Head 221m up to the 31st floor of the Édifice Marie-Guyart for great views of the Old Town, the St Lawrence River and (if it's clear) even the distant Laurentians. It all helps to get your bearings and the information panels along the way will get you up to speed on some of the local history, city superlatives and 'fun facts.'

ÉGLISE ST-ROCH CHURCH

Map p178 (☑418-524-3577; www.eglisesaint roch.com; 590 Rue St-Joseph Est, St-Roch; ☺9am-5pm May-Oct, 10am-4pm Nov-Apr) Measuring over 80m long, 34m wide and 46m high (including the steeples), St-Roch is the largest church in Québec City and can seat 1250 people. Begun in 1914, it was finished off in 1923 in a mixed neo-Gothic and neo-Romanesque style by Louis-Napoléon Audet, the same man who worked on the monumental Ste-Anne-de-Beaupré Basilica 35km to the northeast. The 'marble' (actually limestone) inside the church is from Saskatchewan. See if you can detect faint fossil imprints in it.

In mid-August the church hosts its annual **Bénédiction des Chiens** (Blessing of the Dogs), an event unparalleled elsewhere in Canada (and probably the world).

LE TRAIN DE CHARLEVOIX

Two or three times a day daily from mid-June to late October, this light-rail **train** (☑418-240-4124, 844-737-3282; http://traindecharlevoix.com; Montmorency–Baie St-Paul round-trip adult/child $88/50; ☺mid-Jun–late Oct) travels along a scenic stretch of the St Lawrence River, starting at Parc de la Chute-Montmorency northeast of Québec City and running 125km north to the artists' enclave of Baie St-Paul (2¼ hours).

You can change trains in Baie St-Paul to continue upriver as far as La Malbaie, 142km northeast of Québec City (adult/child $54/34, 1½ hours).

QUÉBEC CITY SIGHTS

ST-ROCH

Sprinkled with stylish nightspots, eclectic eateries, boutiques and vintage shops, St-Roch – a kilometer west of the Old Upper Town – is one of Québec City's trendiest neighborhoods. Long a working-class district for factory and naval workers, it suffered through three decades of dereliction before experiencing a remarkable rebirth in the 1990s, thanks to an ambitious urban-renewal plan that created a public garden, restored a shuttered theater and hired artists to paint frescoes in the neighborhood. Today, the main commercial thoroughfare, Rue St-Joseph, draws a dynamic mix of locals, including many students, immigrants, artists and young professionals.

Thanks to the **Ascenseur du Faubourg** (Suburban Elevator; Rue St-Réal, St-Jean Baptiste; ⊘7am-7pm Mon-Wed, to 10pm Thu & Fri, 10am-10pm Sat, to 7pm Sun), a free elevator that eliminates much of the climb, pedestrians can get from Rue St-Joseph to Rue St-Jean in 15 minutes or so.

ÉGLISE ST-JEAN-BAPTISTE
CHURCH

Map p178 (www.saintjeanbaptiste.org; 470 Rue St-Jean, St-Jean Baptiste) This colossus, named after the patron saint of French Canada, completely dominates the southwest end of Rue St-Jean. The first church was built in 1842 but was destroyed by fire in 1881. It was completely rebuilt in the Second Empire style by architect Joseph-Ferdinand Peachy and open again for business by 1884. Due to lack of funding, it closed its doors for an indeterminate length of time in May 2015.

The architect looked to several well-known churches in Paris for inspiration: Notre-Dame-de-Paris for the pillars, Église St-Sulpice for the vaults and Église de la Trinité for the facade.

CARTIER-BRÉBEUF NATIONAL HISTORIC SITE
MUSEUM

(ww.pc.gc.ca/en/lhn-nhs/qc/cartierbrebeuf; 175 Rue de l'Espinay, Limoilu; ⊘1-5pm late Jun-early Sep) FREE On the St Charles River in Limoilu, northwest of the walled section of the city, this national historic site marks the spot where the Iroquoian people helped Jacques Cartier and his men through the winter of 1535. The small interpretation center features a full-scale replica of Cartier's ship, a reproduction of an aboriginal longhouse, and exhibits about the Jesuit order, established in Canada in 1625 by Jean de Brébeuf. Buses 3 and 801 from the center stop nearby.

PARC DU BOIS-DE-COULONGE
PARK

(☎800-442-0773, 418-528-0773; www.capitale.gouv.qc.ca/parcs-et-places-publiques/parcs/parc-du-bois-de-coulonge; 1215 Grande Allée Ouest, Montcalm & Colline Parlementaire; ⊘7am-11pm) Not far to the southwest of the Plains of Abraham lie the colorful gardens of this park, a paean to the plant world and a welcome respite from downtown. Once the private property of a succession of Québec's and Canada's religious and political elite, this wonderful mix of woodland and extensive horticultural displays has been managed as a public park since 1996.

AQUARIUM DU QUÉBEC
AQUARIUM

(☎418-659-5264, 866-659-5264; www.sepaq.com/ct/paq; 1675 Ave des Hôtels, Ste-Foy; adult/child $20.50/10.25; ⊘9am-5pm Jun–mid-Oct, 10am-4pm mid-Oct–May; 🖃) 🖉 Spread across 40 hectares, Québec's aquarium contains some 10,000 aquatic creatures, including freshwater and saltwater fish, amphibians, reptiles, invertebrates and marine mammals. Among its several habitats are a wetlands region and an Arctic sector complete with underwater window for observing polar bears. Catch daily events like walrus and polar-bear feedings. Times vary throughout the year; see the website for details. There's also a food court with a terrace overlooking the St Lawrence River.

The aquarium is 12km southwest of the city center, at the northern foot of the Pont de Québec. RTC city bus 25 from Place d'Youville stops about 500m from the aquarium. Between late May and early October, a shuttle bus ($10) run by Les Tours de Vieux Québec (p201) links the Place d'Armes in the Old Upper Town and the aquarium, departing at 10:40am and returning at 2pm daily.

✖ EATING

Québec City's restaurant scene has never been better. While the capital has always excelled at classic French food, a number of new arrivals have put a trendy modern spin on bistros. Better places can get a bit pricey, but remember: a carefully chosen *table d'hôte* at lunchtime will give you exactly the same food for a more manageable price.

✖ Old Town & Port

Be choosy about where you spend your money in the Old Upper Town. Though many restaurants have gorgeous settings and may be fine for coffee, tea or a beer, food can often be both costly and disappointing.

In the Old Lower Town, Rue St-Paul, Rue Sault-au-Matelot and Rue du Petit-Champlain are lined with restaurants. In warm weather, they fling their windows open and set up outdoor seating on the streets, creating a terrific atmosphere. In winter the streets outside may be deserted, but the revelry goes indoors, and windows positively glow with warmth and good cheer inside.

CHEZ TEMPOREL CAFE $

Map p170 (✆418-694-1813; www.facebook.com/cheztemporel; 25 Rue Couillard, Old Upper Town; mains $9-20; ☺11am-5pm Mon-Thu, to 8:30pm Fri & Sat, to 7:30pm Sun) Hidden away on a side street just off the beaten path, this charming little cafe serves tasty sandwiches, homemade soups and quiches, pizza plus prodigious salads, fresh-baked goods and excellent coffee. Being slightly off the track, it attracts a healthy mix of locals and travelers.

ACADÉMIE CULINAIRE CAFE QUÉBÉCOIS $

Map p170 (✆418-780-2211; www.academieculinaire.com; 300 Rue St-Paul, Old Lower Town & Port; sandwiches $8.50, salads $9-11; ☺8am-7pm Mon-Fri, to 5pm Sat & Sun) Québec's celebrated

---

QUÉBEC CITY DINING TIPS

Opening Hours & Meal Times

Most restaurants in Québec City are open for lunch and dinner in the off-season and from about 11am to whenever the last customer leaves in peak summer season or during the Carnaval de Québec. Standard lunch hours are noon to 2:30pm, with dinner from 6pm to 10pm. Places really tend to fill up from 8pm onward in the francophone tradition. Note that outside of Winter Carnival, many restaurants in winter may be closed Sunday and Monday, or both. Breakfast cafes open around 7am (later on weekends).

How Much?

Midrange places in Québec City will, on average, charge $15 to $25 for a main course. Top-end restaurants run upward of $25 for a main; a culinary temple of some renown might charge $60 to $100 or more for a four-course gourmet dinner, including wine. Count on $6 to $10 for a glass of drinkable red and $25 to $35 (and up) for a bottle from the house cellar. Federal and provincial taxes amounting to just under 15% apply at all restaurants. Most do not include taxes in their menu prices.

Booking Tables

If you're in Québec City between May and October, or during Winter Carnival, definitely book ahead to dine in one of the finer restaurants. During this peak season, popular places can fill up quickly, even at odd times like Monday nights.

Tipping

A tip of 15% of the pretax bill is customary in restaurants. Most credit-card machines in Québec will calculate the tip for you based on whatever percentage you specify or allow you to tip a dollar amount of your own choosing. Some restaurants may add a service charge for large parties; in these cases, no tip should be added unless the service was extraordinary. If tipping in cash, leave the tip on the table or hand it directly to staff.

Culinary Academy, with branches here and in Montréal, puts its mettle where your mouth is – so to speak – with this simple cafe and takeaway close to the train and bus stations. High-quality precooked meals available to take away, as well as sandwich and salad picnic boxes ($14 to $17).

CASSE CRÊPE BRETON
CRÊPES $

Map p170 (☑418-692-0438; www.cassecrepe breton.com; 1136 Rue St-Jean, Old Upper Town; crepes $5.95-14.50; ⊗7am-10pm; ☑) Tiny and unassuming, this perennial favorite specializes in both sweet and savory crepes, along with sandwiches ($6.50), soups ($4) and salads ($10 to $12.50). Some diners like to sit at the counter and watch the chef at work. Seating is first-come, first-served. Always a warm welcome here. Good ciders too.

PAILLARD
CAFE, BAKERY $

Map p170 (☑418-692-1221; www.paillard.ca; 1097 Rue St-Jean, Old Upper Town; sandwiches $9-11; ⊗7am-9pm Sun-Thu, to 10pm Fri & Sat) At this bright, buzzy and high-ceilinged *café-boulangerie* (cafe-bakery) crammed with tourists, diners seated at long wooden tables tuck into tasty gourmet sandwiches, soups and salads. The attached bakery, with its alluring display cases, is downright irresistible – try the *tentation* ($3), a delicious sweet pastry loaded with berries.

Another favorite here is the savory *fougasse* (Provençal-style bread brushed with olive oil and studded with olives and herbs, $5.60). Paillard is a bit of a madhouse at lunchtime.

LE PACKWOOD
SANDWICHES $

Map p170 (☑418-694-3066; www.facebook.com/ lepackwood; 152 Rue St-Paul, Old Lower Town & Port; sandwiches $5, soup, salad & sandwich $12; ⊗11am-2pm Mon, 9:30am-4pm Tue-Sat; ☑) This delightful boutique opposite the Old Port selling no end of made-in-Québec gift items and souvenirs (jewelry, bags, knitwear, wooden jigsaw puzzles) also has a *comptoir lunch* (lunch counter) with sandwiches, soups, salads and desserts. A lot of good choices for vegetarians too. Lovely and very welcoming host.

LE CHIC SHACK
BURGERS $

Map p170 (☑418-692-1485; www.lechicshack. ca; 15 Rue du Fort, Old Upper Town; mains $7-13; ⊗11am-10pm May-Sep, to 3pm Sun-Wed, to 9pm Thu-Sat Oct-Apr) This lively and very upbeat

place in the heart of the Old Town is mostly about burgers – quality ones made from grass-fed beef and served on brioche rolls. But it's also got a selection of poutine dishes and gourmet salads. Milkshakes are good too.

LE BUFFET DE L'ANTIQUAIRE
DINER $

Map p170 (☑418-692-2661; https://lebuffet delantiquaire.com; 95 Rue St-Paul, Old Lower Town & Port; breakfast $6-15, mains $12-19; ⊗6am-9pm) Tucked in among the antique shops and galleries is this convivial old-school 'diner.' Locals and tourists alike crowd in for hearty breakfasts, steaming plates of poutine ($7 to $13) and savory meat pies like the deep-dish layered *cipaille,* all served with friendly efficiency. Grab a booth, a seat at the narrow counter or a table on the upstairs balcony.

In warm weather, there are also sidewalk tables out front.

LA CANTINE D'ASIE INDOCHINE
VIETNAMESE $

Map p170 (☑418-692-3799; 93 Rue Sault-au-Matelot, Old Lower Town & Port; dishes $10-15; ⊗11:30am-9pm) This hole-in-the-wall in the Lower Town, in place since forever, seats just two dozen people at tables, at the window and along a counter, but serves up some of the best Vietnamese pho (Vietnamese beef noodle soup) and baguettes in town. If you're getting tired of poutine and maple-flavored everything, seek your fix of rice and noodles here.

CHEZ ASHTON
FAST FOOD $

Map p170 (☑418-692-3055; https://chezashton. ca; 54 Côte du Palais, Old Upper Town; mains $4.50-10.50; ⊗11am-10pm Sun-Tue, to midnight Wed-Sat) For a break from fine dining, head to this Québec City fast-food institution with 24 restaurants across town. On weekends, local revelers flock here late at night to refuel with the classic Québécois comfort food, poutine (fries smothered in cheese curds and gravy), which many say is the best in town.

SO-CHO LE SAUCISSIER
FAST FOOD $

Map p170 (☑418-694-9615; www.so-cho.com; 160 Quai St-André, Marché du Vieux-Port, Old Lower Town & Port; sandwiches from $6; ⊗9am-5pm) For a snack on the go, locals favor this humble stand inside Marché du Vieux-Port (p200), with its ever-changing array of de-

THE QUÉBÉCOIS TABLE

French food is king in Québec City. The lack of a significant immigrant population means that there is not the kind of massive ethnic smorgasbord that you'll find in Montréal; even so, the quality of restaurants here is outstanding.

Québec City also boasts at least one drink that you won't find in Montréal. *Caribou* is a potent blend of fortified wine and grain alcohol, sometimes mixed with spices and sweetened with maple syrup. Served hot at outdoor bars and streetside stalls during the Carnaval de Québec, it's designed to warm body and soul in the coldest depths of winter.

lectable homemade sausages. Four to 12 flavors are offered each day, from *fines herbes* to lamb with mint and garlic, to be enjoyed on a roll with sauerkraut and mustard.

The date is not yet firm, but the venerable Marché du Vieux-Port is scheduled to quit its portside location and move to ExpoCité, a multisite entertainment complex that includes the Centre Vidéotron stadium, about 6km north of the Old Town. Once it's moved, look for So-Cho Le Saucissier there.

★LE LAPIN SAUTÉ   FRENCH $$
Map p170 (☑418-692-5325; www.lapinsaute.com; 52 Rue du Petit-Champlain, Old Lower Town & Port; mains $17-29; ⊙11am-10pm Mon-Fri, 9am-10pm Sat & Sun) Naturally, *lapin* (rabbit) plays a starring role at this cozy, rustic restaurant just south of the funicular's lower terminus, in such dishes as rabbit cassoulet or rabbit poutine. Other enticements include salads, French onion soup, charcuterie platters and an excellent-value lunch menu (from $16). In good weather, sit on the flowery patio overlooking tiny Parc Félix-Leclerc.

All of the rabbit served here is raised without hormones or antibiotics on a farm in nearby Beauce.

★1608   CHEESE $$
Map p170 (☑418-692-3861; http://1608baravin.com; 1 Rue des Carrières, Fairmount Le Château Frontenac, Old Upper Town; mains $21-34; ⊙4pm-midnight Sun-Thu, 2pm-1am Fri & Sat) At this Frontenac-based wine-and-cheese bar you can either select some cheeses yourself or let the staff take you down a wine-and-cheese rabbit hole that's difficult to emerge from; platters of three/four/five cheeses are $21/26/30 (five types with charcuterie $34). Wine, *fromage* and an incomparable view of the St Lawrence all make for a very romantic setting.

LE CAFÉ
DU MONDE   BISTRO $$
Map p170 (☑418-692-4455; www.lecafedumonde.com; 84 Rue Dalhousie, Old Lower Town & Port; mains $20-33; ⊙11:30am-10pm Mon-Fri, from 9am Sat & Sun) This Paris-style bistro is the only restaurant in town directly on the St Lawrence River, although actually getting a table with a view can sometimes be a challenge. Persevere. Bright, airy and casually elegant, it swears by bistro classics like *steak frites* (steak and fries) and duck confit, but there's also a great choice of other dishes, from grilled salmon to deer stew.

Gourmet breakfasts ($14 to $25) are served on weekends, and local Québec produce is featured throughout the menu. Weekday three-course lunch menus are $17 to $23, dinner $30.

LÉGENDE   QUÉBÉCOIS $$
Map p170 (☑418-614-2555; http://restaurantlegende.com/restaurant-legende-quebec; 255 Rue St-Paul, Old Lower Town & Port; mains $19-24; ⊙5:30-10pm Wed-Sun) Seasonal cuisine and fine-wine pairings are the name of the game at this classy restaurant under the direction of renowned restaurateurs Karen Therrien and Frédéric Laplante. Québécois oysters, mackerel, lamb and duck share the menu with artisanal cheeses and specialty ingredients such as balsamic-like birch syrup, chanterelle mushrooms and fiddlehead ferns.

All dishes can be ordered as appetizers or main courses, accompanied by sommelier-selected wines ($6 to $16 per glass). The tasting menu is $79 (with wine pairing, add $69). Légende is attached to the **Hôtel des Coutellier** (Map p170; ☑888-523-9696, 418-692-9696; www.hoteldescoutellier.com; 253 Rue St-Paul, Old Lower Town & Port; r $145-295, ste $275-375; ✴@🛜).

CHEZ JULES
FRENCH **$$**

Map p170 (☎418-694-9485; www.chezjules.ca; 24 Rue Ste-Anne, Old Upper Town; mains $18-24; ⊙7:30am-10:30pm May-Oct, 7:30-10am daily, 11:30am-1:30pm Wed-Fri & 5:30-10pm Tue-Sat Nov-Apr) A solid and affordable French meal can be had at this small, central dining room alongside the Auberge Place d'Armes. Chez Jules serves an excellent assortment of traditional French dishes like frogs' legs, bouillabaisse (fish stew), cassoulet (casserole of butter beans and duck confit) and Alsatian *choucroute* (sauerkraut simmered with smoked meats). Its delectable desserts are the coup de grâce.

SAPRISTI ST-JEAN
ITALIAN **$$**

Map p170 (☎418-692-2030; http://sapristi.ca; 1001 Rue St-Jean, Old Upper Town; pizza & pasta $14-19, salads $15.50-17; ⊙11:30am-10:30pm Sun-Wed, to 11:30pm Thu-Sat) This central Italian bistro and bar serves imaginative pizza, pasta and salads. It's very affordable for the location and the glass-and-tile interior gives it an upbeat, of-this-century feel. It's in the same stable as Les Trois Garçons, a fancy burger place across the street.

LE PETIT
COIN LATIN
CAFE **$$**

Map p170 (☎418-692-0700; www.lepetitcoin latin.ca; 8½ Rue Ste-Ursule, Old Upper Town; mains $17.50-26; ⊙7:30am-11pm) For omelets, croissants and bowls of café au lait, this cafe makes a cheerful breakfast stop, especially in summer when the back patio is open. The menu also includes salads, soups and *tourtière* (Québécois elk-meat pie). For a cozy wintertime treat, couples can share a raclette (a make-your-own Swiss dish of melted cheese, potatoes, grilled meat and pickles).

L'ENTRECÔTE SAINT-JEAN
STEAK **$$**

Map p170 (☎418-694-0234; www.entrecote saintjean.com; 1080 Rue St-Jean, Old Upper Town; mains $16-24, steaks $22-28; ⊙11:30am-10pm Mon-Wed, to 10:30pm Thu, 11:30am-11pm Fri, noon-11pm Sat, 5-10pm Sun) 'The secret is in the sauce,' they trumpet, but we'd say it's more in the quality of the meat, which is high at this Québec City institution, in place for over three decades. If you're not in the mood for entrecôte (a long thin sirloin cut) and *frites,* there are other mains such as a croque monsieur and duck confit.

APSARA
ASIAN **$$**

Map p170 (☎418-694-0232; http://restaurant apsara.com; 71 Rue d'Auteuil, Old Upper Town; mains $17-21; ⊙11:30am-2pm Mon-Fri, 5:30-11pm daily, closed Mon winter) Southeast Asian cuisine, from Thai to Vietnamese and Cambodian, all gets a little lumped together at this restaurant in a grand old house opposite the Parc de l'Esplanade and Porte St-Louis. But it's Cambodians who are piloting the ship with delicious results, including thinly sliced beef stir-fry and pork-and-shrimp dumplings. Set menus $30 to $42.

UN THÉ AU SAHARA
MOROCCAN **$$**

Map p170 (☎418-692-5315; 7 Rue Ste-Ursule, Old Upper Town; mains $16-20; ⊙4:30pm-midnight) Bring your own wine or hit the mint tea in this basic but popular Moroccan restaurant in the Old Town. All the classics are available: tabbouleh, hummus and other meze to start, followed by couscous, brochettes and *tagine kefta* (veal croquettes in tomato sauce).

LE COCHON DINGUE
FRENCH **$$**

Map p170 (☎418-692-2013; www.cochondingue. com; 46 Blvd Champlain, Old Lower Town & Port; mains $16-28; ⊙7am-10pm Mon-Fri, from 8am Sat & Sun; ⊛) Since 1979, the ever-popular

---

BAKERIES, SNACKS & FINE DINING

Dozens of boulangeries (bakeries) and patisseries, such as Paillard (p185) and Le Croquembouche (p191), dazzle the eyes and taste buds with perfect croissants and abundant, beautiful displays of éclairs, strawberry tarts and *chocolatines (pain au chocolat)*. For other affordable French-inspired treats, sample the quiches and savory snacks at *traiteurs* (delis) along Ave Cartier or the *crêperies* along Rue St-Jean, or head to the lively Marché du Vieux-Port (p200), where purveyors of artisanal cheeses and sausages mingle with farmers selling fresh produce from nearby Île d'Orléans. If it's fine cuisine you're after, prepare to be spoiled at top-of-the-line restaurants such as Chez Boulay (p188) and Le St-Amour (p188), classy brunch hangouts like Café du Clocher Penché (p192), or trendy bistros like Bistro B (p194) and L'Échaudé (p190).

'Crazy Pig' has been serving straightforward French standbys, from café au lait *en bol* (in a bowl) to croque monsieur, sandwiches, *steak frites*, salads, mussels and quiche. It's all good day-to-day food and a kid-friendly place to boot. There's outside seating in warm weather for crowd-watching.

CHEZ VICTOR

VIEUX-PORT   BURGERS **$$**

Map p170 (☑418-781-2511; www.chezvictor burger.com; 300 Rue St-Paul, Old Lower Town & Port; mains $10.50-19.50; ☺11am-10pm Sun-Fri, to 10pm Sat; ☑) This branch of Québec City's gourmet burger chain is located down by the Vieux-Port close to the bus and train stations. Enter from Rue Abraham-Martin.

★LE ST-AMOUR   FRENCH, QUÉBÉCOIS **$$$**

Map p170 (☑418-694-0667; www.saint-amour. com; 48 Rue Ste-Ursule, Old Upper Town; mains $42-52, tasting menus $72 & $130; ☺11:30am-2pm Mon-Fri, 5:30-10pm daily) One of Québec City's top-end darlings, Le St-Amour has earned a loyal following for its beautifully prepared grills and seafood, and luxurious surrounds. The soaring greenhouse-style ceiling trimmed with hanging plants creates an inviting setting, and the midday *table d'hôte* ($18 to $33; available weekdays) offers that rarest of Upper Town experiences – a world-class meal at an extremely reasonable price.

Perhaps more impressive than the food is the excellent wine selection, with over 12,000 bottles in the cellar. It's in the same stable as Chez Boulay.

★CHEZ BOULAY   QUÉBÉCOIS **$$$**

Map p170 (☑418-380-8166; www.chezboulay. com; 1110 Rue St-Jean, Old Upper Town; lunch menus $18-24, dinner mains $26-35; ☺11:30am-10pm Mon-Fri, 10am-10pm Sat & Sun) ⌀ Renowned chef Jean-Luc Boulay's flagship restaurant serves an ever-evolving menu inspired by seasonal Québécois staples such as venison, goose, blood pudding, wild mushrooms and Gaspé Peninsula seafood. Lunch specials and charcuterie platters for two (served 2pm to 5pm) offer an affordable afternoon pick-me-up, while the sleek, low-lit dining area with views of the open kitchen makes a romantic dinner setting.

★CHEZ MUFFY   FRENCH, QUÉBÉCOIS **$$$**

Map p170 (☑418-692-1022; www.saint-antoine. com/chez-muffy; 10 Rue St-Antoine, Old Lower Town & Port; lunch/dinner menu $22/50, mains $37-50; ☺6:30-10:30am Mon-Fri, 7-11am Sat, 10am-1pm Sun, 6-10pm Wed-Sun) The celebrated restaurant of Auberge St-Antoine (p208) receives top marks for its exquisite, imaginatively prepared Québécois cuisine and top-notch service. Dinners and attractively priced midday *tables d'hôte* feature locally sourced ingredients like sable fish *a la plancha* (grilled), Appalachian red deer with wild-berry sauce or St-Gervais suckling pig. It's set in a stone-walled 19th-century maritime warehouse, with rustic wood beams.

RESTAURANT

CHAMPLAIN   CANADIAN **$$$**

Map p170 (☑418-692-3861; www.restaurant champlain.com; 1 Rue des Carrières, Fairmont Le Château Frontenac, Old Upper Town; mains $29-47; ☺6-9pm Tue-Sat, 10am-1pm Sun) The Fairmont Le Château Frontenac's signature restaurant is the city's most celebrated; you'll be overwhelmed by the fabulous views, the artwork, the stellar service and especially the creative gastronomy. Chef Stéphane Modat likes to juggle ingredients and tastes to universal success – partridge is joined with red-cabbage confit and wild berries, caribou marries wild mushrooms in sweet-and-sour maple.

BELLO RISTORANTE   ITALIAN **$$$**

Map p170 (☑418-694-0030; www.bello ristorante.com; 73 Rue St-Louis, Old Upper Town; mains $17-38; ☺11:30am-11:30pm) Luc Ste-Croix, former student of French master chef Paul Bocuse, brings his passion for Italian cuisine to this stylish and very welcoming eatery near Porte St-Louis. The vast menu ranges from wood-fired pizzas and scrumptious risottos to Parmesan veal scaloppini. Save room at dessert-time for tiramisu ($12), made the right way with real mascarpone.

What we really like is that pastas can be ordered as full ($17 to $34) or half-portions ($10 to $21). Excellent lunch set menu at a budget-busting $16.

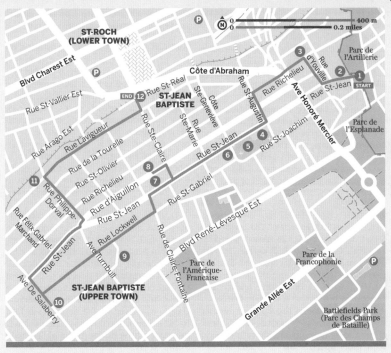

Neighborhood Walk
Hip Hop Through Trendy St-Jean Baptiste

START PORTE ST-JEAN
END ASCENSEUR DU FAUBOURG
LENGTH 3KM; TWO HOURS

This walk takes you through boho St-Jean Baptiste, one of Québec City's best districts for strolling.

Begin at **1 Porte St-Jean**, northernmost of the Old City's three main town gates originally built in 1693. Further along Rue St-Jean on the right is the renovated **2 Théâtre Capitole** (p199), the city's first theater when it opened as the Auditorium de Québec in 1903. Turn right at Rue d'Youville and follow it to the **3 Convent of the Sisters of Charity** and its magnificent galleried chapel.

Walk west along Rue Richelieu, crossing over busy Ave Honoré Mercier and turn left at Rue St-Augustin. At the corner with Rue St-Jean is the onetime Anglican **4 Church of St Matthew** (p182), transformed into a public library in 1980. The adjoining cemetery is now the **5 Parc St-Matthew**. One block along Rue St-Jean is **6 JA Moisan Épicier**

(p203), the oldest grocery store (1871) in North America; at the corner of Rue Ste-Claire is the colossal Second Empire–style **7 Église St-Jean-Baptiste** (p183), rebuilt in 1884 after a devastating fire three years before. Around the church are some colorful **8 wooden clapboard houses** rebuilt after the fires of 1845 and 1881.

Turn left at Rue de Claire-Fontaine and follow Rue Lockwell to the end, passing a residential block called **9 Immeubles Jeffrey Hale**. Near the corner with Ave de Salaberry is the **10 Théâtre Périscope**. Go around the front to see its previous incarnation – the Hebrew letters identify it as the synagogue Beth Israel Ohev Sholom.

Follow Ave de Salaberry north back to Rue St-Jean and turn right. At Rue Philippe-Dorval, turn left and walk north to **11 Martello Tower 4** (p181), one of three such fortifications in town. You can descend steps here but you'll probably prefer continuing east along Rue Lavigueur to the **12 Ascenseur du Faubourg** (p183), an elevator that will take you down to the district of St-Roch.

LAURIE RAPHAËL　　FRENCH **$$$**

Map p170 (📞418-692-4555; https://laurie raphael.com; 117 Rue Dalhousie, Old Lower Town & Port; 7/11 courses $110/155; ⏱5:30-9:30pm Tue-Sat, daily Jul-Oct) One of Québec's finest restaurants, this architecturally stunning, silver-service restaurant with celebrated chefs Daniel and Raphaël Vézina at the helm offers tasting menus of three/five themes and seven/11 courses. Expect such sensations as maple-lacquered smoked and stuffed calamari, and trout-and-leek omelette with a razor clam and celery salad. Seven-course vegetarian menu also available. For wine pairing, add $60 or $80.

L'ÉCHAUDÉ　　BISTRO **$$$**

Map p170 (📞418-692-1299; www.echaude. com; 73 Rue Sault-au-Matelot, Old Lower Town & Port; lunch menus $15-28, dinner mains $23-36; ⏱11:30am-2:30pm & 5:30-11pm Mon-Fri, 10am-2pm & 5:30-11pm Sat, from 9am Sun; 🚲) Everything comes beautifully plated and bursting with flavor at this relaxed but very classy bistro, one of the rare Old Town eateries where locals regularly outnumber tourists. Classics such as duck confit, *steak frites* and salmon tartare share the menu with daily specials like fish and mussel stew in a lobster-and-wine broth. The terrific wine list favors bottles from France.

AUX ANCIENS CANADIENS　　QUÉBÉCOIS **$$$**

Map p170 (📞418-692-1627; www.auxanciens canadiens.qc.ca; 34 Rue St-Louis, Old Upper Town; mains $33-89, 3-course menu from $20; ⏱noon-9pm) Housed in the historic Jacquet House, which dates from 1675, this place is a well-worn tourist destination, specializing in robust country cooking and typical Québécois specialties served by waitstaff in historic garb. The *menu du jour*, offered from noon to 5.45pm, is by far the best deal at around $20 for three courses, including a glass of wine or beer.

Traditional dishes featured on the menu include bison bourguignonne in cream and blueberry wine sauce, duck breast in a maple-syrup reduction, Lac St-Jean game pie, and wild caribou filet mignon. The restaurant gets its name from the novel *Les Anciens Canadiens* (The Canadians of Old) by Philippe-Aubert de Gaspé, who lived in the house from 1815 to 1824. The original rooms have been left intact, resulting in several small, intimate dining areas.

QUÉBEC CITY FOOD & DRINK EXPERIENCES

Académie Culinaire Québec (Map p170; 📞418-780-2211; www.academieculinaire.com; 300 Rue St-Paul, Old Lower Town & Port) The Québec City branch of this well-regarded cooking academy offers courses in French and international cuisine, ranging in length from three hours (from $130) to one week ($475).

Les Tours Voir Québec (Map p170; 📞418-694-2001, 866-694-2001; www.toursvoirque bec.com; 12 Rue Ste-Anne, Old Upper Town; walking tour adult/student/child $23/19.50/11) This group offers excellent tours on the history, architecture and food of Québec City. The popular two-hour 'grand tour,' probably the city's best walking tour, takes in the Old City's highlights, while the food tour includes tastings of wines, cheeses, crepes and chocolate at a variety of shops and restaurants. Buy tickets at and depart from Centre Infotouriste Québec City (p249).

Gourmet Food Tour (Map p170; 📞866-694-2001, 418-694-2001; www.toursvoirquebec. com; 12 Rue Ste-Anne, Old Upper Town; adult/child $46/25; ⏱tours 2pm May-Oct, Tue-Sat Nov-Apr) Wending through the St-Jean Baptiste neighborhood, this 2½-hour culinary tour offers tastings of wines, cheeses, crepes, chocolate and other Québécois specialties at a variety of shops and restaurants. From November through April, a two-person minimum is required. It's one of several city tours offered by Les Tours Voir Québec. Buy tickets at and depart from the Centre Infotouriste Québec City (p249).

Broue-Tours (📞418-554-1233; www.brou-tours.ca; $65) If you're an aficionado of craft beer, join one of this outfit's 'brew tours.' Over three hours you'll visit three microbreweries and down nine sample glasses. Blotter is included in the form of snacks. Check the website for times and places of departure.

CHEZ RIOUX & PETTIGREW

QUÉBÉCOIS **$$$**

Map p170 (📋418-694-4448; www.chezrioux etpettigrew.com; 160 Rue St-Paul, Old Lower Town & Port; mains $27-34; ⏱11:30am-2pm Wed-Fri, from 9:30am Sat & Sun, 5:30-10pm daily) Conveniently placed near the meeting of antiques row and the Vieux-Port, this classy eatery with stone walls and an open kitchen builds its menu around *cuisine du marché,* market-fresh cuisine that changes with the seasons. Scrumptious weekend brunches ($18 to $21), weekday lunch specials ($16 to $21), and full-on three-course dinners ($65) make this an appealing stop anytime of day.

LE BISTRO ST-MALO

BISTRO **$$$**

Map p170 (📋418-692-2004; www.bistrostmalo. com; 75 Rue St-Paul, Old Lower Town & Port; mains $26-34; ⏱11:30am-2pm & 5-10pm) For cozy French bistro atmosphere, you can't beat this cute, very traditional hole-in-the-wall down by the Old Port. The menu abounds in bistro classics like homemade cassoulet, *boudin noir grillé aux légumes racines* (grilled blood sausage with root vegetables) and the unusual rabbit bourguignonne, along with a daily fish choice.

CONTI

ITALIAN **$$$**

Map p170 (📋418-692-4191; www.conticaffe.com; 32 Rue St-Louis, Old Upper Town; mains $26-37; ⏱11:30am-11pm) Set on busy Rue St-Louis, this handsome eatery features an enticing mixture of Italian and Mediterranean flavors. Start off with prosciutto-wrapped shrimp or Cognac-infused lobster bisque, then move on to duck confit risotto or the classic Milanese-style osso buco. The dining room is a warmly lit retreat, with exposed-brick walls trimmed with art and big windows overlooking the street.

The lunchtime *table d'hôte* ($15 to $23 for soup or juice, main dish, coffee and dessert) is one of the Old Town's best deals. It's $40 at dinnertime.

✖ Outside the Old Town

LE CROQUEMBOUCHE

BAKERY **$**

Map p178 (📋418-523-9009; www.lecroquem bouche.com; 225 Rue St-Joseph Est, St-Roch; pastries from $2, sandwiches from $5.25; ⏱7am-6:30pm Tue-Sat, to 5pm Sun; 🖝) Widely hailed as Québec City's finest bakery, Le Croquembouche draws devoted locals from dawn to dusk. Among its seductive offerings are fluffy-as-cloud croissants, tantalizing cakes and éclairs, brioches brimming with raspberries, and gourmet sandwiches on fresh-baked bread. There's also a stellar array of *danoises* (Danish pastries), including orange and anise, cranberry, pistachio and chocolate.

BÜGEL FABRIQUE DE BAGELS

CANADIAN **$**

Map p178 (📋418-523-7666; http://bugel-fabrique.ca; 164 Rue Crémazie Ouest, St Jean-Baptiste; bagel sandwiches $11-12.75, breakfast $7.50-15; ⏱7am-7pm Sat-Wed, to 9pm Thu & Fri) 🖝 Don't be fooled by the title: there's more than plain bagels ($3.60) at this cute neighborhood nook in situ since 1987. More accurately, imagine bagels and then some: served with Brie or goat's cheese, or au gratin with ham and asparagus, or topped with smoked salmon or turkey. Ingredients are locally sourced, and the strong coffee kicks like a mule.

MORENA

BISTRO **$**

Map p178 (📋418-529-3668; www.morena-food. com; 1038 Ave Cartier, Montcalm & Colline Parlementaire; mains $12-16; ⏱8am-7pm Mon-Wed, to 8pm Thu & Fri, to 6pm Sat & Sun) Tucked into a gourmet grocery-deli on chichi Ave Cartier, this Italian-themed neighborhood bistro makes a lively but low-key lunch stop. Daily chalkboard specials are beautifully presented, with fresh veggies on the side and a soup or salad appetizer. After 3pm there's an à la carte snack menu. After your meal it's also a fun place to browse for food-related gifts.

Dine solo at the counter or enjoy a tête-à-tête with your traveling companion at one of the little tables for two.

TORA-YA RAMEN

JAPANESE **$**

Map p178 (📋418-780-1903; www.toraya ramen.com; 75 Rue St-Joseph Est, St-Roch; mains $12-15; ⏱11:30am-2pm Tue-Fri, 5-10pm Tue-Sat) Catering to a young, informal clientele, this straight-ahead noodle house specializes in delicious ramen soups filled with pork, fish, tofu and loads of veggies. Draft beer, wine and a good sake selection make it a cozy place for a sit-down meal, but it's also a great takeout option if you'd rather hunker down in your hotel for a night.

FROMAGERIE
DES GRONDINES
SANDWICHES $

Map p178 (☑581-742-4866; www.fromage riedesgrondines.com; 199 Rue St-Joseph Est, St-Roch; sandwiches $6.75-12; ☺10:30am-6:30pm Mon-Wed & Sat, to 8pm Thu & Fri, to 5pm Sun) Primarily a gourmet cheese shop, this high-ceilinged, brick-walled corner spot raises the humble grilled cheese sandwich to unprecedented heights. The big chalkboard menu lists a dizzying array of choices, from straight-up grilled cheddar 'like Mom used to make' to alternatives that jazz up the concept with fancy cheeses, ham, bacon, mushrooms and dipping sauces.

POUTINEVILLE
QUÉBÉCOIS $

Map p178 (☑581-981-8188; www.poutine ville.com; 735 Rue St-Joseph Est, St-Roch; mains $12-16; ☺11am-10pm Sun-Wed, to 11pm Thu, to midnight Fri & Sat) This could be the place for poutine virgins to try what has become the Québécois national dish – french fries served with cheese curds and swimming in gravy. But don't stop at just the garden-variety poutine: this is *la poutine réinventée*, where you'll find such additions as hot dogs, smoked meat, feta cheese or Mexican chili.

★BATTUTO
ITALIAN $$

Map p178 (☑418-614-4414; www.battuto.ca; 527 Blvd Langelier, St-Roch; mains $21-23; ☺5:30-10pm Tue-Sat) Considered by many Québécois to be the best Italian restaurant in town, this wonderful place on the edge of St-Roch mixes traditional dishes like *vitello tonnato* (veal topped with a tuna sauce) with more inventive pasta ones such as Sicilian *casarecce* served with sweetbreads and sherry. It's a tiny place, with a mere 24 seats, so book well ahead.

★BUVETTE SCOTT
FRENCH $$

Map p178 (☑581-741-4464; www.buvettescott. com; 821 Rue Scott, St-Jean Baptiste; mains $12-18; ☺4:30-11pm Mon-Sat) At this tiny wine bistro with just eight tables and seating at the bar, enlightened French classics like breaded calf's brains, bone marrow and *brandade de morue* (Provençal puree of cod mixed with milk, olive oil and garlic and served with croutons) dominate the menu. The chalkboard wine list is exceptional, with six reds and six whites.

FAITE À L'OS
QUÉBÉCOIS $$

Map p178 (☑418-977-9888; www.faitealos.com; 637 Grande Allée Est, Montcalm & Colline Parlementaire; mains $19-28; ☺11:30am-2:30pm Tue-Fri, 5:30-10pm Tue-Sat) You'll smell this cozy spot well before you arrive; the *fumoir* (smokehouse) would appear to be working overtime. The all-time favorite dish is the Ribs Kenneth Handerson, smoked for eight hours and dressed with homemade barbecue sauce. Also delicious (and less daunting) is the 'Po'boy de Conrad Murphy,' effectively a seafood burger.

L'AFFAIRE EST
KETCHUP
BISTRO $$

Map p178 (☑418-529-9020; www.facebook. com/laffaireest.ketchup; 46 Rue St-Joseph Est, St-Roch; mains $20-28; ☺6-10:30pm Tue-Sun) Book ahead for this quirky local favorite with only eight tables. Dressed in T-shirts and baseball caps, bantering relaxedly with one another as they cook on a pair of electric stoves, founders Olivier Lescelleur St-Cyr and François Jobin specialize in home cooking with a trendy modern twist. Good selection of wines and mixed drinks at the well-stocked bar.

TEMPÉRA QUÉBECOR
QUÉBÉCOIS $$

Map p178 (☑418-644-6780; www.signemc lepage.com; 179 Grande Allée Ouest, Montcalm & Colline Parlementaire; mains $20-29, 3-course set lunch $24; ☺11am-5pm Tue, Thu & Fri, 10am-9pm Wed, 10:30am-5pm Sat & Sun) This beautifully situated and decorated restaurant at the Musée National des Beaux-Arts du Québec (p179) does not require a museum visit; it is worth the trip on its own (though a peek at the galleries is an added bonus). It's chef Marie-Chantal Lepage's flagship restaurant and is like taking a tour around the world with visits to the Mediterranean and Asia.

CAFÉ DU
CLOCHER PENCHÉ
FRENCH $$

Map p178 (☑418-640-0597; www.clocher penche.ca; 203 Rue St-Joseph Est, St-Roch; mains $23-27, brunch & lunch menus $17-20; ☺11:30am-2pm Mon-Fri, from 9am Sat & Sun, 5-10pm Tue-Sat) This splendid, high-ceilinged cafe serves classy bistro fare that proudly shows off local Québécois products. What sets it apart are the delicious – and very rich – weekend brunches,

QUÉBEC WINTER CARNIVAL

Billing itself as the world's largest winter carnival, the **Carnaval de Québec** (Québec Winter Carnival; ☏866-422-7628, 418-626-3716; www.carnaval.qc.ca; ⊘Feb) is an exuberant celebration of ice, snow and wintry community fun. It begins each year on the third weekend before Ash Wednesday and culminates 10 days later when Bonhomme – the giant smiling snowman and official carnival ambassador – bids a wistful adieu to his adoring fans.

In the build-up to the carnival, the city takes on a new look, as a gargantuan ice palace is built opposite the Parliament Building, and the Plains of Abraham get converted into a vast winter playground, with ice slides, snow tubing, sleigh rides, and tire d'érable (maple taffy) served on snow added to the park's usual repertoire of outdoorsy winter activities.

Special events fill the three weekends of the Carnaval de Québec, including ice canoe races across the St Lawrence River, magnificent night parades with whimsical floats, and the infamous bain de neige (snow bath), in which a few dozen scantily clad – and stark raving mad – people court frostbite by volunteering to dance, roll and cavort in the snow with Bonhomme.

Carnaval in its current incarnation dates back to 1955 and carries with it several proud traditions. Many carnival-goers emulate Bonhomme's ceremonial attire, sporting the traditional tuque (hat) and ceinture fléchée (a wide colorful sash worn around the waist). To attend the festivities, you'll need to buy an effigie ($20, or $10 if bought online in advance), a miniature representation of Bonhomme that's sold around town and at the entrance to the fairgrounds. Veteran carnival-goers proudly wear decades worth of past effigies pinned to their sashes as they wander from event to event.

Revelers stave off the frigid weather by drinking caribou – a fortified spiced wine served hot. Buy it by the glass, or follow the locals' lead and pick up a canne, a hollow plastic cane festooned with Bonhomme's likeness, which can be filled to the brim with caribou at stands dotted around town – and used as a walking stick when your gait goes wobbly.

For exact dates and a full schedule of events, see www.carnaval.qc.ca. Bear in mind that the city overflows with tourists during the festival, so it's best to book accommodations and restaurants well in advance. Oh, and don't forget your warm clothes!

featuring homemade brioches with fresh fruit, crème fraîche and maple syrup, bagels topped with smoked mackerel, or veggie chili served with poached eggs, roasted squash and lime sour cream.

DÉLICES D'ARIANA   AFGHANI $$

Map p178 (☏418-948-8680; https://m.facebook.com/RestaurantAriana; 102 Blvd René-Lévesque Ouest, Montcalm & Colline Parlementaire; mains $11-23; ⊘11:30am-2pm Tue-Fri, 5-10pm Sun-Thu, to 11pm Fri & Sat; 🖋) Frequented almost exclusively by locals in the know, this turreted restaurant just north of Ave Cartier is often overlooked by visitors to Québec City. The exotic menu includes sumac-scented kebabs and traditional central Asian curries such as badenjaan bourani (stewed eggplant in tomato sauce with homemade yogurt) and qhurma (an onion-based dish with meat or vegetables).

BATI BASSAC   SOUTHEAST ASIAN $$

Map p178 (☏418-522-4567; http://batibassac.com; 125 Rue St-Joseph Est, St-Roch; mains $16-22; ⊘11am-3pm Mon-Fri, 5-10pm Tue-Thu & Sun, to 11pm Fri & Sat; 🖋) Good Asian food is as scarce as hen's teeth in Québec City, so this bustling Thai-cum-Cambodian eatery is a welcome change of pace, offering a menu full of tasty meat and fish dishes, along with several veggie offerings. Weekday lunch specials offer especially good value at $16 to $18.50, including appetizer, tea and dessert. Lovely decor and service too.

LE RENARD ET
LA CHOUETTE   CAFE $$

Map p178 (☏418-914-5845; http://lerenardetlachouette.com; 125 Rue St-Vallier Ouest, St-Sauveur; mains $14-25; ⊘5-10pm Mon-Wed, 10am-11pm Thu-Sat, to 10pm Sun) The delightful 'Fox and Owl' cafe-bistro nods

LGBTIQ+ VENUES

The city's gay and lesbian club scene is tiny, with pretty much everything centered around Le Drague (p196) and the older, more subdued but even more cruisy **Bar St-Matthew's** (Map p178; 418-524-5000; www.facebook.com/bar.stmatthews; 889 Côte Ste-Geneviève, St-Jean Baptiste; ◷11am-3am). Another address of interest is the all-male **Club Social ForHom** (Map p178; ◪418-522-4918; www.forhom.ca; 221 Rue St-Jean; ◷5pm-1am Thu-Sun) below a gay sauna called **Bloc 225** at the western end of Rue St-Jean; it has drink specials, gay film nights and more four nights a week. Plenty of other bars and clubs are LGBTIQ+ friendly, including **Chez Dagobert** (Map p178; ◪418-522-0393; http://dagobert.ca; 590 Grande Allée Est; ◷10:30pm-3am Thu-Sat), Le Sacrilège, Fou-Bar (p198) and Pub d'Orsay.

In early September the city's LGBTIQ+ community comes out in full force for the annual **Fête Arc-en-Ciel** (Québec City Pride Festival; ◪418-809-3383; www.arcencielque-bec.ca; ◷early Sep), the local version of Pride running over three days and two nights. For info on parties and other LGBTIQ+ events, Fugues (www.fugues.com) is the free gay and lesbian entertainment guide with listings for the entire province of Québec.

to the Middle East with lots of meze ($8 to $12) like baba ghanoush, hummus and tabbouleh, but it also has a wide choice of hot and cold mains that can be meaty (lamb kofta, black pudding) or vegetarian (grilled celeriac, pea and cheese pie). Friendly, helpful service.

BISTRO B
BISTRO $$$

Map p178 (◪418-614-5444; www.bistrob.ca; 1144 Ave Cartier, Montcalm & Colline Parlementaire; mains $25-32; ◷11:30am-2pm Mon-Fri, from 10am Sun, 6-11pm daily) The brainchild of top chef François Blais, this place draws a crowd for business lunches, when reasonably priced specials pop up on the iPad menu. New menus are improvised daily based on whatever ingredients are freshest at the local market. Sit at one of the quiet tables looking over well-heeled Ave Cartier or at the counter fronting the open kitchen.

LE PIED BLEU
BISTRO $$$

Map p178 (◪418-914-3554; https://piedbleu.com; 179 Rue St-Vallier Ouest, St-Sauveur; mains $25-35; ◷11:30am-2pm Wed-Fri, from 10am Sat &Sun, 6-9:30pm Wed-Sat) This bistro in a one-time clothing factory in working-class St-Sauveur is a Québécois take on a Lyonnaise *bouchon*, which means it serves such meaty fare as andouillette sausage made from pork or veal, duck-liver pâté, roast pork and the signature *quenelles* (fish dumplings). The blue-and-white space is a delight, with adorable shopfront seating and places at the counter.

⊖ DRINKING & 🍷 NIGHTLIFE

Let's be honest. Québec City isn't exactly considered a party town. That said, what the city does offer after dark is quite special, fun and refreshingly attitude-free. What the swankier supper clubs and restaurants may lack in urban edge, they more than make up for in friendly ambience and top-notch service; simply put, you get the feeling that everyone's welcome.

For club, bar and other entertainment listings, pick up the monthly *Quoi Faire à Québec* (www.quoifaireaquebec.com), available at bars, clubs, restaurants and tourist offices everywhere. Voir Québec (https://voir.ca) is a good French-language entertainment and listings website. Other useful publications include *Fugues*, a free monthly gay and lesbian entertainment guide, and *Le Clap*, a bimonthly guide to cinema. Have fun!

📍 Old Town & Port

There are several convivial pubs and even some live-music bars on or just off Rue St-Jean in the Old Upper Town and a handful of cozy venues in the Old Lower Town.

L'ONCLE ANTOINE
PUB

Map p170 (◪418-694-9176; 29 Rue St-Pierre, Old Lower Town & Port; ◷11am-1am) Set clandestinely in the vaulted brick cellar of one of the city's oldest surviving houses (dating from 1754), this great tavern pours excellent Québec microbrews (try the Barberie Noir stout), several drafts and various European beers. Its in-house brews include #1 Blonde (lager), #21 Rousse (red) and #29 IPA. Try its famous onion soup on a cold Sunday afternoon.

BAR STE-ANGÈLE
BAR

Map p170 (☑418-692-2171; www.facebook.com/ BarSainteAngele; 26 Rue Ste-Angèle, Old Upper Town; ◷8pm-3am) A low-lit, intimate hipster hangout, where the genial staff will help you navigate the list of cocktail pitchers and local and European bottled craft beers. Live jazz performed by local and visiting musicians on selected nights.

PUB D'ORSAY
PUB

Map p170 (☑418-694-1587; www.dorsayres taurant.com; 65 Rue de Buade, Old Upper Town; ◷11:30am-midnight) Though it has a full menu (mains $17 to $23, steaks $38) and restaurant seating, the main focus of this iconic spot in place since 1973 is the bar, which is really a pub as we see it. Try any of the local microbrews – La Fin du Monde, Boréale, Blanche de Chambly – or the excellent McKeown cider.

PUB DES BORGIA
BAR

Map p170 (☑581-300-9176; www.facebook.com/ pubdesborgia; 12 Rue du Petit-Champlain, Old Lower Town & Port; ◷11am-1am) This hidden nook of a bar huddles by the cobblestones of Old Lower Town and, on the inside, seems to exemplify the colonial coziness you'd expect of drinking establishments in this area. With that said, while the interior has a cellar-esque quality, the adjoining patio adds a bit of fresh air and Rue du Petit-Champlain people-watching.

PUB ST-ALEXANDRE
BAR

Map p170 (☑418-694-0015; www.pubstalex andre.com; 1087 Rue St-Jean, Old Upper Town; ◷11am-3am) High ceilings and dark wood house a loyal mix of tourists and locals at this popular two-level English pub. A near-encyclopedic range of suds (250 sorts!) and over 50 single malts keep the crowds coming back for more. Live music nightly – Celtic, blues, jazz and more – contributes to the animated atmosphere.

PUB ST-PATRICK
IRISH PUB

Map p170 (☑418-694-0618; www.pubsaint patrick.ca; 1200 Rue St-Jean, Old Upper Town; ◷11am-3am) This Irish-style bar is in a historic building with outdoor seating and the usual menu of pub grub. Come here to see the vast system of cellars below, the largest in Québec City. Kids love it here and, unlike at many similar pubs in the area, they are very welcome.

🍸 Outside the Old Town

You'll find the liveliest night spots beyond the walls of the Old Town. There's a cluster of renovated mansions-turned-discos on Colline Parlementaire's Grande-Allée Est where you can dance the night away. Le Drague (p196) in trendy St-Jean Baptiste is essentially LGBTIQ+, though all are welcome.

★LE SACRILÈGE
BAR

Map p178 (☑418-649-1985; www.lesacrilege. com; 447 Rue St-Jean, St-Jean Baptiste; ◷noon-3am) With its unmistakable sign of a laughing, dancing monk saucily lifting his robes, this bar has long been the watering hole of choice for Québec's night owls. Even on Monday, it's standing-room only. There's a quite good selection of beers (including many craft varieties), live music most nights at 8pm and seating on a lovely garden terrace out back.

★GRIENDEL
BRASSERIE ARTISANALE
MICROBREWERY

Map p178 (☑591-742-2884; www.facebook.com/ Brasserie.artisanale.griendel; 195 Rue St-Vallier Ouest, St-Sauveur; ◷3pm-1am Mon-Wed, to 3am Thu & Fri, 1pm-3am Sat, to 1am Sun) Anchor tenant on Rue St-Vallier Ouest in up-and-coming St-Sauveur, Griendel occupies a huge old corner shop with lots of windows and great light. Choose from among the two-dozen *broues* (brews) on the blackboard, most of which are brewed in-house. There are burgers and poutine, but it's generally agreed they serve the best fish 'n' chips ($15) in town.

★NOCTEM ARTISANS BRASSEURS
MICROBREWERY

Map p178 (📞581-742-7979; www.noctem.ca; 438 Rue du Parvis, St-Roch; ⊙11am-3am) One of the most interesting microbreweries in town, Noctem goes beyond the *blonde* (lager), *blanche* (white), *rousse* (red) and IPA tick list to offer a blackboard of up to 18 different beers and ales that change daily. If peckish, eschew the pizza/burger/taco choices in favor of a platter of charcuterie to share.

LE MOINE ÉCHANSON
WINE BAR

Map p178 (📞418-524-7832; www.lemoine echanson.com; 585 Rue St-Jean, St-Jean Baptiste; ⊙4-10pm Sun-Wed, to 11pm Thu-Sat) A darling of the city's wine connoisseurs, this convivial brick-walled wine bar and bistro pours an enticing and ever-changing array of wines from all over the Mediterranean, by the glass and by the bottle, accompanied by hearty and homespun snacks and main dishes such as blood sausage, cheese fondue or lentil soup. Three-/ four-course set menus are $40/45.

Each season brings a new theme, with emphasis placed on a single French region or department (Ardèche, Jura etc) or Mediterranean country. Crowds pour in after work, quickly filling the two rooms to capacity, starting with aperitifs and '5 à 7' snacks ($3 to $10), such as pheasant wings, rillette and scallops, and often lingering on through dinner. During business hours it also doubles as a wine merchant, selling hard-to-find bottles to take away.

BRASSERIE LA KORRIGANE
BREWERY

Map p178 (📞418-614-0932; www.korrigane.ca; 380 Rue Dorchester, St-Roch; ⊙11:30am-1am Sun-Thu, to 3am Fri & Sat) St-Roch's friendliest microbrewery features a full rainbow of flavors, including specialty brews like Emily Carter blueberry beer, maple-laced Croquemitaine and Urbain honey ale, all served up with pub grub such as nachos, chili, burgers and poutine from artisanal producers. You'll also find Sunday improv nights and swing dancing every other Wednesday.

LA BARBERIE
MICROBREWERY

Map p178 (📞418-522-4373; www.labarberie. com; 310 Rue St-Roch, St-Roch; ⊙noon-1am) This cooperative St-Roch microbrewery, in place since 1997, is beloved for its spacious tree-shaded deck and its ever-evolving selection of some 30 home brews. Seasonal offerings range from classic pale ales to quirkier options such as hot pepper amber or a range of sour beers. Undecided? Sample 'em all in the popular eight-beer carousel ($19.75).

Blotters include tapas-size *saucisson sec* (dried-cured sausage), cheese and jerky ($3 to $4.50).

LE DRAGUE
LGBTIQ+

Map p178 (📞418-649-7212; www.ledrague. com; 815 Rue St-Augustin, St-Jean Baptiste; ⊙10am-3am) The star player on Québec City's tiny gay scene, Le Drague is a large club with an attractive outdoor terrace that gets packed in summer, a dance bar and stage on the ground floor where drag shows are held, and a more laid-back cocktail bar on the upper level called Zone 3.

MACFLY BAR ARCADE
BAR

Map p178 (📞418-528-7000; www.macflybar arcade.com; 422 Rue Caron, St-Roch; ⊙3pm-3am) This bar's *Back to the Future*-ish name is no accident: the entire interior evokes the 1980s, or at least an idea of what the '80s were about – old-school arcade consoles, bright countertops, TV set stuck on a test pattern and pinball machines awaiting your wizardry. Not that it's easy to top your highest score after a couple of well-pulled beers...

L'ATELIER
COCKTAIL BAR

Map p178 (📞418-522-2225; www.bistrolatelier. com; 624 Grande Allée Est, Montcalm & Colline Parlementaire; ⊙11:30am-1am Sun-Wed, to 3am Thu-Sat) Bright and buzzy, this classy lounge is a fun spot for late afternoon and evening cocktails. Brick walls, cushioned benches, and a sea of lights and cocktail glasses hanging from the ceiling create a convivial atmosphere for sampling over two dozen creative cocktails such as the house Le Disco (gin and Cointreau) and the Cowgirl (vodka and Cointreau).

QUARTIER GÉNÉRAL BAR

Map p178 (📱418-614-4590; www.qgbarsalon.com; 1 Blvd Charest Ouest, St-Sauveur; ⊙11am-3am Tue-Fri, noon-3am Sat-Mon) Just over the border from St-Roch in up-and-coming St-Sauveur, this wild and crazy place is where to head if you're looking for a raucous and very local experience. There's a jam session on Tuesday, karaoke on Wednesday and a rock-and-roll *soirée dansante* (dance party) with DJs and a set meal ($25) on Friday and Saturday. Great terrace in summer.

LA REVANCHE CAFE

Map p178 (📱418-263-5389; www.facebook.com/publarevanche; 585 Blvd Charest Est, St-Roch; ⊙5pm-midnight Mon, 4pm-1am Tue-Thu, to 2am Fri, noon-2am Sat, to midnight Sun) This eclectic cafe-pub *ludique* (games cafe-pub) with the relevant name 'Revenge' is dedicated to table-top and board gaming. Seriously, there's a wall here that looks like it could have been plucked from a toy store. Staff are on hand to help you learn the ropes of any game. Pro tip: several pints do not, in fact, improve your Jenga performance.

LA SOUCHE LIMOILU MICROBREWERY

(📱581-742-1144; www.lasouche.ca; 801 Chemin de la Canardière, Limoilu; ⊙11am-1am Sun-Wed, to 3am Thu-Sat) This very comfortable pub spread over two large rustic rooms in the Limoilu district across the St-Charles River serves dozens of its own brews, including the unforgettable La Souche Mango #5. (Yes, mango and it is very good.) Normally food at a microbrewery is a second thought, but the poutines ($9 to $16) here are among the best we've tasted.

ENTERTAINMENT

The performing arts are in fine form in Québec City. Live-performance venues abound, from concert halls to open-air amphitheaters, little jazz and rock clubs, and exuberant *boîtes à chanson* (Québec folk-music clubs), where generations of locals dance and sing with uncensored glee. French-language theater is also an interesting scene, with tons of small companies producing a variety of shows.

⭐ Old Town & Port

PAPE GEORGES LIVE MUSIC

Map p170 (📱418-692-1320; https://m.facebook.com/papegeorges; 8 Rue de Cul-de-Sac, Old Lower Town & Port; ⊙11am-3pm) With live music from 10pm on Friday and Saturday night at the very minimum (more in the summer), this charming bar located in a 400-year-old house also serves cheeses, meats and baguettes with a healthy dollop of Québécois culture. It always attracts a lively crowd.

BAR LES YEUX BLEUS LIVE MUSIC

Map p170 (📱418-694-9118; 1117 Rue St-Jean, Old Upper Town; ⊙9pm-3am Mon, Tue & Thu, 8pm-3am Wed, 4pm-3am Fri-Sun, closed Mon-Wed winter) One of the city's better *boîtes á chanson*, this is the place to catch newcomers, the occasional big-name francophone concert and Québécois classics. It's in an old wooden house down a narrow alleyway from Rue St-Jean in the Old Upper Town.

THÉÂTRE PETIT-CHAMPLAIN THEATER

Map p170 (📱418-692-2631; www.theatrepetitchamplain.com; 68 Rue du Petit-Champlain, Old Lower Town & Port; ⊙box office 5-8:30pm show days) This theater and *'maison de la chanson'* (music house) near the base of the funicular in the Old Lower Town is a great place to see and hear Québec's most popular singing stars. It also stages occasional French-language theater productions and comedy gigs.

LES GROS BECS THEATER

Map p170 (📱877-522-2327, 418-522-7880; www.lesgrosbecs.qc.ca; 1143 Rue St-Jean, Old Upper Town; ⊙box office 8am-noon & 3-5pm Tue-Fri; ♿) Devoted to children and young people, this brilliantly creative French-language theater company mounts some 10 shows annually, primarily between September and May. Its colorful catalog and website specifies suggested age ranges – from one to 17 – for every production, and includes everything from drama and comedy to musicals and puppet shows.

ENTERTAINMENT LISTINGS

Lonely Planet (www.lonelyplanet.com/canada/quebec-city) Destination information, independent reviews and more.

Quebec Chronicle-Telegraph (www.qctonline.com) North America's oldest newspaper is a good place to catch up on local happenings.

Québec Cité (www.quebec-cite.com/en) Excellent, all-encompassing website from the city's own tourist office.

Québec Original (www.quebecoriginal.com/en-ca) Excellent multilingual info, travel ideas and events calendar from Québec Tourisme's modern, official website.

Voir (www.voir.ca) Useful French-language entertainment and listings website.

☆ Outside the Old Town

LES VOÛTES
DE NAPOLÉON   LIVE MUSIC
Map p178 (☑418-640-9388; www.voutesde napoleon.com; 680a Grande Allée Est, Montcalm & Colline Parlementaire; ◉9:30pm-3am) At this jubilant *boîte à chanson* (folk-music club), it will likely be just you and the locals. There's lively Québécois music nightly, usually of the 'singer-with-guitar' variety, with lesser-known up-and-coming acts featuring prominently. You'll find 'Napoleon's Vaults' in an atmospheric old cellar with ancient arched stone walls just west of the Hôtel du Parlement (p181).

FOU-BAR   LIVE MUSIC
Map p178 (☑418-522-1987; www.foubar.ca; 525 Rue St-Jean, St-Jean Baptiste; ◉2:30pm-1am Sun & Mon, to 2am Tue & Wed, to 3am Thu-Sat) Laid-back and offering an eclectic mix of bands, this bar is one of the town's classics for good live music. It's also popular for its reasonably priced food menu and its free *pique-assiettes* (literally 'freeloaders' aka appetizers) on Thursday and Friday evenings. There can be a cover charge of up to $20 depending on the band.

GRAND THÉÂTRE
DE QUÉBEC   PERFORMING ARTS
Map p178 (☑877-643-8131, 418-643-8131 , tours 418-643-811, ext 2115; www.grandtheatre.qc.ca; 269 Blvd René-Lévesque Est, Montcalm & Colline Parlementaire; ◉box office noon-5pm Mon-Sat & 30min before performances) Designed by the Polish-Canadian architect Victor Prus in 1971, the 'Great Theater' is Québec City's main performing-arts center, with a steady diet of top-quality classical concerts, opera, dance and theater. Major companies that are based or perform here regularly include the Opéra de Québec, the Orchestre Symphonique de Québec and the **Théâtre du Trident** (☑418-643-8131, 418-643-5873; www. letrident.com; ◉box office 9am-noon & 1:30-4:30pm Mon-Thu).

Guided tours ($5) in English and French are available on Wednesday and Thursday afternoon.

OPÉRA DE QUÉBEC   CLASSICAL MUSIC
Map p178 (☑418-529-0688; www.operade quebec.com; 1220 Ave Taché, Montcalm & Colline Parlementaire; ◉9am-noon & 1:30-5pm Mon-Fri) Under the artistic direction of Grégoire Legendre, this world-class company presents classics like *Aida, Pagliacci, Madame Butterfly, La Traviata, Carmen, Nabucco* and more. Performances take place in the majestic Grand Théâtre de Québec, where you can also buy tickets.

PALAIS MONTCALM   LIVE MUSIC
Map p178 (☑877-641-6040, 418-641-6040; www. palaismontcalm.ca; 995 Place d'Youville, St-Jean Baptiste; ◉box office noon-6pm Mon-Fri, to 5pm Sat) Just outside the walls of the Old Upper Town, this art-deco theater subtitled 'La Maison de la Musique' (The House of Music) hosts a stellar lineup of concerts year-round, featuring everything from opera and chamber music to jazz and rock. The main performance space, the Salle Raoul-Jobin, inaugurated in 2007 is renowned for its 'near perfect' acoustics.

The prestigious Club Musical de Québec of classical musicians is based here.

SCANNER
BISTRO
LIVE MUSIC

Map p178 (☑418-523-1916; www.scanner bistro.com; 291 Rue St-Vallier Est, St-Roch; cover charge $5-12; ⏾4pm-3am Tue-Fri, 8pm-3am Sat-Mon) Ask any local between the ages of 18 and 35 to suggest a cool place for a drink and this is where they might send you. DJs and live bands serve up a potent musical mix, from heavy metal to hard rock to punk to rockabilly. There's a terrace outside in summer, plus table football and pool inside year-round.

LE THÉÂTRE
CAPITOLE
THEATER

Map p178 (☑800-261-9903, 418-694-4444; www. lecapitole.com; 972 Rue St-Jean, St-Jean Baptiste) Québec City's first theater when it opened as the Auditorium de Québec in 1903, this historic and now renovated theater-restaurant offers cabaret and musical revues and is a smaller and more intimate spot to enjoy performing arts. Hitchcock held the premiere of his film *I Confess* here.

The film was largely shot on location in Québec City, with numerous takes of the city's churches and such iconic buildings as the Château Frontenac.

LA ROTONDE
DANCE

Map p178 (☑box office 418-643-8131, information 418-649-5013; www.larotonde.qc.ca; 336 Rue du Roi, St-Roch) This contemporary-dance center has performances by both international touring companies and local dancers, such as those of the influential **Maison pour la Danse** (☑418-649-5013, 418-478-5013; www. maisonpourladanse.ca), including experimental and cutting-edge works. It also offers workshops and classes and is pivotal in keeping dance alive in Québec.

BATEAU DE NUIT
LIVE MUSIC

Map p178 (☑418-977-2626; www.facebook.com/ bateaudenuit; 275 Rue St-Jean, St-Jean Baptiste; ⏾7pm-3am Mon & Tue, from 5pm Wed-Fri, from 8pm Sat & Sun) We really love it when our dive bars come with a heavy dose of live music, which is exactly the case at this sweet little upstairs venue in the heart of St-Jean Baptiste. The in-the-know bartenders can tell you about local musicians or who's carved their initials into the wall – most likely most of the crowd here on both counts.

ORCHESTRE SYMPHONIQUE
DE QUÉBEC
CLASSICAL MUSIC

Map p178 (☑418-643-8131; www.osq.org; 269 Blvd René-Lévesque Est, Montcalm & Colline Parlementaire; ⏾box office noon-5pm Mon-Sat & 30min before performances) Founded in 1902 and boasting the accolade of being the oldest active symphony orchestra in Canada, the internationally recognized Orchestre Symphonique de Québec has performed for more than 100,000 people a year. Concerts are usually broadcast on the radio by public broadcaster Radio Canada. Led by music director Fabien Gabel since 2012, the orchestra is also active in the community.

IMPÉRIAL BELL
LIVE MUSIC

Map p178 (☑877-523-3131, 418-523-3131; www. imperialbell.com; 252 Rue St-Joseph Est, St-Roch; ⏾box office noon-6pm Mon-Fri, to 4pm Sat) One of the hottest venues in town for live music – from rock and pop to cabaret – resides in St-Roch's old Théâtre Impérial, built in 1912.

KIOSQUE
EDWIN-BÉLANGER
LIVE MUSIC

Map p178 (☑418-648-4050; www.ccbn-nbc.gc.ca/ en/activities/kiosque-edwin-belanger; Battlefields Park, Montcalm & Colline Parlementaire) Each summer dozens of free concerts are staged at this bandstand in the middle of Battlefields Park (p179), just a stone's throw (and visible from) the Musée National des Beaux-Arts du Québec (p179). Music covers everything from pop, jazz and world music to blues.

CINÉMA CARTIER
CINEMA

Map p178 (☑418-522-1011; www.cinemacartier. com; 1019 Ave Cartier, Montcalm & Colline Parlementaire; tickets $12.50; ⏾screenings 10:30am-9:30pm) This beloved neighborhood cinema began as a deliciously old-world little place attached to a video shop, with big comfy chairs and nothing but art-house films. Now expanded, it still devotes half of its screen space to independent films, but also shows Hollywood blockbusters and family-oriented fare. Films are screened in their original language with subtitles or dubbed into French.

 SHOPPING

Small, unique and authentic boutiques are Québec City's claim to retail fame, and the town's small size makes it ideal for strolling around and browsing

for surprises. **Find more Québec City shopping tips on p27.**

🏛 Old Town & Port

GALERIE D'ART INUIT BROUSSEAU
ART

Map p170 (☑418-694-1828; www.artinuit.ca; 35 Rue St-Louis, Old Upper Town; ⊘9:30am-5:30pm) Devoted to Inuit soapstone, serpentine and basalt carvings and sculptures from artists all over Arctic Canada, this place is gorgeously set up and elaborately lit, with well-trained staff who knowledgeably answer questions. Works range from the small to the large and intricate. Expect high quality and steep prices. International shipping is available.

The gallery's director, Raymond Brousseau, has been collecting Inuit art since the 1950s, and it is this visionary Québécois' collection that forms the basis of the splendid Brousseau Collection of Inuit Art on the top floor of the Pavillon Pierre Lassonde at the Musée National des Beaux-Arts du Québec (p179).

MARCHÉ DU VIEUX-PORT
FOOD & DRINKS

Map p170 (☑418-692-2517; www.mvpq.ca; 160 Quai St-André, Old Lower Town & Port; ⊘9am-5pm Thu-Sun; 🚇) 🍴 At this heaving local food market, you can buy fresh fruits and vegetables as well as dozens of local specialties, from Île d'Orléans blackcurrant wine to ciders, honeys, cheeses, sausages, chocolates, herbal hand creams and, of course, maple-syrup products. Weekends see huge crowds and more wine tastings than can be considered sensible.

The date is not yet firm, but the venerable Marché du Vieux-Port is scheduled to quit its portside location and move to ExpoCité, a multisite entertainment complex that includes the Centre Vidéotron stadium, about 6km north of the Old Town.

LES BRANCHÉS LUNETTERIE
FASHION & ACCESSORIES

Map p170 (☑418-614-1697; www.lesbranches lunetterie.ca; 155 Rue St-Paul, Old Lower Town & Port; ⊘10am-6pm Mon-Wed, to 8pm Thu & Fri, to 5pm Sat) Displaying a fanciful, wildly colorful mix of designer eyewear from Québec, France and Spain, this is a fun place to browse, even if you're not necessarily in the market for new glasses frames. The collection's centerpiece is the room dedicated to frames from Montures Faniel (www.monturesfaniel.com), a Québécois business founded by opera-singer-turned-designer Anne-Marie Faniel, whose music also fills the store.

ARTISANS CANADA
ARTS & CRAFTS

Map p170 (☑888-339-2109, 418-692-2109; www.artisanscanada.com; 30 Côte de la Fabrique, Old Upper Town; ⊘10am-7pm Sat-Thu, to 9pm Fri) One of our favorite stores to shop and browse, this emporium run by the same family for three generations stocks arts and crafts, clothing, jewelry and quality souvenirs created by 100 different Québécois and Canadian artists. It also stocks the world-renowned (and virtually indestructible) Tilley hat, Canada's greatest contribution to the world of headgear.

GALERIE PERREAULT
ART

Map p170 (☑418-692-4772; www.galerieperreault.com; 205 Rue St-Paul, Old Lower Town & Port; ⊘10am-5pm) Dynamic gallery showing some 16 different North American artists, many of whom got their start here. Don't miss Daniel Gagné's fabulous studies of autumn trees, Normand Boisvert's countryscapes and Marc-Aurèle Fortin's views of Vieux-Québec.

LES TROIS CORBEAUX
GLASS

Map p170 (☑418-887-7655; www.troiscorbeaux.com; 42 Côte de la Fabrique, Old Upper Town; ⊘10am-5pm) This fabulous shop and studio stocks the most exquisite works of art in glass – bowls, candlesticks, paperweights, bric-a-brac – and they're all fired and blown on-site. Watch the master at work in the front of the shop or view more intricate work underway in the glass-fronted atelier out the back.

ZIMMERMANN
JEWELRY

Map p170 (☑418-692-2672; www.zimmermann-quebec.com; 46 Côte de la Fabrique, Old Upper Town; ⊘noon-5:30pm Mon-Wed, to 6pm Thu & Fri, 1-5pm Sat, noon-4pm Sun) The father and son who own this jewelry shop, in the same location since 1963 and almost as much of a landmark as nearby Simons (p202), make every piece of gold and silver jewelry in their workshop just upstairs. The designs are inspired and the workmanship very fine indeed.

**BOUTIQUE MÉTIERS
D'ART DU QUÉBEC** ARTS & CRAFTS

Map p170 (☑418-694-0267, 418-694-0260; www.
metiersdart.ca; 20 Rue Notre-Dame, Old Lower
Town & Port; ☺10am-6pm Mon-Sat, to 5pm Sun)
Run by the organization that oversees
all sorts of arts and crafts disciplines in
Québec, this very stylish boutique in the
Place Royale sells the very best of Québécois porcelain, ceramics, jewelry, wood
carving and a lot of unusual (and fun) gifts.

ANTIQUITÉS BOLDUC ANTIQUES

Map p170 (☑418-694-9558; www.lesantiq
uitesbolduc.com; 89 Rue St-Paul, Old Lower Town
& Port; ☺9:30am-5:30pm Mon-Fri, from 10:30am
Sat) Among the largest and friendliest
stores on 'Antiques Row' in the Old Lower
Town. Bolduc sells furniture, household

QUÉBEC CITY TOURS

Immersion Québec (Map p170; ☑418-204-2592; www.immersionquebec.com; 1191 Rue
St-Jean, Old Upper Town; adult/youth/child $20/15/10; ☺10am-5pm) This is a bizarre
but painless way to 'immerse' yourself in Québec history. Don a wraparound goggle
set then, for a half-hour, 'walk' through the city's past with 360-degree vision (big
screens available for claustrophobes). There are also intuitive games to play yourself
on screens around the rooms, and a couple for competing in teams.

Les Tours de Vieux Québec (Map p170; ☑800-267-8687, 418-664-0460; www.tours-
vieuxquebec.com; 12 Rue Ste-Anne, Old Upper Town) This tour operator offers a variety of
tours: two-hour double-decker bus tours (adult/child $37/22.50) and out-of-town ex-
cursions to Montmorency Falls, Ste-Anne-de-Beaupré and/or Île d'Orléans ($50/30).
It also has whale-watching expeditions ($135/85) in summer. It has a desk at the Cen-
tre Infotouriste Québec City (p249).

Ghost Tours of Québec (Map p170; ☑418-692-9770; www.ghosttoursofquebec.com; 34
Blvd Champlain, Old Lower Town & Port; adult/youth/child under 10 yr $22/19/free; ☺English
tour 8pm May-Oct) This lantern-lit, 90-minute walking tour of the Old Town, led by a
guide in period costume, recounts a series of ghost stories and tales of murders and
hauntings, providing a spooky perspective on Québec City's historic streets. English-
language tours depart from 94 Rue du Petit Champlain in the Old Lower Town. Tickets
may be reserved by phone, online or at its office on Blvd Champlain.

Les Promenades Fantômes (Ghost Walks; Map p170; ☑418-692-0624; www.prom
enadesfantomes.com; 12 Rue Ste-Anne, Old Upper Town; adult/child $20/17; ☺8pm May-Oct,
days vary) Take a nocturnal trip by the light of a swinging lantern and learn about by-
gone Québec City's shadowy side. Buy tickets at the Centre Infotouriste Québec City
(p249). Walks depart from the Centre Morrin (p173).

Les Services Historiques Six-Associés (Map p178; ☑418-573-7815, 418-692-3033;
www.sixassocies.com; 330 Rue St-Roch, office 208; 1½hr walking tours adult/child $18/10)
This outfit offers good themed walking tours like the ever-popular 'Lust and Drunken-
ness,' which illuminates the history of alcohol and prostitution in the city.

Québec Cicerone Tours (Map p170; ☑418-977-8977, 855-977-8977; www.cicerone.ca/en;
12 Rue Ste-Anne, Old Upper Town; adult/youth/child $20/10/free; ☺Château Frontenac tour
10am, 1pm & 3pm late Jun–mid-Oct) Offers four tours of Old Québec by guides in period
costume, including one devoted solely to the Château Frontenac. It has a desk at the
Centre Infotouriste Québec City (p249).

Abraham's Bus Tour (Map p178; ☑418-649-6157, 855-649-6157; www.theplainsof
abraham.ca; 835 Ave Wilfrid-Laurier, Montcalm & Colline Parlementaire; adult/youth/child
incl Plains of Abraham Museum & Martello Tower 1 $15.25/11.25/5; ☺several departures
daily Jul-early Sep) During the summer months, this 40-minute bus tour makes for an
entertaining way to get your bearings at Battlefields Park (p179). An actor in period
costume points out historical sites of interest and throws in some colorful asides. It
departs from the Musée des Plaines d'Abraham (p181). Admission to the museum and
nearby Martello Tower 1 (p181) is included with your bus ticket.

ON TWO WHEELS

There's a large network of bike paths feeding from the Vieux-Port out into the surrounding countryside. Ask for the free *Carte Vélo Officielle/Official Cycling Map* at local tourist offices. Île d'Orléans can also be a fantastic setting for a bicycle outing, but because there are no bike paths and heaps of traffic in summer, this route is not recommended for children.

Corridor du Littoral & Promenade Samuel-de-Champlain (🚲) Starting southwest of Québec City at Cap-Rouge and extending northeast via the Old Lower Town to Montmorency Falls, the Corridor du Littoral is a 48km multipurpose recreation path along the St Lawrence River, popular with cyclists, walkers and in-line skaters. The heart of the path is the Promenade Samuel-de-Champlain, an especially beautiful 2.5km section. The promenade was constructed for Québec's 400th anniversary celebrations in 2008 and is lined with sculptures, sports fields and green space, with a cafe and a 25m observation tower at Quai des Cageux, the eastern end of the Promenade Samuel-de-Champlain.

Vélopiste Jacques-Cartier/Portneuf (📱418-337-7525; www.velopistejcp.com) Formerly a railway line linking St-Gabriel-de-Valcartier and Rivière-à-Pierre, this 68km cycling trail wends its way through verdant country scenery. It's linked to downtown Québec City by another rails-to-trails project, the 22km Corridor des Cheminots. (Incidentally, cyclists can also reach this trail by train from Montréal; VIA Rail offers thrice-weekly service from Montréal to Rivière-à-Pierre, the trail's western terminus.)

Cyclo Services (Map p170; 📱418-692-4052, 877-692-4050; www.cycloservices.net; 289 Rue St-Paul, Old Lower Town & Port; rental per 2/24hr city bike $17/38, electric bike $34/76; ⊙9am-5:30pm Mon-Fri, 10am-5pm Sat & Sun, variable hours Nov-Apr; 🚲) This outfit rents a variety of bikes (city, tandem, road, electric, kids') and organizes excellent cycling tours of the city and outskirts to places such as Wendake (half-day $95) and La Chute Montmorency (four hours $77). The knowledgeable and fun guides frequently give tours in English. In winter it rents snowshoes only ($15), and hours are limited; call ahead.

objects, old paintings and curios from the 19th and 20th centuries. It's more informal than many of the other shops in the area.

SIMONS　　　　　　　　　DEPARTMENT STORE
Map p170 (📱418-692-3630; www.simons.ca; 20 Côte de la Fabrique, Old Upper Town; ⊙9:30am-5:30pm Mon-Wed, to 9pm Thu & Fri, to 5pm Sat, noon-5pm Sun) One of the city's success stories, Simons was started as a dry-goods store in the 1800s by the son of a Scottish immigrant. By 1952 his descendants had turned the business into a successful clothing store. It's popular all over Québec for stocking items more cutting-edge than those at competing department stores. There's been a Simons at this location since 1840.

Don't miss the fabulous *coupole de Saint-Amand-les-Eaux,* a mosaic-tile cupola of Italian glass discovered by owner Peter Simons at a flea market in Paris and installed just inside the store's main entrance to commemorate Simons' 165th anniversary in 2005.

LES 3 TOURS　　　　　　　　　CLOTHING
Map p170 (📱418-694-0525; www.facebook.com/les3tours; 1124 Rue St-Jean, Old Upper Town; ⊙10am-6pm Sun-Wed, 9am-9pm Thu-Sat) Devoted to all things medieval, this Québec shop sells clothes, jewelry, swords and accessories reproduced by Québécois designers from items dating back to the Middle Ages. It's odd when you consider Québec did not even exist in that era, but there is no accounting for taste.

JOAILLERIE
JULES PERRIER　　　　　　　　　JEWELRY
Map p170 (📱418-692-0880; www.julesperrier. com; 39 Rue du Petit-Champlain, Old Lower Town & Port; ⊙10am-5pm Sat-Wed, to 7pm Thu & Fri, to 9pm daily summer) Passion is the inspiration behind this well-known jeweler's stunning designs, with unique earrings, brooches, pendants and more. A family business since 1956, it's full of precious stones, making browsing in this elegant locale feel like perusing art.

**LA PETITE CABANE
À SUCRE DU QUÉBEC** FOOD

Map p170 (☑819-357-2556, 418-692-5875; www.
petitecabaneasucre.com; 94 Rue du Petit-Champlain, Old Lower Town & Port; ☺9:30am-5:30pm Sat-Wed, to 9pm Thu & Fri) Maple syrup is a massive industry in Québec, and the 'Little Québec Sugar Shack' sells it in every guise: candies, delicacies, ice cream, snacks, cotton candy, popcorn, syrup-related accessories and, of course, the very nectar itself.

**VITRAIL
ORIGINAL** GLASS

Map p170 (☑418-522-5888; www.facebook.com/
VitrailOriginal; 97 Rue St-Paul, Old Lower Town & Port; ☺10am-5pm Mon-Fri, from noon Sat & Sun) You may not be in the market for *vitrail* (stained glass), but this is a lovely and original shop in which to browse; some of the inspired lampshades would put Tiffany to shame. Check out, too, the wonderful wooden boxes by master carver André Dorais and the adorable animal sculptures by Alain Mailhot.

KETTŐ FASHION & ACCESSORIES

Map p170 (☑418-977-3337; www.kettodesign.
com; 1039 Rue St-Jean, Old Upper Town; ☺10am-5pm Sat-Wed, to 7pm Thu & Fri) Illustrator Julie St-Onge-Drouin started up Kettő with her partner Catherine Fafard after her illustrative designs kept finding their way onto ceramic surfaces. Now at this bright and colorful boutique, they're on bags – from gym and school bags to backpacks. Kettő designs are sold in small boutiques throughout Québec, but the selection here is better than you'll find elsewhere.

And if you were wondering, *kettő* means 'two' in Hungarian, denoting the two women who set up the company.

**CIDRERIE
PEDNEAULT** FOOD & DRINKS

Map p170 (☑418-558-2365; www.verger
pedneault.com; 73 Rue du Petit-Champlain, Old Lower Town & Port; ☺9:30am-5:30pm Sat-Wed, to 6:30pm Thu & Fri, to 9pm daily summer) This Old Lower Town outlet of the famous *cidrerie* based on the Isle-aux-Coudres in the St Lawrence River stocks any number of types of alcoholic cider – dry, fruity, sparkly, sherry-like 'ice' etc ($17 to $25 a bottle). It also sells jams, fruit butters, syrups and vinegars.

**LE RENDEZ-VOUS DU
COLLECTIONNEUR** ANTIQUES

Map p170 (☑418-692-3099; www.facebook.com/
aurendezvousducollectionneur; 123 Rue St-Paul, Old Lower Town & Port; ☺10am-5pm) Antique lamps and silverware from Château Frontenac are among the many items crowding the shelves at this well-established shop on the Lower Town's antiques row. It stocks some Inuit carvings as well.

CANDEUR COSMETICS

Map p170 (☑418-353-1683; www.candeur.ca;
117 Rue St-Paul, Old Lower Town & Port; ☺10am-5pm, Sat & Sun only winter) A great spot for small gifts, this sweet boutique specializes in artisanal soaps made with goat's milk, herbal oils and other natural ingredients. The beautifully displayed soap selection features a pleasing array of colors and charming French touches, such as soap bars imprinted with fleur-de-lis motifs.

🏠 Outside the Old Town

★JA MOISAN ÉPICIER FOOD

Map p178 (☑418-522-0685; www.jamoisan.
com; 695 Rue St-Jean, St-Jean Baptiste; ☺8:30am-7pm Mon-Wed & Sat, to 9pm Thu & Fri, 10am-7pm Sun, extended hours summer) Established in 1871, this charming store bills itself as North America's oldest grocery. It's a browser's dream come true, packed with beautifully displayed edibles and kitchen and household items alongside antique cash registers and wood shelving. You'll find items here you've never seen before, along with heaps of local goods and gift ideas.

ÉRICO CHOCOLATE

Map p178 (☑418-524-2122; www.ericochoco
latier.com; 634 Rue St-Jean, St-Jean Baptiste; ☺10:30am-6pm Mon-Wed & Sat, to 9pm Thu & Fri, 11am-6pm Sun, to 9pm daily summer) The sights and smells in this delectable boutique will send chocophiles into conniptions of joy. The main shop brims with truffles, chocolate-chip cookies, ice cream and seasonal chocolate treats, while the quirky museum next door has a dress made entirely of chocolate, old-fashioned gumball machines dispensing sun-dried cocoa beans, and a window through which you can watch the chocolatiers work.

Don't miss Érico's inspired and ever-changing seasonal offerings (chocolate roses for Valentine's Day, chocolate bunnies and chickens at Easter etc) as well as what many say is the city's best hot chocolate ($2.85 to $5).

LES HALLES CARTIER
FOOD & DRINKS

Map p178 (www.hallesdupetitquartier.com; 1191 Ave Cartier, Montcalm & Colline Parlementaire; ⊘7am-9pm Mon-Fri, to 7pm Sat & Sun) Montcalm's very popular and somewhat pricey indoor food market (sometimes referred to by its old name Les Halles du Petit-Quartier) features individual stalls for bakers, chocolatiers, and fruit, vegetable, cheese, meat and fish vendors, plus a number of cafes and restaurants on two levels.

BENJO
TOYS

Map p178 (☑877-236-5622, 418-640-0001; www.benjo.ca; 543 Rue St-Joseph Est, St-Roch; ⊘10am-5:30pm Mon-Wed, to 9pm Thu & Fri, 9:30am-5pm Sat & Sun) This toy shop gives a glimpse into what the world would be like if kids ran the show. Even the front doors are pint-sized (the grown-ups door is in the center). The enormous store is stocked to the rafters with educational toys, model trains and cars, costumes, stuffed animals and lots more.

There's a train that goes around the store on weekends, and arts and crafts for little ones during the week. Note the bronze statue of the store's mascot, Benjo the Frog, out front.

CAMELLIA SINENSIS
TEA

Map p178 (☑418-525-0247; www.camellia-sinensis.com; 624 Rue St-Joseph Est, St-Roch; ⊘10am-6pm) This modern and very elegant Japanese-inspired shop, which takes its name from the botanical name for 'tea,' stocks some 200 varieties of said commodity; just count the large canisters lining the shelves. Buy to take away or sip some tea ($3 to $4.85) on the premises. It stocks some incredibly beautiful teapots and cups as well.

LATULIPPE
SPORTS & OUTDOORS

(☑418-529-0024; www.latulippe.com; 637 Rue St-Vallier Ouest, St-Sauveur; ⊘8:30am-5:30pm Mon-Wed, to 9pm Thu & Fri, 9am-5pm Sat, from 10am Sun) If you're in the market for sporting goods or outdoor gear and this enormous store in St-Sauveur doesn't have it, it doesn't exist. Visit Latulippe for skins, kayaks, tents, fishing tackle, bird guidebooks – or just about anything that will take you to the great outdoors.

SPORTS & ACTIVITIES

Whether it's summer or deepest, darkest winter, you can expect to find Québec City locals enjoying life outdoors. Inside the city limits there are picturesque parks and paths ideal for an early morning jog or bike ride, as well as a host of winter sports – skating, cross-country skiing and tobogganing – when the weather turns cold.

★ BATTLEFIELDS PARK
OUTDOORS

Map p178 (Parc des Champs-de-Bataille; ☑418-649-6157, 855-649-6157; www.theplainsofabraham.ca; Ave George VI, Montcalm & Colline Parlementaire; ⊘9am-5:30pm;) Conveniently close to the Old Upper Town and boasting fine views of the St Lawrence River, this vast park is Québec City's green lung and prime venue for outdoor activities. You can walk or run along the network of trails, or pound the pavement of a terrific jogging track built atop a former horse-racing course.

The park is also ideal for in-line skating and a host of winter activities, including cross-country skiing, skating and snowshoeing. All equipment can be rented at the Anneau de Glace des Plaines d'Abraham in season.

GLISSADE DE LA TERRASSE
SNOW SPORTS

Map p170 (Terrace Slide; ☑418-528-1884; www.au1884.ca; Terrasse Dufferin, Old Upper Town; per person 1/4 slides $3/10; ⊘10am-5pm Sun-Thu, to 6pm Fri & Sat mid-Dec–mid-Mar;) Next to the Château Frontenac, the scenic Terrasse Dufferin (p172) on the riverfront stages this invigoratingly fast, triple-chute toboggan run all winter long (weather permitting). Toboggans accommodating up to four people are available for rent at the bottom; buy tickets at the Au 1884 kiosk, then grab your toboggan, walk up to the top and let 'er rip.

PATINOIRE DE LA
PLACE D'YOUVILLE ICE SKATING
Map p178 (Place d'Youville Skating Rink; ☑418-641-6256; www.quebec-cite.com/en/businesses/outdoor-activities/snow/skating/patinoire-de-la-place-dyouville; 995 Place d'Youville, St-Jean Baptiste; skating free, skate rental $9.25; ☺noon-10pm Mon-Thu, 10am-10pm Fri-Sun mid-Nov–mid-Mar; 🖈) In the shadow of the Old Town walls and the Palais Montcalm (p198), this improvised outdoor rink is one of the most scenic and popular places for ice skating once winter rolls around. It's a great place to mingle with locals, and you can also rent skates at the nearby Pavillon des Services.

ANNEAU DE GLACE DES
PLAINES D'ABRAHAM SKATING
Map p178 (Plains of Abraham Ice Rink; ☑581-777-0700, 418-691-6733; www.ccbn-nbc.gc.ca/en/activities/plains-abraham-skating-rink; 255 Grande Allée Ouest, Plains of Abraham; skating free, skate rental per 2hr $9.25; ☺10am-10pm late Dec–mid-Mar; 🖈) With a circumference of 400m, this giant open-air skating rink accommodating 350 skaters on the Plains of Abraham offers free skating in winter, including illuminated night skating, skate rental and a snack shack selling hot chocolate to keep you nice and toasty.

COIN DES COUREURS RUNNING
Map p178 (Running Room; ☑418-522-2345; www.runningroom.com; 1049 Ave Cartier, Mont-calm & Colline Parlementaire; ☺10am-9pm Mon-Fri, 9:30am-7pm Sat, 8:30am-5pm Sun) This Alberta-based athletic-shoe chain offers free employee-led group runs at 6pm on Wednesdays and 8:30am on Sundays. Just meet at the store. Its website also has downloadable maps of Québec City running routes ranging from 3km to 20km in length.

ROC GYMS CLIMBING
(☑418-647-4422; www.rocgyms.com; 2350 Ave du Colisée; ☺9am-10pm) Offers indoor climbing and excursions to the canyons and crevices around Québec City. During the evenings and weekends, 30-minute 'try out' sessions are available from $20.

🛏 SLEEPING

From old-fashioned B&Bs to stylish boutique hotels, Québec City has some fantastic overnight options. The best choices are the numerous small European-style hotels and Victorian B&Bs scattered around the Old Town. Make reservations well in advance, especially for weekends. Prices rise in the high-season summer months and during Winter Carnival. At other times of year, you can usually save 30% or so off the high-season prices.

ON THE WATER

Just outside of town, you can go rafting along the Jacques Cartier River. If you prefer a more sedentary approach, take a train ride along the St Lawrence River, or check out the cluster of boat-tour operators moored near Place-Royale; these cross the St Lawrence to Lévis or go upriver toward the Montmorency Falls and Île d'Orléans.

Lévis Ferry (Map p170; ☑877-787-7483; www.traversiers.com; 10 Rue des Traversiers, Gare Fluviale de Québec, Old Lower Town & Port; car & driver/adult/child one way $8.65/3.65/2.45) For city views, you can't beat the 12-minute ferry ride to Lévis; boats operate from 6am to 2am, departing every 30 to 60 minutes depending on the time, day and season. If you purchase a round-trip ticket, you must disembark for security reasons. There's usually a 20-minute layover in Lévis.

Croisières AML (Map p170; ☑800-563-4643, 866-856-6668; www.croisieresaml.com; 10 Rue Dalhousie, Old Lower Town & Port) Enjoy fantastic city perspectives from AML's small vessels, including the classic sightseeing trip along the St Lawrence River (adult/child $35/20) and a brunch cruise ($60/35), each 90 minutes in length. Four-hour summer evening cruises (adult/child $60/35) culminate in July/August with five-course dinner-and-fireworks cruises ($115/87) during the **Grands Feux Loto-Québec** (Loto-Québec Fireworks; www.lesgrandsfeux.com; ☺Jul/Aug) festival.

1. Parc de la Chute-Montmorency 2. Basilique Ste-Anne-de-Beaupré
3. Wendake International Pow Wow 4. Autumn colors, Île d'Orléans

ANDRIY BLOKHIN/SHUTTERSTOCK ©

Day Trips from Québec City

Québec City is surrounded by stunning countryside filled with attractions. Most sights, except for Wendake, can be reached via Rte 138 northeast of town.

Île d'Orléans

This stunning island 15km northeast of Québec City can be visited on a day trip but is easily worth two days or more. Cut off from the rest of Québec for centuries (the Pont de l'Île d'Orléans – once called the Taschereau Bridge – was only built in 1935), its attractions include gorgeous pastoral scenery, riverside villages and 300-year-old stone homes.

Parc de la Chute-Montmorency

This **park** (www.sepaq.com/montmorencyfalls; 5300 Blvd Ste-Anne) containing an 83m-high waterfall is right by the bridge crossing over to the Île d'Orléans. While it tops Niagara Falls by about 30m, it's not nearly as wide, but what's cool is walking over the falls on a suspension bridge, with the water thundering below. The park is about 14km northeast of Québec City. It is the terminus of Métrobus 800 from Place d'Youville in Québec City.

Wendake

The major attraction at this Huron Aboriginal reserve is the **Onhoüa Chetek8e** (www.huron-wendat.qc.ca; 575 Rue Chef Stanislas Koska; ⊙9am-5pm mid-May–Sep, 10am-4pm Oct–mid-May; adult/youth/child $14.75/11.75/9.75), a reconstructed Huron village, and the nearby and more ambitious **Huron-Wendat Museum** (http://tourismewendake.ca; 5 Place de la Rencontre; ⊙10am-noon & 1-4pm May-Oct, 3-6pm Mon-Fri, 10am-noon & 1-4pm Sat & Sun Nov-Apr; adult/child $14.50/7.25) of Aboriginal culture.

Ste-Anne-de-Beaupré

About 35km from Québec City, this village is known for **Basilique Ste-Anne-de-Beaupré** (www.sanctuairesainteanne.org; 10018 Ave Royale; ⊙7am-9:30pm Jun-Aug, 8am-5pm Mon-Sat, to 6pm Sun Sep-May) and its role as a pilgrimage site. Try to visit on July 26, Ste-Anne's feast day, when the faithful flock in droves.

QUÉBEC'S COOLEST HOTEL

Visiting the **Ice Hotel** (Hôtel de Glace; ☑888-384-5524, 418-844-2200; www.valcartier. com/en; 1860 Blvd Valcartier, Village Vacances Valcartier; r per person from $495, day pass adult/youth/child $21/16/free; ☉Jan-Mar; ℙ❋☎) is like stepping into a wintry fairy tale. Nearly everything here is made of ice: the reception desk, the sink in your room, your bed – all ice. Some 500 tons of ice and 15,000 tons of snow go into the five-week construction of this perishable hotel. First impressions are overwhelming – in the entrance hall, tall, sculpted columns of ice support a ceiling where a crystal chandelier hangs. To either side, carved sculptures, tables and chairs fill the labyrinth of corridors and guest rooms. A highlight is the ice bar, where stiff drinks are served in cocktail glasses made of ice (there's hot chocolate for the kids too).

The Ice Hotel usually opens from January to March and offers packages starting at around $400 per double. Sleeping here is more about the adventure, and less about getting a good night's sleep, although thick sleeping bags laid on plush deer pelts do keep things cozier than you might expect.

If you don't want to overnight, you can buy a day pass (adult/youth/child $21/16/free), which allows you to visit the guest rooms and all of the hotel's public spaces, including the ice bar and chapel.

The Ice Hotel is about 30km north of Québec City, in the Village Vacances Valcartier amusement park. Get there via Hwy 73/175 north (exit 154) and Rte 371.

🛏 Old Town & Port

AUBERGE DE LA PAIX   HOSTEL $
Map p170 (☑418-694-0735; www.auberge delapaix.com; 31 Rue Couillard, Old Upper Town; dm $29-34, s/d/tr with shared bath $60/80/102; @☎) With welcoming staff, cheerfully painted rooms and a tree-filled garden, this funky old-school hostel on a quiet backstreet feels less institutional than the official HI hostel to thesouthwest. The eight dorms with four to eight solid wooden bunkbeds are complemented by five coveted private rooms (with shared bath) that must be booked wellin advance. Continental breakfast included.

★LE MONASTÈRE
DES AUGUSTINES   HISTORIC HOTEL $$
Map p170 (☑418-694-1639, 844-694-1639; https://monastere.ca/fr/hebergement; 77 Rue des Remparts, Old Upper Town; r $184-230, with shared bath $130-160; ℙ❋☎) Attached to the convent museum (p169), this fabulous hostelry is the most atmospheric place to stay in Québec City. Choose among 32 'authentic' rooms (shared bath) – former cells inhabited by the nuns when it was a much larger working convent – or 33 'modern' rooms in a new wing with all the usual commodities.

There's an attached restaurant serving multicourse set meals ($24) at 6pm and 7pm Thursday to Saturday. The monastery is a nonprofit organization and all proceeds go to the Augustinian Sisters Heritage Fund.

★LA MARQUISE
DE BASSANO   B&B $$
Map p170 (☑877-692-0316, 418-692-0316; www.marquisedebassano.com; 15 Rue des Grisons, Old Upper Town; r $129-279; ❋@☎) The congenial owners have done a beautiful job with this welcoming family home dating from 1888, outfitting its five rooms with thoughtful touches, whether it's a canopy bed or a claw-foot bathtub. It's peacefully placed on a low-traffic street surrounded by period homes, minutes from the important sights. Only two rooms – including the delightful Library – have private baths.

★HÔTEL
MARIE-ROLLET   INN $$
Map p170 (☑800-275-0338, 418-694-9271; www.hotelmarierollet.com; 81 Rue Ste-Anne, Old Upper Town; r from $129; ❋☎) This lovely inn overlooking the Hôtel de Ville was once owned by the Ursuline nuns at the nearby convent, which is why you'll spot tell-tale signs like ecclesiastical stained glass in some of the public areas. The 13 rooms are on the smallish side and there's no elevator, but the warmth of the place and lovely furnishings excuse all that.

★MAISON HISTORIQUE
JAMES THOMPSON   B&B $$

Map p170 (📞418-694-9042; www.bedandbreak
fastquebec.com; 47 Rue Ste-Ursule, Old Upper
Town; r $75-135; P❄🛜) History buffs will
get a real kick out of staying in the 18th-
century former residence of James Thompson, a veteran of the Battle of the Plains of
Abraham. The beautifully restored house
comes complete with the original murder
hole next to the front door. The three rooms
are spacious – check out the High Priestess.

MANOIR D'AUTEUIL   BOUTIQUE HOTEL $$

Map p170 (📞418-694-1173, 866-662-6647; www.
manoirdauteuil.com; 49 Rue d'Auteuil, Old Upper
Town; r $99-229, junior ste $289-329; P❄🛜)
Friendly American expatriate owners Daniel and Linda have thoroughly renovated
this pair of 19th-century manor houses
opposite the Old Town walls, creating a
supremely comfortable 30-room hotel replete with modern amenities. Rooms range
in size; the nicest offer high ceilings, stone
walls, fireplaces and canopy beds, or, in
the case of the Edith Piaf suite, an ultra-
spacious blue-tiled bath with armchair.

HÔTEL CLARENDON   HISTORIC HOTEL $$

Map p170 (📞418-692-2480, 888-554-6001; www.
hotelclarendon.com; 57 Rue Ste-Anne, Old Upper
Town; r from $165; P❄🛜) Opening to great
fanfare in 1870, the four-star Hôtel Clarendon has continued to set standards in
Québec City for a century and a half. Half
of the 143 rooms look to its main competi-
tor, the Fairmont Le Château Frontenac,
the other to a quiet courtyard. Interesting
features include an old piano in the library
that attracts musicians – talented or otherwise.

CHÂTEAU
FLEUR-DE-LYS   BOUTIQUE HOTEL $$

Map p170 (📞418-694-1884, 877-691-1884; www.
lhotel.ca; 15 Ave Ste-Geneviève, Old Upper Town;
d $100-180, q $254-400; ❄🛜) Delightfully
sited opposite Jardin des Gouverneurs, this
rambling old home has 16 rooms of various
dimensions outfitted with hand-chosen
antiques by its European owners Romuald
and Olivier. Top picks include spacious
Suite Florence Adelaide White overlooking
Château Frontenac and the St Lawrence
River, and the *chambre d'amis,* a snug,
budget-priced cutie with sink and its own
bath down the hall.

MANOIR SUR LE CAP   INN $$

Map p170 (📞418-694-1987, 866-694-1987; www.
manoir-sur-le-cap.com; 9 Ave Ste-Geneviève, Old
Upper Town; r $85-209, ste $185-245; P❄🛜)
Attractions at this 16-room hotel include
the wonderful, quiet location away from the
tourist throngs, and the architectural details of the better rooms: attractive stone or
brick walls and views of the Jardin des Gouverneurs (especially from room 1), the Château or the river. On the downside, some of
the smaller rooms have dated furnishings.

HÔTEL CAP DIAMANT   GUESTHOUSE $$

Map p170 (📞418-684-0313, 888-694-0313; www.
hotelcapdiamant.com; 39 Ave Ste-Geneviève, Old
Upper Town; r $115-175; ❄🛜) This wonderful
B&B in two houses dating from the early
19th century oozes charm, its nine period-style rooms and public areas boasting
features like ancient stained glass, marble
fireplaces and hardwood floors. The room
of choice is the loft suite with its own rooftop balcony and views across the Old Town
to the Château Frontenac.

HÔTEL LE PRIORI   BOUTIQUE HOTEL $$

Map p170 (📞800-351-3992, 418-692-3992; www.
hotellepriori.com; 15 Rue Sault-au-Matelot, Old
Lower Town & Port; r $139-239, ste $209-399;
❄🛜) Housed in the high-ceilinged former workshop of the renowned Baillairgé
family of architects, the Lower Town's
original boutique hotel offers 20 rooms and
eight suites in separate buildings with tall
windows, exposed brick and stone walls,
stylish Italian and Québécois furniture, and
other classy amenities such as stainless-
steel sinks and slate floors.

LES LOFTS
DU TRÉSOR   APARTMENT $$

Map p170 (📞418-431-9905; https://loftsvieux
quebec.com/les-lofts-du-tresor; 1 Rue du Trésor,
Old Upper Town; studios $80-110, apt $170-300;
❄🛜) One of a dozen properties offering
mostly self-catering apartments across
Québec City, this welcoming pied-à-terre
in the heart of the Old Upper Town and
opposite the basilica has gorgeously refurbished and bright, high-ceilinged apartments. Comfortable bedding, full kitchens,
ultramodern bathrooms and laundry facilities make each loft a cozy home away from
home.

QUÉBEC CITY SLEEPING

★FAIRMONT LE
CHÂTEAU FRONTENAC   HOTEL $$$
Map p170 (☑866-540-4460, 418-692-3861;
www.fairmont.com/frontenac; 1 Rue des Car-
rières, Old Upper Town; r $229-700, ste $408-
2700; P❄🐾📶🐾) More than a hotel, the
iconic Frontenac is Québec City's most
enduring symbol. Its 611 rooms come in a
dozen-plus categories. The coveted river-
view rooms – beg, borrow or steal room
1001 – range in price from Deluxe units
tucked under the 18th-floor eaves to the 60
ultraspacious Fairmont Gold rooms, with
concierge service, curved turret windows
and vintage architectural details.

The hotel has over 2000 windows, a
variety of elegant salons, bars and restau-
rants, and 12km of corridors lined with
photos of famous guests including Alfred
Hitchcock and Paul McCartney. Service
is professional and staff are adept at han-
dling the big crowds. Everyone enjoys con-
necting with a little slice of Québec City
history; the lobby (which puts on special
exhibits) is often filled with more visitors
than guests. Check the website for special
deals, especially outside the peak summer
and Winter Carnival seasons. Or just sam-
ple one of a trio of romantic outlets includ-
ing the 1608 (p186) *bar à vin et fromage*
(wine and cheese bar) and the silver-ser-
vice Restaurant Champlain (p188).

★AUBERGE
ST-ANTOINE   DESIGN HOTEL $$$
Map p170 (☑888-692-2211, 418-692-2211;
www.saint-antoine.com; 8 Rue St-Antoine, Old
Lower Town & Port; r $259-429, ste $720-1450;
P❄@📶) Auberge St-Antoine is probably
Québec's finest smaller hotel, with phenomenal service and endless amenities.
The 95 plush and spacious rooms come
with high-end mattresses, goose-down
duvets, luxury linens and atmospheric
lighting, while the halls resemble an art
gallery, filled with French-colonial artifacts from the 18th and 19th centuries
uncovered during excavations to expand
the hotel.

HÔTEL LE
GERMAIN QUÉBEC   BOUTIQUE HOTEL $$$
Map p170 (☑418-692-2224, 888-833-5253;
www.legermainhotels.com/en/quebec; 126
Rue St-Pierre, Old Lower Town & Port; r $199-

335; P❄@📶🐾) The flagship of a classy
Québécois chain with 18 properties, this
hotel combines understated luxury with
superb service. It occupies two adjacent
historic buildings, one once a bank, the
other a fruit-and-vegetable market. The
60 rooms are quiet, cozy and tastefully
designed, with sumptuous mattresses,
Egyptian-cotton bedding, fluffy towels
and bathrobes, good lighting, big win-
dows, attractive woodwork and glow-in-
the-dark basins.

LE CLOS ST-LOUIS   BOUTIQUE HOTEL $$$
Map p170 (☑800-461-1311, 418-694-1311; www.
clossaintlouis.com; 69 Rue St-Louis, Old Upper
Town; r $229-365; ❄@📶) At this three-star
boutique hotel between Porte St-Louis
and Château Frontenac, the owners have
retained the building's natural 1844 Victorian charm while adding modern amenities. Most of the 18 spacious and lavishly
decorated rooms come with Jacuzzis,
beautifully tiled baths, and canopy or
four-poster beds. The suites (check out No
18) resemble Victorian apartments, apart
from the TV.

HOTEL MANOIR VICTORIA   HOTEL $$$
Map p170 (☑800-463-6283, 418-692-1030; www.
manoir-victoria.com; 44 Côte du Palais, Old Upper
Town; r $199-369, ste $329-550; P❄@📶🐾)
A historical, old-world facade gives way to
a stylishly chic lobby and lounge, and 156
modern rooms decked out with flat-screen
TVs and sometimes a glass-fronted fire-
place. The fabulous indoor swimming pool,
on-site spa and gym will keep the chill at
bay after walking through the Old Town in
winter.

HÔTEL 71   BOUTIQUE HOTEL $$$
Map p170 (☑888-692-1171, 418-692-1171; www.
hotel71.ca; 71 Rue St-Pierre, Old Lower Town &
Port; r $179-399, ste $259-539; P❄@📶) Set
in an imposing former Bank of Canada,
this 60-room hotel provides a boutique experience par excellence. Sleek, minimalist
rooms offer unstinting comfort, with fantastic mattresses, linens partially made of
birch fiber, 4m-high ceilings and dramatically lit baths. The penthouse suite, with
its wraparound windows, commands some
of Québec City's most astounding perspectives on the St Lawrence River and Château
Frontenac.

🛏 Outside the Old Town

MAEVA HOSTEL
HOSTEL **$**

Map p178 (☎418-914-9578; www.auberge maeva.ca; 671 St-François Est, St-Roch; dm $20-35, d $50-70; @🕸) One of just a handful of hostels in town, this welcoming place has dorms with between five and 12 beds as well as two private rooms. Dorms, including a females-only one, have attached baths and lockers, and there's a giant kitchen. Decor is cheery, with lots of Inuit art. Maeva means 'welcome' in Tahiti, where affable owner Roberto comes from.

CENTRE DE PLEIN AIR DE BEAUPORT
CAMPGROUND **$**

(☎877-641-6113, 418-641-6112; www.centre pleinairbeauport.ca; 95 Rue de la Sérénité, Beauport; campsites & RV sites $38-48; ☼Jun-early Sep; 🅿) This excellent campground near Montmorency Falls is green, peaceful and just a 15-minute drive from the Old Town. To get there, take Hwy 40 toward Montmorency, get off at exit 321 and turn north.

★AUBERGE JA MOISAN
B&B **$$**

Map p178 (☎418-529-9764; www.jamoisan.com; 695 Rue St-Jean, St-Jean Baptiste; s $110-170, d $120-180; 🅿🕸🕸) This lovely B&B above the historical JA Moisan (p203) grocery store has four relatively small bedrooms tucked under the eaves and gorgeously furnished in period style. The floor below holds common areas, including a parlor, tearoom, solarium, terrace and computer room. Gregarious host Clément St-Laurent makes guests feel right at home. Rates include breakfast, afternoon tea and valet parking.

CHÂTEAU DES TOURELLES
B&B **$$**

Map p178 (☎866-346-9136, 418-647-9136; www.chateaudestourelles.qc.ca; 212 Rue St-Jean, St-Jean Baptiste; r $99-183, ste $129-245; 🅿🕸@🕸) You'll recognize this B&B by its soaring turret, which mirrors the steeple of the Church of St-Jean Baptiste to the east. The affable Breton owner has completely refurbished this old house, equipping the 11 rooms with wood floors, triple-paned windows, hi-def TV and new bath; other perks include the bright-orange-hued breakfast area and lounge, and rooftop terrace with great views.

HÔTEL PUR
DESIGN HOTEL **$$**

Map p178 (☎418-647-2611, 800-267-2002; www. hotelpur.com; 395 Rue de la Couronne, St-Roch; r $125-225; 🅿🕸@🕸🕸) Not sure how 'Pure' this place is, but we love its style, good humor and huge swimming pool and spa. The reception has a white woolen backdrop that looks like a raging snowstorm, and the fox and moose portraits in the lobby are hysterical. Some of the 242 rooms have floor-to-ceiling windows, framing the distant mountains and river.

AU CROISSANT DE LUNE
B&B **$$**

Map p178 (☎418-523-9946; www.aucroissant delune.com; 594 Rue St-Gabriel, St-Jean Baptiste; r with shared bath $92-140; 🕸) Patricia, Olivier and their two children offer three comfortable and colorful rooms with shared bath at this unpretentious family-friendly B&B in St-Jean Baptiste. Easily the most charming is the two-level Green Room, with its main bedroom under the

---

ℹ PARKING

Compact Old Québec lends itself better to exploration on foot than by car. If you're driving up here, plan to park your vehicle for as much of your stay as possible.

Parking garages in and around the Old Town typically charge a day rate of $17.50 to $25 Monday to Friday, and $8 to $12 overnight and on weekends. In the Old Upper Town, the most central garage, and one of the cheapest, is underneath the **Hôtel de Ville** (Rue Pierre-Olivier-Chauveau, Old Upper Town; weekday/weekend/overnight $17.50/8/8), just a couple of blocks from the Château Frontenac. In the Old Lower Town, there are a couple of convenient lots along Rue Dalhousie. Metered street parking is also widely available, but expensive (from $2 per hour). Many guesthouses provide discount vouchers for nearby parking garages.

In winter nighttime snow removal is scheduled on many streets between 11pm and 6:30am. Don't park during these hours on any street with a 'Déneigement' (snow removal) sign and a flashing red light, or you'll wake up to a towed vehicle and a hefty fine!

eaves and a kid-friendly smaller room below. Breakfast, featuring homemade yogurt, fresh fruit, waffles and/or French-style crepes, is another plus.

C3 HÔTEL

ART DE VIVRE BOUTIQUE HOTEL **$$**
Map p178 (☏800-782-9441, 418-525-9726; www.lec3hotel.com/en; 170 Grande Allée Ouest, Montcalm & Colline Parlementaire; r $129-189; P❄@⌛) This rechristened and rebranded hotel around the corner from restaurant-lined Ave Cartier offers modern rooms and professional service. The two-dozen rooms range in size from small and modestly furnished to spacious numbers with nice extras, such as a fireplace. They're done up in a sleek, modern style that tries to reflect the well-heeled neighborhood and nearby fine-arts museum.

LE CHÂTEAU

DU FAUBOURG B&B **$$**
Map p178 (☏418-524-2902; www.lechateaudu faubourg.com; 429 Rue St-Jean, St-Jean Baptiste; r $139-179; P❄⌛) Built by the massively rich Dussault family (of Imperial Tobacco fame) in the 1800s, this is one of the city's most atmospheric B&Bs – the frosty 'welcome' notwithstanding. The interior is pure British-lord-of-the-manor-meets-French-marquis style, replete with old oil paintings, antique furnishings and shimmering chandeliers. The three rooms and two suites – all themed – are packed with old-world details.

RELAIS

CHARLES-ALEXANDRE HOTEL **$$**
Map p178 (☏418-523-1220; www.relaischarles alexandre.com; 91 Grande Allée Est, Montcalm & Colline Parlementaire; r $109-179; ❄⌛) This small, delightful hotel in a former officers' residence is on the edge of Battlefields Park (p179). The 23 rooms are all different and are best described as low-key and comfortable with modern furnishings. Standard rooms are bright, but have a view onto the parking lot. Some superior rooms have big bay windows and fireplaces. Parking costs $15 extra.

Understand Montréal & Québec City

Old Montréal (p46)

History

Originally the home of Iroquois people, Montréal has a dynamic history as a small French colony, a fur-trading center and a base for industrialists who laid the foundation of Canada. Later eclipsed by Toronto, it has rebranded itself as a powerhouse of French-speaking business and culture.

The Early Settlement

The Island of Montréal was long inhabited by the St Lawrence Iroquois, one of the tribes that formed the Five Nations Confederacy of Iroquois. In 1535 French explorer Jacques Cartier visited the Iroquois village of Hochelaga (Place of the Beaver Dam) on the slopes of Mont-Royal, but by the time Samuel de Champlain founded Québec City in 1608, the settlement had vanished. In 1642 Paul de Chomedey, sieur de Maisonneuve founded the first permanent mission, despite fierce resistance by the Iroquois. Intended as a base for converting Aboriginal people to Christianity, this settlement quickly became a major hub of the fur trade. Québec City became the capital of the French colony Nouvelle-France (New France), while Montréal's *voyageurs* (trappers) established a network of trading posts into the hinterland.

As part of the Seven Years' War, Britain clashed with France over its colony in New France. The British victory on the Plains of Abraham outside Québec City heralded the Treaty of Paris (1763), which gave Britain control of New France; it also presaged the creation of Canada itself with Confederation in 1867.

The American army seized Montréal during the American Revolution (1775–83) and set up headquarters at Château Ramezay. But even the formidable negotiating skills of Benjamin Franklin failed to convince French Québécois to join their cause, and seven months later the revolutionaries decided they'd had enough and left empty-handed.

When Jacques Cartier arrived around the time of the feast of St Lawrence in 1535, he gave thanks by naming Montréal's river after the early Christian saint. It has had many other names – the River That Walks, the Canada River and the Cod River – but St Lawrence eventually stuck.

TIMELINE

1500	1535	1608
Semisedentary Iroquois groups frequent the island, settling one permanent village, Hochelaga (Place of the Beaver Dam), near present-day McGill University.	French gold-seeker Jacques Cartier sets foot on the island. He encounters the Iroquois, returning home with 'gold' and 'diamonds' – later revealed to be iron pyrite and quartz.	French explorer Samuel de Champlain establishes a new city 250km downriver from Montréal and names it Kebec, from the Algonquian word meaning 'where the river narrows.'

Industry & Immigration

In the early 19th century Montréal's fortunes dimmed as the fur trade shifted north to Hudson Bay. However, a new class of international merchants and financiers soon emerged, founding the Bank of Montréal and investing in shipping as well as a new railway network. Tens of thousands of Irish immigrants came to work on the railways and in the factories, mills and breweries that sprang up along the Canal de Lachine. Canada's industrial revolution was born, with the English clearly in control.

The Canadian Confederation of 1867 gave Québécois a degree of control over their social and economic affairs and acknowledged French as an official language. French Canadians living in the rural areas flowed into the city to seek work and regained the majority. At this time, Montréal was Canada's premier railway center, financial hub and manufacturing powerhouse. The Canadian Pacific Railway opened its head office there in the 1880s, and Canadian grain bound for Europe was shipped through the port.

In the latter half of the century, a wave of immigrants from Italy, Spain, Germany, Eastern Europe and Russia gave Montréal a cosmopolitan flair that remains unique in the province. By 1914 the metropolitan

HISTORY BOOKS

➡ *A Short History of Quebec* (John A Dickinson and Brian Young; 1993, revised 2008). Social and economic portrait of Québec from the pre-European period to modern constitutional struggles.

➡ *City Unique: Montreal Days and Nights in the 1940s and '50s* (William Weintraub; 1996). Engaging tales of Montréal's twilight period as Sin City and an exploration of its historic districts.

➡ *The Road to Now: A History of Blacks in Montreal* (Dorothy Williams; 1997). A terrific and rare look at a little-known aspect of the city's history and the Black experience in New France.

➡ *All Our Yesterdays: A Collection of 100 Stories of People, Landmarks and Events From Montreal's Past* (Edgar Andrew Collard; 1988). An insightful look at the city's history, streets and squares, with wonderful illustrations.

➡ *Canadiens Legends: Montreal's Hockey Heroes* (Mike Leonetti; 2004). Wonderful profiles of some of the key players that made this team a National Hockey League (NHL) legend and a mythological part of Montréal's 20th-century cultural history.

➡ *The Illustrated History of Canada* (Craig Brown, ed; 2002). Several historians contributed to this well-crafted work with fascinating prints, maps and sketches.

1642	1721	1760	1763
Maisonneuve and a group of 50 settlers found the colony of 'Ville-Marie.' Frenchwomen Jeanne Mance and Marguerite Bourgeoys establish New France's first hospital and school.	After years of on-and-off fighting with the Iroquois, the town erects a stone citadel. The colony continues to grow, fueled by the burgeoning riches of the fur trade.	One year after a resounding victory outside of Québec City, the British seize Montréal.	France officially cedes its territories to Britain under the Treaty of Paris, bringing an end to French rule in Canada.

population exceeded half a million residents, of whom more than 10% were neither British nor French.

War, Depression & Nationalism

In 1775 two American revolutionary armies marched on Québec; one of them seized Montréal and the other, under the command of patriot-turned-traitor Benedict Arnold, headed for Québec City. But even the formidable negotiating skills of Benjamin Franklin failed to convince Québécois to join the American Revolution, and seven months later the revolutionaries withdrew.

The peace that existed between the French and English citizens ran aground after the outbreak of WWI. When Ottawa introduced the draft in 1917, French Canadian nationalists condemned it as a plot to reduce the francophone population. The conscription issue resurfaced in WWII, with 80% of francophones rejecting the draft and nearly as many English-speaking Canadians voting for it.

During the Prohibition era Montréal found a new calling as 'Sin City,' as hordes of free-spending, pleasure-seeking Americans flooded over the border in search of booze, brothels and betting houses. But with the advent of the Great Depression, the economic inferiority of French Canadians became clearer than ever.

Québec's nationalists turned inward, developing proposals to create cooperatives, nationalize the anglophone electricity companies and promote French Canadian goods. Led by the right-wing, ruralist, ultraconservative Maurice Duplessis, the new Union Nationale party took advantage of the nationalist awakening to win provincial power in the 1936 elections. The party's influence would retard Québec's industrial and social progress until Duplessis died in 1959.

Grand Projects

By the early 1950s, the infrastructure of Montréal, by now with a million-plus inhabitants, badly needed an overhaul. Mayor Jean Drapeau drew up a grand blueprint that would radically alter the face of the city, including the metro, a skyscraper-filled Downtown and an underground city. The harbor was extended for the opening of the St Lawrence Seaway.

SUZANNE TAKES YOUR HAND...

Leonard Cohen, one of the city's most famous sons, grew up in the wealthy Anglo enclave of Westmount, but was drawn to the streets of Downtown and the Old Port. His celebrated 1967 ballad 'Suzanne' was based on his experiences with Suzanne Verdal, then wife of sculptor Armand Vaillancourt. Fans have tried to pinpoint the location of the meeting, and the most likely spot is an old waterfront building along Rue de la Commune in the Old Port. The lyrics refer to a lady within the harbor, thought to be the statue atop the Chapelle Notre-Dame-de-Bon-Secours at 400 Rue St-Paul Est.

1775	1832	1833	1840s
Two American revolutionary armies march on Québec, but fail to convince Québécois to join the American Revolution and withdraw after seven months.	Montréal is incorporated as a city following the prosperous 1820s. The Canal de Lachine dramatically improves commerce and transportation.	Jacques Viger is elected as Montréal's first mayor.	Bad times arrive, with violent protests over colonial reform, and an 1847 typhus epidemic that kills thousands.

IRISH IN MONTRÉAL

The Irish have been streaming into Montréal since the founding of New France, but they came in floods between 1815 and 1860, driven from Ireland by the Potato Famine. Catholic like the French settlers, the Irish easily assimilated into Québécois society. Names from this period still encountered today include 'Aubrey' or 'Aubry,' 'O'Brinnan' or 'O'Brennan,' and 'Mainguy' from 'McGee.' In Montréal, most of these immigrants settled in Griffintown, then an industrial hub near the Canal de Lachine. The first St Patrick's Day parade in the city was held in 1824 and has run every year since; it's now one of the city's biggest events. For some terrific reads on the Irish community, check out *The Shamrock and the Shield: An Oral History of the Irish in Montreal* by Patricia Burns and *The Untold Story: The Irish in Canada*, edited by Robert O'Driscoll and Lorna Reynolds.

Along the way Drapeau set about ridding Montréal of its 'Sin City' image by cleaning up the shadier districts. His most colorful nemesis was Lili St-Cyr, the Minnesota-born stripper whose affairs with high-ranking politicians, sports stars and thugs were as legendary in the postwar era as her bathtub performances.

The face of Montréal changed dramatically during the 1960s as a forest of skyscrapers shot up. Private developers replaced Victorian-era structures with landmark buildings such as Place Bonaventure, a modern hotel-shopping complex, and the Place des Arts performing-arts center. The focus of the city shifted from Old Montréal to Ville-Marie, where commerce flourished.

In 1960 the nationalist Liberal Party won control of the Québec assembly and passed sweeping measures that would shake Canada to its very foundations. In the first stage of this so-called Quiet Revolution, the assembly vastly expanded Québec's public sector and nationalized the provincial hydroelectric companies.

Francophones were able to work in French because more corporate managers supported French-language working conditions. For instance, the nationalization of power companies saw the language of construction blueprints change from English to French.

Still, progress wasn't swift enough for radical nationalists, and by the mid-1960s they were claiming that Québec independence was the only way to ensure francophone rights.

As the francophones seized power, some of the old established anglophone networks became spooked and resettled outside the province. By 1965, Montréal had lost its status as Canada's economic capital to Toronto. But new expressways were laid out and the metro was finished

In 1940 UK Prime Minister Winston Churchill shipped $5 billion in foreign reserves from the Bank of England to Montréal. The fortune was placed in a vault in the Sun Life Building, to fund a British government in exile should the Nazis invade and occupy Britain.

1852	1865	1867	1867
The Great Fire burns much of the city to the ground.	Lured by big industry, immigrants arrive by the thousands; francophones soon outnumber anglophones. Over the next 40 years, the population quadruples.	Railways and an active harbor bring wealth to Montréal.	Tired of colonial rule, representatives of colonies on the Atlantic coast meet and form a Confederation; modern Canada is born.

in time for Expo '67 (the 1967 World's Fair), a runaway success that attracted 50 million visitors. It was the defining moment of Montréal as a metropolis, and would lay the foundations for its successful bid to host the 1976 Olympics – an event that would land the city in serious debt.

Meanwhile, things continued heating up in the Quiet Revolution. To head off clashes with Québec's increasingly separatist leaders, Prime Minister Pierre Trudeau proposed two key measures in 1969: Canada was to be made fully bilingual to give francophones equal access to national institutions; and the constitution was to be amended to guarantee francophone rights. Ottawa then pumped cash into French-English projects, which nonetheless failed to convince francophones that French would become the primary language of work in Québec.

In 1976 this lingering discontent spurred the election of René Lévesque and his Parti Québécois, committed to the goal of independence for the province. The following year the Québec assembly passed Bill 101, which not only made French the sole official language of

THE QUIET REVOLUTION

In the 1960s the so-called Quiet Revolution began to give French Québécois more sway in industry and politics, and ultimately established the primacy of the French language.

The 'revolution' itself refers to the sweeping economic and social changes initiated by nationalist Premier Jean Lesage and others that were intended to make Québécois more in control of their destiny. It was an effort to modernize, secularize and Frenchify Québec after years of conservatism under Premier Maurice Duplessis. But this tide of nationalism also had extreme elements.

The Front de Libération du Québec (FLQ), a radical nationalist group committed to overthrowing local power structures (as personified by the church and big business), was founded in 1963. Initially the FLQ attacked military targets and other symbols of federal power, but soon became involved in labor disputes. In the mid-1960s the FLQ claimed responsibility for a spate of bombings, and in October 1970 it kidnapped Québec's labor minister Pierre Laporte and a British trade official in an attempt to force the independence issue. Prime Minister Pierre Trudeau declared a state of emergency and called in the army to protect government officials. The next day Laporte's body was found in the trunk of a car. By December the crisis had passed, but the murder discredited the FLQ in the eyes of many supporters. In the years that followed, the FLQ effectively ceased to exist as a political movement.

While support for Québec independence still hovers around 30% to 45% in the polls, there's little appetite for another referendum on separation from Canada. Rather, the current generation of voters seems to prefer a path of strong Québécois autonomy within the existing Canadian framework.

1917	1959	1967	1970
As war rages in Europe, Québécois feel no loyalty to France or Britain and resent being conscripted to fight. Tensions seethe between Anglos and French Canadians.	St Lawrence Seaway opens, permitting freighters to bypass Montréal. Toronto slowly overtakes Montréal as Canada's commercial engine.	Expo '67 in Montréal marks the centenary of Canadian Confederation, drawing people from across the country and around the world.	The separatist-minded Front de Libération du Québec kidnaps labor minister Pierre Laporte (later killing him). Although the FLQ is discredited, separatism gains support.

Québec but also stipulated that all immigrants enroll their children in French-language schools. The trickle of anglophone refugees from the province turned into a flood. Alliance Québec, an English-rights group, estimates that between 300,000 and 400,000 Anglos left Québec during this period.

The Not-Quiet Nation Of Québec

The Quiet Revolution heightened tensions not only in Québec but across Canada. After their reelection in 1980, federal Liberals, led by Pierre Trudeau, sold most Québécois on the idea of greater rights through constitutional change, helping to defeat a referendum on Québec sovereignty the same year by a comfortable margin. Québec premier Robert Bourassa then agreed to a constitution-led solution – but only if Québec was recognized as a 'distinct society' with special rights.

In 1987 the federal Conservative Party was in power and Prime Minister Brian Mulroney unveiled an accord that met most of Québec's demands. To take effect, the Meech Lake Accord needed ratification by all 10 provinces and both houses of parliament by 1990. Dissenting premiers in three provinces eventually pledged their support, but incredibly the accord collapsed when a single member of Manitoba's legislature refused to sign.

The failure of the Meech Lake Accord triggered a major political crisis in Québec. The separatists blamed English-speaking Canada for its demise, and Mulroney and Bourassa subsequently drafted the Charlottetown Accord, a new, expanded accord. But the separatists picked it apart, and in October 1992 the second version was trounced in Québec and five other provinces. The rejection sealed the fate of Mulroney, who stepped down as prime minister the following year, and of Bourassa, who left political life a broken man.

Referendum & Rebirth

In the early 1990s Montréal was wracked by political uncertainty and economic decline. No one disputed that the city was ailing as the symptoms were everywhere: corporate offices had closed and moved their headquarters to other parts of Canada, shuttered shops lined Downtown streets, and derelict factories and refineries rusted on the perimeter. Relations between anglophones and francophones, meanwhile, plumbed new depths after Québec was denied a special status in Canada.

The victory of the separatist Parti Québécois in the 1994 provincial elections signaled the arrival of another crisis. Support for an independent Québec rekindled, and a referendum on sovereignty was called the

1976	1980	1993	1994
The Parti Québécois gains power and passes Bill 101, declaring French the official language. Many businesses leave Montréal, taking 15,000 jobs with them.	The first referendum on independence ends in a comfortable defeat.	Prime Minister Brian Mulroney steps down after failing to get support for the revised Charlottetown Accord.	Voters go to the polls again, narrowly defeating Québec gaining sovereignty. Over the next decade the separatist movement slowly fizzles.

When Mayor Camilien Houde was faced with the proposal of building a road over Mont-Royal, he famously retorted that it would only be built over his dead body. After he died, and was duly buried on the side of the mountain, Mayor Jean Drapeau built the aptly named Voie Camilien-Houde.

following year. While it first appeared the referendum would fail by a significant margin, the outcome was a real cliff-hanger: Québécois decided by 52,000 votes – a razor-thin majority of less than 1% – to stay part of Canada. In Montréal, where the bulk of Québec's anglophones and immigrants live, more than two-thirds voted against sovereignty.

In the aftermath of the vote, the locomotives of the Quiet Revolution (economic inferiority and linguistic insecurity among francophones) ran out of steam. Exhausted by decades of separatist wrangling, most Montréalers put aside their differences and went back to work.

Oddly enough, a natural disaster played a key role in bringing the communities together. In 1998 a freak ice storm – some blamed extramoist El Niño winds, others cited global warming – snapped power masts like matchsticks across the province, leaving over three million people without power and key services in the middle of a Montréal winter. Some people endured weeks without electricity and heat, but regional and political differences were forgotten as money, clothing and offers of personal help poured into the stricken areas. Montréalers recount memories of those dark days with a touch of mutual respect.

As the political climate brightened, Montréal began to emerge from a fundamental reshaping of the local economy. The city experienced a burst of activity as sectors such as software, aerospace, telecommunications and pharmaceuticals replaced rust-belt industries like textiles and refining. Québec's moderate wages became an asset to manufacturers seeking qualified, affordable labor, and foreign investment began to flow more freely. Tax dollars were used to recast Montréal as a new-media hub, encouraging dozens of multimedia firms to settle in the Old Port area.

Today the Place des Arts area teems with restaurants and entertainment venues; Old Montréal buzzes with designer hotels and trendy restaurants; and once-empty warehouses around town have been converted to lofts and offices.

Montréal's renewed vigor has lured back some of the Anglophones who left in the 1980s and '90s, and language conflicts have slipped into the background. The impassioned separatists who came of age during the heady days of the Quiet Revolution are older now, and most young Montréalers are at least bilingual. In the 2014 Québec general election, the Parti Québécois earned its smallest share of the popular vote since its inaugural run in 1970. The PQ's defeat, brought about in part by candidate Pierre Karl Péladeau's strong endorsement of Québécois sovereignty, has led some to speculate that the demographic opportunity for separatism may have ended for good – a sentiment exacerbated by Péladeau's retirement from politics in 2016 and the victory by anti-independence Coalition Avenir Québec (CAQ) in 2018.

1998	2005	2011–12	2014
The Great Ice Storm leaves thousands in Montréal and southern Québec without heat or electricity as power lines are severed by ice.	Canada becomes the fourth country in the world to legalize same-sex marriage. Montréaler Michaëlle Jean is installed as 27th governor-general of Canada.	Montréal is wracked by months of street protests by students opposed to government plans to increase tuition. Hundreds are arrested.	The Parti Québécois suffers its worst electoral showing in decades, reflecting anemic public support for Québécois sovereignty.

The federalist Québec Liberal Party dominated provincial government for almost a decade. In 2012 the party suffered its greatest challenge when students staged months of street protests against Premier Jean Charest's plans to end a long freeze on tuition increases. The controversy resulted in hundreds of arrests, passage of a tough new law to curb the protests and a brief return to power in September 2012 for the Parti Québécois, which had promised to do away with Charest's proposed tuition hike. However, the Liberals regained supremacy in Québec's April 2014 elections under Philippe Couillard. They in turn were ousted by a landslide victory by the conservative CAQ, which was only formed in 2011. A new era of politics without Québec Liberal Party dominance began.

Montréal Today

Montréal's urban rush of redevelopment in recent years reflects a city finally hitting the big time and shaking off its quaint Québec image. International students, workers and migrants have brought newfound wealth and the numbers to justify redevelopment projects. All these aspirations are pinned on Valérie Plante, the city's first female mayor.

LIVABLE CITY

In business and industry, Montréal does well for itself, boasting the highest number of research centers in Canada, an impressive high-tech sector and the third-largest fashion industry in North America (after New York and Los Angeles). While overall the cost of living here is low compared to most Canadian cities, and home prices remain about 40% to 50% cheaper than in Toronto or Vancouver, Montréal saw rental prices soar by as much as 30% in 2020, and gentrification has become a hot topic. The Plateau used to be the affordable bohemian place to live; now those without cash to pay for ever-increasing rents are being pushed out. Consequently, the creative scene is moving up to Little Italy, Mile End and Park Ex. Other pressing issues are the city's aging infrastructure, its high unemployment relative to other Canadian cities, and a city government that many see as cumbersomely complex, inefficient and costly. Montréalers also complain about paying the highest taxes of any province in Canada.

In spite of the city's shortcomings, Montréalers remain proud, citing the city's burgeoning film and music industries, its vibrant multiculturalism and its rich intellectual life. Not surprisingly, Montréal does quite well in quality-of-life surveys (often ranking well ahead of Paris, Barcelona and San Francisco for instance). A 2018 survey by the *Economist* rated Montréal as the world's 12th most livable city, while the annual Mercer Quality of Living rankings regularly list Montréal among the top 25 cities globally.

2017	2018	2019	2021
Montréal elects its first female mayor, Valérie Plante. Her victory was propelled by promises to improve public transit and making the city more family friendly.	Anti-independence Coalition Avenir Québec (Coalition for Québec's Future) party wins a landslide victory in the Québec assembly, gaining 74 of the 125 seats.	Bill 21 is passed. This controversial law bans teachers, police officers and other civil servants from wearing religious symbols such as crosses, hijabs and turbans.	Valérie Plante is reelected as Montréal's mayor in late 2021.

Spirit of Montréal

Montréal's social scene is nothing if not passionate. Political apathy can turn into fiery protest overnight, while the potent mix of French, English and many other languages bubbles away in a stew that's sometimes tense. But a love of music, festivals and food somehow makes it all work.

Politics

At the local level, Montréal is seeking to regain political equilibrium after a turbulent period in 2012–13 that saw major student protests and three changes of mayor within 12 months. Yet tumultuous times have been seen with every mayor since then. Denis Coderre, elected in November 2013, came into office on the heels of corruption scandals that spelled the doom of longtime mayor Gérald Tremblay and his immediate successor, Michael Applebaum. Coderre barely squeaked into office with 32% of the vote with a populist, nonpartisan style earning high approval ratings, especially among younger voters concerned about the environment. Still, he was ousted in 2017 by the first ever female mayor in the city's history, Valérie Plante. While she rejected an election-time proposal to heat the sidewalks on Rue St-Catherine, Plante is finally going ahead on the key election promise of a new Pink metro line. Yet it was when her Projet Montréal party announced a new bylaw requiring all new large residential projects to include social housing that there was hope that Plante might finally live up to her claims of being for the people.

Carved in stone on Québec City's Parliament building and emblazoned on every license plate in the province, the simple motto *'Je me souviens'* ('I remember') eloquently expresses the Québécois sense of pride and identity as North America's largest and oldest French-speaking culture.

Language

French is the official language of Québec and French Québecers are passionate about it, seeing their language as the last line of defense against Anglo-Saxon culture. What makes Montréal unique in the province is the interface of English and French – a mix responsible for the city's dynamism as well as the root of many of its conflicts.

According to Québec's latest census, native French speakers in the Montréal metropolitan area number 2,395,525, while native English speakers number 439,845. More than 50 per cent of Montréalers from a variety of backgrounds speak both official languages.

To Francophone Québecers, the French spoken in France sounds desperately posh. To people from France, the French spoken in Québec sounds terribly old-fashioned and at times unintelligible – an attitude that instantly ruffles feathers in Québec, as it's felt to be condescending.

Québecers learn standard French in school, hear standard French on newscasts and grow up on movies and music from France, so if you speak French from France, locals will have no difficulty understanding you – it's you understanding them that will be the problem. Remember, even when French-language Québécois movies are shown in France, they are shown with *French* subtitles.

Young Montréalers today are not particularly concerned about language issues. Most grew up speaking both languages, and people you meet in daily life – store owners, waiters and bus drivers – switch effort-lessly between French and English.

Media

Montréal is the seat of Québec's French-language media companies and has four big TV networks. New-media firms such as Autodesk Media and Entertainment are renowned for their animation and special effects, and the Cité du Multimédia center in Old Montréal is an incubator for start-ups.

The *Montreal Gazette* (www.montrealgazette.com) is the major English-language daily, with coverage of national affairs, politics and the arts. The big French dailies are the federalist *La Presse* (www.cyber presse.ca) and the separatist-leaning *Le Devoir* (www.ledevoir.com).

Le Journal de Montréal (www.journaldemontreal.com) is *the* city's rollicking tabloid, replete with sensational headlines and photos. Though much derided, the *Journal* does the brashest undercover and investigative reporting in town and has the city's biggest daily circulation.

Montréal's last free alternative weekly is the French-language *Voir* (www.voir.ca); it covers film, music, books, restaurants and goings-on about town.

Canada's only truly national papers are the left-leaning Toronto *Globe and Mail* (www.theglobeandmail.com) and the right-leaning *National Post* (www.nationalpost.com). *The Walrus* (www.thewalrus.ca) is a Canadian *New Yorker/Atlantic Monthly*–style magazine, with in-depth articles and musings from the country's intellectual heavyweights. Canada's weekly news magazine *Maclean's* (www.macleans.ca) and the sophisticated general-interest magazine *Maisonneuve* (www.maisonneuve.org) are also full of high-quality writing.

L'Actualité (www.lactualite.com) is Québec's monthly news magazine in French. The Canadian Broadcasting Corporation's site (www.cbc.ca) is an excellent source for current affairs.

Fashion

One of the things visitors first notice here is how well dressed people are – and it's not just the women that stop traffic. Conservative colors prevail in law and banking, but in media, IT and other businesses, local men might sport a chic olive-green suit with a lavender tie, which their counterparts in Vancouver, Toronto or even New York wouldn't dream of donning.

Radio & TV Stations

CJAD 800AM
(www.cjad.com)
Talk radio

CBC Radio One 88.5 FM *(www.cbc.ca/radio)*
News and current events

CHOM 97.7 FM
(www.chom.com)
Classic rock

Global Montreal
(www.globalnews.ca/montreal)
Television

CTV Montreal
(www.montreal.ctvnews.ca)
Television

CBC Montreal
(www.cbc.ca/montreal) Television

SIGNS OF PRIDE

Québec's French Language Charter, the (in)famous Bill 101, asserts the primacy of French on public signs across the province. Stop signs in Québec read 'ARRÊT,' a word that actually means a stop for buses or trains (even in France, the red hexagonal signs read 'STOP'). Apostrophes had to be removed from storefronts like Ogilvy's in the 1980s to comply with French usage, and English is only allowed on signage provided it's no more than half the size of the French lettering. Perhaps most bewildering of all is the acronym PFK (Poulet Frit Kentucky) for a leading fast-food chain.

The law is enforced by language police who, prompted by complaints from French hardliners, roam the province with tape measures (yes – for real!) and hand out fines to shopkeepers if a door says 'Push' more prominently than 'Poussez.' These days, most Québecers take it all in their stride, and the comical language tussles between businesses and the language police that once featured regularly on evening newscasts and phone-in shows have largely disappeared.

Whether artists, students or entrepreneurs, it seems like everybody knows the look they're going for and pulls it off well. Label-watchers put it down to the perfect fusion of European and American fashion – Paris' bold willingness to experiment coupled with an American practicality that makes people choose what's right for them rather than what's necessarily in fashion. In short, Montréalers have fun with clothes and are happy to flaunt it.

Sports

Québecers are active year-round, jogging, cycling and kayaking on warm summer days, with cold wintry days bringing ice-skating, cross-country skiing and pickup hockey games on frozen lakes.

Sporting events – which can essentially be subcategorized as hockey followed by everything else – draw huge numbers of Montréalers. The essential experience is to journey into the great hockey hall of the Bell Centre to catch the Canadiens (www.canadiens.nhl.com) gliding to victory.

Other key spectator moments include watching the mighty Alouettes (www.montrealalouettes.com), a Canadian football team with plenty of muscle (despite being named after a songbird), rooting for the Montréal Impact (www.impactmontreal.com) soccer team, and attending the Formula One Grand Prix du Canada (www.gpcanada.ca).

For those who'd rather join the fray, there are plenty of outdoorsy events. The Tour de l'Île, for instance, is one of Montréal's best-loved participatory bike rides, when tens of thousands fill the streets for a fun cycle (28km or 50km) around Montréal. There's a palpable energy in the city that even nonpedalers enjoy.

In winter green spaces become cross-country ski trails, and ponds and lakes transform into outdoor skating rinks at places like the Old Port and Parc La Fontaine.

Other great ways to enjoy the scenery include white-water rafting down the Lachine Rapids (or surfing them if your life-insurance policy is in order), kayaking idly down the Canal de Lachine, or simply heading to 'the Mountain' (Parc du Mont-Royal) for a bit of running, pedal-boating, ice-skating, sledding, snowshoeing, bird-watching or – if it's Sunday – gyrating and/or pounding your drums at the free-spirited tam-tam jam (p112).

The Québécois have swear words centered on the church. Where an English speaker might yell 'fuck!' a Québecer will unleash *'tabarnac'* (from tabernacle); instead of 'oh, shit!' they'll cry *'sacrament!'* (from sacrament). There are also combos like *'hostie de câlisse de tabarnac!'* ('host in the chalice in the tabernacle!').

Head to social media for pics from French- and English-language fashion influencers such as Justine Brouil (@justinebrouil), who promotes local brands, and Kelsey (@mskelslevy) for looks with Montréal attractions as backdrops.

Music & the Arts

Montréal is both the undisputed center of the French-language entertainment universe in North America and the cultural mecca of Québec. It is ground zero for everything from Québec's sizable film and music industries to visual and dramatic arts and publishing.

Music

From Leonard Cohen to Arcade Fire and the Jazz Fest, sometimes it seems Montréal is all about the music. A friend to experimentation of all genres and styles, the city is home to more than 250 active bands, embracing anything and everything from electropop, hip-hop and glam rock to Celtic folk, indie punk and *yéyé* (exuberant 1960s-style French rock) – not to mention roots, ambient, grunge and rockabilly.

Rock & Pop

On the rock scene, Arcade Fire remains one of Montréal's top indie rock bands. Their eclectic folk/rock/indie sound and manic ensemble of instruments have made them critics' darlings since their first album *Funeral* hit the US and UK top 10 lists in 2004. Their 2010 album *The Suburbs* topped charts in several countries and won Album of the Year at the 2011 Grammy Awards, and their 2014 release *Reflektor* was nominated as Best Alternative Music Album at the 2015 Grammies.

In the francophone music industry, the market is crowded with talented artists. Eternal favorites include alternative rocker Louis-Jean

A hit TV show in French is *Tout le Monde en Parle* (Everybody is Talking About It), a current-affairs program hosted by comedian Guy A Lepage. It's controversial, snappy and the first stop for anyone doing anything in Québec's public arena, from politicians and actors to war heroes.

SOUNDS OF MONTRÉAL: THE WORLD-RENOWNED JAZZ FESTIVAL

In a city that loves festivals, the **Festival International de Jazz de Montréal** (www.montrealjazzfest.com) is the mother of them all – erupting in late June each year and turning the city into an enormous stage for 10 days. No longer just about jazz, this is one of the world's biggies, with hundreds of top-name performers bringing reggae, rock, blues, world music, Latin, reggae, Cajun, Dixieland and even pop to audiophiles from across the globe.

It started as the pipe dream of a young local music producer, Alain Simard, who tried to sell his idea to the government and corporate sponsors, with little success. Now it's the single biggest tourist event in Québec, attracting nearly two million visitors to 400 concerts – many say it's the best jazz festival on the planet. Miles Davis, Herbie Hancock, Al Jarreau, Sonny Rollins, Wayne Shorter, Stevie Wonder, Al Dimeola, James Cotton, Booker T Jones, Taj Mahal, John Scofield and Jack DeJohnette are but a few of the giants who have graced the podiums over the years.

Practicalities

The festival website provides all the details; free festival programs are at kiosks around the Place des Arts. Some concerts are held indoors, others on outdoor stages; several Downtown blocks are closed to traffic. The music starts around noon and lasts until late evening when the clubs take over.

Cormier, who won both a Juno and a Félix (Québec music award) for his 2013 release *Le Treizième Étage,* keyboardist Pierre Lapointe, rocker Jean Leloup, and singer-songwriter Ariane Moffatt.

More recent arrivals include: singer-songwriter Alex Nevsky, who made a clean sweep of the Félix awards in 2014, taking honors for Best Male Vocalist, Best Pop Album *(Himalaya Mon Amour)* and Best Song ('On Leur A Fait Croire'); indie pop artist Coeur de Pirate, whose first two albums were nominated for Junos; crooner Patrick Watson, known for singing in English and French, as well as playing unusual instruments, such as a bicycle on his song 'Beijing'; and singer-songwriter Marie-Pierre Arthur, whose awards include best new singer-songwriter of 2012 and best album for her 2013 release *Aux Alentours.*

Rue Rufus Rockhead near Marché Atwater is named for the Jamaican-born owner of Rockhead's Paradise, the hottest downtown jazz club in the 1930s and '40s. It hosted the likes of Billie Holiday, Sarah Vaughan and Sammy Davis Jr.

Jazz

In the 1940s and '50s, Montréal was one of North America's most important venues for jazz music. It produced a number of major jazz musicians, such as pianist Oscar Peterson and trumpeter Maynard Ferguson. The scene went into decline in the late 1950s but revived after the premiere of the jazz festival in 1979.

The city's other celebrated jazz pianist, Oliver Jones, was already in his 50s when he was discovered by the music world. Since the 1980s he

---

MONTRÉAL'S CULTURAL CLASSICS

Best on Film

The Apprenticeship of Duddy Kravitz (1974) Mordecai Richler's timeless story of a Jewish upbringing.

Jesus of Montreal (1989) A prizewinning take on Montréal and Catholicism.

Incendies (2010) Two siblings confront the mystery of their mother's past.

Funkytown (2011) Bilingual film set against the backdrop of Montréal's 1970s club scene and the burgeoning secession movement.

Mommy (2014) The collapse between mother and son set on the South Shore by Montréal upstart Xavier Dolan.

Best in Print

Two Solitudes (Hugh MacLennan; 1945) One man's struggles with his English- and French-Canadian background.

The Tin Flute (Gabrielle Roy; 1947) A waitress looks for love in the slums of St-Henri.

How to Make Love to a Negro Without Getting Tired (Dany Laferrière; 1985) Provocative debut novel from this Haitian-Québécois author.

Barney's Version (Mordecai Richler; 1997) Richler's acclaimed murder mystery, told by a pair of less-than-reliable narrators.

Best in Music

'Oblivion' (Grimes; 2012) Vancouver electronic artist who studied at McGill and filmed her first big hit at the university and Olympic Stadium.

'Suzanne' (Leonard Cohen; 1967) Montréal local's ode to the St Lawrence River, Old Port and Chapelle Notre-Dame-de-Bon-Secours.

'Hometown Waltz' (Rufus Wainwright; 2004) He cut his chops on the club circuit of Montréal and this is his bittersweet ode to the city.

'Je Reviendrai à Montreal' (Robert Charlebois; 1976) A French classic oozing longing to see Montréal's winter again.

has established himself as a major mainstream player with impressive technique and a hard-swinging style.

Singer and pianist Diana Krall has enjoyed mass appeal without sacrificing her bop and swing roots. In 1993 she launched her career on Montréal's Justin Time record label, and she remains a perennial local favorite during regular appearances at Montréal's jazz festival.

Originally from New York City, singer Ranee Lee is known for her virtuosity that spans silky ballads, swing standards and raw blues tunes. She has performed with many jazz notables and is a respected teacher on the McGill University music faculty.

Classical

The backbone of Montréal's classical-music scene is the Orchestre Symphonique de Montréal. The OSM has won a host of awards including two Grammys and 12 Junos, and it was the first Canadian orchestra to achieve platinum (500,000 records sold), on its 1984 recording of Ravel's *Bolero*.

The smaller Orchestre Métropolitain du Grand Montréal is a showcase of young Québec talent and as such is staffed by graduates from the province's conservatories. The director is Yannick Nézet-Séguin, a Montréaler who became one of Canada's youngest major orchestra directors when he took the baton at age 25 in 2000.

Opera

Over the past 25 years, the Opéra de Montréal has become a giant on the North American landscape. It has staged dozens of operas and hundreds of performances, and collaborated with numerous international companies. Many great names have graced its stages including Québec's own Leila Chalfoun, Lyne Fortin, Suzie LeBlanc and André Turp, alongside a considerable array of Canadian and international talent. The company stages several new operas every season, including classics like *Madame Butterfly* and *The Magic Flute*.

Locally, new operas are not created, but in 1989 the Opéra de Montréal won a Félix for the most popular production of the season for *Nelligan,* an opera created in Québec about the life of poet Émile Nelligan by André Gagnon; Michel Tremblay wrote the libretto.

Montréal boasts two great contemporary-dance festivals: the Festival TransAmériques (www.fta.qc.ca; late May/early June) focuses on new creations by Canadian and international performers. The Quartiers Danses festival (www.quartiersdanses.com; September) stages performances at venues ranging from the Atwater Market to the Montreal Museum of Fine Arts and Parc du Mont-Royal.

Folk

Best known as an icon of the 1960s, Montréal's late native son Leonard Cohen remains one of the world's most eclectic folk artists. Beloved worldwide for his song 'Suzanne,' Cohen experienced a second burst of major creativity in the 1980s and early 1990s that suddenly made him hip again to younger audiences. Into his 80s, Cohen re-emerged with another cycle of albums and embarked on a series of wildly successful world tours to rapturous audiences. He was chosen as Artist of the Year at the 2013 Juno awards, while *Popular Problems* took Album of the Year at the 2015 Junos. He finished with *You Want It Darker,* released to critical acclaim 19 days before his death in late 2016.

Other English-language folk singers are few and far between, but it's well worth hearing Montréal-based folk quartet the Barr Brothers if you get a chance.

Chanson

It's hard to understand music in Québec without understanding what they call *chanson*. While France has a long tradition of this type of French folk music, where a focus on lyric and poetry takes precedence over the music itself, in Québec the *chanson* has historically been tied in with politics and identity in a profound way. With the Duplessis-era Québec stifling any real creative production, Québecers were tuned into only what was coming out of France, like Edith Piaf or Charles Aznavour.

The social upheaval of the Quiet Revolution in the 1960s changed all that, when a generation of musicians took up their guitars, started to sing in Québécois and penned deeply personal lyrics about life in Québec and, often, independence.

Longtime favorite Gilles Vigneault is synonymous with the *chanson Gens du pays* (People of the Country), often played on nationalist occasions. Other iconic *chansonniers* include Félix Leclerc, Claude Léveillé, Richard Desjardins and Jean-Pierre Ferland.

These days, younger performers who embrace the style (such as Coeur de Pirate or the Soeurs Boulay) are usually referred to as *auteurs-compositeurs-interprêtes* (singer-songwriters) rather than *chansonniers,* and their repertoire may include pop and rock as well as *chanson.* To experience this Québécois tradition for yourself, visit a *boîte á chanson* (club where this type of music is played).

Reflecting the strength and diversity of Québec's film industry, three consecutive Québécois directors earned Oscar nominations in the Best Foreign Film category between 2010 and 2012: Denis Villeneuve for *Incendies,* Philippe Falardeau for *Monsieur Lazhar* and Kim Nguyen for *Rebelle* (War Witch).

Film & Television

The foundations of Québec cinema were laid in the 1930s when Maurice Proulx, a pioneer documentary filmmaker, charted the colonization of northwestern Québec's gold-rich Abitibi region. In the 1960s directors were inspired to experiment by the likes of Federico Fellini and Jean-Luc Godard, but rural life remained the subject of most Québécois films. The 1970s were another watershed moment when erotically charged movies like Claude Jutra's *Mon Oncle Antoine* (1971) and Gilles Carle's *La Vraie Nature de Bernadette* (1972) sent the province a-twitter.

Montréal finally burst onto the international scene in the 1980s with a new generation of directors such as Denys Arcand, Louis Archambault, Michel Brault and Charles Binamé. That trend has continued into the 21st century with the emergence of acclaimed directors such as Denis Villeneuve, Philippe Falardeau and Kim Nguyen. Films are produced in French but dubbing and subtitling have made them accessible to a wider audience.

Animation, 3D and multimedia technologies have also been a Montréal specialty. Companies such as Softimage and Discreet Logic – now both folded into the much bigger, but still Montréal-based, Autodesk Media and Entertainment – have masterminded the special effects used in countless Hollywood blockbusters, including *Jurassic Park* (1993), *The Mask* (1994), *Godzilla* (2014), *Titanic* (1997), *Avatar* (2009), *Harry Potter and the Deathly Hallows* (2010) and the *Life of Pi* (2012).

In late August or early September, the Festival du Film de Montréal (www.ffm-montreal.org), one of Canada's largest and most prestigious cinema festivals, brings in filmmakers from all over Québec and around the world.

Montréal resident Margie Gillis is a modern dancer of international renown who combines performing, teaching and choreography all over the world. She has choreographed solo shows for Cirque du Soleil and in 2013 was named an Officer of the Order of Canada for her lifelong artistic achievement.

Theater

Founded in 1968, the Centaur Theatre is Québec's premier English-language stage for drama. Initially it featured contemporary international playwrights such as Arthur Miller, Bertolt Brecht and Harold Pinter, but the addition of a second stage for experimental theater in the 1970s helped fuel the rise of English-speaking playwrights such as David Fennario, whose award-winning *Balconville,* first performed in 1979, remains a classic. The theater stages its 10-day Wildside Theatre Festival every January.

QUÉBEC'S MASTER FILMMAKER

No director portrays modern Québec with a sharper eye than Montréal's own Denys Arcand. His themes are universal enough to strike a chord with international audiences: modern sex in *The Decline of the American Empire* (1986), religion in *Jésus of Montréal* (1989) and death in the brilliant tragicomedy *The Barbarian Invasions* (2003), which won the Academy Award for Best Foreign Film (the first, and so far the only, Canadian film to ever win an Oscar in that category).

Born in 1941 near Québec City, Arcand studied history in Montréal and landed a job at the National Film Board making movies for Expo '67. The young director was a keen supporter of francophone rights and the Quiet Revolution, but became deeply disillusioned with Québec politics in the 1970s. His most recent works include *L'Âge des Ténèbres* (2007), which was the closing film of the Cannes Film Festival, and *Le Règne de la Beauté* (2014).

Québec's fabulously successful Cirque du Soleil set new artistic boundaries by combining dance, theater and circus in a single power-packed show. Now an international phenomenon with $1 billion-plus in annual revenues, the company produces touring shows in places as far flung as Colombia, Australia and multiple hotels on the Las Vegas Strip; performances in Québec are not as common as they once were, but if you're lucky you may still catch a first look at one of their new shows in Montréal's Old Port or elsewhere around the province.

One of Québec's most famous playwrights is Michel Tremblay, whose plays about people speaking in their own dialects changed the way Québecers felt about their language.

Dance

Montréal's dance scene crackles with innovation. Virtually every year a new miniseries, dance festival or performing-arts troupe emerges to wow audiences in wild and unpredictable ways. Hundreds of performers and dozens of companies are based in the city and there's an excellent choice of venues for interpreters to strut their stuff; Agora de la Danse and Circuit-Est Centre Chorégraphique are two of the best.

Several major companies have established the city's reputation as an international dance mecca. Les Grands Ballets Canadiens attracts the biggest audiences, while Les Ballets Jazz de Montréal, La La La Human Steps, Compagnie Marie Chouinard, Cas Public, O Vertigo, Daniel Léveillé Danse and Par B.L.eux are troupes of international standing.

'Le Chandail de Hockey' (The Hockey Sweater; Roch Carrier; 1979), is a well known short story. Through a mail-order mix-up, a child is forced to wear a Toronto Maple Leafs jersey in a town teeming with Montréal Canadiens fans. It's a parable about the friction between French and English populations.

Literature

Montréal proudly calls itself the world's second cradle of French-language writers – after Paris, of course. But the city also boasts intimate links to many English-language writers of repute.

Caustic, quick-witted and prolific, Mordecai Richler was the 'grumpy old man' of Montréal literature in the latter part of the 20th century. Richler grew up in a working-class Jewish district in Mile End and, for better or worse, remained the most distinctive voice in anglophone Montréal until his passing in 2001. Most of his novels focus on Montréal and its wild and wonderful characters. For another engaging English-language perspective on the province, check out the award-winning mystery novels of Louise Penny, whose protagonist Chief Inspector Armand Gamache unravels murders set in both small-town and urban Québec.

MONTRÉAL'S LITERARY STAR

Émile Nelligan (1879–1941) is one of Québec's literary icons, a star like Oscar Wilde or Lord Byron whose mix of talent and tragedy keeps them in the public consciousness long after their era is over. A poetic genius, Nelligan created most of his famous works by the age of 20 before being committed and spending the rest of his life in mental institutions.

Born in Montréal to an Irish father and a Québécois mother, his bohemian traits were in evidence from the time he was a teenager. He sailed in and out of school to the dismay of his parents and seemed interested in little other than romantic poetry. After submitting two samples of his work, he was accepted by the l'École Littéraire de Montréal (Literary School of Montréal); public readings followed and his poems exploring love and loneliness were regularly published in French-language magazines around town. Nelligan had always marched to a different drum but by 1899 it was apparent his problems were more than just those of a temperamental artist and there was something seriously wrong.

His father had him committed to a mental institution that year. Though he tried briefly to rejoin society in 1925, he was back in care within days. What was he dealing with? Historians who've examined his hospital records believe he may have suffered from schizophrenia.

Though there has been both a movie and play about Nelligan's life, and he was immortalized in a painting by master Québec artist Jean-Paul Lemieux, there is no museum devoted to his work or life. Hunting his ghost around town is the best you'll be able to do. The Château Ramezay (p53) is where l'École Littéraire de Montréal used to meet and where Nelligan's poems were first read in public. Nelligan lived in a house on the west side of Carré St-Louis (p101). The square is also the setting for the famous Lemieux painting. Further along, St Patrick's Basilica (p75) is where Nelligan was baptized; there's a plaque at the back commemorating this event, along with a plaque devoted to Montréal's other famous Irishman, D'Arcy McGee.

On the French side, Québec writers who are widely read in English include Anne Hébert, Marie-Claire Blais, Hubert Aquin, Christian Mistral and Dany Laferrière. For stories about everyday life on the Plateau, try Michel Tremblay's short stories.

William Shatner left his native Montréal long ago, but the city still loves him. McGill University, his alma mater, awarded him an honorary doctorate in 2011. 'Don't be afraid of making an ass of yourself,' he told students. 'I do it all the time and look what I got.'

Painting & Visual Arts

Québec's lush forests and icy winter landscapes have been inspiring landscape artists since the 19th century. Horatio Walker was known for his sentimental interpretations of Québec farm life such as *Oxen Drinking* (1899). Marc-Aurèle Fortin (1880–1970) is famed for his watercolors of the Québec countryside. His portraits of majestic elms along Montréal avenues can be viewed in the Musée des Beaux-Arts. Québec's surrealist-influenced Automatistes movement of the 1940s produced a number of artists, including Jean-Paul Riopelle (1923–2002), whose works are on permanent display at Montréal's Musée d'Art Contemporain and Québec City's Musée National des Beaux-Arts.

Brilliant Architecture

Montréal's split personality is nowhere more obvious than in its architecture, a beguiling mix of European traditionalism and North American modernism. Lovingly preserved Victorian mansions and stately beaux-arts monuments rub shoulders with the sleek lines of modern skyscrapers, lending Montréal's urban landscape a creative, eclectic sophistication all of its own.

Old-World Icons

Architectural Montréal is perhaps most easily understood by its neighborhoods and its icons. In Old Montréal, a plethora of 19th-century and some 18th-century buildings crowd in cobblestone streets, where horse-drawn carriages impart a flavor of Europe some 100 years ago; no wonder it's the setting for so many films. The representative structure here is the stunning Basilique Notre-Dame (p50) from the mid-19th century. Indeed, for most of its modern history, the city's architecture has been characterized by churches, reflecting the Catholic and Protestant churches' influence on its development. Their innumerable metallic roofs earned Montréal its nickname – La Ville aux Cent Clochers (City of 100 Steeples). When Mark Twain visited in 1881, he famously remarked, 'This is the first time I was ever in a city where you couldn't throw a brick without breaking a church window.'

Today, however, Old Montréal is also home to modern eyesores that clash with the heritage structures: the 500 Place d'Armes building and the Palais de Justice building, relics of the 1960s and 1970s, make no attempt to fit in. Still, Old Montréal is one of the most homogenous neighborhoods of the city. Today's strict building codes require extensive vetting before new construction can begin.

For many visitors, the weathered greystones, such as the old stone buildings along Rue St-Paul, offer the strongest images of Old Montréal. The style emerged under the French regime in Québec (1608–1763), based on Norman and Breton houses with wide, shallow fronts, stuccoed stone and a steep roof punctuated by dormer windows. But the locals soon adapted the blueprint to Montréal's harsh winters, making the roof less steep, adding basements and extending the eaves over the walls for extra snow protection.

From the 19th century, architects tapped any number of retro styles: classical (Bank of Montréal), Gothic (Basilique Notre-Dame) and Italian renaissance (Royal Bank), to name a few. As Montréal boomed in the 1920s, a handful of famous architects such as Edward Maxwell, George Ross and Robert MacDonald left their mark on handsome towers in Old Montréal and downtown. French Second Empire style continued to be favored for comfortable francophone homes and some public buildings, such as the Hôtel de Ville (City Hall).

Downtown is a multifaceted jumble of buildings where run-down 20th-century brick buildings abut shiny new multipurpose complexes. Sometimes one building straddles the historical divide: the Centre Canadien d'Architecture (p131) integrates a graceful historical greystone

Must-Sees in Montréal

Basilique Notre-Dame (p48)

Hôtel de Ville (p52)

Biosphère (p68)

Oratoire St-Joseph (p129)

Stade Olympique (p104)

Top: Hôtel de Ville (p52)

Bottom: Victorian-era houses, Plateau Mont-Royal (p99)

VICTORIAN BEAUTIES

Montréal boasts the largest collection of Victorian row houses in all of North America. Numerous examples can be viewed in the Plateau, along Rue St-Denis north of Rue Cherrier or Ave Laval north of Carré St-Louis. Visitors are inevitably charmed by their brightly painted wrought-iron staircases, which wind up the outside of duplexes and triplexes. They evolved for three important reasons: taxes (a staircase outside allowed each floor to count as a separate dwelling, so the city could hike property taxes), fuel costs (an internal staircase wastes heat as warm air rises through the stairwell) and space (the 1st and 2nd floors were roomier without an internal staircase).

right into its contemporary facade. Other important buildings were meant to break with the past. **Place Ville-Marie** (www.placevillemarie.com; 1 Pl Ville-Marie; MMcGill), a multitowered complex built in the late 1950s, revolutionized urban architecture in Montréal and was the starting point for the underground city.

Transforming Downtown

Since the 1960s, the government has spent billions developing tourist attractions and infrastructure in Montréal, and the resultant architectural boom has greatly transformed the city. Expo '67 spurred the construction of experimental edifices such as Habitat 67 (p130), a controversial apartment building designed by Montréal architect Moshe Safdie when he was only 23; located on a promontory off the Old Port, it resembles a child's scattered building blocks. Other structures with 1960s roots include Buckminster Fuller's Biosphère (p68), which once wore a skin made of spherical mesh, and the Casino de Montréal (p69), which cleverly merges two of the most far-out pavilions of Expo '67. The 1976 Olympics saw an explosion of large-scale projects, the most notorious of which, the Olympic Stadium (p104), serves as a reminder of the pitfalls of constructing costly white elephants. Despite its reputation, many admire the stadium's dramatic tower, which leans at 45 degrees and is home to an observation deck.

In the 1880s enterprising locals took advantage of the frigid temperatures and built castles made of ice for the Winter Carnivals. By 1889 they were more than 10 stories tall made of thousands of ice blocks, as many extant art prints held by the Musée McCord attest.

One of the largest redevelopment projects in Canada was Montréal's $200-million Palais des Congrès (p53) convention center, inaugurated in 1983 and expanded between 1999 and 2002. The Palais and its adjacent squares form a mini-district known as the Quartier International that unites Downtown and Old Montréal by concealing an ugly sunken expressway. Nearby, in the Quartier Latin, the 33,000-sq-meter Bibliothèque et Archives Nationale du Québec opened to huge success in 2005, with crowds of Montréalers visiting the building each day.

The government has also invested millions of dollars in Montréal's public thoroughfares. 'The Main' (Blvd St-Laurent) has been spruced up with the widening of sidewalks, the planting of trees and the addition of street lights in certain stretches. A similar face-lift for Rue Ste-Catherine, completed in 2012, involved the installation of new sidewalks and paving stones. Rue Notre-Dame, long a two-lane nightmare pocked with potholes (but nonetheless an important artery into Old Montréal), is also slated for a major overhaul that will convert it into a landscaped boulevard with four lanes in each direction, flanked by multipurpose recreation paths.

Into the Future

Never a city to rest on its laurels, Montréal continues to jazz up its urban landscape with new architectural ventures. Several new spaces

CANADA'S STAR ARCHITECT, MOSHE SAFDIE

Born in Haifa, Israel in 1938, Moshe Safdie graduated from McGill University's architecture program in 1961 and became almost an instant star. He was only 23 when asked to design Habitat 67 (p130), which was actually based on his university thesis. Now based in Boston, Safdie has crafted a stellar career gravitating toward high-profile projects where he can unleash innovative buildings with just the right dash of controversy to get people talking about them.

Most notably, Safdie designed the $56-million, 4000-sq-meter Holocaust Memorial in Jerusalem, Israel, which opened in 2005. He also designed Ottawa's National Gallery of Canada, which opened in 1988 with its trademark soaring glass front, and the Vancouver Library Square, which evokes the Roman Colosseum.

More recently, Safdie's design for the Kauffman Center for the Performing Arts in Kansas City, Missouri, which opened in 2011, features dramatic swooping curves and resembles a giant paper lantern or beehive.

Safdie was made a companion of the Order of Canada in 2005, Canada's highest civilian honor.

were constructed for its 375th anniversary celebration in 2017. In addition, a new square is planned near Champ-de-Mars; this will improve pedestrian access between Old Montréal (Vieux-Montréal) and Downtown as well as having the aesthetic benefit of covering over part of the Ville-Marie Expressway with grass and colourful crushed stones. A flower-laden inclined urban forest will be installed at the Champ-de-Mars metro exit, as designed by a local female artist to honor the memory of 14 female Montréalers. Nearby Pl Jacques-Cartier in Vieux-Montréal will also get a major face-lift.

Downtown, the refurbishment of aging infrastructure has seen the main artery torn up from Blvd Robert-Bourassa to Rue Bleury in a 400m stretch with a new road. Similarly Rue Peel has seen a rip up and refresh.

The most disruptive, but ultimately beneficial, project in view is the construction of the new REM light rail. The network will link downtown to the West Island, South Shore and Montréal North and, promisingly for visitors, Trudeau Airport. No small project, it will become the fourth-largest automated transportation system in the world.

Montréal's most ambitious urban-renewal project in recent years has been the Quartier des Spectacles, on the edge of the Quartier Latin and downtown. Since 2007, the $150-million project has completely revitalized a 1-sq-km area bordered roughly by Rue Berri, Rue Sherbrooke, Blvd René-Lévesque and Rue City Councillors. The result is a culturally rich district that currently houses 80 arts venues, including 30 concert halls and numerous galleries and exhibition spaces. The Quartier is now home to 12,000 residents and hosts several big-ticket festivals, including the Montréal Jazz Festival. Its success has inspired arts and urban-planning professionals from around the world, who have come from as far away as New Zealand to study it as a model for integrating the arts with urban living and work spaces.

Major milestones in the Quartier des Spectacles' development include the 2009 opening of the Place des Festivals, a vast open-air entertainment venue with a colorfully lit 235-jet fountain, and the 2011 inauguration of the Maison Symphonique de Montréal – the new home of Montréal's symphony orchestra. In 2017 the National Film Board of Canada opened its own headquarters here.

Québec City's History & Culture

While Montréal reigns supreme as Québec's largest and most cosmopolitan city, Québec City's cultural identity rests on its dual role as the seat of provincial government and the cradle of French civilization in the Americas. The capital of Nouvelle France still exudes the spirit of days past, revealing deep French roots in everything from its atmospheric 17th- and 18th-century architecture to the overwhelming prevalence of French language and cuisine. Despite its strong historic ties, the city also has a vibrant modern side, with a flourishing arts scene and a jam-packed cultural calendar.

History

The first significant settlement on the site of today's Québec City was a 500-strong Iroquois village called Stadacona. The Iroquois were semi-nomadic, building longhouses, hunting, fishing and cultivating crops until the land got tired, when they moved on.

French explorer Jacques Cartier traveled to the New World in 1534, making it as far as the Gaspé Peninsula before returning to France. His second trans-Atlantic voyage in 1535 brought him further up the St Lawrence River, where he spent a long and difficult winter encamped at the foot of the cliffs of present-day Québec City. Cartier lost 30 of his men to scurvy (the rest survived in large part thanks to traditional remedies provided by the Iroquois) before beating a retreat back to France in May 1536. Cartier returned in 1541 hoping to start a post upstream in the New World, but again faced a winter of scurvy and disastrous relations with the indigenous population; this last failed attempt set back France's colonial ambitions for more than half a century.

Explorer Samuel de Champlain is credited with founding the city in 1608, calling it Kebec, from the Algonquian word meaning 'the river narrows here.' Champlain established forts and dwellings around present-day Place-Royale, laying the groundwork for the thriving capital of Nouvelle-France (New France). The English successfully attacked in 1629, but Québec was returned to the French under a treaty in 1632. As the 17th century progressed, Ursuline and Jesuit missionaries arrived, bolstering Québec City's status as the most important French settlement in the New World.

Great Britain continued to keep its eye on Québec, launching unsuccessful campaigns to take the city in 1690 and 1711. In 1759 General Wolfe finally led the British to victory over Montcalm on the Plains of Abraham. One of North America's most famous battles, it virtually ended the long-running conflict between Britain and France. The Treaty of Paris gave Canada to Britain in 1763. And in 1775, the American revolutionaries tried to capture Québec but were promptly pushed back. In 1864 meetings were held in the city that led to the formation of Canada in 1867. Québec City became the provincial capital.

History Hot Spots

Battlefields Park (p179)

Immersion Québec (p201)

La Citadelle (p165)

Musée de la Civilisation (p167)

Musée des Plaines d'Abraham (p181)

Fortifications of Québec National Historic Site (p173)

Cartier-Brébeuf National Historic Site (p183)

In the 19th century the city lost its status and importance to Montréal, but when the Great Depression burst Montréal's bubble in 1929, Québec City regained some stature as a government center. Then, in the 1950s, a group of business-savvy locals launched the now-famous Winter Carnival to incite a tourism boom.

Poor urban planning led to an exodus to the suburbs, leaving downtown depopulated and prone to crime. Things started to turn round in the 1990s, with the rejuvenation of the St-Roch neighborhood and diversification of the economy. Université Laval also moved some of its apartments downtown, bringing an influx of young students.

In 2008 Québec City threw a monumental bash in honor of its 400th anniversary, an expression of local pride that drew in tens of thousands of visitors and added several features to the city's landscape, including new public green spaces along the St Lawrence River. The city's cultural scene continues to thrive with the opening of the Amphithéâtre du Québec in 2015 and the expansion of the Musée National des Beaux-Arts in 2016.

Arts & Architecture

Visual Arts

Many artists have been bewitched by the beauty of Québec City and its surrounding countryside.

Jean-Paul Lemieux (1904–90) is one of Canada's most accomplished painters. Born in Québec City, he studied at L'École des Beaux-Arts de Montréal and later in Paris. He is famous for his paintings of Québec's vacant and endless landscapes and Québecers' relationship to these. Many of his paintings are influenced by the simple lines of folk art. There's a hall devoted to his art at the Musée National des Beaux-Arts du Québec (p179).

Alfred Pellan (1906–88) is another renowned artist who studied at the local École des Beaux-Arts before moving to Paris. He later became famous for his portraits, still lifes, figures and landscapes, before turning to surrealism in the 1940s.

Amsterdam-born Cornelius Krieghoff (1815–72) was acclaimed for chronicling the customs and clothing of 19th-century Québecers in his

QUÉBEC CITY CULTURAL CLASSICS

Best in Print

Shadows on the Rock (Willa Cather; 1931) Detailed portrait of a year in the lives of Cecile Auclair and her father Euclide, 17th-century colonists in Québec.

To Quebec and the Stars (HP Lovecraft; 1976) Collection of 17 essays on subjects as diverse as astronomy, poetry, literature and travel.

Bury Your Dead (Louise Penny; 2010) Murder mystery that takes in the Winter Carnival, Québec founder Samuel de Champlain and a 400-year-old secret.

Best on Film

I Confess (1953) Alfred Hitchcock's lens caresses the city in this old-world film-noirish suspense thriller.

Les Yeux Rouges (Red Eyes; 1982) A Québec City–set thriller with two cops on the trail of a deranged/arsonist strangler.

Le Confessionnal (The Confessional; 1995) A man's quest to uncover a family secret that sometimes follows in Hitchcock's footsteps.

paintings. He is known especially for the portraits of the Aboriginal Wendats, who lived around Québec City.

Francesco Iacurto (1908–2001) was born in Montréal but moved to Québec City in 1938. His acclaimed works are dominated by the town's streetscapes, landscapes and portrayals of Île d'Orléans.

Music

Québec City has plenty to offer music lovers. The respected Orchestre Symphonique de Québec (p199) and the terrific Opéra de Québec (p198) both perform at the Grand Théâtre de Québec (p198) between September and May. Some of the province's biggest rock and pop-music stars, such as Jean Leloup and Bruno Pelletier, also started out here, as did the politically charged hip-hop trio Loco Locass. There's a brash and independent spirit among the eclectic mix of active bands here, but because the scene is so small, most musicians eventually relocate to Montréal for its thriving club scene and ties to the music industry.

For the latest developments in local music, visit a club like Scanner Bistro (p199), or check out entertainment listings at Quoi Faire à Québec (www.quoifaireaquebec.com) and Voir Québec (www.voir.ca).

Film

The beginnings of Québec cinema can be traced to the 1930s, when Maurice Proulx, a pioneer documentary filmmaker, charted the colonization of northwestern Québec's gold-rich Abitibi region. In the 1960s directors were inspired to experiment by the likes of Federico Fellini and Jean-Luc Godard, but rural life remained the subject of most Québécois films. The 1970s were another watershed moment, when erotically charged movies like Claude Jutra's *Mon Oncle Antoine* and Gilles Carle's *La Vraie Nature de Bernadette* sent the province atwitter.

But Montréal has always been the undisputed capital of the film industry in Québec and remains so today. Virtually nothing is produced in Québec City though its dramatic setting does appear from time to time in location, most notably in Alfred Hitchcock's *I Confess* (1953).

Theater

Canada's French-language TV and film industries are firmly based in Montréal, but Québec City's active theater scene still holds its own – though its tight-knit nature cuts both ways. An actor here with a creative or original idea can write a script and have it produced – something that might take years, if it happened at all, in Montréal. On the other hand, plays produced here can't always draw an audience in Montréal. To cite one famous example, the brilliant one-woman show *Gros et Détail* by Québec City actor Anne-Marie Olivier about people in the St-Roch neighborhood was a hit in Québec City, France and several countries in francophone Africa, yet when Olivier tried to get it produced in Montréal, she was rejected on the basis that it focused too much on Québec City.

In the performing-arts realm, Québec City's most famous native son is award-winning playwright and director Robert Lepage. While his best-known works feature Québec City, he has also achieved major international success, becoming the first North American to direct a Shakespeare play at London's Royal National Theatre (1992's *A Midsummer Night's Dream*); directing Richard Wagner's Ring Cycle for New York's Metropolitan Opera in 2010–12; and creating two major touring shows for Cirque du Soleil (*Kà* and *Totem*). Recent projects closer to home include the 2013 film *Triptyque* (Lepage's first movie in 10 years); the *Image Mill*, a gigantic sound-and-light show exploring

A VOICE FOR THE NATION

In 1965 poet and singer-songwriter Gilles Vigneault stepped into a studio in Montréal to record the song *'Mon pays ce n'est pas un pays, c'est l'hiver'* for a documentary film now long forgotten. Québec immediately had a hit song and its own motto: 'My county is a not a country, it's winter,' which seemed to celebrate both the province's natural beauty and its free spirit. Never resting on his laurels, a decade later Vigneault performed his 'Gens du Pays,' which opened with the lyrics 'People of the land/it is your turn/to let yourself speak of love' at the Fête National du Québec on Mont Royal in Montréal. It immediately became a folk classic and is today looked upon as the de facto national anthem of Québec. What's more, with the first three words replaced by 'my dear friend,' it has become the Québécois version of the happy birthday song.

This is probably not how his parents – a fisherman and a school teacher – imagined the future of their only male child to reach adulthood when he was born in 1928 in remote Natashquan in the Côte-Nord, 1000km northeast of Québec City and accessible only by boat until 1996. He was passionate about poetry when he studied at the Séminaire de Rimouski, on the St Lawrence River about 400km northeast of Québec City, and wrote songs for other performers in the 1950s. He made his singing debut in 1960 at the Arlequin club on the Rue St-Jean and has effectively never stopped. His fame both at home and abroad outlived his initial successes, and he has recorded more than 30 albums, most recently *Vivre Debout* (Living Standing Up) in 2014. Vigneault continues to perform live and remains – in every sense – a true living legend.

Québec City's history, which was projected against oversized grain silos in the Vieux-Port between 2008 and 2013; and an ambitious project to build a $60-million, 625-seat new theater, Théâtre Le Diamant, just outside Québec City's Old Town walls.

Québec City Architectural Gems

Le Château Frontenac (p166)

Cathedral of the Holy Trinity (p176)

Hôtel du Parlement (p181)

Église Notre-Dame-des-Victoires (p177)

La Maison Henry-Stuart (p181)

Architecture

Québec City boasts some stunning architecture – from the colorful vernacular wooden houses of the St-Jean Baptiste district and the delightful Maison Henry-Stuart in Montcalm to the stately Hôtel du Parlement and the audacious Château Frontenac. But even more important than the unique style of New France architecture is the fact that Québec City is the only remaining walled city north of Mexico. For this reason it was added to Unesco's World Heritage list in 1985.

Cultural Events

Québec City loves a good festival. Warm weather here lasts only a few short months, so locals make the most of it. In midsummer you'll find residents celebrating in city parks and streets, especially on June 24, Québec's **national holiday** (www.fetenationale.quebec), and during the fabulous 11-day **Festival d'Été** (www.infofestival.com) in July, when Québécois musicians share the stage with performing artists from around the globe.

Winter, the longest season, holds an equally special place in the hearts of Québec City residents. The annual 17-day Winter Carnival (p193) is perhaps Québec's most beloved cultural event, presided over by Bonhomme de Neige, a giant snowman clad in a traditional Québécois hat and sash who has become one of the city's most beloved symbols. Local residents join Bonhomme in droves to celebrate the joys of the northern winter – staging ice canoe races across the St Lawrence River, horse-drawn sleigh competitions, colorful night parades, and rides for all ages on dogsleds, snow tubes and ice slides.

MARC BRUXELLE/SHUTTERSTOCK ©

Survival Guide

Lionel-Groulx metro station, Montréal

Transportation

ARRIVING IN MONTRÉAL

Most travelers arrive in Montréal by air. It's easy to drive to Montréal from elsewhere in Canada as well as from the US if you have the time, or take the train or intercity coach from cities such as Toronto or New York.

Air

Montréal is served by **Montréal-Pierre Elliott Trudeau International Airport** (Trudeau, YUL; www.admtl.com; Dorval), known in French as Aéroport Montréal-Trudeau, or simply as Trudeau Airport. It's about 21km west of downtown and is the hub of most domestic, US and overseas flights. Trudeau Airport (still sometimes known by its old name, Dorval Airport) has decent connections to the city by car and shuttle bus.

To/from the Airport

BUS

Bus 747 (www.stm.info), the cheapest way to get into town, takes 25 to 60 minutes. Buses run round the clock, leaving from just outside the arrivals hall and dropping passengers downtown, first at Lionel-Groulx metro station, then on to Berri-UQAM metro station in the Quartier Latin. The $10 fare can be paid by Visa, MasterCard or cash at vending machines in the international arrivals area, or tickets may be bought on board (coins only, no change given). Your ticket gives you unlimited travel on Montréal's bus and metro network for 24 hours. Multiday tickets loaded onto the Opus transport card also provide free use of bus 747.

CAR

Driving to or from Downtown takes 20 to 30 minutes (allow an hour during peak times). As you exit the airport, follow signs for Autoroute 20 Est, which will take you into the heart of Downtown along the main Autoroute Ville Marie (the 720).

BORDER CROSSINGS

Continental US highways link with their Canadian counterparts along the border at numerous points. The main US highways leading directly into Québec include the I-87 in New York, I-89 and I-91 in Vermont, and US-201 in Maine. During summer and on holiday weekends, waits of several hours are not uncommon at major USA–Canada border crossings such as Detroit, Michigan; Windsor, Ontario; Fort Erie, Ontario; Buffalo, New York; Niagara Falls; and Rouse's Point, New

CLIMATE CHANGE & TRAVEL

Every form of transport that relies on carbon-based fuel generates CO_2, the main cause of human-induced climate change. Modern travel is dependent on aeroplanes, which might use less fuel per kilometre per person than most cars but travel much greater distances. The altitude at which aircraft emit gases (including CO_2) and particles also contributes to their climate change impact. Many websites offer 'carbon calculators' that allow people to estimate the carbon emissions generated by their journey and, for those who wish to do so, to offset the impact of the greenhouse gases emitted with contributions to portfolios of climate-friendly initiatives throughout the world. Lonely Planet offsets the carbon footprint of all staff and author travel.

York. Smaller crossings are generally much quieter.

Visitors with US or British passports are allowed to bring their vehicles into Canada for up to six months.

SHUTTLES

Several hotels run shuttles from the airport to downtown or further afield. **Autocars Skyport** (☎514-631-1155; www.skyportinternational.com; one way/return $105/182) runs express shuttles to the Mont-Tremblant ski resort in winter and summer.

TAXI

It takes at least 20 minutes to get Downtown from the airport and the fixed fare is $40. Limousine services ($55 and up) are also available.

Bus

Most long-distance buses arrive at Montréal's **Gare d'Autocars** (Map p276; ☎514-842-2281; www.gamtl.com; 1717 Rue Berri; Ⓜ Berri-UQAM).

If buying tickets here for other destinations in the province, allow about 45 minutes before departure; most advance tickets don't guarantee a seat, so arrive early to line up at the counter.

Car & Motorcycle

All the major international car-rental companies have branches at the airport, main train station and elsewhere around town. **Auto Plateau** (☎514-281-5000; www.autoplateau.com; 3585 Rue Berri; Ⓜ Sherbrooke) is a reputable local company.

Kangaride (☎855-526-4274; www.kangaride.com) is a reliable online ride-share agency. It connects you with

drivers with spare seats in their car. A sample fare is around $15 to Québec City.

Train

Canada's trains are arguably the most enjoyable and romantic way to travel the country. Long-distance trips are quite a bit more expensive than those by bus, however, and reservations are crucial for weekend and holiday travel. A few days' notice can cut fares a lot.

Gare Centrale (Central Train Station; ☎arrivals & departures 888-842-7245, info & reservations 514-989-2626; www.viarail.ca; 895 Rue de la Gauchetière Ouest; Ⓜ Bonaventure) is the local hub of **VIA Rail** (☎888-842-7245, 514-989-2626; www.viarail.ca; Ⓜ Bonaventure), Canada's vast rail network, which links Montréal with cities all across the country.

Amtrak (www.amtrak.com) provides service between New York City and Montréal on its Adirondack line. The trip, though slow (11 hours), passes through lovely scenery along Lake Champlain and the Hudson River.

ARRIVING IN QUÉBEC CITY

Montréal is Québec City's gateway, and many travelers arrive here from there by car, bus or rail. The drive is about three hours. VIA Rail's trains take only slightly longer (3¼ hours).

Highway networks connect Québec's capital with the rest of the province. Québec City has frequent air connections to Canadian and some US destinations, as well as less-frequent – usually seasonal – flights to Mexico and the Caribbean.

Air

Québec City's petite **Aéroport International Jean-Lesage de Québec** (YQB; ☎418-640-3300; www.aeroportdequebec.com; 505 Rue Principal, Ste-Foy) lies about 15km west of the Old Town. It mostly has connections to Montréal, but there are also flights to Toronto, Ottawa, Chicago, Newark, New York City (JFK) and resorts in the Caribbean (including Cuba) and Mexico. Check the website for additional destinations.

Regularly scheduled flights (45 minutes) on Air Canada and several other budget airlines, including Air Transat, PAL Airlines and Pascan, run between Montréal and Québec City's airport.

To/from the Airport

BUS

RTC (RTC Information Center; Map p178; ☎418-627-2511; www.rtcquebec.ca; 884 Rue St-Joachim, St-Jean Baptiste; ⊙10:30am-6pm Mon-Thu, to 9pm Fri, noon-5pm Sat) has launched a bus service linking Jean-Lesage Airport with the train and bus stations in Ste-Foy, from where you can catch city bus 11 to the Old Town or Métrobus 800 or 801 to Colline Parlementaire. Bus 76 leaves the airport about every 15 minutes from 5:30am to 11pm daily; the trip takes about 30 minutes.

CAR

It takes about half an hour to drive from Québec City's airport to the Old Town. The most straightforward route is to take Autoroute Duplessis/Rte 540 Sud, merge onto Rte 175 Nord, then follow this northeast as it changes names from Blvd Laurier to Grand Allée, crosses through the Porte St-Louis, and finally becomes Rue St-Louis.

TAXI

A taxi is the fastest option but most expensive for travel between the airport and downtown Québec City. A taxi costs a flat fee of just over $35 to go into the city, or just over $15 if you're only going to the boroughs surrounding the airport. Returning to the airport, you'll pay the metered fare, which should be less than $30. **Transport Accessible du Québec** (Québec Accessible Transport; ☑418-641-8294; www.taq.qc.ca) offers a transit service for people with disabilities.

Bus

If you're coming from Montréal, your bus may first stop at **Gare d'Autocars de Ste-Foy** (Ste-Foy Bus Station; ☑418-650-0087; 3001 Chemin des Quatre Bourgeois, Ste-Foy), which is 12km southwest of the center, so ask before you get off.

Orléans Express (☑418-525-3000; www.orleans express.com) runs services from Montréal's main bus station, Gare d'Autocars, to Québec City's **bus station** (Québec Bus Station; Map p170; ☑418-525-3000; 320 Rue Abraham-Martin) at the **Gare du Palais** (Palace Station;☑888-842-7245; www. viarail.ca; 450 Rue de la Gare du Palais, Old Lower Town & Port) between 6am and 11pm daily. From Québec City they run on the half-hour between 6:30am and 10:30pm daily. Prices for the journey (2¾ to 3¼ hours) start at $55/89 for a one-way/return ticket.

Car & Motorcycle

Québec City lies about 260km northeast of Montréal (three hours by car). The most common routes are Autoroute 20, on the south shore of the St Lawrence River, and the slightly longer Autoroute 40 along the north shore.

Train

VIA Rail (☑514-989-2626; www.viarail.ca; Ⓜ Bonaventure) has between four and six daily trains between Montréal's Gare Centrale and Québec City's **Gare du Palais** (Palace Station;☑888-842-7245; www.viarail.ca; 450 Rue de la Gare du Palais, Old Lower Town & Port). Normal prices for the 3¼-hour journey start at $42/87 for a one-way/return ticket. Some trains stop at the suburban **Gare de Ste-Foy** (Ste-Foy Train Station;☑888-842-7245; www.viarail.ca; 3255 Chemin de la Gare, Ste-Foy) as well.

Service is also good along the so-called Québec City–Windsor corridor that connects Québec City with Montréal, Ottawa, Kingston, Toronto and Niagara Falls.

GETTING AROUND MONTRÉAL & QUÉBEC CITY

Bus & Metro

Montréal

STM (Société de Transport de Montréal;☑514-786-4636; www.stm.info) is the city's bus and metro (subway) operator. Schedules vary depending on the line, but trains generally run from 5:30am to midnight from Sunday to Friday, slightly later on Saturday night (to 1:30am at the latest).

A single bus or metro ticket costs $3.25 – and allows transfers between bus and metro. Two-ride tickets ($6) are also available in metro stations. If you're sticking around Montréal for longer, you'll save money by buying a rechargeable Opus card; the card costs $6 up front, but can be recharged at a discounted rate for 10 rides ($28), one day of unlimited rides ($10, actually 24 hours), three days ($19), a week ($26.25) or a month ($85).

Buses take tickets or cash but drivers won't give change. If transferring from the metro to a bus, use your

---

LONG-DISTANCE BUS LINES

Galland Laurentides (☑450-687-8666; www.galland-bus.com; 1717 Rue Berri; Montréal- Mont-Tremblant one-way/round trip $32/57) Provides bus service from Montréal to Mont-Tremblant and other destinations in the Laurentians.

Greyhound (www.greyhound.ca) Operates long-distance routes to Ottawa, Toronto, Vancouver, Boston, New York City and other points throughout Canada and the United States.

Limocar (www.limocar.ca) Offers bus service from Montréal to the Eastern Townships.

Moose Travel Network (www.moosenetwork.com) Popular with backpackers, this network operates several circuits around Canada, allowing travelers to jump on and jump off along the way. Pickup points are in Montréal, Québec City, Ottawa and Toronto, among other places. Destinations within Québec include Mont-Tremblant and the Gaspé Peninsula.

Orléans Express (www.orleansexpress.com) Makes the three-hour run between Montréal and Québec City.

original metro ticket as a free bus transfer. If you're switching between buses, or between bus and the metro, ask the driver for a free transfer slip (*correspondance* in French).

Québec City

Single rides paid in cash on **RTC** (RTC Information Center; Map p178; ☑418-627-2511; www.rtcquebec.ca; 884 Rue St-Joachim, St-Jean Baptiste; ⊙10:30am-6pm Mon-Thu, to 9pm Fri, noon-5pm Sat) buses cost $3.50. The most convenient hub for catching multiple buses is on Place d'Youville, just outside the Old Town walls.

Bus 1 links the Old Lower Town and ferry terminal with St-Roch and St-Sauveur via the Gare du Palais train and bus stations.

Bicycle

Montréal

Montréal's bicycle paths are extensive, running more than 500km around the city, and often protected from vehicular traffic. Useful bike maps are available from the tourist offices.

Top bike paths follow the Canal de Lachine and then up along Lac St-Louis; another popular route goes southwest along the edge of the St Lawrence River, passing the Lachine Rapids, then meeting up with the Canal de Lachine path.

BIXI

One of the best ways to see the city is by the public bike-rental service **Bixi** (☑514-789-2494; http://montreal.bixi. com; per 30min $2.95; ⊙24hr mid-Apr–Oct) ☒. Short-term subscription fees allowing you to use the system for one day are very reasonably priced and allow unlimited free 30-minute rides (with fees rising steeply after 45 minutes). The 500-plus rental stations are almost ubiquitous.

Québec City

Québec City has an extensive network of bike paths (more than 70km in all), including a route along the St Lawrence that connects to paths along the Rivière St-Charles. Pick up the free *Carte Vélo Officielle/Official Cycling Map* at local tourist offices or bike shops.

Just across from Québec City's train station, **Cyclo Services** (Map p170; ☑418-692-4052, 877-692-4050; www.cycloservices.net; 289 Rue St-Paul, Old Lower Town & Port; rental per 2/24hr city bike $17/38, electric bike $34/76; ⊙9am-5:30pm Mon-Fri, 10am-5pm Sat & Sun, variable hours Nov-Apr; ☒) rents a wide variety of bikes, including city, tandem, road, electric and kids' models. It also organizes cycling tours in the Québec City region.

Boat

Montréal

Cruise vessels ply the St Lawrence River for day trips and longer cruises.

St Lawrence Cruise Lines (☑800-267-7868; www.stlawrencerivercruise.com; from $1673) Offers a four- to six-night Canadian Connection Cruise between Kingston, Ontario and Québec City.

CTMA Group (☑888-986-3278; www.ctma.ca; per person from $1019) Runs weeklong cruises from Montréal to the picturesque Îles de la Madeleine in the Gulf of St Lawrence, with intermediate stops in Québec City and the Gaspé Peninsula.

Calèche

In Québec City, horse-drawn coaches called **calèches** (Map p170; ☑418-683-9222, 418-520-1555; Place d'Armes, Old Upper Town; 35/80/120min rides $90/180/270) cost $90 for a 35-minute tour for up to four passengers. You'll find them just inside the Porte St-Louis, in the Parc de l'Esplanade and, most frequently, in the Place d'Armes near the Château Frontenac.

Car & Motorcycle

Car Rental

Trudeau Airport has many international car-rental firms, and there's a host of smaller operators in Montréal. Rates will swing with demand so it's worth phoning around to see what's on offer. Advance bookings via online sites often offer the best rates, and airport rates are normally better than those in town.

To rent a car in the province of Québec you must be at least 21 years old and have had a driver's license for at least a year.

Motorcycle Rental

Harley-Davidson Laval
(☑450-973-4501; www.
premonthdlaval.com; 3255 Rue
Jules-Brillant, Laval; ☺9:30am-
6pm Mon-Wed, to 8pm Thu
& Fri, 10am-4pm Sat & Sun)
rents motorcycles by half-day,
full day, weekend or longer out
of Laval in suburban Montréal.

Road Rules

➡ Fines for traffic violations,
from speeding to not wearing
a seat belt, are stiff in Québec.
You may see few police cars
on the roads, but radar traps
are common. Motorcyclists are
required to wear helmets and to
ride with their lights on.

➡ Traffic in both directions must
stop when school buses stop to
let children get off and on. At the
white-striped pedestrian crosswalks, cars must stop to allow
pedestrians to cross the road.

➡ Turning right on red lights is il-
legal in Montréal. (It is legal everywhere else in Québec, as long as
there is no sign posted specifi-
cally prohibiting such turns.)

➡ A flashing green light means
that you are allowed to turn
left (similar to a green left-turn
arrow in the United States).

➡ Québec's blood-alcohol
limit while driving is 0.08%, as
opposed to the 0.05% limit in
most other Canadian provinces.
Driving motorized vehicles
(including boats and snowmo-
biles) under the influence is a
serious offense in Canada. You
could land in jail with a court
date, heavy fine and suspended
license. The minimum drinking
age is 18 – the same age as for
obtaining a driver's license.

➡ In winter parking on city
streets is periodically prohibited
to facilitate snow removal.
Yellow and black signs marked
'Déneigement' (snow removal)
or 'Opération Neige' (operation
snow) indicate the hours when
parking is prohibited (usually

7am to 7pm, or 7pm to 7am).
Heed the signs, or you could
find yourself with a towed vehicle and a hefty fine.

➡ Québec mandates that cars
have snow tires on during winter.

Taxi & Ride Share

Flag fall in both Montréal and
Québec City is a standard
$3.50, plus another $1.70 per
kilometer and 65¢ per minute
spent waiting in traffic.

Uber is currently available
in both Montréal and Québec
City (although it is presently
in a state of flux).

Kangaride (☑855-526-4274;
www.kangaride.com) Get drivers
and passengers together for
rides to other parts of Québec.

Taxi Champlain (☑514-271-
1111; http://taxichamplain.com)
Montréal taxi service.

Taxi Co-Op (☑514-725-9885;
www.taxi-coop.com) Provides
taxi service in Montréal.

Taxis Coop (☑418-525-5191;
www.taxiscoop-quebec.com)
Taxi service in Québec City.

Funicular

In Québec City, a **Funicular**
(www.funiculaire-quebec.com;
Rue du Petit-Champlain; one
way $3.50; ☺7:30am-10:30pm,
to 11:30pm summer) links the
Old Upper and Lower Towns.

TOURS

Excellent bilingual tours are
especially common in Old
Montréal, where day and
evening tours trace history,
and even specific topics such
as crimes and legends. Mile
End is an interesting place for
a food or street art tour.

Montréal

Guidatour (Map p268; ☑514-
844-4021; www.guidatour.
qc.ca; ticket office 360 Rue
St-François-Xavier; adult/child

$30/17; ☺scheduled tours
Fri-Sun May & daily Jun-Oct,
private tours year-round)

AML Cruises (Map p268;
☑514-842-9300; www.croi
sieresaml.com; 200 Rue de la
Commune Ouest, ticket office;
adult/youth/child under 4yr
$30/18/free; ☺departures
11:30am, 2pm & 4pm May–
mid-Sep; MPlace-d'Armes)

**Les Fantômes du Vieux-
Montréal** (Map p268; ☑514-
844-4021; www.fantommontreal.
com; 360 Rue St-François-Xavier,
ticket office; adult/youth $25/16;
☺scheduled tours 8:30pm Sat
May-Jun, daily Jul-Aug & late
Oct-early Nov, Fri & Sat early
Sep–mid-Oct)

Amphi Tours (Map p268;
☑514-849-5181; www.montreal-
amphibus-tour.com; boarding
location 2 Rue de la Commune
Ouest; 1hr tour adult/youth/
child $39/25/18; ☺May-Oct)

Québec City

Croisières AML (Map p170;
☑800-563-4643, 866-856-
6668; www.croisieresaml.com;
10 Rue Dalhousie, Old Lower
Town & Port)

Les Tours de Vieux Québec
(Map p170; ☑418-664-0460;
www.toursvieuxquebec.com; 12
Rue Ste-Anne, Old Upper Town)

Gourmet Food Tour (Map p170;
☑418-694-2001; www.tours-
voirquebec.com; 12 Rue Ste-
Anne, Old Upper Town; adult/
child $46/25; ☺tours 2pm
May-Oct, Tue-Sat Nov-Apr)

Broue-Tours (☑418-554-1233;
www.brou-tours.ca; $65)

Cyclo Services (Map p170;
☑418-692-4052; www.cyclo
services.net; 289 Rue St-Paul,
Old Lower Town & Port; rental
per 2/24hr city bike $17/38,
electric bike $34/76; ☺9am-
5:30pm Mon-Fri, 10am-5pm
Sat & Sun, variable hours
Nov-Apr; 🚲)

Directory A–Z

Accessible Travel

Most public buildings in Montréal and Québec City – including tourist offices, major museums and attractions – are accessible for people in wheelchairs. Many restaurants and hotels also have facilities for the mobility-impaired but not in Québec City's Old Town, where very few buildings (including places to stay) have elevators.

Montréal's public-transport system is quite accessibility friendly, provided weather conditions permit. Check the STM page (www.stm.info/en/access). Featured accessible accommodation is searchable on Québec For All (http://quebecforall.com). Download Lonely Planet's free Accessible Travel guides from https://shop.lonelyplanet.com/categories/accessible-travel.

The nonprofit **Kéroul** (☑514-252-3104; www.keroul.qc.ca) provides themed accessible travel itinerary suggestions covering Montréal and Québec City.

Customs Regulations

For the latest customs information, contact the Canadian embassy or consulate at home, or go to the 'Visit as a Tourist' section of the Canadian government website (www.cic.gc.ca).

➡ All fruit, vegetables and plants must be declared when crossing into Canada. For current restrictions, visit www.inspection.gc.ca.

➡ Visitors to Québec aged 18 and older can bring up to 8.5L of beer or ale, 1.5L of wine or 1.14L (40oz) of other liquor without paying duty or taxes. In addition, the following quantities of tobacco products may be brought into the country duty-free: 50 cigars, 200 cigarettes, 200g of tobacco and 200 tobacco sticks. Individual gifts valued at $60 or less are also duty-free.

➡ US residents may bring back $800 worth of goods duty-free, plus 1L of alcohol (but you must be aged 21 or over), as well as 200 cigarettes and 100 non-Cuban cigars.

Discount Cards

The **Montréal Museum Pass** (www.museesmontreal.org; 3-day pass $80) allows free access to 39 museums for three days of your choice within a 21-day period ($80). It comes with three consecutive days of free access to bus and metro. It's available from the city's tourist offices, major museums, or you can buy it online.

Emergency

Canada's country code	☑1
International access code	☑1
Operator	☑0
Emergencies	☑911
Police, non-emergencies	☑514-280-2222

Health

There are no required vaccinations for visitors to Montréal but ensure you are up to date for routine vaccines including the measles-mumps-rubella (MMR) vaccine, diphtheria-tetanus-pertussis vaccine, varicella (chickenpox) vaccine and the polio vaccine.

Medical Checklist

➡ acetaminophen (eg Tylenol) or aspirin

➡ anti-inflammatory drugs (eg ibuprofen)

➡ antihistamines (for hay fever and allergic reactions)

➡ antibacterial ointment (eg Neosporin) for cuts and abrasions

➡ steroid cream or cortisone (for poison ivy and other allergic rashes)

➡ bandages, gauze, gauze rolls

➡ adhesive or paper tape

→ tweezers
→ thermometer
→ insect repellent
→ sunblock

Environmental Hazards

Cold exposure is a significant problem here. Keep all body surfaces covered, including the head and neck. Watch out for the 'Umbles' – stumbles, mumbles, fumbles and grumbles – which are signs of impending hypothermia.

Health Insurance

Québec offers some of the finest health care in the world. However, unless you are a Canadian citizen, it can be prohibitively expensive. It's essential to purchase travel health insurance if your regular policy doesn't cover you when you're abroad.

Pharmacies are abundant, but prescriptions can be expensive without insurance. Bring medications you may need clearly labeled in their original containers. A signed, dated letter from your physician that describes your medical conditions and medications, including generic names, is also a good idea.

Internet Access

Wi-fi is widely available throughout Montréal and Québec City – and with the exception of a few high-end hotels, it's generally free of charge. That said, many cafes and restaurants still do not offer wi-fi, making Montréal less wi-fi saturated than other large cities such as London or New York.

For a map of hundreds of places where you can get online for free, see Zap (zap-wifipublic.ca). For info on free wi-fi hot spots around the province, visit Zap Québec (www.zapquebec.org).

Electricity

Type A
120V/60Hz

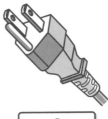

Type B
120V/60Hz

Legal Matters

If you're charged with an offense, you have the right to public counsel if you can't afford a lawyer.

Generally speaking, it's an offense to consume alcohol anywhere other than at a residence or licensed premises, which technically puts parks, beaches and the rest of the great outdoors off-limits. Montréal has side-stepped this restriction with a city ordinance that allows for alcohol to be 'consumed in a park with a meal'; even so, it's best to be discreet, and bear in mind that disturbance of the peace or loitering in any park between 11pm and sunrise remains a criminal offense.

LGBTIQ+ Travelers

Fugues (www.fugues.com) is the free, French-language, authoritative monthly guide to the gay and lesbian scene for the province of Québec. It's an excellent place to find out about the latest clubs and gay-friendly accommodations, with some information in English online.

Montréal

Montréal is a popular getaway for lesbian, gay and bisexual travelers. The gay community is centered in The Village, and it's huge business. The weeklong **Montréal Pride** (Fierté Montréal; ☎514-903-6193; http://fiertemtl.com; ☉Aug) attracts hundreds of thousands every August, while the **Black & Blue Festival** (☎514-875-7026; www.bbcm.org; ☉Oct) in early October features major dance parties along with cultural and arts events.

Gay and lesbian travelers are an accepted part of Montréal life. In neighborhoods such as the Plateau, for example, two men holding hands in public will scarcely raise an eyebrow.

Montréal Gay & Lesbian Community Centre & Library (☎514-528-8424; www.ccglm.org; 2075 Rue Plessis; ☉center 2-9pm Mon, to 6pm Tue-Thu; library 1-8pm Mon & Wed, 1-6pm Thu & Fri; Ⓜ Beaudry) Ⓕ Ⓡ Ⓔ Ⓔ has been around since 1988 and provides an extensive library and loads of info on the city's gay and lesbian scene.

Québec City

Québec City's LGBTIQ+ community is tiny but well established, with its own Pride festival, the **Fête Arc-en-Ciel** (Québec City Pride Festival; ☎418-809-3383; www.arcencielquebec.ca; ⊗early Sep), in early September, and a handful of popular nightspots along Rue St-Jean in the St-Jean Baptiste district.

Québec City tends to be a bit more conservative than big brother Montréal, and open displays of affection between same-sex couples may attract more attention.

Fugues (www.fugues.com) is a free gay and lesbian entertainment guide with listings for the entire province of Québec, including Québec City.

Medical Services

Medical treatment is pricey (less so by US comparison), and long waits – particularly in the emergency room – are common. Avoid going to the hospital if possible.

Call the **Québec Poison Control Centre** (☎1800-463-5060) immediately if you suspect that you or a child has been poisoned.

Clinics

If you're sick and need some advice, call Québec's provincial **Health Hotline** (☎811), which is staffed by nurses 24 hours a day.

For minor ailments in Montréal, visit the **CLSC** (Centre Local de Services Communautaires; ☎514-934-0354; www.santemontreal.qc.ca/en; 1801 Blvd de Maisonneuve Ouest; ⊗8am-8pm Mon-Fri, 8:30am-4:30pm Sat & Sun; Ⓜ Guy-Concordia) clinic Downtown.

Emergency Rooms

MONTRÉAL
MUHC Glen Hospital

(☎514-934-1934; www.muhc.ca; 1001 Blvd Décarie; Ⓜ Vendôme) Montréal's state-of-the-art emergency hospital, affiliated with McGill University Health Centre, opened in April 2015. This is the best option for English-speaking patients.

Montréal General Hospital (☎514-934-1934; www.muhc.ca/mgh; 1650 Ave Cedar, emergency entrance cnr Ave des Pins & Rue Chemin de la Côte-des-Neiges; ⊗24hr; Ⓜ Guy-Concordia)

QUÉBEC CITY
L'Hôtel-Dieu de Québec (☎418-525-4444, 418-691-5042; www.chuq.qc.ca; 11 Côte du Palais, Old Upper Town; ⊗consultations 2-9pm, emergency 24hr) Québec City's oldest and most centrally located hospital.

Centre Hospitalier de l'Université Laval (CHUL; ☎418-525-4444; www.chudequebec.ca/visiteur/centre-hospitaliers/centre-hospitalier-de-l'universite-laval-(chul).aspx; 2705 Blvd Laurier, Ste-Foy; ⊗2-9pm) Affiliated with Université Laval, this emergency facility is 8.5km southwest of the center.

Pharmacies

The big pharmacy chains are Pharmaprix (www.pharmaprix.ca) and Jean Coutu (www.jeancoutu.com). Some branches stay open late.

Money

ATMs

Montréal and Québec City have droves of ATMs, not only in banks but also in pubs, convenience stores and hotels. Many charge a small fee per use, and your own bank may levy an extra fee – it's best to check before leaving home. Some users report that Banque Nationale charges no usage fees.

Changing Money

The main shopping streets in Montréal, including Rue Ste-Catherine, Blvd St-Laurent and Rue St-Denis, have plenty of banks. There are also foreign-exchange desks at the main tourist office, the airport and the casino.

Note that many credit-card machines only take chip-enabled cards.

Taxes & Refunds

Québec has two taxes: a 5% federal goods and services tax (GST) and the 9.975% Québec sales tax (QST). In addition, an accommodations tax of 3.5% of the room price per night applies. Taxes are not generally included in prices given; they're added on afterward.

CLAIMING TAX REFUNDS

You might be eligible for a rebate on some taxes. If you've booked your accommodations in conjunction with a rental car, plane ticket or other service (ie if it all appears on the same bill from a 'tour operator'), you should be eligible to get 50% of the tax refunded from your accommodations. Fill out the GST/HST Refund Application for Tour Packages form, available from the Canada Revenue Agency (www.canada.ca/en/revenue-agency.html).

Opening Hours

The following are typical, though individual businesses hours may vary:

Banks 10am–3pm Monday to Friday (later on Thursday).

Bars & Pubs 11:30am–midnight or later; those not serving food may not open until 5pm or later.

Government Offices 9am–5pm Monday to Friday.

Museums 10am or 11am to 6pm. Most close Monday, but stay open late one day a week (typically Wednesday or Thursday).

Post Offices 8am–5pm Monday to Friday.

Restaurants 11:30am–2:30pm and 5:30pm–11pm; cafes serving breakfast open between 7am and 9am.

Post

For general information, contact **Canada Post** (Postes Canada; ☑416-979-3033; www.canadapost.ca).

Montréal's **main post office** (677 Rue Ste-Catherine Ouest, Eaton Centre; ⊙7am-6pm Mon & Tue, to 7pm Wed-Fri, 10am-5pm Sat, 11am-5pm Sun; Ⓜ McGill) is the largest but there are many convenient locations around town. Stamps are also available at newspaper shops, convenience stores and some hotels.

Public Holidays

New Year's Day January 1

Good Friday & Easter Monday Late March to mid-April

Victoria Day May 24 or nearest Monday

National Aboriginal Day June 21 (unofficial)

St-Jean-Baptiste Day June 24

Canada Day July 1

Labour Day First Monday in September

Canadian Thanksgiving Second Monday in October

Remembrance Day November 11

Christmas Day December 25

Boxing Day December 26

Responsible Travel

Overtourism is a small but growing problem in Montréal and Québéc City but visitors can still do their bit to help. To get across town in Montréal, the city's bike-rental service Bixi is a carbon neutral alternative to the already efficient public transport system. Bixi bike-rack stations are solar-powered and close only in winter, allowing even short-term visitors to easily rent bicycles to ride on over 200 miles of bike paths.

Between regions, go overland instead of by air. Long-distance buses are not the only option either. Carpooling not only saves money but means one less single-passenger car. Popular car-pooling sites used across Québéc include www.kangaride.com and www.kijiji.ca.

In Montréal, single-use plastic shopping bags are banned, with restaurants to follow. A total ban on styrofoam cups, take-out containers and plastic utensils will follow by 2023. Visitors can bring their own reusable shoppers and refillable water bottle.

Safe Travel

➡ Violent crime is rare (especially involving foreigners). Even so, as in all big cities, it's best to stay alert for petty theft and use hotel safes where available.

➡ Cars with foreign registration are occasionally targeted for smash-and-grab theft. As in any big city, don't leave valuables in the car.

➡ Take special care at pedestrian crosswalks: unless there's an *arrêt* (stop) sign, drivers largely ignore these crosswalks.

Telephone

The area code for the entire island of Montréal is ☑514; Québec City is ☑418. When you dial, even local numbers, you will need to punch in the area code as well.

Toll-free numbers begin with ☎800, ☎866, ☎877 or ☎888 and must be preceded with 1. Some numbers are good throughout North America, others only within Canada or one particular province.

Dialing the operator (☎0) or the emergency number (☎911) is free of charge from both public and private phones. For directory assistance, dial ☎411. Fees apply.

With the advent of cell phones, public phones have become a rarity. When you do find them they will either be coin-operated (local calls cost 50¢) or accept phone cards and credit cards.

Cell Phones

The only foreign cell phones that will work in North America are unlocked triband models operating on GSM 1900 – this is nearly every smartphone made in the last few years. If you don't have one of these, your best bet is to buy an inexpensive phone with prepaid minutes and a rechargeable SIM card at a consumer electronics store such as Best Buy (www.bestbuy.ca). If you just need data and not calls, you can still use wi-fi.

US residents traveling with their phone may have service (though they'll pay roaming fees). Get in touch with your cell-phone provider for details.

Time

Montréal is on Eastern Time (EST/EDT), as is New York City and Toronto – five hours behind GMT.

Canada switches to daylight-saving time (one hour later than Standard Time) from the second Sunday in March to the first Sunday in November.

Train schedules, film screenings and schedules in French use the 24-hour clock (eg 6:30pm becomes 18:30), while English schedules use the 12-hour clock.

Tourist Information

Montréal

Centre Infotouriste Montréal (Map p272; ☎514-844-5400; www.mtl.org; 1255 Rue Peel; ☺9am-6pm May-Sep, to 5pm Oct-Apr; Ⓜ Peel) Information about Montréal and all of Québec. Free hotel, tour and car reservations, plus currency exchange.

Tourisme Montréal (☎877-266-5687; www.mtl. org; ☺9am-noon & 1-5pm Mon-Fri, from 10am Wed) The Montréal tourist office has reams of information and a last-minute hotel search engine with guaranteed best price.

Tourist Welcome Office – Old Montréal (Map p268; www.mtl.org; 174 Rue Notre-Dame Est; ☺9am-7pm Jun-Sep, 10am-6pm May & Oct; Ⓜ Champ-de-Mars) Just off bustling Place Jacques-Cartier, this helpful little office is always humming.

Québec City

Centre Infotouriste Québec City (Québec Original; Map p170; ☎418-641-6290; www.quebecoriginal.com; 12 Rue Ste-Anne, Old Upper Town; ☺9am-5pm Nov-Jun, to 6pm Jul-Oct) Québec City's main tourist office, in the heart of the Old Town, opposite Château Frontenac.

Frontenac Kiosk (Map p170; ☎418-648-7016; www.pc.gc.ca/eng/lhn-nhs/qc/fortifications/index.aspx; off Rue St-Louis, Old Upper Town; adult/child $4/free; ☺10am-5pm mid-May–early Oct, to 6pm Jul & Aug) In summer this kiosk offers tourist information for (and entry to) the Fortifications of Québec and St-Louis Forts & Châteaux national historic sites.

Musée des Plaines d'Abraham (Plains of Abraham Museum); Map p178; ☎418-649-6157; www.theplains ofabraham.ca; 835 Ave Wilfrid-Laurier, Montcalm & Colline Parlementaire; adult/youth/child $12.25/10.25/4, incl Abraham's bus tour & Martello Tower 1 Jul-early Sep $15.25/11.25/5; ☺9am-5:30pm) Reception in the museum's lower-ground floor provides information on the Plains of Abraham and Battlefields Park.

Visas

Citizens of dozens of countries – including the USA, most Western European countries, Australia, Japan, Mexico and New Zealand – don't need visas to enter Canada for stays of up to 180 days. US permanent residents are also exempt. Note that you still need an Electronic Travel Authorization (eTA) to fly into Canada. The eTA costs $7 and you can apply for one online at https://eta-canada.com; the approval process usually only takes a few minutes but can take up to 72 hours. US citizens and US permanent residents do not require eTAs.

Nationals of around 150 other countries must apply to the Canadian visa office in their home country for a temporary resident visa (TRV). See www.cic.gc.ca for full details. Note that if you have a visa, you are not required to purchase an eTA.

Single-entry visitor visas are valid for six months, while multiple-entry visas can be used for up to 10 years, provided that no single stay exceeds six months. Either type of visa costs $100. Extensions cost the same price as the original and must be applied for at a Canadian Immigration Center one month before the current visa expires. A separate visa is required if you intend to work in Canada.

Language

Canada is officially a bilingual country with the majority of the population speaking English as their first language. In Québec, however, the dominant language is French. The local tongue is essentially the same as what you'd hear in France, and you'll have no problems being understood if you use standard French phrases (provided in this chapter).

Of course, there are some differences between European French and the Québec version (known as 'Québécois' or joual). For example, while standard French for 'What time is it?' is Quelle heure est-il?, in Québec you're likely to hear Y'est quelle heure? instead. Other differences worth remembering are the terms for breakfast, lunch and dinner: rather than petit déjeuner, déjeuner and dîner you're likely to see and hear déjeuner, dîner and souper. Québec French also employs a lot of English words; eg English terms are generally used for car parts – even the word char (pronounced 'shar') for car may be heard.

The sounds used in spoken French can almost all be found in English. If you read our pronunciation guides as if they were English, you'll be understood. There are a couple of exceptions: nasal vowels (represented in our guides by o or u followed by an almost inaudible nasal consonant sound m, n or ng), the 'funny' u (ew in our guides) and the deep-in-the-throat r. Syllables in French words are, for the most part, equally stressed. As English speakers tend to stress the first syllable, try adding a light stress on the final syllable of French words to compensate.

WANT MORE?

For in-depth language information and handy phrases, check out Lonely Planet's French phrasebook. You'll find it at **shop. lonelyplanet.com**.

BASICS

Hello.	Bonjour.	bon·zhoor
Goodbye.	Au revoir.	o·rer·vwa
Excuse me.	Excusez-moi.	ek·skew·zay·mwa
Sorry.	Pardon.	par·don
Yes./No.	Oui./Non.	wee/non
Please.	S'il vous plaît.	seel voo play
Thank you.	Merci.	mair·see

How are you?
Comment allez-vous?   ko·mon ta·lay·voo

Fine, and you?
Bien, merci. Et vous?   byun mair·see ay voo

What's your name?
Comment vous appelez-vous?   ko·mon voo·za·play voo

My name is ...
Je m'appelle ...   zher ma·pel ...

Do you speak English?
Parlez-vous anglais?   par·lay·voo ong·glay

I don't understand.
Je ne comprends pas.   zher ner kom·pron pa

ACCOMMODATIONS

Do you have any rooms available?
Est-ce que vous avez   es·ker voo za·vay
des chambres libres?   day shom·brer lee·brer

How much is it per night/person?
Quel est le prix   kel ay ler pree
par nuit/personne?   par nwee/per·son

Is breakfast included?
Est-ce que le petit   es·ker ler per·tee
déjeuner est inclus?   day·zher·nay ayt en·klew

dorm	dortoir	dor·twar
guesthouse	pension	pon·syon
hotel	hôtel	o·tel
youth hostel	auberge de jeunesse	o·berzh der zher·nes

I'd like to reserve a table for ...	Je voudrais réserver une table pour ...	zher voo·dray ray·zair·vay ewn ta·bler poor ...
(eight) o'clock	(vingt) heures	(vungt) er
(two) people	(deux) personnes	(der) pair·son

Signs

Entrée	Entrance
Femmes	Women
Fermé	Closed
Hommes	Men
Interdit	Prohibited
Ouvert	Open
Renseignements	Information
Sortie	Exit
Toilettes/WC	Toilets

a ... room	une chambre ...	ewn shom·brer ...
single	à un lit	a un lee
double	avec un grand lit	a·vek un gron lee

with (a) ...	avec ...	a·vek ...
air-con	climatiseur	klee·ma·tee·zer
bathroom	une salle de bains	ewn sal der bun
window	fenêtre	fer·nay·trer

DIRECTIONS

Where's ...?
Où est ...? — oo ay ...

What's the address?
Quelle est l'adresse? — kel ay la·dres

Can you write down the address, please?
Est-ce que vous pourriez écrire l'adresse, s'il vous plaît? — es·ker voo poo·ryay ay·kreer la·dres seel voo play

Can you show me (on the map)?
Pouvez-vous m'indiquer (sur la carte)? — poo·vay·voo mun·dee·kay (sewr la kart)

EATING & DRINKING

What would you recommend?
Qu'est-ce que vous conseillez? — kes·ker voo kon·say·yay

What's in that dish?
Quels sont les ingrédients? — kel son lay zun·gray·dyon

I'm a vegetarian.
Je suis végétarien/ végétarienne. — zher swee vay·zhay·ta·ryun/ vay·zhay·ta·ryen (m/f)

Cheers!
Santé! — son·tay

That was delicious.
C'était délicieux! — say·tay day·lee·syer

Please bring the bill.
Apportez-moi l'addition, s'il vous plaît. — a·por·tay·mwa la·dee·syon seel voo play

Key Words

appetizer	entrée	on·tray
bottle	bouteille	boo·tay
breakfast	déjeuner	day·zher·nay
cold	froid	frwa
delicatessen	traiteur	tray·ter
dinner	souper	soo·pay
fork	fourchette	foor·shet
glass	verre	vair
grocery store	épicerie	ay·pees·ree
hot	chaud	sho
knife	couteau	koo·to
lunch	dîner	dee·nay
market	marché	mar·shay
menu	carte	kart
plate	assiette	a·syet
spoon	cuillère	kwee·yair
wine list	carte des vins	kart day vun
with/without	avec/sans	a·vek/son

Meat & Fish

beef	bœuf	berf
chicken	poulet	poo·lay
crab	crabe	krab
lamb	agneau	a·nyo
oyster	huître	wee·trer
pork	porc	por
snail	escargot	es·kar·go
squid	calmar	kal·mar
turkey	dinde	dund
veal	veau	vo

Fruit & Vegetables

apple	pomme	pom
apricot	abricot	ab·ree·ko
asparagus	asperge	a·spairzh
beans	haricots	a·ree·ko
beetroot	betterave	be·trav
cabbage	chou	shoo

celery	*céleri*	sel·ree
cherry	*cerise*	ser·reez
corn	*maïs*	ma·ees
cucumber	*concombre*	kong·kom·brer
gherkin (pickle)	*cornichon*	kor·nee·shon
grape	*raisin*	ray·zun
leek	*poireau*	pwa·ro
lemon	*citron*	see·tron
lettuce	*laitue*	lay·tew
mushroom	*champignon*	shom·pee·nyon
peach	*pêche*	pesh
peas	*petit pois*	per·tee pwa
(red/green) pepper	*poivron (rouge/vert)*	pwa·vron (roozh/vair)
pineapple	*ananas*	a·na·nas
plum	*prune*	prewn
potato	*pomme de terre*	pom der tair
prune	*pruneau*	prew·no
pumpkin	*citrouille*	see·troo·yer
shallot	*échalote*	eh·sha·lot
spinach	*épinards*	eh·pee·nar
strawberry	*fraise*	frez
tomato	*tomate*	to·mat
turnip	*navet*	na·vay
vegetable	*légume*	lay·gewm

Other

bread	*pain*	pun
butter	*beurre*	ber
cheese	*fromage*	fro·mazh
egg	*œuf*	erf
honey	*miel*	myel
jam	*confiture*	kon·fee·tewr
oil	*huile*	weel
pepper	*poivre*	pwa·vrer
rice	*riz*	ree
salt	*sel*	sel
sugar	*sucre*	sew·krer
vinegar	*vinaigre*	vee·nay·grer

Drinks

beer	*bière*	bee·yair
coffee	*café*	ka·fay
(orange) juice	*jus (d'orange)*	zhew (do·ronzh)
milk	*lait*	lay
red wine	*vin rouge*	vun roozh
tea	*thé*	tay
(mineral) water	*eau (minérale)*	o (mee·nay·ral)
white wine	*vin blanc*	vun blong

EMERGENCIES

Help!
Au secours! — o skoor

Leave me alone!
Fichez-moi la paix! — fee·shay·mwa la pay

I'm lost.
Je suis perdu/perdue. — zhe swee·pair·dew (m/f)

Call a doctor.
Appelez un médecin. — a·play un mayd·sun

Call the police.
Appelez la police. — a·play la po·lees

I'm ill.
Je suis malade. — zher swee ma·lad

It hurts here.
J'ai une douleur ici. — zhay ewn doo·ler ee·see

I'm allergic (to ...).
Je suis allergique (à ...). — zher swee za·lair·zheek (a...)

SHOPPING & SERVICES

I'd like to buy ...
Je voudrais acheter ... — zher voo·dray ash·tay ...

Can I look at it?
Est-ce que je peux le voir? — es·ker zher per ler vwar

I'm just looking.
Je regarde. — zher rer·gard

I don't like it.
Cela ne me plaît pas. — ser·la ner mer play pa

How much is it?
C'est combien? — say kom·byun

It's too expensive.
C'est trop cher. — say tro shair

There's a mistake in the bill.
Il y a une erreur dans la note. — eel ya ewn ay·rer don la not

bank	*banque*	bonk
internet cafe	*cybercafé*	see·bair·ka·fay
tourist office	*office de tourisme*	o·fees der too·rees·mer

Question Words		
What?	*Quoi?*	kwa
When?	*Quand?*	kon
Where?	*Où?*	oo
Who?	*Qui?*	kee
Why?	*Pourquoi?*	poor·kwa

Numbers

1	*un*	un
2	*deux*	der
3	*trois*	trwa
4	*quatre*	ka·trer
5	*cinq*	sungk
6	*six*	sees
7	*sept*	set
8	*huit*	weet
9	*neuf*	nerf
10	*dix*	dees
20	*vingt*	vung
30	*trente*	tront
40	*quarante*	ka·ront
50	*cinquante*	sung·kont
60	*soixante*	swa·sont
70	*soixante-dix*	swa·son·dees
80	*quatre-vingts*	ka·trer·vung
90	*quatre-vingt-dix*	ka·trer·vung·dees
100	*cent*	son
1000	*mille*	meel

TIME & DATES

What time is it?
Y'est quelle heure?   il ay kel er

It's (eight) o'clock.
Il est (huit) heures.   il ay (weet) er

Half past (10).
(Dix) heures et demie.   (deez) er ay day·mee

morning	*matin*	ma·tun
afternoon	*après-midi*	a·pray·mee·dee
evening	*soir*	swar
yesterday	*hier*	yair
today	*aujourd'hui*	o·zhoor·dwee
tomorrow	*demain*	der·mun

Monday	*lundi*	lun·dee
Tuesday	*mardi*	mar·dee
Wednesday	*mercredi*	mair·krer·dee
Thursday	*jeudi*	zher·dee
Friday	*vendredi*	von·drer·dee
Saturday	*samedi*	sam·dee
Sunday	*dimanche*	dee·monsh

TRANSPORTATION

I want to go to ...
Je voudrais   zher voo·dray
aller à ...   a·lay a ...

At what time does it leave/arrive?
À quelle heure est-ce   a kel er es
qu'il part/arrive?   kil par/a·reev

Does it stop at ...?
Est-ce qu'il s'arrête à ...?   es·kil sa·ret a ...

I want to get off here.
Je veux descendre   zher ver day·son·drer
ici.   ee·see

a ... ticket	*un billet ...*	un bee·yay ...
1st-class	*de première classe*	der prem·yair klas
2nd-class	*de deuxième classe*	der der·zyem las
one-way	*simple*	sum·pler
return	*aller et retour*	a·lay ay rer·toor

aisle seat	*côté couloir*	ko·tay kool·war
boat	*bateau*	ba·to
bus	*bus*	bews
cancelled	*annulé*	a·new·lay
delayed	*en retard*	on rer·tar
first	*premier*	prer·myay
last	*dernier*	dair·nyay
plane	*avion*	a·vyon
platform	*quai*	kay
ticket office	*guichet*	gee·shay
timetable	*horaire*	o·rair
train	*train*	trun
window seat	*côté fenêtre*	ko·tay fe·ne·trer

I'd like to hire a ...	*Je voudrais louer ...*	zher voo·dray loo·way ...
car	*une voiture*	ewn vwa·tewr
bicycle	*un vélo*	un vay·lo
motorcycle	*une moto*	ewn mo·to

child seat	*siège-enfant*	syezh·on·fon
helmet	*casque*	kask
mechanic	*mécanicien*	may·ka·nee·syun
petrol/gas	*essence*	ay·sons
service station	*station-service*	sta·syon·ser·vees

Can I park here?
Est-ce que je peux   es·ker zher per
stationner ici?   sta·syo·nay ee·see

I have a flat tyre.
Mon pneu est à plat.   mom pner ay ta pla

I've run out of petrol.
Je suis en panne   zher swee zon pan
d'essence.   day·sons

GLOSSARY

allophone – a person whose mother tongue is neither French nor English

anglophone – a person whose mother tongue is English

beaux arts – architectural style popular in France and Québec in the late 19th century, incorporating elements that are massive, elaborate and often ostentatious

Bill 101 – law that asserts the primacy of the French language in Québec, notably on signage

boîte à chanson – club devoted to *chanson française* (folk music from Québec or France)

brochette – kebab

cabane à sucre – place where the collected maple sap is distilled in large kettles and boiled as part of the production of maple syrup

calèche – horse-drawn carriage that can be taken around parts of Montréal and Québec City

Cantons de l'Est – Eastern Townships, a former Loyalist region southeast of Montréal toward the US border

cinq à sept – literally means five-to-seven, but refers to happy hours

correspondance – a transfer slip like those used between the métro and bus networks in Montréal

côte – a hill, as in Côte du Beaver Hall

dépanneur – called 'dep' for short, this is a Québec term for a convenience store

Estrie – a more recent term for *Cantons de l'Est*

First Nations – a term used to denote Canada's indigenous peoples, sometime used instead of Native Indians or Amerindians

francophone – a person whose mother tongue is French

Front de Libération du Québec (FLQ) – a radical, violent political group active in the 1970s that advocated Québec's separation from Canada

gîte (du passant) – French term for B&B or similar lodging

Hochelaga – name of early Iroquois settlement on the site of present-day Montréal

Je me souviens – this Québec motto with a nationalist ring ('I remember') appears on license plates across the province

loonie – Canada's $1 coin, named for the loon stamped on one side

Mounties – Royal Canadian Mounted Police (RCMP)

Québecois – the French spoken in Québec; someone from the province of Québec; someone from Québec City

Refus Global – the radical manifest of a group of Québec artists and intellectuals during the Duplessis era (1944–59)

SAQ – Société des Alcools du Québec, a state-run agency that sells wines, spirits, beer etc

téléroman – a type of Québec TV program that's a cross between soap opera and prime-time drama, in French

toonie – also spelled 'twonie,' the Canadian $2 coin introduced after the *loonie*

MENU DECODER

ailes wings

allongé watered-down espresso

apportez votre vin or AVV bring your own bottle

boire drink

bouteille bottle

brochette kebab

casse-croûte a snack bar

cretons pork spread with onions and spices

entrée appetizer

escalopes tenderized, boneless meat

foie de veau calf liver

le déjeuner breakfast

le dîner lunch

le souper dinner

maison homemade, by the chef

manger to eat

menu dégustation a multi-course tasting menu

pâté pâté, as in pâté de foie gras

pâtes pasta

plat dish

plat du jour daily special

plat principal main dish

poutine French fries served with gravy and cheese curds

rillettes pastelike preparation of meat

ris de veau veal sweetbreads

service compris service included

stimés hotdog with a steamed bun

table d'hôte fixed-price meal (of the day)

taxes incluses taxes included

toastés hotdog with a toasted bun

tourtière Québec meat pie usually made of pork and beef or veal, sometimes with game meat

verre glass

Behind the Scenes

SEND US YOUR FEEDBACK

We love to hear from travelers – your comments keep us on our toes and help make our books better. Our well-traveled team reads every word on what you loved or loathed about this book. Although we cannot reply individually to your submissions, we always guarantee that your feedback goes straight to the appropriate authors, in time for the next edition. Each person who sends us information is thanked in the next edition.

Visit **lonelyplanet.com/contact** to submit your updates and suggestions or to ask for help. Our award-winning website also features inspirational travel stories and news.

Note: We may edit, reproduce and incorporate your comments in Lonely Planet products such as guidebooks, websites and digital products, so let us know if you are happy to have your name acknowledged. For a copy of our privacy policy visit **lonelyplanet.com/legal**.

WRITER THANKS

Phillip Tang

Thank you to Ben Buckner and the destination editors for your expertise and legacy. *Muchas gracias a Lalo* (José Eduardo García Sánchez) *por tu apoyo y consejo sobre estilo y mucho más desde lejos.* Thank you to Felix, Nick Zhang and all the other Montréalers who offered guidance; and to Manuelle González Goretti for advice on the Eastern Townships and adventures in the Village.

Steve Fallon

Thanks to Gab Danjou Drouin in Québec City for pointing me in so many correct directions, and to fellow Lonely Planet writers Mark Baker, Gregor Clark, Daniel McCrohan, Zora O'Neill and Kevin Raub for guidance and advice before I set out. Thanks, too, to Vicky Drolet in La Malbaie and Sylvie Senécal and Pierre Lachance in Ville de Mont-Tremblant for their hospitality. And to all the wonderful Québécois I met along the way, *Merci beaucoup pour (surtout à -22° C) la chaleur et la gentillesse!* As always, I'd like to dedicate my share of this to partner (and erstwhile Quebecker) Michael Rothschild, with love and gratitude.

ACKNOWLEDGEMENTS

Cover photograph: Le Château Frontenac, Québec City, mervas/Shutterstock ©

THIS BOOK

This 6th edition of Lonely Planet's *Montréal & Québec City* guidebook was curated by Regis St Louis and researched and written by Steve Fallon and Phillip Tang. The previous three editions were written by Regis, Gregor Clark and Timothy N Hornyak.

This guidebook was produced by the following:

Destination Editor
Ben Buckner

Senior Product Editors
Kate Chapman, Martine Power, Saralinda Turner

Product Editors
Amy Lysen, Ross Taylor

Cartographer
Corey Hutchison

Book Designers
Gwen Cotter, Meri Blazevski

Assisting Editors
Judith Bamber, Michelle Bennett, Jennifer Hattam, Jodie Martire, Charlotte Orr, Gabbrielle Stefanos

Cover Researcher
Kat Marsh

Thanks to
Ronan Abayawickrema, Imogen Bannister, Joel Cotterell, Kate James, Sonia Kapoor, Craig Ramsay

Index

see also separate subindexes for:

🍴 **EATING P260**

🍺 **DRINKING & NIGHTLIFE P261**

☆ **ENTERTAINMENT P262**

🛍 **SHOPPING P263**

🏃 **SPORTS & ACTIVITIES P263**

🛏 **SLEEPING P264**

✕ EATING

DRINKING & NIGHTLIFE

Montréal Maps

Sights
- Beach
- Bird Sanctuary
- Buddhist
- Castle/Palace
- Christian
- Confucian
- Hindu
- Islamic
- Jain
- Jewish
- Monument
- Museum/Gallery/Historic Building
- Ruin
- Shinto
- Sikh
- Taoist
- Winery/Vineyard
- Zoo/Wildlife Sanctuary
- Other Sight

Activities, Courses & Tours
- Bodysurfing
- Diving
- Canoeing/Kayaking
- Course/Tour
- Sento Hot Baths/Onsen
- Skiing
- Snorkeling
- Surfing
- Swimming/Pool
- Walking
- Windsurfing
- Other Activity

Sleeping
- Sleeping
- Camping
- Hut/Shelter

Eating
- Eating

Drinking & Nightlife
- Drinking & Nightlife
- Cafe

Entertainment
- Entertainment

Shopping
- Shopping

Information
- Bank
- Embassy/Consulate
- Hospital/Medical
- Internet
- Police
- Post Office
- Telephone
- Toilet
- Tourist Information
- Other Information

Geographic
- Beach
- Gate
- Hut/Shelter
- Lighthouse
- Lookout
- Mountain/Volcano
- Oasis
- Park
- Pass
- Picnic Area
- Waterfall

Population
- Capital (National)
- Capital (State/Province)
- City/Large Town
- Town/Village

Transport
- Airport
- BART station
- Border crossing
- Boston T station
- Bus
- Cable car/Funicular
- Cycling
- Ferry
- Metro/Muni station
- Monorail
- Parking
- Petrol station
- Subway/SkyTrain station
- Taxi
- Train station/Railway
- Tram
- Underground station
- Other Transport

Routes
- Tollway
- Freeway
- Primary
- Secondary
- Tertiary
- Lane
- Unsealed road
- Road under construction
- Plaza/Mall
- Steps
- Tunnel
- Pedestrian overpass
- Walking Tour
- Walking Tour detour
- Path/Walking Trail

Boundaries
- International
- State/Province
- Disputed
- Regional/Suburb
- Marine Park
- Cliff
- Wall

Hydrography
- River, Creek
- Intermittent River
- Canal
- Water
- Dry/Salt/Intermittent Lake
- Reef

Areas
- Airport/Runway
- Beach/Desert
- Cemetery (Christian)
- Cemetery (Other)
- Glacier
- Mudflat
- Park/Forest
- Sight (Building)
- Sportsground
- Swamp/Mangrove

Note: Not all symbols displayed above appear on the maps in this book

MAP INDEX

Key on p270

OLD MONTRÉAL

A B C D

Rue Ste-Catherine Ouest

Sq Phillips

Rue St-Edward

Pl Phillips

Rue St-Alexandre

Blvd St-Laurent

Rue St-Dominique

Blvd René-Lévesque Ouest

Rue St-Urbain

Rue Clark

57

66

43

78

26

7

Rue Belmont

Côte du Beaver Hall

Rue Carmichael

Rue de Bleury

Rue Anderson

Rue Jeanne-Mance

Rue Dowd

Rue de la Gauchetière Ouest

54 52

50

56

55

38

Ave Viger Ouest

CHINATOWN
Place-d'Armes

See map p272
Square-Victoria

20

Autoroute Ville-Marie

24

61

Rue St-Antoine Ouest

103

Sq Victoria

Rue Square Victoria

Rle des Fortifications

Rue St-François-Xavier

45

2

106

100

Rue St-Jacques

22

17

46 79

30

15 104

65

70

1

33

Basilique Notre-Dame

Rue de Brésoles

Blvd St-Laurent

62

51

Rue de l'Hôpital

Rue Notre-Dame Ouest

59

99

60

72

8

94

Rue Ste-Hélène

37

9

OLD MONTRÉAL

Rue St-Maurice

63

Rue Le Moyne

98

68

Rue St-Sulpice

92

77

41

31

101

83

Rue St-Henri

Rue de Longueuil

Rue McGill

44

53 64

80

18

105

Rue St-Paul Ouest

58

25

Pl Royale

102

75

4

34 36

40 89

14

27

93

Pl d'Youville

Rue William

49

42

Pl d'Youville

3

73

10

Rue Ottawa

47

Rue des Soeurs-Grises

Rue Normand

Rue St-Pierre

Rue de la Commune Ouest

28

Conveyor Pier

Rue Wellington

Rue Marguerite d'Youville

16

Promenade du Vieux-Port

Quai Alexandra

67

Rue Prince

Rue Queen

Rue King

Parc des Écluses

Bassin Alexandra

39

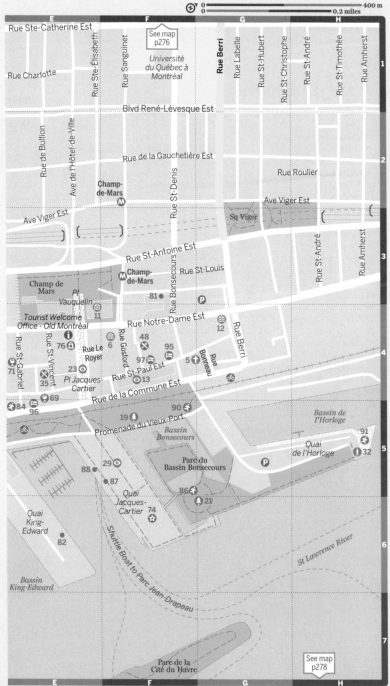

0   400 m
0   0.2 miles

Rue Ste-Catherine Est
Rue Charlotte
Rue Ste-Élisabeth
Rue Sanguinet
See map p276
Université du Québec à Montréal
Rue Berri
Rue Labelle
Rue St-Hubert
Rue St-Christophe
Rue St-André
Rue St-Timothée
Rue Amherst

1

Blvd René-Lévesque Est

Rue de Bullion
Ave de l'Hôtel-de-Ville
Rue de la Gauchetière Est
Rue St-Denis
Rue Roulier

2

Champ-de-Mars
Ave Viger Est
Sq Viger
Ave Viger Est
Rue St-André
Rue Amherst

Ave Viger Est

Rue St-Antoine Est
Champ de Mars
Champ-de-Mars
Rue St-Louis
Pl Vauquelin
11
81
Rue Bonsecours
Tourist Welcome Office - Old Montréal
Rue Notre-Dame Est
12
Rue Berri

3

76
Rue Le Royer
6
Rue Gosford
48
95
5
Rue Bonneau
Rue St-Gabriel
Rue St-Vincent
71
23
97
13
Pl Jacques-Cartier
35
Rue St-Paul Est
Rue de la Commune Est

4

84
96
69
19
90
Promenade du Vieux-Port
Bassin Bonsecours
Bassin de l'Horloge
91
Quai de l'Horloge
32

5

88
29
87
Quai Jacques-Cartier
74
Parc du Bassin Bonsecours
86
21
St Lawrence River

Quai King-Edward
82
Shuttle Boat to Parc Jean-Drapeau

6

Bassin King-Edward

7

Parc de la Cité du Havre
See map p278

E   F   G   H

OLD MONTRÉAL *Map on p268*

DOWNTOWN

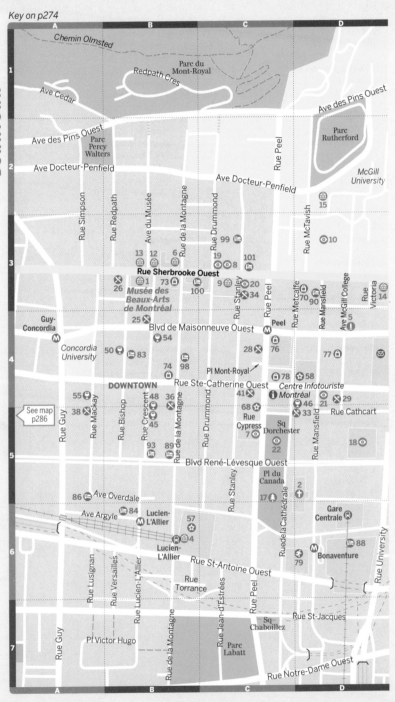

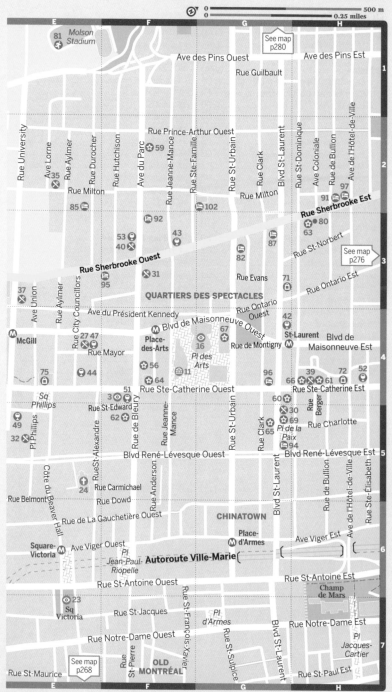

0   500 m
0   0.25 miles

81 Molson Stadium

See map p280

Ave des Pins Ouest

Ave des Pins Est

Rue Guilbault

Rue University

Ave Lorne

Rue Aylmer

Rue Durocher

Rue Hutchison

Ave du Parc

Rue Jeanne-Mance

Rue Ste-Famille

Rue Prince-Arthur Ouest

Rue St-Urbain

Rue Clark

Blvd St-Laurent

Rue St-Dominique

Ave Coloniale

Rue de Bullion

Ave de l'Hôtel-de-Ville

35

59

Rue Milton

Rue Milton

97

91

Rue Sherbrooke Est

85

102

92

80

63

53

43

40

87

Rue Sherbrooke Ouest

Rue St-Norbert

82

See map p276

31

95

Rue Evans

71

QUARTIERS DES SPECTACLES

Rue Ontario Est

37

Ave Union

Ave Aylmer

Rue City Councillors

Ave du Président Kennedy

Rue Ontario Ouest

42

Blvd de Maisonneuve Ouest

67

St-Laurent

Blvd de Maisonneuve Est

McGill

27 47

Place-des-Arts

16

Rue de Montigny

Rue Mayor

Pl des Arts

39

72

52

75

44

56

11

96

66

61

Rue Ste-Catherine Ouest

64

Rue Ste-Catherine Est

Sq Phillips

51

3

60

Rue Berger

Rue St-Edward

62

30

69

Rue Charlotte

49

Rue de Bleury

Rue Jeanne-Mance

Rue St-Urbain

Rue Clark

65

Pl de la Paix

32

Rue St-Alexandre

94

Pl Phillips

Blvd René-Lévesque Ouest

Blvd René-Lévesque Est

24

Rue Carmichael

Rue Anderson

Blvd St-Laurent

Rue de Bullion

Ave de l'Hôtel-de-Ville

Rue Ste-Élisabeth

Rue Belmont

Rue Dowd

Côte du Beaver Hall

Rue de La Gauchetière Ouest

CHINATOWN

Place-d'Armes

Square-Victoria

Ave Viger Ouest

Ave Viger Est

Jean-Paul-Riopelle

Autoroute Ville-Marie

Rue St-Antoine Est

Champ de Mars

Rue St-Antoine Ouest

23

Sq Victoria

Rue St-Jacques

Pl d'Armes

Rue Notre-Dame Est

Pl Jacques-Cartier

Rue Notre-Dame Ouest

Rue St-François-Xavier

Rue St-Pierre

Rue St-Sulpice

Blvd St-Laurent

See map p268

Rue St-Maurice

OLD MONTRÉAL

Rue St-Paul Est

DOWNTOWN *Map on p272*

DOWNTOWN

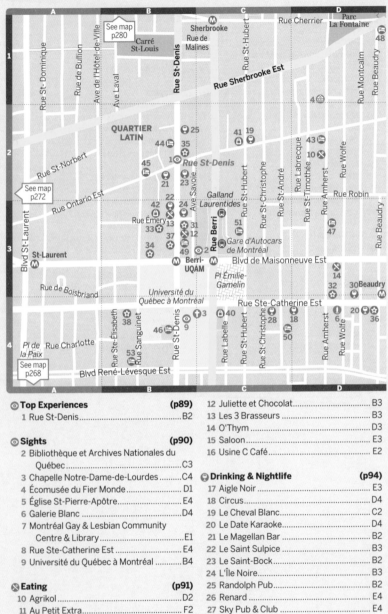

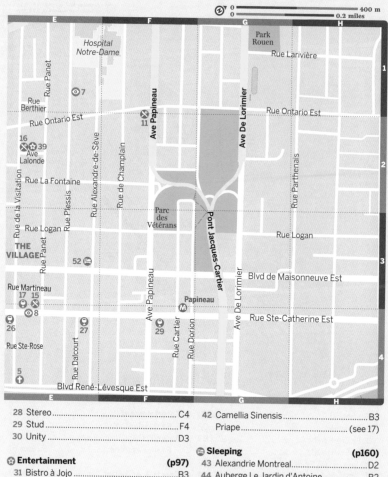

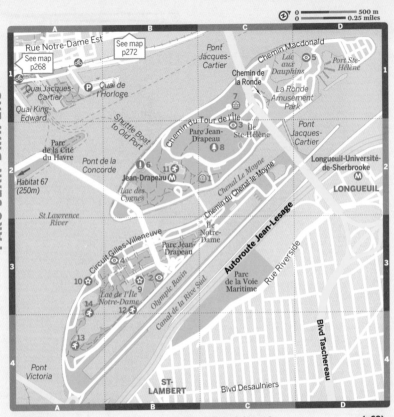

PLATEAU MONT-ROYAL

PLATEAU MONT-ROYAL *Map on p280*

PLATEAU MONT-ROYAL

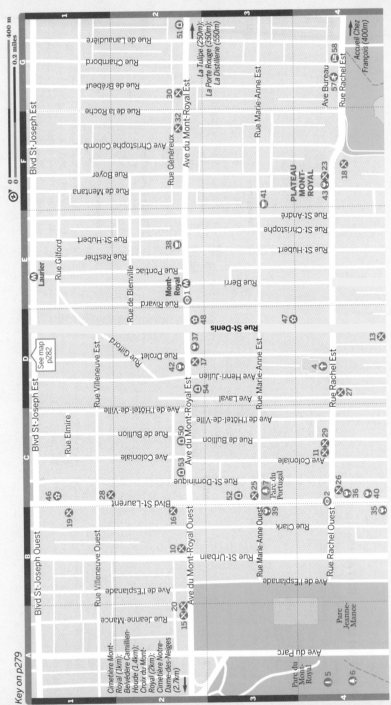

Key on p279

See map p282

0   400 m
0   0.2 miles

Cimetière Mont-
Royal (1km);
Belvédère Camillien-
Houde (1.4km);
Croix du Mont-
Royal (2km);
Cimetière Notre-
Dame-des-Neiges
(2.7km)

La Tulipe (250m);
La Porte Rouge (350m);
La Distillerie (550m)

Accueil Chez
François (400m)

Blvd St-Joseph Est

Blvd St-Joseph Ouest

Rue Villeneuve Ouest

Rue Villeneuve Est

Rue Gilford

Rue Émire

Rue de l'Esplanade

Rue Jeanne-Mance

Blvd St-Laurent

Rue St-Urbain

Rue Clark

Rue de Bullion

Ave Coloniale

Rue St-Dominique

Ave de l'Hôtel-de-Ville

Ave Laval

Ave Henri-Julien

Rue Drolet

Rue Rivard

Rue St-Hubert

Rue Resther

Rue Berri

Rue St-Christophe

Rue St-André

Rue de Mentana

Rue Boyer

Ave Christophe Colomb

Rue de Bienville

Rue Pontiac

Rue de la Roche

Rue de Brébeuf

Rue Chambord

Rue de Lanaudière

Rue Marie-Anne Ouest

Rue Marie-Anne Est

Rue Rachel Ouest

Rue Rachel Est

Ave du Mont-Royal Ouest

Ave du Mont-Royal Est

Ave du Parc

Ave de l'Esplanade

Ave Bureau

Rue Généreux

Parc du
Mont-Royal

Parc
Jeanne-Mance

Parc du
Portugal

PLATEAU
MONT-ROYAL

Laurier

Mont-
Royal

Rue St-Denis

M Laurier
M Mont-Royal

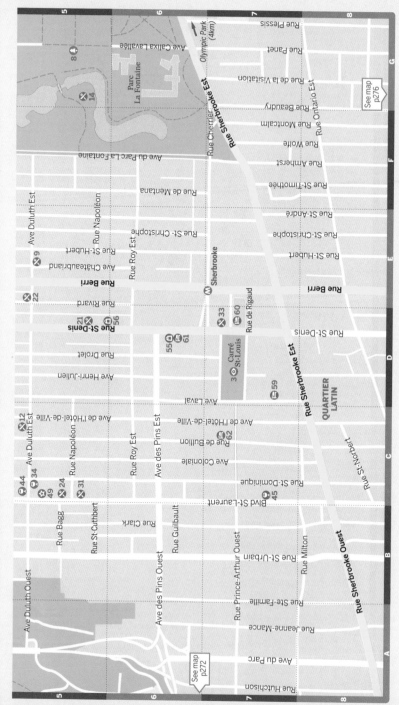

See map p276

See map p272

Olympic Park (4km)

Rue Plessis

Rue Panet

Rue de la Visitation

Rue Beaudry

Rue Montcalm

Rue Ontario Est

Rue Wolfe

Rue Amherst

Rue St-Timothée

Rue St-André

Rue St-Christophe

Rue St-Hubert

Rue Berri

Rue St-Denis

Rue de Rigaud

QUARTIER
LATIN

Rue Sherbrooke Est

Rue St-Norbert

Ave Calixa Lavallée

Parc La Fontaine

Rue Cherrier Est

Rue Sherbrooke Est

Ave du Parc La Fontaine

Rue de Mentana

Ave Duluth Est

Rue Napoléon

Rue St-Christophe

Rue St-Hubert

Rue Roy Est

Ave Châteaubriand

Rue Berri

Rue Rivard

Rue St-Denis

Rue Drolet

Ave Henri-Julien

Sherbrooke

Carré
St-Louis

Ave Laval

Ave de l'Hôtel-de-Ville

Rue Roy Est

Ave des Pins Est

Ave de l'Hôtel-de-Ville

Rue de Bullion

Ave Coloniale

Rue St-Dominique

Blvd St-Laurent

Ave Duluth Est

Rue Napoléon

Ave Duluth Ouest

Rue Bagg

Rue St-Cuthbert

Rue Clark

Rue Guilbault

Ave des Pins Ouest

Rue Prince-Arthur Ouest

Rue St-Urbain

Rue Ste-Famille

Rue Milton

Rue Jeanne-Mance

Ave du Parc

Rue Hutchison

Rue Sherbrooke Ouest

8

14

9

22

96

12

33

60

55

61

59

62

45

44

34

49

24

31

3

LITTLE ITALY, MILE END & OUTREMONT

Key on p284

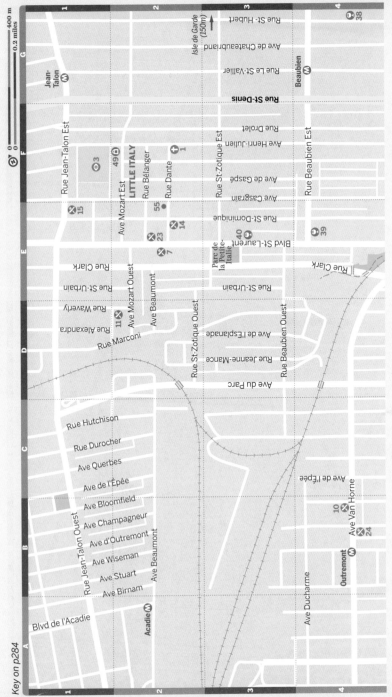

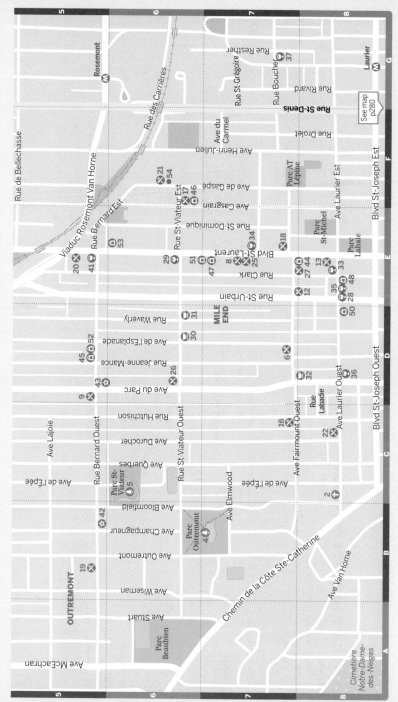

See map p280

LITTLE ITALY, MILE END & OUTREMONT Map on p282

LACHINE CANAL, LITTLE BURGUNDY & THE SOUTHWEST *Map on p286*

LACHINE CANAL, LITTLE BURGUNDY & THE SOUTHWEST

Key on p285

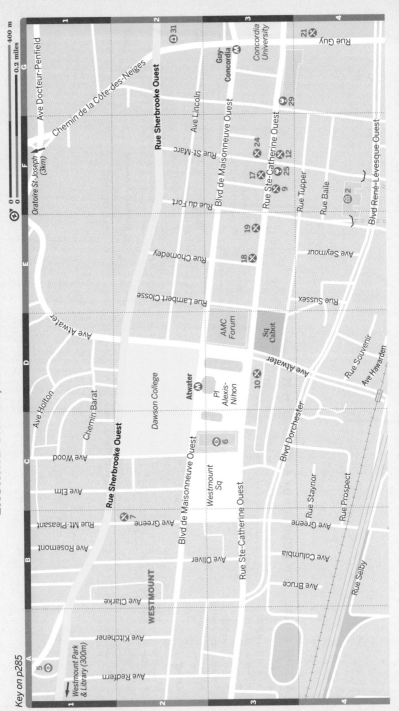

LACHINE CANAL, LITTLE BURGUNDY & THE SOUTHWEST

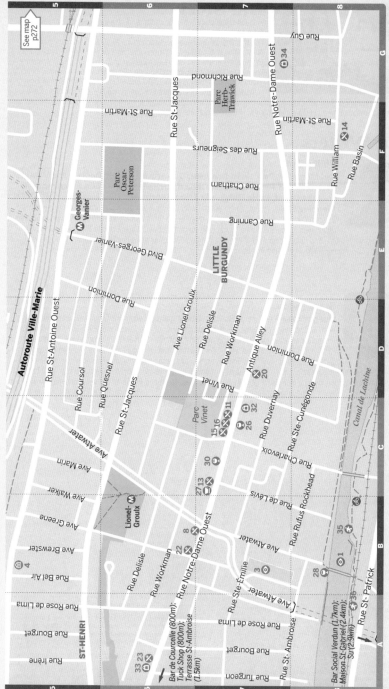

See map p272

Our Story

A beat-up old car, a few dollars in the pocket and a sense of adventure. In 1972 that's all Tony and Maureen Wheeler needed for the trip of a lifetime – across Europe and Asia overland to Australia. It took several months, and at the end – broke but inspired – they sat at their kitchen table writing and stapling together their first travel guide, *Across Asia on the Cheap*. Within a week they'd sold 1500 copies. Lonely Planet was born.

Today, Lonely Planet has offices in the US, Ireland and China, with a network of over 2000 contributors in every corner of the globe. We share Tony's belief that 'a great guidebook should do three things: inform, educate and amuse'.

Our Writers

Phillip Tang

Old Montréal; Parc Jean-Drapeau; Downtown; Rue St-Denis & the Village; Plateau Mont-Royal & the Northeast; Little Italy, Mile End & Outremont; Lachine Canal, Little Burgundy & the Southwest; Day Trips from Montréal; Sleeping Phillip grew up on a typically Australian diet of pho and fish 'n' chips before moving to Mexico City. A degree in Chinese and Latin American cultures launched him into travel and then writing about it for Lonely Planet's Canada, China, Japan, Korea, Mexico, Peru and Vietnam guides. Writing at hellophillip.com, photos on Instagram @mrtangtangtang and tweets @philliptang. Phillip also wrote the Plan, Understand and Survival Guide sections.

Steve Fallon

Québec City A native of Boston, Steve graduated from Georgetown University with a Bachelor of Science in modern languages. After working for several years for an American daily newspaper and earning a master's degree in journalism, his fascination with the 'new' Asia led him to Hong Kong, where he lived for over a dozen years, working for a variety of media and running his own travel bookshop. Steve lived in Budapest for three years before moving to London in 1994. He has written or contributed to more than a hundred Lonely Planet titles. Visit his website on www.steveslondon.com. Steve also wrote The Laurentians section of the Day Trips from Montréal chapter as well as the Québec City–related parts of the Plan, Understand and Survival Guide sections.

Published by Lonely Planet Global Limited
CRN 554153
6th edition – Jul 2022
ISBN 978 1 78868 450 7
© Lonely Planet 2022   Photographs © as indicated 2022
10 9 8 7 6 5 4 3 2 1
Printed in China

Although the authors and Lonely Planet have taken all reasonable care in preparing this book, we make no warranty about the accuracy or completeness of its content and, to the maximum extent permitted, disclaim all liability arising from its use.